S0-ARM-730

FORTRAN PROGRAMMING

FORTRAN PROGRAMMING

A SPIRAL APPROACH

With WATFOR/WATFIV and Standard FORTRAN

CHARLES B. KREITZBERG

Educational Testing Service

BEN SHNEIDERMAN

Indiana University

HARCOURT BRACE JOVANOVICH, INC.

New York   Chicago   San Francisco   Atlanta

To Valerie and to Nancy

© 1975 by Harcourt Brace Jovanovich, Inc.

All rights reserved. No part of this publication may be reproduced
or transmitted in any form or by any means, electronic or mechanical,
including photocopy, recording, or any information storage and
retrieval system, without permission in writing from the publisher.

ISBN: 0-15-528012-0

Library of Congress Catalog Card Number: 75-852

Printed in the United States of America

PHOTO CREDITS

Page 1, Ken Knowlton, Bell Laboratories
Page 28, Harbrace Photo
Page 50, Sema Marks
Page 86, Grace C. Hertlein, California State University, Chico, California
Page 126, © 1968, CalComp
Page 158, © Computra, Inc., compliments of Computra, Inc., Upland, Ind.
Page 196, © Computra, Inc., compliments of Computra, Inc., Upland, Ind.
Page 238, Courtesy of Control Data Corp.
Page 272, © Computra, Inc., compliments of Computra, Inc., Upland, Ind.
Page 298, Lou Katz
Page 326, Charles Curtis Rhode
Page 352, © Computra Inc., compliments of Computra, Inc., Upland, Ind.
Page 372, Lou Katz

PREFACE

Why another book on FORTRAN? We asked ourselves this question when it was suggested that we write a FORTRAN text. Surely most students and professors could find an adequate introduction to FORTRAN among the hundreds of FORTRAN texts already available. But a survey of the current texts convinced us there was indeed a need for yet another FORTRAN book; one that met the following criteria, which we believe are essential in such a text:

First, the text should be organized in accordance with sound principles of educational psychology to encourage the student's development of programming skills and mastery of meaningful concepts and to discourage rote memorization.

Second, the text should be truly a text (not merely a programming manual) and should focus on computing as a creative activity. Professional programmers know well that learning a second programming language requires far less effort than was required to learn the first; thus, the *difficult* aspect of learning to program is not the language itself but initially learning to conceptualize a problem in algorithmic terms. [One of the authors was recently involved in conducting a survey of student attitudes toward introductory FORTRAN courses. Students at several universities agreed that the two most difficult problems they faced were *learning how to develop an algorithm* (30% reported this) and *learning how to debug the required programs* (30% found this most difficult). At the end of a one semester course, fewer than 10% of these students reported that they felt "competent" to write a computer program.] Thus, the text should teach programming itself, not simply a programming language.

Third, the text should not require more than a high school mathematics background. Examples should be accessible to students in a wide range of fields, such as business, the social sciences, the humanities, urban affairs, economics, and education as well as the physical and engineering sciences. But ease of understanding must not mean compromising depth of presentation.

Fourth, the text must include numerous examples, exercises, and worked-out examples so that the student may apply those concepts presented. Short "do-it-now" problems should be inserted at critical points to encourage the student to test his or her mastery of important concepts. Answers to these problems and to selected exercises should be provided to facilitate self-study and review. Finally, the problems and exercises should be thoughtful and interesting—not meaningless and mechanical—and should cover many subject areas, to reflect the wide range of possible computer applications.

Fifth, the text should be organized for reference as well as for study so that the student can use it in the laboratory as well as in the classroom.

Sixth, the text should encourage the development of good programming habits. Programming style, design, documentation, and debugging should be prominent topics.

In *FORTRAN Programming: A Spiral Approach* we have tried to meet these six criteria. The "spiral" in the title refers to our use of the "spiral curriculum" recommended by educational psychologists D. P. Ausubel and J. S. Bruner. In spiral learning the student is not presented with every detail and possible option when a concept is introduced; rather, the presentation starts slowly, gradually adding new concepts in a rational way at appropriate intervals. In the spiral approach the student is first provided with a simple-to-use subset of the language, which is expanded as the student's sophistication in programming grows. (Care has been taken so that misconceptions will not develop because of incomplete information.) We think that instructors will find this method of organization natural and congenial for teaching. There should be little need to advise students to skip sections and return to them later or to ignore confusing details. There is an appendix summarizing the details of FORTRAN syntax; after the student has learned a concept, this appendix will serve as a reference guide for the entire language. A detailed exposition of the psychological model underlying the organization of this text may be found in C. Kreitzberg and L. Swanson, "A Cognitive Model for Structuring an Introductory Programming Curriculum," *Proceedings of the National Computer Conference,* Volume 47 (Montvale, N. J.: AFIPS Press, 1974).

Each chapter begins with a *chapter organizer.* These brief sections provide an overview of the key concepts to be learned in the chapter. The student who studies a chapter organizer before embarking on the chapter itself will find the "new" concepts somewhat familiar and therefore easier to learn. Each chapter ends with a summary and review questions; in some of the longer chapters there are also summaries at key points.

Exercises, Programming Exercises, Advanced Exercises, and Spiral Problems are provided for homework and self-study. Answers to selected exercises are in an appendix; answers to the remaining exercises appear in the Instructor's Manual. Programming Exercises require the student to apply the concepts learned in short programs, whereas Advanced Exercises are more ambitious. The Spiral Problems appearing in every chapter allow the student to select a short programming project in an area of interest. Most chapters have three Spiral Problems, each of which exercises the same computational techniques in a different area of application. The Spiral Problems test the student's understanding of the key concepts presented in the chapter and become progressively more complex as the student's expertise grows. The Spiral Problems are designed to provide the student with an opportunity to use the computer center facilities from the very first day of the course.

Debugging is an essential aspect of programming, and each chapter contains a Debugging Clinic with useful hints for debugging programs and avoiding common errors. In addition, many chapters contain set-off materials on *programming style.* These enrichment sections introduce the techniques of programming and program design, to help the student gain insight into what constitutes a good program. The style readings are brief adaptations from our book *The Elements of FORTRAN Style* (New York: Harcourt Brace Jovanovich, 1972), which may be used as a supplementary text.

Techniques of program design are also discussed in Chapter 12, which introduces the process of designing a modular, modifiable programming system. This chapter, like the flow-charts presented throughout the book, has been designed to allow the instructor to introduce discussion of structured programming techniques if desired. The program design chapter and the sections on subroutines and functions stress the idea of program modularity. However, structured programming is not explicitly discussed and thus its inclusion is left to the instructor.

Because of their widespread acceptance in academic computing, we discuss such WATFOR/WATFIV language extensions as simplified input/output and CHARACTER declarations. However, WATFOR/WATFIV extensions are clearly indicated as such, and standard FORTRAN techniques for performing the computations are also provided. The use of parallel examples and parallel text where necessary should allow *FORTRAN Programming: A Spiral Approach* to be used by instructors in either a WATFOR/WATFIV or a standard FORTRAN environment.

We wish to thank the numerous friends and colleagues who provided us with the encouragement and feedback necessary for this project. The detailed comments of Thomas De Lutis (Ohio State University) and Daniel Friedman (Indiana University) helped in the refinement of the manuscript. Len Swanson wrote the *Instructor's Manual* and was an active participant in formulating the psychological theory that underlies the text. Others who participated were John Buck, Barbara Gordon, Allan J. Mayer, Roger Rubinstein, Stuart C. Shapiro, Mitchell Wand, and the 1500 students at Indiana University who worked through early versions of the manuscript. We hope we have produced a text that is appealing and accessible to the reader.

Charles B. Kreitzberg
Ben Shneiderman

CONTENTS

FORTRAN PROGRAMMING

BASIC CONCEPTS

The purpose of computing is insight—not numbers.

R. W. Hamming

CHAPTER 1

Computers are electronic devices which perform calculations in millionths of a second. Unlike other computational aids, such as adding machines, computers must be designed to operate with limited human attention. The comparatively slow reactions of human users would severely reduce the computer's tremendous productivity.

Since computers operate without human intervention, before the computer can be utilized it is necessary to specify completely the calculations to be performed. A set of instructions prepared for the computer is called a program.

The program specifies the computations to be performed upon a set of data. Data are the values which are used in the calculations. Data are gathered in advance and data values are ready when the program is run. A program may be run with many sets of data.

Different sets of data may require slightly different calculations. For example, in a payroll calculation some employees may have a certain deduction while others may not. In order to permit the program to run with many sets of data, a programmer may specify conditional instructions that indicate actions are to be taken only if the data have certain values.

Programs are usually prepared in a special programming language. For academically oriented users, the most popular language is FORTRAN. Learning to write FORTRAN programs is simplified by its similarity to traditional algebraic notation.

Introduction

People study computer programming for several reasons. Most people learn how to program because they want to use computers to solve problems; other people learn programming because they are curious about computers and the things computers can do. Still others learn to program because programming is fun; some programmers spend hours writing programs which play games, draw pictures, or create music. Whatever your motivation in studying computer programming, you will be exploring a fascinating discipline.

Computer programmers develop an approach to problem analysis which is also productive in many noncomputational situations. In order to program the solution to a problem a programmer must understand exactly how to solve it. Because there is no room for fuzzy thinking while programming, programmers learn how to analyze a problem into a series of steps which, when followed, lead to a solution.

Another reason for learning programming is that the computer, one of the most significant inventions in history, has the potential for profoundly altering the structure of society. In learning about computers you will become aware of one of the most important forces in contemporary society and the ways in which it can be used and misused.

The computer has done for our intellect what tools and machines did for our muscles— it has allowed us to overcome the physiological limits to our creativity. The computer permits the consideration of problems whose solutions would be beyond the reach of the unaided mind, just as mechanical tools permit the creation of structures which would be beyond the reach of the unaided builder. The increased power that computers provide has led the well-known mathematician Richard Hamming to characterize the computer as an "intelligence amplifier." Recognizing that computers have more significance than their ability to perform rapid calculation, Dr. Hamming noted that "the purpose of computing is insight—not numbers."

We could roughly divide the evolution of mechanical aids to calculation into three periods. During the first period nonmechanical aids such as pen and paper, pebbles,[1] and sticks were used. The problems which people could solve were limited by their patience and lifespan. The second period was characterized by mechanical calculation aids; the slide rule, the adding machine, and later the tabulating machine permitted the solution of problems of far greater complexity. In the third period electronic computers have provided a vast increase in computational ability and a corresponding increase in the magnitude of the problems which we can solve.

In order to comprehend the magnitude of the effect which the computer has had, consider the analogy of increased ability to travel. When Columbus sailed for the New World, transportation was difficult. Most people traveled on foot or by horseback and their knowledge of the world was limited. The development of the automobile changed all that; instead of traveling 30 miles in a day, a person could travel 300 miles. Suddenly many aspects of life changed. The airplane provided another ten-fold increase in traveling ability, so that a trip of 3000 miles became a single day's affair. The most important result of the increased power of transportation is not that more distance can be covered but that distance is no longer a limiting factor in human activities. Because of the airplane you can open a seafood restaurant in Arizona, ship a parcel coast to coast overnight, or decentralize a manufacturing plant. The changes resulting from our increased ability to travel may not have always been good, but they have certainly been profound.

---

[1] The word "calculate" comes from the Latin *calculus,* "pebble."

In the same way, the development of the computer has made it possible to consider problems whose computational requirements are beyond the abilities of unaided calculation. The unaided problem solver is like the person traveling on foot who must depend upon limited power to achieve the goal. Like the automobile, mechanical calculators (such as adding machines) provide their users with increased calculating ability which permits them to approach more complex problems. Like the airplane, the computer has made previously unapproachable areas accessible to the human intellect.

To illustrate the computer's ability to reduce massive calculations to manageable size, consider the task of finding the sum of 1000 five-digit numbers. Calculation of the sum by hand might require several hours; with an adding machine, about 30 minutes would be needed; a typical computer could compute the sum within 1/10 second.

Of course, computers can do more than just add numbers and we shall shortly explore their capabilities. Computers routinely are used to solve problems in mathematics, accounting, business, medicine, music, literature, engineering, statistics, psychology, and urban affairs; in fact, there are few areas in which computers do not have some application.

From Adding Machine to Computer

If you have never used computers, they may seem esoteric and complex. Actually, the complexity of computers is more apparent than real; the basic concepts of computer organization are quite simple. Every aspect of the design of a computer is predicated upon the functions it must perform.

In order to introduce the basic concepts of computer organization we shall consider a related, but very simple device—the "adding machine." The purpose of the computer is to perform very fast calculations; the purpose of the adding machine is to perform calculations. We will develop the basic concepts by considering the characteristics of adding machines and overcoming their limitations by adding the features of a computer.

Consider the design of an "adding machine" that adds, subtracts, multiplies, and divides numbers. The user of such a machine would need a means for entering numbers (*data*) and *instructions* which describe the operations to be performed. Adding machines use keys for entering both data and instructions. For example, data are often put in by means of ten keys corresponding to the digits 0–9; instructions are entered by special keys. An adding machine's keyboard might look something like Figure 1.1. (The four instruction keys stand for *add, subtract, multiply,* and *divide,* respectively.) Unfortunately, these manual keys, while suitable for an adding machine, would delay a fast computer. A simple operation such as adding 59 to 19 would require punching five separate keys, one at a time. For this reason, computers are equipped with devices that enter or "read" the data at much higher speeds than a person can key them in manually.

One common way of preparing data for a computer to read is the familiar *punch card.* A punch card is a square of cardboard about 3 X 7 inches in which small rectangular holes are punched. A computer reads the holes by sensors (usually photoelectric). Many punch cards have printing on them; these are for human eyes only—the computer reads only the holes.

If an adding machine had a card reader attached, we would no longer need the digit entry keys. We would, however, need a method of causing a card to be read. The addition of

Data Keys   Instruction
                             Keys

1	2	3		+
4	5	6		–
7	8	9		*
	0			/

Figure 1.1

a new instruction—a READ key—would accomplish this task. Every time this key was depressed a number might be read from a punched card in the card reader. A means of printing a result on command—a PRINT key and a *printer*—would also be useful. Having redesigned the adding machine to (1) read data prepared in advance and (2) print results on command, we arrive at a device like Figure 1.2.

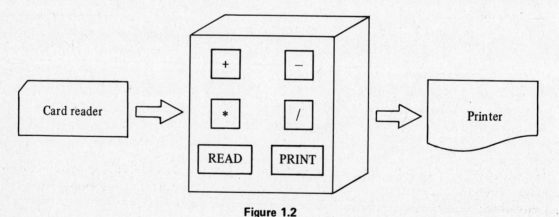

Figure 1.2

The redesign of the ten manually operated data entry keys has eliminated one of the bottlenecks in the original design—the slow speed of manual data entry. In the process we added two new instructions. Our "computer" now has six instructions: *add, subtract, multiply, divide, read,* and *print*. It is no longer necessary to enter data by hand, but it is still necessary to enter these instructions manually. Because our "computer" cannot operate at electronic speeds (being limited by the speed with which the operator can enter instructions), a further design change is required.

Computer Programs

The technique of preparing the data in advance so they can be read at high speed can be adapted to instructions as well. Instructions can be stored *in* the computer so that the computer will execute them without human intervention. Such a set of instructions, prepared in advance, is called a *program*. The computer circuits in which the program is stored constitute the computer's *memory* (Figure 1.3).[2]

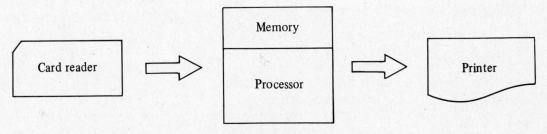

Figure 1.3

The card reader and printer may not be the only input and output devices utilized; a more general diagram is shown in Figure 1.4.

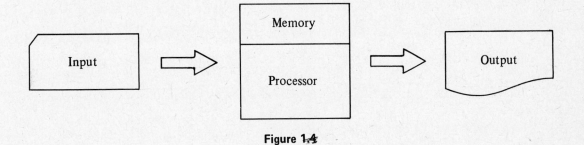

Figure 1.4

The addition of a memory to store a program has transformed our adding machine into a "real" computer. The three functions which our computer performs ~~are exactly~~ the functions which all computers perform:

- *Input*—reading data into the memory of the processing unit

- *Processing*—performing calculations on the data read in

- *Output*—communicating the results of processing to the ouside world

This is the reason that computers are sometimes called *data processors*.

Let us review the steps by which we moved from an "adding machine" to a "computer":

1. We wanted to design a very fast calculating device.

---

[2] A more correct term is *store*, but "memory" is in common use and we adopt it in this text.

2. We needed to eliminate human intervention so that our device could operate rapidly.
3. We therefore developed a means of putting in data prepared in advance so the computer could obtain it at high speeds.
4. We stored our instructions for performing the calculations (program) in the computer so the instructions could be executed rapidly.
5. The result is a device which can perform calculations at electronic speeds.

A Simple Program

You will recall that our simple computer had six instructions: *add, subtract, multiply, divide, read,* and *print.* A computer program is constructed from the available instructions arranged in an appropriate order for execution. For example, a program which would add two numbers and print the sum might look like this:[3]

```
INSTRUCTION #1   READ
            #2   READ
            #3   ADD
            #4   PRINT
```

To run this program on the "computer" we developed in the preceding section, we would enter the program into the computer's memory and place two punch cards with our data on them in the card reader. When the program was started, the following four actions would take place:

1. The computer would execute the first READ instruction by reading the first punch card.
2. The computer would execute the second READ instruction by reading the second punch card.
3. The computer would add the two numbers read in.
4. The computer would print the sum.

As you can see, once the program was started no human intervention would be required. Note that the results of executing the program depend on the data as well as the program. If we had punched

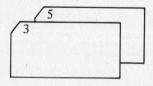

in our card deck of data, the computer would print "8," whereas if we had punched

---

[3] Note that these "instructions" are invented for discussion purposes. They are neither actual computer instructions nor FORTRAN.

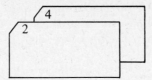

in our data deck, the computer would print "6." Thus, one program may be used with many sets of data; the program itself is general. Naturally, most programs are more complicated than adding two numbers, but even a program as simple as this could conceivably be useful. Suppose the two numbers which we punched on the data cards were an employee's weekly salary and his overtime pay. Then the program which we wrote could be used to compute the amount of the employee's paycheck.

The GO TO Statement

In the program above there was an implicit "flow of control"; the computer first executed instruction #1, then instruction #2, and so on. A new instruction—GO TO—can be added to create a program like this:

```
INSTRUCTION  #1   READ
             #2   READ
             #3   ADD
             #4   PRINT
             #5   GO TO INSTRUCTION #1
```

Then, when the computer reaches instruction #5, it is commanded to go back to instruction #1. In this modified program the computer will execute the instructions

$$\#1 \ \#2 \ \#3 \ \#4 \ \#5 \ \#1 \ \#2 \ \#3 \ \#4 \ldots.$$

A diagram of the flow of control of this program would look like this:

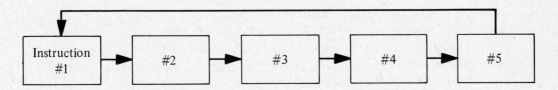

For obvious reasons, a program with a flow of control like this one is said to be a *loop*. Compare the program with the GO TO instruction to the original program:

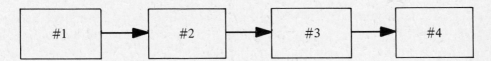

The original program does not have a loop.

The simple addition of the GO TO instruction to the computer's repertoire increases the power of the computer by a vast amount. With the GO TO instruction a single program can process many sets of data; one, ten, or 1000 sets of data can all be processed with the same five instructions.

Suppose we had prepared a data deck with six cards as follows:

Card 1—employee 1/salary

Card 2—employee 1/overtime pay

Card 3—employee 2/salary

Card 4—employee 2/overtime pay

Card 5—employee 3/salary

Card 6—employee 3/overtime pay

Our deck might look like this:

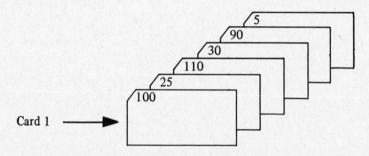

If our program were run with these data, the computer would follow these steps:

1. The computer would execute instruction #1 by reading the first card.
2. The computer would execute instruction #2 by reading the second card.
3. The computer would execute instruction #3 by adding the two numbers read.
4. The computer would execute instruction #4 and print the first employee's wage ($125).
5. The computer would execute instruction #5 which tells it to go to instruction #1.
6. The computer would execute instruction #1 again by reading the third card.
7. The computer would execute instruction #2 by reading the fourth card.
8. The computer would execute instruction #3 by adding the two numbers read.
9. The computer would execute instruction #4 by printing the second employee's wage ($140).
10. The computer would execute instruction #5 which tells it to go to instruction #1.
11. The computer would execute instruction #1 by reading the fifth card.
12. The computer would execute instruction #2 by reading the sixth card.
13. The computer would execute instruction #3 by adding the two numbers read.
14. The computer would execute instruction #4 by printing the third employee's wage ($95).
15. The computer would execute instruction #5 which tells it to go to instruction #1.
16. The computer would attempt to execute instruction #1 but as there is no card in the card reader it would stop.

The GO TO instruction is powerful in several ways. First, even though the program is only five instructions long, it caused the computer to perform 15 operations because each instruction was executed three times. If there had been more data, the program would have processed them. Given an infinite amount of data, it would have run forever. Second, the GO TO instruction caused our five-statement program:

```
#1   READ
#2   READ
#3   ADD
#4   PRINT
#5   GO TO INSTRUCTION # 1
```

to execute as if it had been a 12-statement program:

```
#1   READ
#2   READ
#3   ADD
#4   PRINT
#5   READ
#6   READ
#7   ADD
#8   PRINT
#9   READ
#10  READ
#11  ADD
#12  PRINT
```

The instruction specified as the object of the GO TO is identified by a *label*. Had we written "go to instruction #3" (for example), the program would have operated differently. It would still be an executable program but it would not do what we want.

Problem 1.1

a. Write a program that will read an employee's hourly salary (on a punch card) and the number of hours he has worked this week (on a second punch card), calculate his weekly salary, and print out the result.

b. What changes are necessary for this program to process a series of employees?

c. For this program, does it matter which one of each pair of cards is read in first?

Instruction Classes

The computer we designed has a seven-instruction repertoire. Computers may have a repertoire of several hundred instructions; however, most are similar to the ones we have discussed. Many are computational; but we want to be able to do more than simple arithmetic, so some are similar to the READ and PRINT instructions. There is, however, one type of instruction that we have not yet discussed which is important and powerful.

This instruction type is the *conditional* or *decision* instruction class. Conditional instructions are necessary because when a task is performed on many data it is often necessary to introduce variations for special cases. In a payroll computation, for example, several conditions which might influence the processing could be:

- If the employee earns more than $10,000 per year, do not compute overtime pay.

- If the employee's deductions exceed his salary, carry some deductions until the next pay period.

- If the employee was ill, deduct the number of days he was absent from his available sick time.

Each decision specifies an action to be taken if a condition occurs.

Decision capability must be built into the computer's instruction set since a human should not need to intervene during the program's execution. The idea of a machine's making decisions somehow sounds esoteric, but many mechanical devices have this capability. A soda vending machine that charges 10¢ for a glass of soda might have the following decision rule:

- If coin input is 25¢, then return 15¢ change.

A parking meter can decide using two rules:

- If input is 5¢, then allow 30 minutes.

- If input is 10¢, then allow 60 minutes.

Other machines such as slot machines and pinball machines have even more complicated decision ability.

In general, the decision instructions in a computer's repertoire are *data comparison* instructions which compare two items of data. If *A* and *B* are two values in the computer, a comparison may be made for *A equal to B, A greater than B,* or *A less than B,* and different actions selected as a result of the comparison. While the principle is simple, very complex decision procedures may be constructed by combining a number of conditional instructions.

The addition of decision instructions completes our discussion of instruction types. The instructions of any computer, no matter how complex, may be partitioned into the following instruction classes: *input/output, computational, transfer of control,* and *decision.* The instructions we have considered so far are classified in Table 1.1.

Table 1.1

Class	Instruction
Input/Output	READ
	PRINT
Computational	ADD
	SUBTRACT
	MULTIPLY
	DIVIDE
Transfer of Control	GO TO
Decision	COMPARISON

Loading the Program

Having prepared a program and the data for a problem to be solved, we are ready to go except for one rather important logistical point. How do we load the program into the computer? Without a means of loading the program into the computer we have no way of making it run; it is as if we built an automobile with no doors—we are ready to go but we have no way of getting into the driver's seat.

Like data, programs are inscribed on a suitable input medium such as punch cards, magnetic tape, or magnetic disks and are loaded into the computer at high speeds. Thus, the computer's data input devices also serve as program input devices. The data are normally placed immediately behind the program; the program is loaded and begins execution with the data positioned correctly for reading.

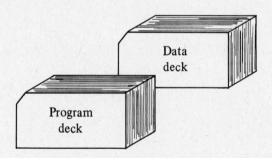

A Recapitulation

A computer of the sort we have been discussing is most properly called a *general purpose stored program digital computer.* By *general purpose* we mean that the computer can be made to do many different types of tasks. A computer may process a payroll one minute and calculate a rocket trajectory the next—it all depends on the programs. For this reason, some people consider a computer to be a general purpose machine which is made into a specific machine by the addition of a program. In other words, loading a program into a computer turns it temporarily into a payroll machine or into a rocket tracking machine, depending on the program.

By *stored program* we mean that the program is stored in the computer's memory. The fact that a computer has a stored, changeable program differentiates it from other computational aids such as slide rules, adding machines, and tabulating machines.

By *digital computer* we mean a device that computes with digits (numbers). Perhaps this is in some sense a misnomer since digital computers are able to manipulate letters and symbols as well as numbers. However, digital computers were first used for computing with numbers and this is still one of their major functions. The term "digital" serves two other purposes as well. First, it indicates that the computer operates upon numbers expressed in terms of digits; it does not have infinite precision. Thus, a digital computer can represent the fraction 1/3 as .33 or .3333 or even .3333333, but it cannot carry an infinite amount of precision. Secondly, a *digital computer* is called digital to differentiate it from a different type of computer known as an *analog computer.* As analog computers are not general purpose and do not have stored programs, they are not of any interest to us.

Thus, a *general purpose stored program digital computer* is a device capable of doing many kinds of processing. It is given a specific task by means of a program, and it is capable of manipulating numbers, letters, and symbols.

A computer consists of three major parts: a *processor, a memory* and *input/output* units. The processor, or CPU (for *central processing unit),* contains the circuitry for executing instructions and is connected to the computer's memory where data and programs are stored while the computer is processing them. The input/output devices (also known as I/O devices or *peripheral devices*) are connected to the central processing unit and serve as the means for data to be read into memory or written from memory. Some I/O devices are bidirectional and can be used for both input and output; some devices are unidirectional and can be used for either input or output but not both. The Table 1.2 lists some common input/output devices.

Table 1.2

Device	Method of Recording Information	Used for	
		Input	Output
Card Reader	Holes punched in cardboard card	X	
Card Punch	Holes punched in cardboard card		X
Magnetic Tape	Magnetized spots on recording tape	X	X
Magnetic Disk	Magnetized spots on the surface of a disk	X	X
Magnetic Drum	Magnetized spots on the surface of a drum	X	X
Printer	Ink on paper		X
Terminal	Cathode ray tube or paper	X	X
Microfilm	Light on film		X
Paper tape reader	Holes punched in paper ribbon	X	
Paper tape punch	Holes punched in paper ribbon		X

There are many other more esoteric peripherals, such as optical character recognizers, devices to sense pencil marks on cards or paper, and laser storage devices. One device in common use which we have not yet discussed is the *terminal*. Terminals include typewriter-like devices with the ability to transmit data to computers over telephone lines. Some terminals have typewriter printers attached and produce printed output; other terminals have screens somewhat like a television on which they display letters or pictures.

Programming Languages and Translators

When we designed the simple computer, we utilized seven instructions: READ, PRINT, ADD, SUBTRACT, MULTIPLY, DIVIDE, and GO TO. Real computers have many more instructions than this, often several hundred. The internal representations of the instructions are not easy words like ADD or READ but difficult-to-remember strings of ones and zeroes. For example, on the IBM 360 and 370 series of computers, the instruction ADD is written as 01011010. When you have several hundred such instructions, remembering which is which can be a problem. Even worse, the instructions for one type of computer are usually unique for that type of computer. For an IBM 7040 computer, the instruction ADD is written as 000110000000 and for a Data General Nova it is written as 001000011010100000. Programmers, faced with a computer age Tower of Babel, certainly have sufficient motivation for seeking an alternative approach to programming. Fortunately, one exists—"high-level" languages.

High-Level Languages

A high-level language is a language which is convenient for human programmers. High-level languages cannot be understood by computers; therefore, a program first written in a high-level language is then *translated* into the machine's language. This may seem to introduce an extra amount of work for the programmer, but this is not the case. The burden of translating the high-level language into machine language is placed upon a special program.

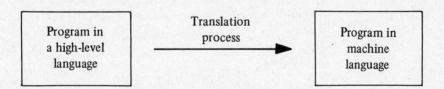

It may seem strange that the computer can translate a language that it does not understand, but consider the following analogy.

A telegram written in French with the message *"après moi le déluge"* could be transmitted by an operator who spoke only English. It is not necessary to understand French in order to translate the sentence into its Morse Code equivalent if you have the following table:

A ·—	H ····	O ———	V ···—
B —···	I ··	P ·——·	W ·——
C —·—·	J ·———	Q ——·—	X —··—
D —··	K —·—	R ·—·	Y —·——
E ·	L ·—··	S ···	Z ——··
F ··—·	M ——	T —	
G ——·	N —·	U ··—	

and these instructions:

1. Look at the first letter.
2. Write the Morse Code equivalent of the letter at which you are looking.
3. If there are no more letters in the message, you are done. Otherwise, look at the next letter and go to step 2.

Applying the above instructions to the French message yields the string

A P R E S M O T F E D E L U G E
·— ·——· ·—· · ··· —— ——— — ··—· · —·· · ·—·· ··— ——· ·

which is the original message translated into Morse Code. The translation instructions are expressed in an unusual manner; they could have been written more concisely as

1. Replace every letter by its Morse Code equivalent.

However, the first set captures the flavor of a computer program; there is a lot of similarity between the way the first set of instructions is written and the way a computer program is written. We will have much more to say about this in later chapters.

The Morse Code translation example given above has many characteristics in common with the translation process used for high-level languages. First, we translated a human-oriented language into a machine-oriented language by a mechanical process. In the same way a high-level language is translated into machine language by a mechanistic process. The algorithmic language[4] to be translated is called the *source language* and the language into which the program is translated is called the *object language*. Second, it would be possible to translate the same source statement into many different codes by changing the code table. In the same way, a *source program* can be translated into the appropriate *object program* for different computers by selecting the appropriate machine language codes. Thus, we solve the "Tower of Babel problem" by forcing the programmer to learn only one language, the source language, and providing an appropriate translator for each machine on which the program is to be run.

The program which performs the language translation is called a *compiler*. Compilers are written by highly skilled programmers.

---

[4] An *algorithmic language* is one that deals with the use of algorithms (sets of instructions) to solve problems. There are other types of high-level computer languages, but we will talk only about algorithmic languages.

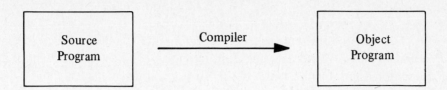

There have been many high-level languages designed, because none has been totally satisfactory to all users. The language most widely in use is FORTRAN. FORTRAN is an acronym which is derived from FORmula TRANslation language and, as its name implies, FORTRAN is particularly suited for arithmetic manipulation. Other high-level languages in widespread use include COBOL (*CO*mmon *B*usiness *O*riented *L*anguage), BASIC (*B*eginner's *A*ll-purpose *S*ymbolic *I*nstruction *C*ode), SNOBOL (*St*ri*N*g *O*riented Sym*BO*lic *L*anguage), and ALGOL (*ALGO*rithmic *L*anguage). Although we shall be concentrating on FORTRAN in this text, most of the concepts you will learn are applicable to other languages.

Introduction to FORTRAN

High-level languages come in many flavors; since high-level languages are compiled (translated) into the computer's machine language, the language designer has the freedom to design the language in any way that he wants. This assumes, of course, that a compiler can be written for the language. Fortunately, we are not concerned with language design, as the FORTRAN language is already defined. Although different compiler writers may make small changes in the language, on the whole, FORTRAN is FORTRAN no matter which computer you are using.

This is fortunate as it means that you will be able to program many different computers while learning only a single language—something that would not be possible if you were learning a specific machine language. In fact, in order to insure that a FORTRAN program will compile on every computer that has a FORTRAN compiler, a national standard has been adopted by the American National Standards Institute (ANSI). When a compiler is written, it must be able to process the FORTRAN language as defined in the ANSI standard. In addition to processing ANSI standard FORTRAN a compiler may, if the designer so chooses, include some additional features.

Two very popular compilers, WATFOR and WATFIV, are FORTRAN compilers written at the University of Waterloo. In addition to the standard FORTRAN accepted by WATFOR and WATFIV, the Waterloo compilers have added a few extensions to the language which make it easier to learn.

In this text we will discuss standard FORTRAN; however, since WATFOR and WATFIV are so widely used, we will include some of the extensions they provide. *In every case this is done explicitly and a standard method of performing the same operation is provided.* Thus, if you have a WATFOR or WATFIV compiler to use, you may use either the extension discussed or the standard language. If you are using a different compiler, you will have to use the standard FORTRAN operations.

FORTRAN Programs

A FORTRAN program consists of a series of statements which are arranged one after the other. A statement in FORTRAN is something like a sentence in English and is an instruction to the computer. Consider the following set of English instructions:

1. A student had three test scores.
    The score of test 1 = 75%.
    The score of test 2 = 83%.
    The score of test 3 = 42%.
2. Add the three scores and divide by three in order to compute the average.

If you were to follow these instructions, you would compute the student's average. In FORTRAN, these instructions could be written as

```
TEST1 = 75.0
TEST2 = 83.0
TEST3 = 42.0
AVER = (TEST1 + TEST2 + TEST3)/3.0
```

Notice that every statement is written in all capital letters. Also note the lack of explanatory filler such as "a student had three test scores." FORTRAN statements tend to be concise, although it is possible to insert comments in a program (Chapter 3). Aside from these minor differences, the FORTRAN program above should be understandable. As you can see, it is much closer to English than the ones and zeroes of the computer's machine language. Table 1.3 shows the English statement, the FORTRAN equivalent, and the machine language instructions into which it would be translated if it were to be run on an IBM 360 or 370 computer.

Table 1.3

English	*FORTRAN*	*IBM 360/370 Machine Code*
The score on test 1 = 75%.	`TEST1 = 75.0`	0111 1000 0000 0000 1101 0000 1011 0000 0111 0000 0000 0000 1101 0000 0110 1000 0111 0000 0000 0000 1101 0000 1011 0100
The score on test 2 = 83%.	`TEST2 = 83.0`	0111 0000 0000 0000 1101 0000 0111 0110 0111 1000 0000 0000 1101 0000 1011 1000 0111 0000 0000 0000 1101 0000 0111 0000
The score on test 3 = 42%.	`TEST3 = 42.0`	0111 1000 0000 0000 1101 0000 0110 1000 0111 1010 0000 0000 1101 0000 0110 1100 0111 1010 0000 0000 1101 0000 0111 0000
Add the three scores and divide by three.	`AVER = (TEST1 + TEST2` `         + TEST3)/3.0`	0111 1101 0000 0000 1101 0000 1011 1000 0111 0000 0000 0000 1101 0000 0111 0100

The FORTRAN program shown above is not complete. For one thing, the computer was never instructed to print the average it computed. This means that we would never see the results of our computation. (Programmers sometimes inadvertently make this error!) A second reason that the FORTRAN program shown above is incomplete is that every program is required to have a special statement as the last line of the program. That statement is, very reasonably, END. A complete FORTRAN program to compute the test average could be written like this:

```
TEST1 = 75.0
TEST2 = 83.0
TEST3 = 42.0
AVER = (TEST1 + TEST2 + TEST3)/3.0
PRINT, AVER⁵
STOP⁶
END
```

Recall that when we designed our "computer" we found it necessary to build in four types of instructions:

- input/output instructions

- computational instructions

- conditional instructions

- transfer instructions

FORTRAN statements also fall into the same five categories. Here are some examples:

Input
```
        READ, A, B, C
        READ (1,10) RATE, TIME
```
Output
```
        PRINT, DIST, COST
        WRITE(2,20) PAY, TAX
```
Computation
```
        DIST = RATE * TIME⁷
        AVERGE = SUM/A
```
Conditional
```
        IF (WIDTH .EQ. HEIGHT) STOP
        IF (DED .GT. PAY) CALL DEFER
```
Transfer
```
        GO TO 10
        GO TO 987
```

---

[5] This particular PRINT statement is a WATFOR/WATFIV format.
[6] The STOP and END statements will be discussed in Chapter 3.
[7] The symbol * indicates multiplication.

These are examples of valid FORTRAN statements. As you can see, they often use English words like *if, go to, read,* and *write.* The computational statements look very much like arithmetic expressions which should not be too surprising since the acronym FORTRAN is derived from the words FORmula TRANslation.

The transfer statement, GO TO, is very similar to the "go to" statement which we used in the "computer." When we instruct the computer to go to another statement in the program, we need a means of specifying which statement we want to go to next. There are a number of ways in which the FORTRAN language designers might have solved this problem; the technique they adopted was to allow the programmer to place a *label* on a statement to which a transfer is to be made. A label is a number which identifies the statement. For example, the statement

```
DIST = RATE * TIME
```

could have a label on it:

```
10 DIST = RATE * TIME
```

This means that the statement has the name 10. The choice of 10 is completely arbitrary; the programmer could have chosen any name, such as

```
47 DIST = RATE * TIME
1092 DIST = RATE * TIME
```

The fact that 10 was selected does not mean that the statement is the tenth; statement numbers do not need to be in order.

```
50 X = Y + Z
24 S = X - 2.0
```

is a perfectly valid sequence. Not all statements need be numbered. The rules for statement numbering will be explained in detail later on; for now it is sufficient to be aware that they exist and to recognize their function as the object of a GO TO statement.

Recall the program which was presented in this chapter to compute an employee's pay by adding weekly salary and overtime pay. Here is that program in FORTRAN:

```
10 READ, WAGE
   READ, OVTIME
   PAY = WAGE + OVTIME
   PRINT, PAY
   GO TO 10
   END
```

This program is a complete FORTRAN program (although the READ and PRINT statements are not quite standard, they are WATFOR/WATFIV extensions), and the FORTRAN program will run in the same way as was analyzed before.

PROGRAMMING STYLE

Programming style is difficult to define but it is something that most programmers eventually acquire. The elusive nature of programming style has led some computer scientists to characterize computer programming as an "art" rather than as a science. In these brief sections, we will attempt to provide you with some guidance as to what we consider good style to be. As you develop as a programmer you will undoubtedly begin to define your own rules for good programming style.*

Style is subjective. As programmers, we rarely share a common background because of the variations among compiler dialects, operating systems, hardware configurations, and programming environments. These variations make it impossible to specify a complete, consistent, and universal set of programming rules. In consequence, programming style must be approached functionally—in terms of the specific uses of each program, and the specific equipment it is run on.

A *correct* program is one that produces the desired results. Obviously, a "good" program must be correct. There are usually many correct programs that will solve a particular problem; of these some are faster than others, some are more accurate than others, some require less storage than others, and some are beautifully structured and easy to modify. The ideal program would embody all these qualities. However, there are very few ideal programs in the real world, because the factors which make a program "good" are not mutually independent. Increasing computational efficiency will often produce an increase in the storage requirement. Elegant algorithms are often difficult to understand. Thus, style must always be tempered by the programming environment. The programmer who has a mini-computer will almost certainly have different design goals from the programmer with a gigantic "number cruncher" at his disposal. Deadlines, too, often force a programmer to write hastily, for the most elegant program is useless until it is running.

What then, should be the goal? To write the best possible program in the available time using the available resources. As far as possible the program should be accurate, well documented, frugal in its use of storage, computationally efficient, modular, and compiler-independent.

If a critical design goal is to minimize execution time, then a complex but fast algorithm is in order. If storage space is at a premium, effort should be applied to eliminate useless information and to compress the remaining data. If development time is limited or if other programmers may modify your code, the simplest and most obvious algorithm should be selected.

Some programmers eagerly implement the first technique that comes to mind and worry about resolving difficulties after a few runs. The temptation to begin keypunching and get results is great, but it must be overcome. You should carefully consider alternative methods and design the entire program before coding a single line. Extra thought at the early stages of problem solving can save a great deal of effort at the later stages.

Program Flow

A source of confusion for many beginning programmers is the order in which statements are processed. It is really simple; the program starts with the first statement and executes the statements in sequential order unless a GO TO statement alters that order. Thus, in the program

*For a more extensive discussion of style in the FORTRAN language, you may wish to consult: Kreitzberg, C. and Shneiderman, B. *The Elements of FORTRAN Style: Techniques for Effective Programming.* New York: Harcourt Brace Jovanovich, Inc., 1972.

```
RATE = 10.0
TIME = 5.0
DIST = RATE * TIME
PRINT, DIST
STOP
END
```

the computer will first execute

```
RATE = 10.0
```

then

```
TIME = 5.0
```

then

```
DIST = RATE * TIME
```

then

```
PRINT, DIST
```

and finally

```
STOP
```

which is a special statement which stops the program.

The above program could be reordered to

```
TIME = 5.0
RATE = 10.0
DIST = RATE * TIME
PRINT, DIST
STOP
END
```

without affecting the results. *You could not reorder the program to be*

```
TIME = 5.0
DIST = RATE * TIME
RATE = 10.0
PRINT, DIST
STOP
END
```

and expect it to work. A statement such as

```
DIST = RATE * TIME
```

is not a passive statement of fact; it is a command to multiply the value of RATE by the value of TIME and assign that result to DIST. The computer looks at one statement at a time. When it executes a statement like

```
DIST = RATE * TIME
```

it will not look around to see if the programmer has defined RATE and TIME somewhere in the program. If it has previously executed a statement like

```
RATE = 10.0
```

or has obtained the value from a card by means of a statement like

```
READ, RATE
```

the value of RATE has been defined. If the value was never defined, as in the example above, the results will be unpredictable.

Summary

An *algorithmic language* is a language designed to allow programmers to state their instructions in a reasonably natural manner. Algorithmic languages are sometimes called *problem-oriented* languages since they are designed to allow the programmer to state instructions in terms of the problem rather than the computer. Since computers cannot understand algorithmic languages, a program written in an algorithmic language is *compiled* (translated) into the appropriate machine instructions by a program called a *compiler*.

FORTRAN is an algorithmic language in common use and most computers have a FORTRAN compiler. All FORTRAN compilers are capable of translating ANSI standard FORTRAN; some, like WATFOR and WATFIV, can translate additional language extensions.

The FORTRAN language is written as a series of *statements* arranged in the order in which they are to be executed. The GO TO statement may be used to jump to a statement in the program other than the next sequential one; the statement to which the jump is made is *labeled*.

In this chapter you have been introduced to a number of very important concepts. It would not be an exaggeration to say that if you understand these concepts you will have learned most of the fundamental ideas you need to become a programmer. Much of the material that follows is an extension of the concepts presented in this chapter and the next.

In presenting these concepts, we have tried to explain why computers are built the way they are. The "laws" governing computing are not, after all, "natural laws" that must be discovered but human design decisions made to solve specific needs. Thus, we have presented these concepts in a developmental manner, pointing out a problem and presenting the solution. Table 1.4 summarizes some of the major ideas discussed in this chapter.

Table 1.4

Concept	Problem	Solution
Program	Need to automate calculation so as not to be limited by human speeds.	Prepare instructions in advance at human speeds; then execute them at electronic speeds.
Data preparation	Need to avoid human intervention during program execution in order not to limit computational speed.	Prepare data in advance; then obtain it at high speed by program request without human intervention.
Transfer instructions (GO TO)	Need to process many sets of data.	Use transfer instructions to execute a group of statements many times.
Conditional instructions (IF)	All data may not use the same computation; special cases require different processing.	Provide the ability to make decisions and choose different instruction sequences depending on the data.
Statement labels	The transfer statement must refer to its destination.	Prefix a label to "name" a statement to which a transfer is to be made.

In the next chapter we will discuss the problem of organizing a program; that is, deciding how to put statements together to solve a problem.

DEBUGGING CLINIC

If every program worked the first time, programming would be a far easier task than it is. Unfortunately, even professional programmers make errors and it is a rare program indeed that works the first time it is run. The process of locating errors and correcting them is known as *debugging,* and getting the "bugs" out of a program can sometimes require more time and effort than the actual writing of the program. The errors that programmers make fall into two basic categories: errors of syntax and errors of logic. Syntactical errors occur when statements in a program do not conform to the rules of FORTRAN; they include typographic errors when keypunching the program as well as programming slips such as the use of a comma where a left parenthesis is required. Logical errors occur when the program does not operate as anticipated; they include such items as forgetting to define a variable before it is used or transferring control to the wrong statement number. Fortunately, the FORTRAN compiler makes a careful check of the syntax of the statements and reports syntactical errors to the programmer. Logical errors are more difficult for the compiler to catch since the compiler cannot "understand" the intentions of the programmer.

Therefore, while a program that violates the rules of FORTRAN will not compile, the computer will not detect invalid logic as long as the FORTRAN statements are syntactically correct. It is up to the programmer to figure out from the output what has gone wrong and correct the program.

Debugging has been called an art, not so much because the process is esthetically pleasing, but because there are no set procedures for catching and destroying bugs. In the debugging clinic section in each chapter, we will provide clues as to where bugs often occur and hints for bug prevention.

REVIEW QUESTIONS

1. What is a computer program and why are programs necessary?
2. Does it matter in what order the statements of a program are arranged? Why?
3. What are the five classes of statements? What is the purpose of each?
4. What is an algorithmic language? Why is it used? What is a compiler?
5. Why are data prepared before running the program? What are some devices that may be used for data input? For data output?

EXERCISES

1. Classify each of the following FORTRAN statements as *input, output, computational, conditional,* or *transfer.* A conditional statement may also be in another class.

   a. READ, MONTH, DAY, YEAR   *input*

   b. IF (DIV .EQ. 0.0) DIV = 1.0   *conditional*

   c. IF (DIV .LT. 2.0) GO TO 54   *conditional – transfer*

   d. DINNER = CAT + RAT   *computational*

   e. GO TO 17   *transfer*

   f. FALL = HOUSE/SELF   *computational*

   g. PRINT, X, Y, SUM   *output*

   h. WRITE (1,10) A, B, Q   *output*

   i. IF (TAX .GT. 0.0) PRINT, TAX   *conditional – output*

   j. RING = HOBBIT + ELF - ORC   *computational*

2. Fill in the blank with the most appropriate word or words.

   a. A(n) _____program_____ is a set of statements which instruct the computer to carry out a specific task.

   b. An algorithmic language is translated into machine language by a program called a(n) _____compiler_____.

   c. A source program is translated into a(n) _____object_____ program, which is the set of machine language instructions corresponding to the source program.

   d. In addition to FORTRAN, three well-known algorithmic languages are _____cobol_____, _____snobol_____, and _____basic_____. algol

   e. A(n) _____transfer (go to)_____ statement may be used to alter the sequence of statement execution.

   f. A(n) _____end_____ statement must always be the last statement in a program.

   g. A(n) _____conditional_____ is used to name a statement so that it can be jumped to by a GO TO.

   h. When the computer executes the following program:

```
SIDE = 5.0
AREA = SIDE * SIDE
PRINT, AREA
STOP
END
```

   the value printed will be _____25.0_____.

3. What two things are wrong with the following program?

```
10 READ, STOCK
20 PRINT, STOCK
30 NEW = STOCK + CHANGE
40 READ, CHANGE
50 PRINT, CHANGE, NEW
```

stop
end

SPIRAL PROBLEMS

At the end of each chapter there is a series of Spiral Problems designed to help develop your programming ability. These problems increase in difficulty gradually from chapter to chapter. By doing one or more of the spiral problems in each chapter you will gain experience in programming by using the knowledge acquired by reading the chapter.

The spiral problem for this chapter is to find the computer center and to learn to use the keypunch. Prepare two punch cards with the following information:

Columns	Information
1–40	Your name
41–66	Alphabet from A to Z
70–79	Numbers from 0 to 9

PRINCIPLES
OF PROGRAMMING

The same problem. . .should be completely represented by diagrams to the imagination, for thus it will be more distinctly perceived by the intellect.

René Descartes, Rules for the Direction of the Mind *(1628)*

CHAPTER 2

This chapter is concerned with the principles of program design. A program is a set of instructions that specify the precise operations which the computer must carry out. The FORTRAN language is a medium in which instructions can be formulated. FORTRAN provides the programmer with a means of writing a concise and unambiguous program to solve a given problem.

While the epigram, "a picture is worth a thousand words," was not originally applied to computer programming, the process of diagramming (making a flow chart for) the steps to be followed is an extremely productive technique for the development of a program.

In Chapter 1, the GO TO statement, which causes a group of instructions to be repeated, was introduced. In this chapter we expand this powerful concept of writing repetition into a program. We also develop the concept of executing alternate sets of instructions, depending on the data values. To do so, we utilize the conditional instructions discussed in Chapter 1.

The Nature of Algorithms

How many times have you asked someone to perform some task for you, only to find the person didn't get the message and did the wrong thing? Human nature and the ambiguity inherent in natural languages frequently tend to turn a simple request, imprecisely communicated, into a confusing, complex, sometimes chaotic experience.

A digital computer simplifies the computation of a problem but it cannot think about the specific steps it is following. In fact, since computers can perform only a limited number of special instructions and since they cannot make assumptions based on previous experience, it is often more difficult to direct a computer than it is to direct another person.[1] The computer can only carry out the computations which have been specified. If the programmer were not correct in analyzing the problem and specified an incorrect sequence of steps, the program would produce erroneous results. Verifying that a program is correct and eliminating the errors (*debugging*) is an important aspect of programming.

Students are often confused as to what can and cannot be programmed. It is not possible to construct a program in FORTRAN beyond the capability of the computer because the language permits only those things that a computer can do. Of course, it is possible to write programs that produce meaningless results or require much computer time to execute. However, every syntactically correct program can be executed—even if the results are not useful.

In FORTRAN, unlike English, no ambiguity exists; a statement always means the same single thing: precisely and immutably. The design of a programming language is no small task and constitutes a specialization in computer science.

A program is composed of a series of steps, consisting of statements. Thus, writing a FORTRAN program consists simply of constructing statements in the FORTRAN language and arranging them so that when executed they will produce the desired results. In the course of reading this book you will be learning about the different FORTRAN statement types and how they may be combined in order to create programs.

Many students find that the most fundamental obstacle is in learning the skill of analyzing a problem into a set of executable steps. The technique is first to think about the problem and loosely outline several possible methods of solution. When a technique has been chosen, the programmer formalizes the steps in an *algorithm*. *An algorithm is a set of instructions which when followed will produce the solution to a given problem.*[2] Algorithms must be precise, every detail must be considered, and there must be no loose ends. Computers are simplistic machines and must be fully instructed.

Algorithms occur in noncomputing contexts as well as programming. You can think of the recipe for baking a cake as an algorithm—certainly a recipe is a set of instructions which, when followed, will result in a cake. Likewise, the instructions in a stereo kit are steps which, when followed, will produce a properly assembled electronic device. If the instructions are poorly written or if they are not followed precisely, the result is a soggy cake or too much static.

---

[1] Attempts to utilize the computer to *analyze* and *solve* problems are the subject of much current research in *artificial intelligence*.

[2] It may help to consider an algorithm as the same thing as a program. Actually, the algorithm is the *technique* or *procedure* upon which the program is constructed, but the two words are often used interchangeably.

Flowcharts

Consider the following instructions we found in a neighborhood laundromat:

1. Put clothes in washing machine.
2. Add half cup of soap.
3. Select water temperature.
4. Insert quarter and push plunger.

Do you see what is wrong? The instructions never mentioned that the door of the washing machine should be closed. Of course, a human would probably compensate for the inadequate instructions by making some assumptions. A machine, however, would not and this "program" would not work properly.

The instruction "close the door" could reasonably follow step 2 or 3. If it were inserted after step 2, the clothes washing algorithm would look like this:

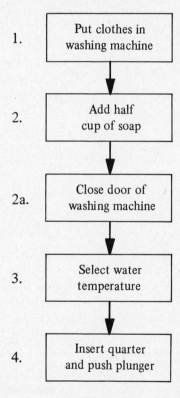

1. Put clothes in washing machine

2. Add half cup of soap

2a. Close door of washing machine

3. Select water temperature

4. Insert quarter and push plunger

Note that in this diagram we have enclosed each instruction in a box and drawn an arrow to the instruction that follows. This type of diagram, called a *flowchart,* is very useful as a means of visualizing the relationships among the statements in the algorithm. Of course, the clothes washing algorithm is quite straightforward, and the diagram is not needed; but many algorithms are far more complex. Consider a series of steps you might follow if you were invited to a friend's house for dinner. Part of the algorithm might be

.

.

.

Get dressed.
Drive to friend's house.

.

.

.

If you feared you might be delayed, your plans might include the possibility of telephoning to say you would be late. To include this possibility you must introduce a decision point into the algorithm:

.

.

.

10. Get dressed.
11. If you are not late, go to step 13.
12. Telephone friend.
13. Drive to friend's house.

.

.

.

Statement 12 will be executed only if you were late and will not be executed otherwise. The decision statement is statement 11. The flowchart for this algorithm is shown in Figure 2.1.

The exact way in which this algorithm will be executed depends on the data (that is, whether you are late or not):

If late	*If not late*
Get dressed.	Get dressed.
Telephone friend.	Drive to friend's house.
Drive to friend's house.	

Both paths are implicit in the algorithm; the specific path executed will depend on the circumstances.

Next, let's take a look at a task a bit more complex—getting to school in the morning. We call this our plan for making school more fun; you'll see why in a while.

1. Turn off alarm.
2. Get up.
3. If there is no time to get washed, go to step 6.
4. Enter bathroom.
5. Get washed.
6. If there is no time to make breakfast, go to step 10.
7. Enter kitchen.
8. Get breakfast.

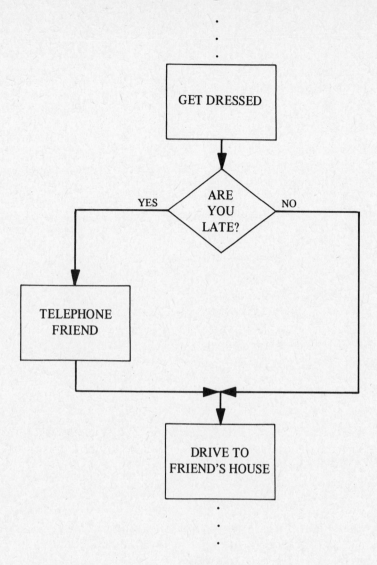

Figure 2.1

   9. Go to step 11.
10. Grab cookies.
11. Get in car.
12. Drive to school.

To make this algorithm complete and more formal we add two steps:

   0. Start.
13. End.

   Normally, we begin at step 0 and go to the next highest numbered statement unless directed to do otherwise by a GO TO instruction. Notice that this algorithm, like the previous one, contains an IF statement. IF statements permit jumping around and skipping some instructions. GO TO and IF statements cause a program to *branch*—that is, to make an out-of-sequence jump from one statement to another.

It is difficult to follow the branches; so in order to make the logic of the algorithm more clear, it is useful to represent the algorithm as a flow chart. Our set of instructions for getting to school might be converted to the flow chart in Figure 2.2.

Each *block* in the flowchart has a characteristic shape. *Start* and *end blocks* look like this:

A *process or operation block* which gives instructions for work to be done looks like this:

and a *decision block* which asks a question and has two or more outputs looks like this:

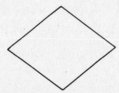

In this algorithm the start block indicates where the algorithm begins. First, we turn off the alarm clock, then we get up. The first decision asks if there is time to get washed; if the answer is yes, then we enter the bathroom and wash. The block labeled "get washed" could, of course, be expanded to include instructions such as "wash face," "brush teeth," and "comb hair." After completing the bathroom chores, or skipping them, the next step asks if there is time for breakfast. If so, then the kitchen is entered for breakfast. If there is no time for breakfast, we grab some cookies. In either case we then get into the car and drive to school.

Anyone following this algorithm precisely would be embarrassed on arriving at school because nowhere was there an instruction to dress. When programming, it is easy to make this type of mistake, leaving out some obvious detail. Computers make no assumptions and all details must be carefully and explicitly taken care of.

Program Loops and Decisions

Algorithms are usually easier to follow when they are represented as flowcharts. Frequently, when developing an algorithm for the solution of a problem, the programmer begins by drawing a flowchart. If the logic of an algorithm is complicated with many branch statements, flowcharts may be a tremendous aid in the design of a program. For example, look at Figure 2.3, a flowchart for getting a date.

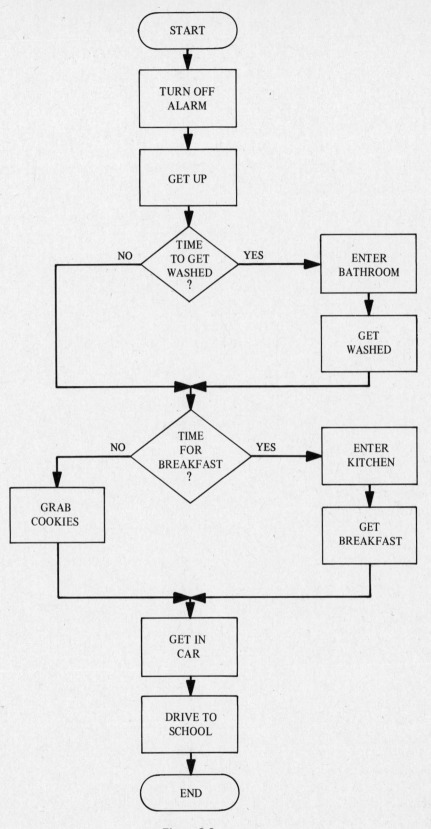

Figure 2.2

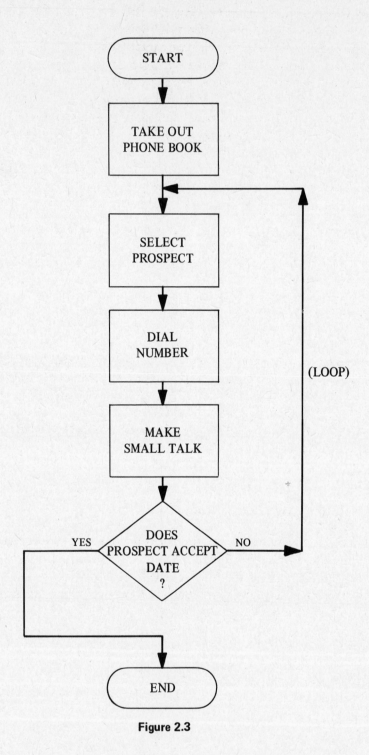

Figure 2.3

As before, the start block shows where the algorithm begins. First, take out your book of phone numbers and select a likely prospect. Dial the number, make small talk, and finally ask for a date. If she (he) accepts, then you're done. If you are refused, then go back and select another number. In this simplified example, we've left out the "Maybe" or "Call me back on Thursday" answer. The essential concept in this algorithm is the branch back to an earlier statement to create a *loop*. A loop is a sequence of instructions which is repeated several times. Note that each time the program goes through the loop a different telephone number is used; the instructions remain unchanged but the data operated on differs. If you eventually get an acceptance, you would reach the end block. However, if you keep getting rejections, then you re-execute the loop instructions. Since you only have a finite number of telephone numbers in your book, you must stop when the data run out. Converting this flowchart to a series of instructions in English is straighforward:

0. Start.
1. Take out phone book.
2. Select prospect.
3. Dial number.
4. Make small talk.
5. If prospect does not accept, go to step 2.
6. End.

A similar algorithm could be constructed to find the right blood donor in a medical emergency. The program might be used if there were an urgent need for a donor with type B-positive blood. If the medical records of the students at a college were kept on machine readable punch cards, the computer could be used to search the collection of data (called the *file*). *Input* and *output* are represented by specially shaped blocks:

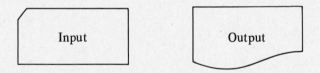

The algorithm reads a card with a student's name and blood type. If the blood type is B-positive, then the name is printed; otherwise it loops back to read the next card. This process continues until all cards have been read.

A programmer might begin by mapping the steps visually, using a flowchart like Figure 2.4. Then the algorithm could be written out:

0. Start.
1. Read NAME, TYPE.
2. If TYPE not equal to B-positive, go to step 1.
3. Print NAME.
4. Go to step 1.
5. End.

Note that this program will print the names of *all* students who have type B-positive blood. If statement 4 in the program were missing, the program would stop when the first B-positive card was encountered.

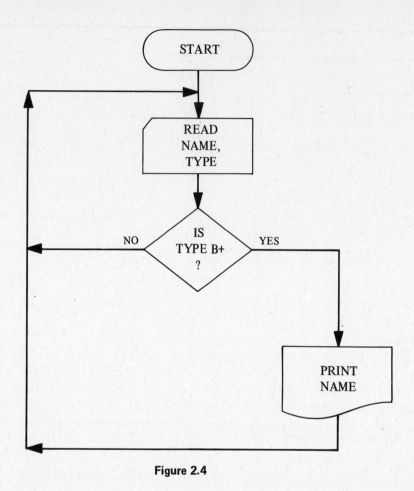

Figure 2.4

This simple example gives an indication of how computers are used for medical purposes. This type of *information retrieval* program has already had widespread impact on many facets of society.

The use of computers to solve business problems has revolutionized the nature of American enterprises in the last twenty years. One of the most common applications is the calcution of employee payrolls. Consider a file of records containing each employee's identification number, the number of hours worked in the past week, and rate of pay. The program must read the ID, HOURS, and RATE information for each employee to calculate his earnings for the week. In this example, overtime will be calculated at twice the normal rate.

As usual, the flowchart (Figure 2.5) begins with a START block and reads the ID, HOURS, and RATE from a data record. The algorithm then checks to see if this employee has worked more than 40 hours. If not, then the wages are simply the product of HOURS and RATE. If this employee has worked overtime, then the regular pay is computed by multiplying 40 and the RATE, and the overtime pay is calculated at twice the basic RATE multiplied by the hours worked in excess of 40. The total wages are calculated as the sum of regular wages plus overtime wages. Finally, the ID number and the wages are printed out. (With a few more instructions, they could be printed directly onto a check.) After printing, the program loops back to get the next employee's record.

All of the calculations for overtime wages can be combined into the single formula:

```
WAGES = (40.0 + (HOURS-40.0)*2.0)*RATE
```

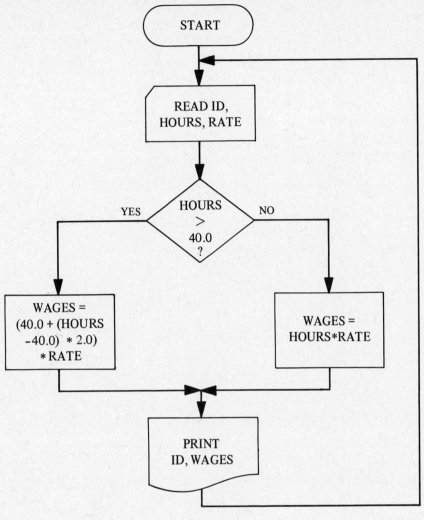

Figure 2.5

The instructions in this case might be

    0. Start.
    1. Read ID, HOURS, RATE.
    2. If HOURS > 40.0 go to step 6.
    3. WAGES = HOURS*RATE
    4. Print ID, WAGES.
    5. Go to step 1.
    6. WAGES = (40.0 + (HOURS − 40.0) *2.0) *RATE
    7. Go to step 4.
    8. End.

Note that in step 7 the algorithm transfers to step 4 in order to print the wages. Thus, there are two alternate formulas for computing wages; the decision as to which should be used depends on whether the number of hours worked is greater than 40 or not.

This example is an oversimplification of the actual payroll problem. The complicated rules for Federal withholding tax, Social Security tax, state and local taxes, health and pension plans, union dues, and charitable contributions make life difficult for the personnel payroll departments and keep several programmers busily employed at most major companies.

Problem 2.1

Draw a flow chart for the following program:

A local telephone company prepares its customers' bills by allowing each customer a basic monthly allowance of up to 50 calls for minimum service charge of $6.00. For each additional call, there is a 10¢ charge, and any long-distance charges are added to get the final bill.

The program statements are

```
0.  START
1.  READ, NAME, NCALLS, TOLLS
2.  BILL = 6.00
3.  IF ( NCALLS < 51 ) GO TO 6
4.  OVER = NCALLS-50
5.  BILL = BILL+(OVER*0.10)
6.  BILL = BILL+TOLLS
7.  PRINT, NAME, BILL
8.  GO TO 1
9.  END
```

Program Design

As a final example, consider the case of a professor who decided to grade students on the basis of the highest of three test scores rather than on the average. Assume that each student's name and test scores are punched onto a data card and the program must read each of the cards and find the largest of the three test scores. The basic flow of the algorithm (Figure 2.6) is similar to those which we have looked at before.

As the first step, the algorithm reads the student's name and three test scores. It then selects the largest of the three scores and prints the student's name and highest grade. The program then loops back to read the next card if one is there. If no card is there, the program will stop (the attempt to read a card when none remains is called an *end of file* condition). While the basic algorithm is simple, the step that selects the largest score is complex. As no single instruction in FORTRAN will select the largest of three scores, it will be necessary to expand this step.[3] For simplicity, assume that all three scores are different; that is, no two are the same.

[3] In Chapter 4, when we study *functions,* a simpler method will be possible.

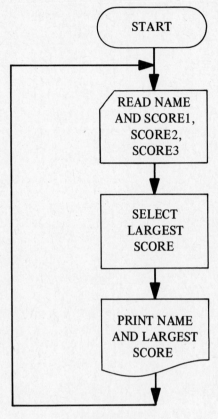

Figure 2.6

There are a number of ways in which the largest of three numbers can be found. Perhaps the most reasonable is the following:

1. Compare the first number with the second number and select the larger.
2. Compare the number chosen in step 1 with the third number and select the larger.

The result will be the largest of the three numbers.

This algorithm is like a playoff in sports among three players, A, B, and C: A plays B and the winner plays C. To demonstrate, suppose our three numbers are 91, 87, and 72.

1. Compare the first two and select the larger:

91   87
91

2. Compare the "winner" with the third number and select the larger:

91   72
91

Suppose our three numbers are 53, 75, and 42.

1.   53   75
       └────┬────┘
            75

2.   75   42
       └────┬────┘
            75

Suppose our three numbers are 63, 89, and 97.

1.   63   89
       └────┬────┘
            89

2.   89   97
       └────┬────┘
          97

Thus, the algorithm works if the largest number is in the first, second, or third position.[4]
We may rewrite the steps of the algorithm in more general terms as follows:

1. Set P to the larger of SCORE1 and SCORE2.
2. Set Q to the larger of P and SCORE3.

When step 2 has been executed, Q will be equal to the largest of the three scores. P may be set equal to the larger of SCORE1 and SCORE2 by these steps:

1. Set P to SCORE1.
2. If SCORE1 is larger than SCORE2, go to step 4.
3. Set P to SCORE2.
4. . . .

This segment starts by assuming that SCORE1 is the larger and sets P equal to SCORE1. It then compares SCORE1 with SCORE2 and, if the assumption was correct, *it skips step 3 and goes on to step 4* (which is not specified here). However, if the assumption were wrong and SCORE1 were less than SCORE2, it corrects by executing step 3 and setting P equal to SCORE2. The flowchart for this segment of the algorithm looks like Figure 2.7.
The entire algorithm may be written

0. Start.
1. Read NAME, SCORE1, SCORE2, SCORE3.
2. Set P = SCORE1.
3. If SCORE1 is larger than SCORE2, go to step 5.
4. Set P = SCORE2.

---

[4] In general, an algorithm should be tested on several different sets of data to insure its correctness.

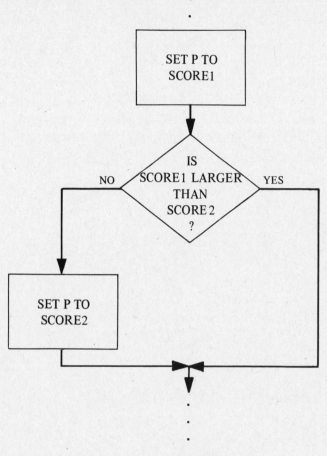

Figure 2.7

   5. Set Q = P.
   6. If P is larger than SCORE3, go to step 8.
   7. Set Q = SCORE3.
   8. Print NAME, Q.
   9. Go to step 1.
10. End.

Problem 2.2

Draw a flowchart for an algorithm that finds the smallest of three scores.

SOME BASIC AXIOMS OF GOOD STYLE

In 1919, a Cornell University professor, William Strunk, published a remarkable book which he called *The Elements of Style.** In only 44 pages Professor Strunk laid down a comprehensive set of rules for literary style.

The similarities between program structure and prose structure are striking. Consider the following maxims which are set down in *The Elements of Style:*

- work from a suitable design

- be clear

- revise and rewrite

- do not take shortcuts at the expense of clarity

- omit needless words

- prefer the standard to the offbeat

- do not use dialect

- do not overwrite

These rules provide a basis for defining programming style.
Consider Professor Strunk's rules and how they apply to program construction.

Work from a suitable design. Without careful planning, a program will become a disaster when it comes to debugging and modifying. The temptation to begin coding a program fragment is tremendous but must be overcome. The program should be designed before any coding begins. The organization should be logical and meaningful so that debugging is easy.

Be clear. You are not the only person who will read your program, and six months after you complete the program you will have forgotten what you did, anyway. It takes very little time to insert comments into a program listing and to choose meaningful variable and subprogram names. A program is not complete until good documentation is available.

Revise and rewrite. After writing a program, go through it. Do you expect it to run correctly? Is it understandable? Could you make it more efficient? If there is substantial room for improvement (there usually is), then revisions should be considered.

Do not take shortcuts at the expense of clarity. Shortcuts usually lead to trouble; they rarely pay off. If you absolutely must take shortcuts, carefully document your intent and check with someone else to see if your explanation is comprehensible. Don't be clever for the sake of being clever—the computer can't appreciate it anyway.

Omit needless words. To paraphrase Professor Strunk "vigorous programming is concise. A statement should contain no unnecessary computations, a routine no unnecessary statements, for the same reason that a drawing should have no unnecessary lines and a machine no unnecessary parts." Make every statement count.

Prefer the standard to the offbeat. There are times when little-used language features or unusual algorithms pay off. In general, however, it is best to be straightforward. Offbeat programming can make debugging difficult and later program modifications an impossibility.

---

*Now available in revised edition, W. S. Strunk, Jr. and E. B. White, *The Elements of Style,* Macmillan, 1962.

Do not use dialect. The number of different versions of FORTRAN, each with its own idiosyncrasies and advantages, makes this difficult. It is tempting to use statements unique to your system, since they may offer advantages in simplicity and efficiency. However, the cost of creating a compiler-dependent program may be great since transferring the program to another system will be difficult, tedious, and unsure. The American National Standards Institute (ANSI) has defined the FORTRAN language, and programs which adhere to the ANSI standard will compile on any FORTRAN system.

Do not overwrite. There is a limit to how much effort should be spent on a program. Don't try to squeeze out every excess instruction or every wasted location. There is a point of diminishing returns after which additional effort is wasted.

These rules are basic to good programming. Programs should not have excessive, wasteful, or unnecessary statements. Each programmer must decide whether his program is suitable for the environment in which he works. Only by understanding the hardware, the software, and the job requirements is it possible to evaluate the quality of a program.

Summary

In order to program effectively, we need an unambiguous language. Such a language does not exist among the naturally occurring languages human beings speak. We have traded off the ability to say many subtle (sometimes nonsensical) things for the clarity and conciseness of an artificial language like FORTRAN. Any set of FORTRAN statements that specifies an algorithm is a FORTRAN program.

When you write a computer program, there are many, many details to remember. Using a flowchart allows you to see more clearly the relationships between each of your statements or groups of statements.

One group of statements we use frequently in programming is a loop. When we combine loops with decision statements, we have a way of specifying an algorithm without a great amount of effort. These two concepts allow us to design a wide range of programs with only a few lines of instructions.

DEBUGGING CLINIC

The conversion of a handwritten program to FORTRAN statements is a clerical process with a large number of precise constraints. Statement numbers must appear in columns 1 through 5 and the program statements must be within columns 7 through 72. Violation of either of these rules will cause a syntactical error during compilation. It is helpful to write out the FORTRAN statements carefully on a special *coding sheet* in order to minimize the chance of error. Columns 73–80 are used for identification and are not part of the FORTRAN statement field.

In preparing programs for keypunching make sure to distinguish between the following pairs of often confusing characters:

Number	Letter
zero 0	O
one 1	I
two 2	Z

An incorrect version of the program shown earlier in this chapter was run using the WATFIV compiler; the output is shown in Figure 2.8. The errors in this program are quite obvious and the sample diagnostic output will give you an idea of what to expect when you make mistakes.

The following incorrect version of Spiral Problem 2A was run using the WATFIV compiler:

```
                TEST1 = 80.0
                TEST2 = 75.0
                AVERAG = (TEST1 + TEST2 + TEST3 /3.0
***ERROR***  UNMATCHED PARENTHESIS
                TEST3 = 85.0
                PRINT, TEST1, TEST2, TEST3, AVERAG
                STO6
***ERROR***  UNDECODEABLE STATEMENT
                END
```

Figure 2.8.

REVIEW QUESTIONS

1. Explain the purpose and construction of a flow chart.

2. What is an *algorithm?*

3. Explain the effect of an IF statement in an algorithm.

4. Explain the meaning of a *loop* in an algorithm. Why are loops useful?

5. List the flow chart symbols for start, end, process (operation), decision, input, and output.

6. How does an artificial language differ from a natural language?

EXERCISES

1. a. Write an algorithm for changing a flat tire and draw a flow chart for it.

   b. Draw a flow chart for the student grading algorithm on page 41, including a detailed section covering the choosing of the highest of the three scores.

   c. Modify the student grading algorithm so as to eliminate the use of Q in the second comparison. (Hint: Consider what would happen if you compared P with SCORE3 directly.)

   d. Draw a flow chart for the following series of statements:

```
0.  START
1.  READ X, Y
```

```
2. COMPUTE Z = (X + Y)/2
3. PRINT X, Y, Z
4. GO TO STEP 1
5. END
```

What will this algorithm accomplish? When will it terminate?

e. Write a series of English statements corresponding to the flow chart in Figure 2.9. What algorithm does this flowchart represent? What are the *two* conditions under which it will terminate?

2. Fill in the missing word(s):

a. A(n) _flowchart_ is a graphical representation of an algorithm.

b. An *end of file* occurs when a program _loops back to read a card & there is none._

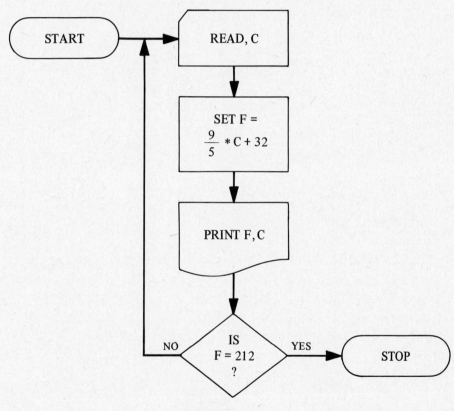

Figure 2.9

c. On an *end of file* a program will _stop_ .

d. A sequence of steps which, when followed, will lead to the solution of a problem is called a(n) _algorithm_ .

e. Whenever a(n) _decision_ statement is executed, a branch will occur.

f. A branch which may or may not be taken depending on the data (*conditional* branch) may be included in an algorithm by means of a(n) _____ statement.

g. Consider the following algorithm:

0. Start
1. Wake up
2. If you have missed train, go to step 5
3. Take train to school
4. Go to step 6
5. Drive to school
6. Attend class

If you miss the train, which sequence of steps will be executed? _drove to school & attend class_.

h. If you do not miss the train, which sequence of steps will be executed? _take train to school & attend class_.

3. a. Select the best answer(s). If a program has a loop in it, it

    1) Won't stop when it runs out of cards.
    2) Will read cards.
    3) Executes some instructions more than once.
    4) Does not need an END card.
    5) Needs fewer instructions.

b. Which of the following flowchart segments are incorrect? Why?

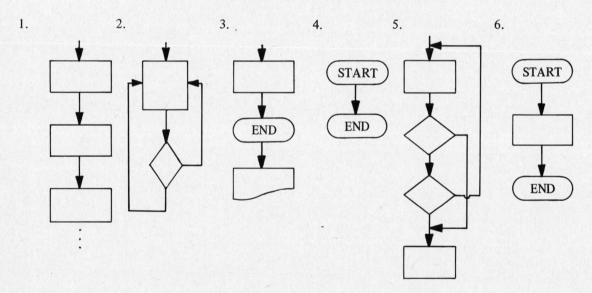

1.   2.   3.   4.   5.   6.

c. Write a flowchart that will describe the following algorithm:

    1. Read in a number, NUMB.
    2. If it is less than zero, set it equal to zero.
       If it equals zero, set it equal to 1.
       If it is larger than zero, set it equal to -1.
    3. Then, print the new number out.
    4. Stop.

SPIRAL PROBLEMS[5]

A. Student Grading

Keypunch and run the following program:

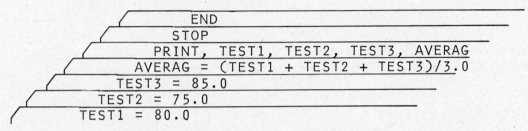

```
              END
            STOP
          PRINT, TEST1, TEST2, TEST3, AVERAG
        AVERAG = (TEST1 + TEST2 + TEST3)/3.0
      TEST3 = 85.0
    TEST2 = 75.0
  TEST1 = 80.0
```

B. Commercial Application: Salesperson Commissions

Keypunch and run the following program:

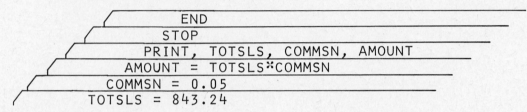

```
              END
            STOP
          PRINT, TOTSLS, COMMSN, AMOUNT
        AMOUNT = TOTSLS*COMMSN
      COMMSN = 0.05
    TOTSLS = 843.24
```

C. Mathematical Application

Keypunch and run the following program:

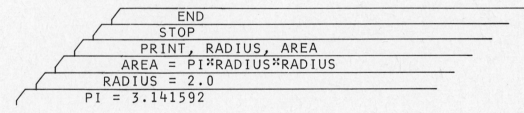

```
              END
            STOP
          PRINT, RADIUS, AREA
        AREA = PI*RADIUS*RADIUS
      RADIUS = 2.0
    PI = 3.141592
```

---

[5]Your instructor will indicate the special "control cards" needed in order to run the program. Be sure to follow the coding conventions (page 45). If no WATFOR or WATFIV compiler is available, you must punch a slightly different form of the PRINT statement; consult your instructor, or see page 72.

FORTRAN FUNDAMENTALS

If, in a series of things being investigated, we come upon one which our intellect cannot adequately comprehend, we must immediately call a halt. We should not examine what follows, but refrain from a useless task.

René Descartes, Rules for the Direction of the Mind *(1628)*

CHAPTER 3

FORTRAN, like English, has rules of grammar which must be observed if statements written in it are to be meaningful. FORTRAN statements are normally written on punched cards, one statement per line. The most commonly used FORTRAN statement is the assignment statement which is used to compute arithmetic results and assign the results of the computation to a variable. While the use of variables in FORTRAN is similar to their use in algebraic notation there are conceptual differences between a mathematical variable and a programming variable which will be discussed in this chapter.

The four most fundamental FORTRAN statements are the assignment statement, the READ statement, the PRINT statement, and the GO TO statement. The assignment statement allows the programmer to store and manipulate values by arithmetic operations such as addition, subtraction, multiplication, division, and exponentiation. The READ statement permits data values to be put in, the arithmetic assignment statement permits these values to be computationally manipulated, and the PRINT statement permits the results of the computations to be displayed. The use of the GO TO statement, introduced in the first chapter, permits program loops to be created similar to those discussed in Chapter 2.

The FORTRAN Statement

Any language, natural or artificial, has rules of syntax. "Natural" languages, like English, adhere to certain conventions about the way in which statements are written; these conventions, while arbitrary, must be observed. For example, in English we agree to write our sentences from left to right:

"How are you today?" ⟶

while Hebrew reads from right to left:

?מה שלומך היום ⟵

and Chinese from top to bottom:

你今天好嗎

It is important that these conventions be observed, because a deviation like

"?yadot uoy era woH"

makes communication difficult.

FORTRAN, like natural languages, has certain conventions which must be observed. The basic unit in FORTRAN is the *statement*. Statements, which are similar to English sentences, are either *instructions* ("Sit on this chair!") or *declarations* ("This is an early American antique chair."). Statements are written one to the line. Some examples of FORTRAN statements are

```
A = B + 2.3
GO TO 23
END
```

Note that only capital letters are needed in FORTRAN; there are no lower-case letters on keypunches.

The form in which FORTRAN text is written is 80 characters long, corresponding to the 80 character positions available on a punch card. The 80-character line is divided into four parts (*fields*).

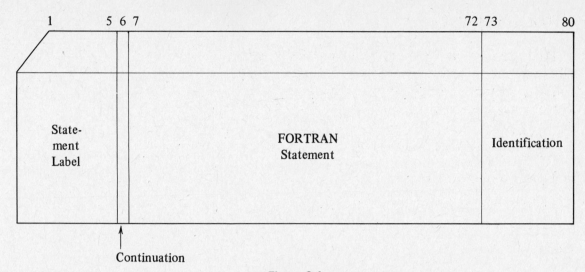

Figure 3.1

Field 1 is the *label field*. FORTRAN statements may be labeled for later reference, as we learned in Chapter 1. FORTRAN labels consist of one to five digits. Any arbitrary label may be chosen for a statement. The label field occupies columns 1–5 of a FORTRAN line and the label may appear anywhere within these columns.

Field 2 is a single character in column 6. If a FORTRAN statement is too long for a single card it may be continued on as many cards as required by placing a nonblank (non-zero) character in column 6 of each continuation card. For the first or only card of a statement column 6 must be blank (or zero).

Field 3 is columns 7–72 of the FORTRAN line and contains the FORTRAN statement itself. The statement may appear anywhere within columns 7–72 inclusive and may contain blanks anywhere the programmer desires. Typically, the statement begins in column 7 and continues in column 7 of the succeeding card if required.

Field 4, comprising the remaining columns 73–80, is available for any use the programmer desires. In general, programmers use this field to number the cards so that the deck may be restored to correct sequence if it should accidently be shuffled. If this is done, it is usual to number the cards by tens (10, 20, 30. . .) so that room is left to insert additional statements later without renumbering the deck.

Examples of coded FORTRAN statements are shown in Figures 3.2, 3.3, and 3.4.

Special forms are available for writing FORTRAN programs (Figure 3.5). On these forms you can divide your statements properly into fields. Therefore, a program coded on these forms is easy to keypunch.

A FORTRAN programmer may also take advantage of a *comment card* to insert comments into the program (Figure 3.6). These comments are for human readers only and have no effect whatsoever on the program. A comment card has the letter C in column 1; the rest of the card may contain any information the programmer desires.

Figure 3.7 shows a short, complete FORTRAN program.

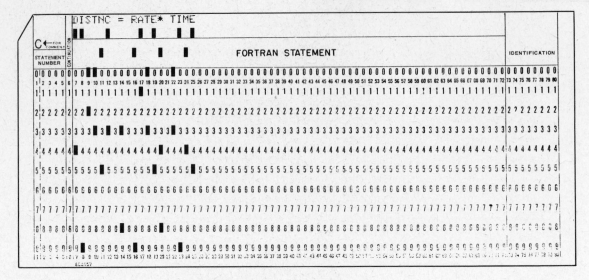

Figure 3.2 A FORTRAN statement.

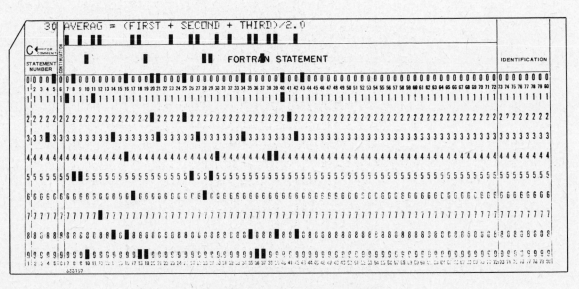

Figure 3.3 A FORTRAN statement with a label.

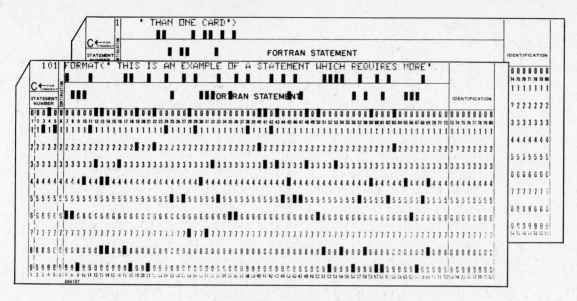

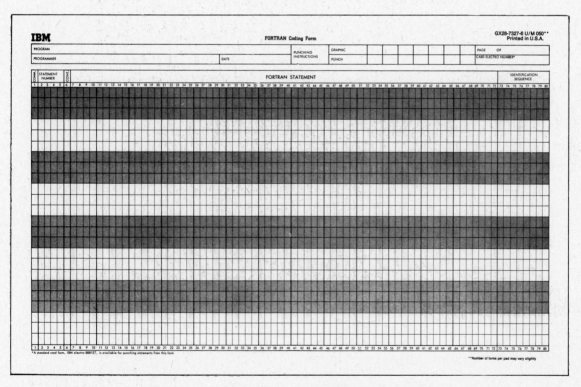

Figure 3.4   A statement requiring two cards.

Figure 3.5   A FORTRAN coding form.

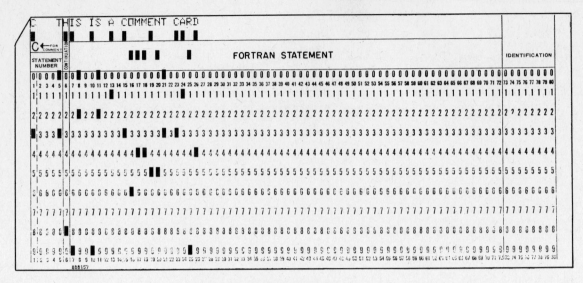

Figure 3.6   A comment card.

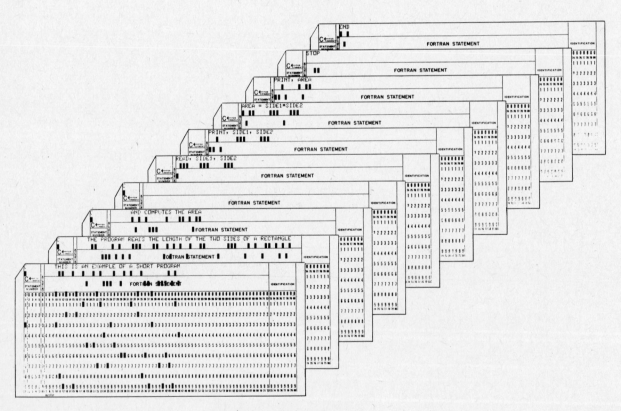

Figure 3.7   A short program.

Problem 3.1

Here is a program which converts temperature readings from degrees Fahrenheit to degrees Centigrade. Transcribe the FORTRAN statements onto coding forms or punch cards, being careful to utilize the correct fields.

```
C      THIS IS A SMALL FORTRAN PROGRAM
  100  READ, TEMPF
       TEMPC = (5./9.)*(TEMPF - 32.)
       PRINT, TEMPF, TEMPC
       GO TO 100
       END
```

Simple Assignment Statements

In Chapter 1 we noted that the computer stores data in its "memory." Since the purpose of a program is to specify operations to be performed upon data, it is important to learn how these data may be stored and retrieved.

A computer's memory may be thought of as though it were divided into little "boxes":

Each "box" is capable of storing a single value at any time. Thus, a particular box may have the value:

$$\boxed{64.0}$$

or it may have the value

$$\boxed{-128.6}$$

However, it may only have one value in it at a time. There are just two things that you can do with a "box":

- You can put a value into it.

- You can use the value in it in a statement.

When you put a new value into a box, the value that is currently in the box will be destroyed:

Destructive read-in

but when you *use* a value in the box, it is not destroyed. These operations are known as *destructive read-in* and *nondestructive read-out*.

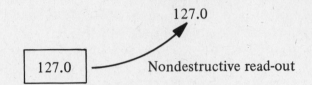

There are many such memory "boxes" in a computer; some computers have millions of boxes. Therefore, the programmer must have some means of referring to a specific box. This is accomplished by giving each box a *name*.

SAM
–14.3

RUTH
128.2

FIDO
.007

The name chosen is completely up to the programmer; the rule is that it must contain from one to six letters and numbers of which the first *must* be a letter. Since the contents of a box may vary, they are called *variables* and the name of a variable is called, logically enough, a *variable name*.

Variables are of two main types, *INTEGER variables* and *REAL variables*. The convention is that if the first letter of a variable name begins with I, J, K, L, M, or N, the variable is an *INTEGER variable*. Otherwise, the variable is a *REAL variable*.

The following names are valid REAL variable names:

X	Y	Z	ALPHA
SAM	YES	Q1	FIDO
A1234X	B1Q2	REDSPX	

REAL variable names

The names of REAL variables, then, will be one to six characters in length. The first character must be chosen from the letters A–H or O–Z; the second through sixth characters may be alphabetic or numeric. The following are invalid REAL names. Why?

MINI   TYPEWRITER   K   3HJK   HB(7

While you may choose any legal combination of letters and numbers to make up a variable name, it is best to choose meaningful names so you will remember what value you are storing in the variable. Here are examples of meaningful names:

PI   RATE   TIME
RADIUS   SALARY   FICA

Of course, the variable names are completely arbitrary. The value of π (PI) is about 3.14, but if you decide to name a variable PI and put some value other than 3.14 in it

PI
98.6

that is perfectly legal. It is not a good idea because anyone who has to read your program will be confused, but it is nonetheless legal.

Problem 3.2

Which of the following are valid REAL variables?

a. A	f. 1K	k. ONE
b. A1	g. SAM	l. VAR
c. 1A	h. JOAN	m. ZQ1234
d. K	i. WILLIAM	n. F19D6
e. K1	j. ALPHA	o. N14

REAL variables may take on *real values*. A REAL value is a number consisting of from one to seven digits with a decimal point[1]; it may also have a sign. Examples of REAL numbers are

1.5	2.	127.3
−4.	+3.14	.0000006
−.05	33.33	1234567.

In general, you write a REAL number just the way you would expect to. One caution: you must not write commas in REAL numbers. The numbers

1,000.0   7,344,266.

are *not* valid REAL numbers.

---

[1] The maximum size of the value is dependent upon the computer. The restriction of REAL values to seven digits exists on the IBM 360/370 series of computers and similar computers. For other computers, check the manufacturer's manual.

Problem 3.3

Which of the following are valid REAL numbers?

a. 1   b. 1.   c. 1.0

d. 1,972.   e. 1276.321   f. .007

Assume you have a variable named PI and you want to put the value 3.14 into it. The statement

PI = 3.14

will cause the value 3.14 to be placed in the variable PI:

PI
3.14

The statement

PI = 3.14

is not quite the same as the mathematical statement

$$\pi = 3.14$$

The mathematical statement is a fact. It is always true by definition. The programming statement is an *instruction.* It says, "take the value 3.14 and put it in the variable named PI." To see why this distinction is so important, consider the statement

B = 17.0

This is to be interpreted as "take the value 17.0 and put it into the variable named B." The result is

B
17.0

If later in the program the statement

B = -24.2

is executed, then the value will change; it will become

B
−24.2

Here is a complete (if useless) FORTRAN program:

```
A = 0.0
B = 1.
C = -43.246
A = .05
STOP
END
```

Let us see what will happen to the variables in it. Remember that this program must be translated by the computer into the computer's language (compiled). When this occurs, the compiler program will note that you have used three variables (A, B, and C) and will assign them to memory locations:

A	B	C
?	?	?

Before the program is executed the variables do not have known values. Whatever value they have will depend on what is left in the computer from the last program or will be indeterminate. The program is executed as follows.

First, the statement

```
A = 0.0
```

is executed. This causes the value 0.0 to be put into variable A:

A	B	C
0.0	?	?

Next the statement

```
B = 1
```

results in

A	B	C
0.0	1.	?

Then the statement

```
C = -43.246
```

will cause the variable C to assume the value −43.246:

A	B	C
0.0	1.	−43.246

When the statement

```
A = .05
```

is executed, the value in the variable A will be changed:

A	B	C
.05	1.	−43.246

The STOP statement will cause the execution of the program to terminate. (The END statement serves no function except to signal the end of the program deck.)

INTEGER Arithmetic and REAL Arithmetic

We have mentioned that there is another kind of variable besides REAL variables. The second kind of variable is the *INTEGER variable.* Just as REAL variables may assume REAL values, INTEGER variables assume INTEGER values. Integers are whole numbers; they have no decimal point and no fractional part. Examples of integers are

2	−4	837	0
+17	128	1234567	

It may seem that INTEGER variables are unnecessary since REAL variables may take on integral values:

INTEGER	REAL
0	0.
23	23.
−4	−4.
1234	1234.

as well as values which cannot be assumed by INTEGER variables:

INTEGER	2				3
REAL	2.0	2.1	2.5	2.9	3.0

However, we shall see that INTEGER variables have some special properties which can be useful when programming.

INTEGER variable names, like their REAL variable counterparts, are composed of from one to six letters and numbers, but the first *must* be one of the letters I, J, K, L, M, or N. Examples of INTEGER variable names are

I	MPG	MARY
K9	JOYFUL	IAMBIC

The following are invalid INTEGER names. Why?

XBH	MONSTER	KHU*G
8JKT	Q7	

Problem 3.4

Which of the following are valid INTEGER variable names?

a. KAT	d. KILOMETER	g. 4
b. CAT	e. K9	h. 4.0
c. MILE	f. DOG	i. FOUR

Problem 3.5

After the following programs have been executed, what are the contents of each of the storage locations?

```
1.  A = 5.4      2. N = 9      3. RESULT = 8.675
    B = 6.3         K = N         TEST = 9.6
    C = A           K5 = 5        VALUE = TEST
    D = B           NOW = K       X = VALUE
    E = C
    C = 2.4
```

Summary

There are two numbering systems in FORTRAN: the INTEGER and the REAL. The INTEGER constants are the whole numbers and they may be stored in a location whose name is six or less characters in length, the first of which must be I, J, K, L, M, or N. The REAL constants contain a decimal point and may be stored in a location whose name is six or less characters in length, the first of which must be taken from the letters A–H or O–Z.

Copying a Value

The assignment statement can do more than simply assign a value to a location. It can also be used to copy a location to another location. If in our program on page 61 it were necessary to save the first value of A, it could be copied into a location named AY by the statement

AY = A

which means "*copy the value of the location whose name is A into the location whose name is A Y.*" If this were done, the following values would result.

A	B	C	AY
.05	1.	−43.246	0.0

providing the statement AY = A *were placed before the statement* A = .05. (What would be the result if it were placed after A = .05?)

Notice that

AY = A

is *not* the same as

A = AY

Why?

The important point to note here is that the content of A is unchanged. In an assignment statement the contents of the locations whose names appear on the right-hand side of the equals sign are not altered. Only the content of the single variable name which appears on the left-hand side of the equals sign is changed. *Each assignment statement changes the contents of one and only one location.*

Addition

The assignment statement is even more powerful than the preceding discussion has indicated. In addition to being used to assign a numerical value to a variable and to copy a location, the assignment statement can also be used for performing mathematical computations. The general form of an assignment statement is

variable = expression

The statement is interpreted as *compute the value of the expression* and *copy it into the variable.*

An expression may be as simple as a number (*constant*):

$$A = 43.7$$

Variable   Expression

or a variable:

$$B = C$$

Variable   Expression

or it may be more complex and include *variables, constants,* and *operators*:

$$CAT = DOG + 7.2$$

Variable   Expression

Operators specify the operations (such as addition, subtraction, multiplication, and division) to be performed.

Expressions, and therefore assignment statements, can become quite complex. In every case, however, the interpretation of the statement is to evaluate the expression and *assign* its value to the variable on the left of the equals sign. In this chapter we shall be concerned only with simple expressions containing one operator. In Chapter 4, we shall consider more complex forms.

If the following program fragment were executed:

```
          .
          .
          .
PI = 3.141592
RADIUS = 6.5
NOVER = 40
NREG = 150
RADCPY = RADIUS
          .
          .
          .
```

the relevant section of memory would look like this:

PI	RADIUS	NOVER
3.141592	6.5	40
NREG	RADCPY	
150	6.5	

The inclusion later in the program of the assignment statement

```
NTOTAL = NREG + NOVER
```

directs the computer to take the contents of the location whose name is NREG, add it to the contents of the location whose name is NOVER, and store the results in the location whose name is NTOTAL. This calculation would result in variables with these values:

PI	RADIUS	NOVER	
3.141592	6.5	40	
NREG	RADCPY	NTOTAL	
150	6.5	190	

Notice that INTEGER and REAL values can both appear in the same program.

This assignment statement utilized INTEGER variables. An assignment statement utilizing REAL numbers is executed in a similar way. The following sequence of three statements assigns the cost of a dinner at a restaurant to the REAL variable COST, the sales tax amount is stored in SLSTAX, and the total charge is calculated and stored in CHARGE:

```
COST = 9.08
SLSTAX = .63
CHARGE = COST + SLSTAX
```

If the restaurant had an additional nontaxable cover charge of two dollars, it could be added to the bill by the following assignment statement:

```
CHARGE = CHARGE + 2.00
```

This statement instructs the computer to take the contents of the location called CHARGE, add 2.00 to it, and put the result back into the location CHARGE. How much is the total bill in this case? Notice that all the variable names satisfy the FORTRAN rules of formation.

Problem 3.6

A building is 945.5 feet tall and a television tower 135.2 feet tall is erected on the top of the building. Write three assignment statements to store the height of the building and store the height of the tower. Then calculate and store the total height of the building with the tower on top.

Problem 3.7

A student receives a mark of 78 on a test but the professor announces a bonus of 5 points for everyone. Write the assignment statements to calculate the new grade.

Subtraction

Subtraction may also be performed in an arithmetic assignment statement. Assume that the PRICE of a can of cleanser is 0.29 (29 cents) and that there is a customer coupon for a reduction of 0.05 (5 cents). The FINAL price could be calculated as follows:

```
PRICE = 0.29
COUPON = 0.05
FINAL = PRICE - COUPON
```

Computer programs may have several steps to include both addition and subtraction. A university registration system might have a sequence of steps to calculate the number of students in a class after students were added or dropped from the course. The number of students registered could be stored in NSTUD, the number added in NADD, and the number dropped in NDROP. To calculate the final number of students (stored in NFINAL), one can use

```
NSTUD = 34
NADD = 6
NDROP = 3
NFINAL = NSTUD + NADD
NFINAL = NFINAL - NDROP
```

After execution of this program fragment, the content of location NFINAL is 37.

Multiplication

The multiplication operator is represented by an asterisk (*). One might use this operation to calculate the AREA of a rectangle whose HEIGHT and WIDTH were known (LENGTH is not REAL):

```
HEIGHT = 12.1
WIDTH = 9.4
AREA = HEIGHT * WIDTH
```

The perimeter of this rectangle can be found by doubling the sum of the HEIGHT and the WIDTH:

```
SUM = HEIGHT + WIDTH
PERIM = 2.0 * SUM
```

To calculate the total number of ounces in 19 twelve-ounce jars, you could write this:

```
NUMBER = 19
NOUNCE = 12
NTOTAL = NUMBER * NOUNCE
```

Division

The division operator is represented by a slash (/). First, consider an example of REAL division. Imagine that a trip of 224.1 miles required a total of 12.7 gallons of gasoline. To calculate the miles achieved per gallon, the following assignment statements could be used:

```
DIST = 224.1
GALS = 12.7
RMPG = DIST/GALS
```

Division involving REAL numbers takes place exactly as we expect and the result is 17.6 miles per gallon.

There is a peculiarity in INTEGER division since fractions are not permitted in INTEGER arithmetic. If you divided 6 by 3:

```
NRESLT = 6/3
```

the result would be 2. But the situation becomes more complicated when we try to divide 6 by 4:

```
NVALUE = 6/4
```

This result is mathematically 1.5, but decimal fractions are not permitted in INTEGER arithmetic. In INTEGER division, *the fractional parts of results are dropped*. In this case the location named NVALUE would contain the INTEGER value 1 without any decimal point or fraction. The convention of dropping the fractional part of the result produces the following results:

$3/2 = 1$	$19/5 = 3$	$497/50 = 9$
$5/6 = 0$	$-3/2 = -1$	$7/(-2) = -3$

This rule is simple, but it can produce some surprising results. For example, in taking the average of two INTEGER numbers such as 10 and 13 (that is, $23/2$), the result will be 11. As another example, imagine that six quarts of apple cider were to be divided among 18 campers. Using INTEGER division:

```
NQUART = 6
NCAMPR = 18
NSHARE = NQUART/NCAMPR
```

You would find that the share (NSHARE) for each camper is 0. To avoid this, REAL arithmetic must be used:

```
QUART = 6.0
CAMPR = 18.0
SHARE = QUART/CAMPR
```

Using REAL division, each camper's share is computed as 0.333333 quarts, or one-third of a quart. The subject of REAL and INTEGER arithmetic will be discussed in greater depth in the next chapter. Although it may seem awkward to you now, INTEGER arithmetic can be used in some very productive ways.

Exponentiation

A number may be raised to a power by the use of the exponentiation operator (**). One could find the area of a circle whose radius is 2.3 inches by executing the following program fragment[2]:

```
RADIUS = 2.3
RADSQ = RADIUS**2.0
AREA = 3.141592*RADSQ
```

Exponentiation may also be used to find the square root of a number. This is possible since $\sqrt{X} = X^{1/2} = X^{0.5}$. To find the length of the side of a square whose area is known (length of a side $= \sqrt{\text{area}}$) we could write

```
AREA = 64.
SIDE = AREA**0.5
```

As an example of exponentiation with INTEGER values, consider a designer of light fixtures who has an order for a discotheque. He has red, green, blue, and yellow bulbs and a large number of light fixtures with three sockets. He would like to know how many different lighting arrangements he can make. He could put any of the four colors in any of the three sockets. The following program fragment finds the number of combinations:

```
NCOLOR = 4
NSOCKT = 3
NCOMBS = NCOLOR**NSOCKT
```

In this case there are 4^3 or 64 combinations.

Summary

The arithmetic assignment statement may be used to compute the operations of addition, subtraction, multiplication, division, and exponentiation on REAL and INTEGER variables. When dividing INTEGER values, the fractional part is dropped from the result.

Simple Input and Output

We have seen that a value may be stored in a variable by means of an assignment statement. For example, the statement

---

[2]The formula for the area of a circle is $A = \pi r^2$, where π is the constant 3.141592 and r is the radius.

```
A = 43.0
```

will cause the value 43.0 to be stored in the variable A.

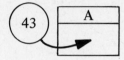

The statement

```
A = B
```

will cause the value currently contained in variable B to be copied and stored in variable A. This will not destroy the value of B. The statement

```
A = B * 2.
```

will cause the current value of B to be multiplied by 2. and the result will be stored in variable A.

Another way to store a value in a variable is to read it from a data card. Reading data is a very important process because it allows one to write a program and run it with many different sets of data. For example, look at the simple payroll program below:

```
10  READ,RATE,HOURS
    WAGE = RATE*HOURS
    PRINT,WAGE
    GO TO 10
    END
```

The program reads data values into the variables RATE (that is, rate of pay) and HOURS (hours worked), then multiplies the values in RATE and HOURS to compute a wage and store the result in WAGE. Since the program does not depend upon *specific* values in RATE and HOURS, any values read from the data card will work. The program loops back after printing to read a new set of values, and uses the same code again to process the new data. The program flow is diagrammed in Figure 3.8.

Printing the results of a computation is also extremely important; the values resulting from a computation are useless unless someone can read them. Throughout the previous chapters we have used examples of output statements, so you should have some feel by now for when and where output statements are used. Many programs use the following sequence of operations:

1. Read data.
2. Process data.
3. Print data.
4. Loop back to read more data.

and terminate when an end of file condition (no more data) occurs.

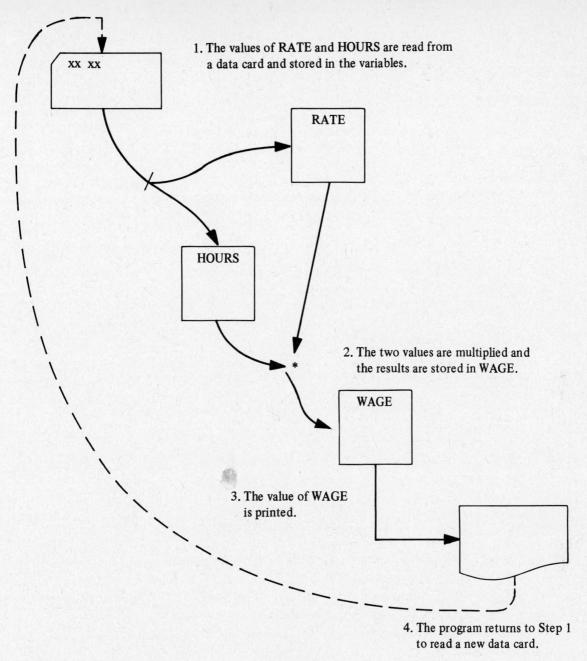

1. The values of RATE and HOURS are read from a data card and stored in the variables.

2. The two values are multiplied and the results are stored in WAGE.

3. The value of WAGE is printed.

4. The program returns to Step 1 to read a new data card.

Figure 3.8

In introducing the FORTRAN input/output statements, a problem of presentation arises. FORTRAN I/O, while not difficult, is a bit detailed and often confusing to the novice programmer. For this reason the WATFOR and WATFIV compilers accept simplified FORTRAN READ and PRINT statements that are easy to use although they do not have the flexibility and power of the standard FORTRAN input/output statements. We will introduce the simplified statements in this chapter and discuss them in more detail in the next. We must, however, make provision for readers who do not have a WATFOR or WATFIV compiler at their disposal. Therefore, if you will run your programs on a WATFOR or WATFIV compiler, skip to the section titled "Format-Free Output"; otherwise continue to read.

Output for non-WATFOR/WATFIV Compilers

If you do not have a WATFOR or WATFIV compiler, you cannot use the simple input and output statements described in this chapter. The reason is that the WATFOR and WATFIV simplified input and output statements are not part of the standard FORTRAN language. Rather than attempt to explain the standard FORTRAN I/O statements at this time, we suggest the following procedure.

1. Add the following statement to every FORTRAN program:

```
1000 FORMAT(5G16.8)
```

This statement will never be executed and can be placed anywhere before the END statement.
2. Wherever the WATFOR statement

```
PRINT, list of variables
```

is used, substitute the statement

```
PRINT 1000, list of variables
```

Here are some examples:

WATFOR	Standard FORTRAN
PRINT, V1,V2,V3	PRINT 1000,V1,V2,V3
PRINT, ALPHA	PRINT 1000,ALPHA

Note that the standard FORTRAN statement does not have a comma after the word PRINT, whereas the WATFOR/WATFIV simplified I/O does.

The format of the printed output resulting from the PRINT 1000 statement will be similar to the format described for the simplified output statement.

Input may be handled in a similar manner. The statement

```
1000 FORMAT(5G16.8)
```

must be added to the program. It should be added only once to a program and will serve for both input and output. Wherever a WATFOR statement of the form

READ, *list of variables*

occurs, substitute a statement of the form

READ 1000, *list of variables*

Compare these examples:

WATFOR	Standard FORTRAN
`READ,X,Y,Z`	`READ 1000,X,Y,Z`
`READ,GAMMA`	`READ 1000,GAMMA`

One data card can read in up to five numbers. When you punch numbers onto a card for input, the numbers should be right justified within the following columns:

First number	1–16
Second number	17–32
Third number	33–48
Fourth number	49–64
Fifth number	65–80

Thus, the statement

`READ 1000,SAM`

would read a single (REAL) number punched in columns 1–16 and the statement

`READ 1000,DAVID,LISA`

would read a (REAL) number punched in columns 1–16 and an (INTEGER) number punched in columns 17–32. *Right justified* means that the number may have leading blanks but should not have trailing blanks. Thus

Card column number: <u>1</u> . . . <u>13</u> <u>14</u> <u>15</u> <u>16</u> <u>17</u> . . . <u>31</u> <u>32</u> . . .
                                      1   2   5   .   1   4

would be a valid data card for the above statement. Each READ statement will read a new card.

Free-Format PRINT Statement

The WATFOR and WATFIV compilers have a simplified input/output capability that is very convenient. The PRINT statement can be used to print the contents of a variable on the line printer. The statement which will print the value of a variable is simply

PRINT, *variable list*

where *variable list* contains the name of one or more variables separated by commas. Examples of PRINT statements are

```
PRINT,X
PRINT,N
PRINT,RATE
PRINT,ALPHA
PRINT,A,NUM,XVAL
PRINT,Q,Z123
```

Note that both REAL and INTEGER variables may be mixed in a single statement. The PRINT statement is executed as soon as it is reached in the program; the value printed is the current value stored in the variable. If the following program were executed:

```
N = 1
PRINT,N
N = N + 1
PRINT,N
STOP
END
```

the printed output would be

```
1
2
```

Similarly, in the following program to calculate the number of hours in a week:

```
NHRDAY = 24
NDAYWK = 7
NHRWK = NHRDAY*NDAYWK
PRINT,NHRWK
```

the result will appear on the output as

```
168
```

To print the values which produced the result on the line preceding the result, we add another print statement:

```
NHRDAY = 24
NDAYWK = 7
PRINT,NHRDAY,NDAYWK
NHRWK = NHRDAY*NDAYWK
PRINT,NHRWK
```

This new program gives the following output:

```
 24        7
168
```

This is somewhat more meaningful, since we can see the values that have produced the result. Notice that each PRINT statement begins printing on a new line. If there is more than one value to be printed in a single PRINT statement, printing continues across the page.

As part of a student grading program, it is necessary to compute the average of two grades stored in locations MARK1 and MARK2:

```
MARK1 = 87
MARK2 = 81
PRINT,MARK1,MARK2
NSUM = MARK1 + MARK2
NAVER = NSUM/2
PRINT,NAVER
```

The output of this program fragment is

```
87      81
84
```

Notice that the grades were selected so that the average was a whole number. Consider the case where the result is not a whole number. For example, if the two marks were 87 and 84, the average would be 85.5 which would be stored as 85 under the rules for INTEGER division. In order to compute the average and retain the fractional part, we must use REAL arithmetic for the computation.

There is a rather peculiar convention used for the output of REAL values; REAL values are printed in a format known as *E notation*.

The student grading program rewritten using REAL values:

```
GRADE1 = 87.0
GRADE2 = 81.0
PRINT,GRADE1,GRADE2
SUM = GRADE1 + GRADE2
AVERAG = SUM/2.0
PRINT,AVERAG
```

produces the output

```
0.870000E 02      0.810000E 02
0.840000E 02
```

This strange-looking result is not quite what you might have expected. The values printed are expressed in *E notation*. This exponential notation, or power-of-ten notation, is commonly used to represent very large or very small quantities. Instead of having many rules, the creators of WATFOR/WATFIV decided to print all REAL quantities in E notation. It is not difficult to translate the output to a more recognizable quantity. The value 0.870000E 02 is the computer's representation of $.87 \times 10^2$ which is 87., just as expected. The other two values translate into $.81 \times 10^2$ and $.84 \times 10^2$, or 81. and 84.

The REAL number 0.870000E 02 is composed of two parts. The first part,

$$0.870000$$

is called the *mantissa*; the second part,

$$E\ 02$$

is called the *exponent*. The number after the E indicates how many places the decimal point should be shifted to get the number's true value. For example, to interpret the number

$$0.100000E\ 01$$

the decimal point should be shifted one (= E 01) place to the right.

$$0.100000E\ 01 = 1.$$

Similarly,

$$0.100000E\ 02 = 10.$$
$$0.100000E\ 03 = 100.$$

If the exponent negative, the decimal is shifted to the left instead of the right. Thus:

$$0.100000E\text{-}01 = .01$$
$$0.100000E\text{-}02 = .001$$

E notation is an adaptation of the often used "scientific notation" which represents numbers as values multiplied by a power of 10. The speed of light is 186,000 miles per second. In scientific notation, this number would be written as $.186 \times 10^6$; in E notation it is written as 0.186000E 06.

E notation is useful when printing numbers which are very large:

$$0.250000E\ 30 = 250000000000000000000000000000$$

or very small:

$$0.250000E\text{-}30 = .00000000000000000000000000000025$$

In general, E notation is of the form

$$0.xxxxxxEspp$$

where 0.xxxxxx is a decimal number between 0.100000 and 0.999999, s is the sign (blank for plus or minus sign for minus), and pp is a power or exponent which indicates how many places the decimal point is to be shifted. In the previous example we had to shift the decimal point two places to the right to get the value. A negative power indicates that the decimal point is to be moved to the left. These examples give a better idea of how E notation is used:

$$0.140000E\ 02 = 14.0$$
$$0.874936E\ 03 = 874.936$$
$$-0.957800E\ 01 = -9.57800$$
$$0.800000E\text{-}05 = 0.000008$$
$$-0.100000E\text{-}16 = -0.00000000000000001$$
$$0.123456E\ 00 = 0.123456$$

$$0.140000E\ 04 = 1400.0$$
$$0.783000E\ 12 = 783000000000.$$
$$0.123064E\text{-}01 = 0.0123064$$
$$-0.840000E\text{-}02 = -0.0084$$

Returning to the example of adding the sales tax to the cost of a dinner, we now include a PRINT statement to have the final charge printed:

```
COST = 9.08
SLSTAX = .63
CHARGE = COST + SLSTAX
PRINT,CHARGE
```

The computer would print out

```
0.971000E 01
```

We could also instruct the computer to print out the COST and the SLSTAX as well:

```
COST = 9.08
SLSTAX = .63
CHARGE = COST + SLSTAX
PRINT,COST,SLSTAX,CHARGE
```

which would produce the following results:

```
0.908000E 01    0.630000E 00    0.971000E 01
```

We could change the program to print one item per line:

```
COST = 9.08
SLSTAX = .63
CHARGE = COST + SLSTAX
PRINT,COST
PRINT,SLSTAX
PRINT,CHARGE
```

which would result in the following output:

```
0.908000E 01
0.630000E 00
0.971000E 01
```

The general form of the format-free PRINT statement is

$$PRINT, f1, f2, \ldots, fn$$

where $f1, f2, \ldots, fn$ represent *fields* of data that may be printed. A field is one whole piece of data; it may be an INTEGER or a REAL variable, a constant or even an expression. Since expressions are permitted as fields of a PRINT statement, one might write the statement

```
PRINT,7,24,7*24
```

for the output of our program to calculate the number of hours in a week. One could also substitute the following PRINT statement and get the same results:

```
NHRDAY = 24
NDAYWK = 7
PRINT,NDAYWK,NHRDAY,NDAYWK*NHRDAY
```

Notice that we are taking a short-cut: instead of first doing the calculation, then printing it, we let the PRINT statement take care of both jobs. When a calculation is performed in a PRINT statement, the result of the computation gets printed but is not stored for later use.

Free-format READ Statement (WATFOR/WATFIV)

Just as WATFOR/WATFIV offers us a simpler PRINT statement, it lets us read data on cards more conveniently than standard FORTRAN (page 73). Obtaining data punched on cards is conveniently done with the simplified READ statement. In the student grading example, the values of the marks might be read by the following statements:

WATFOR/WATFIV	*Standard FORTRAN*
`READ,MARK1,MARK2`	`READ 1000,MARK1,MARK2`
`PRINT,MARK1,MARK2`	`PRINT 1000,MARK1,MARK2`
`NSUM = MARK1 + MARK2`	`NSUM = MARK1 + MARK2`
`NAVER = NSUM/2`	`NAVER = NSUM/2`
`PRINT,NAVER`	`PRINT 1000,NAVER`
.	`1000 FORMAT(5G16.8)`
.	.
.	.
	.

This program is more general than the one presented earlier in the chapter since this program may be used with many different sets of test marks.

In this system, the data would be punched on data cards as

```
87     81
```

or as

```
87,81
```

Fields of data on the punch card are separated by blanks (as on the first card) or by commas (as on the second card). The convenience of free-format input is that it is *not* necessary to punch the data in specific columns; they can be entered anywhere on the card, just so long as each field is separated from its neighbor by at least one blank or by a single comma. Each READ statement begins reading from a new card, but there may be as many fields on a data card as you can squeeze in.

REAL values are read in exactly the same way except that decimal points are punched in the numbers on the data cards. If the following program fragment were run:

```
READ,COST,SLSTAX
CHARGE = COST + SLSTAX
PRINT,COST,SLSTAX,CHARGE
```

the input could be punched as

```
9.08     .63
```

or if commas were used to separate the fields

```
9.08, .63
```

The output of this program would be identical to the earlier example.

If it were preferred to read each value using a separate READ statement:

```
READ,COST
READ,SLSTAX
```

it would be necessary to punch each data item on a separate card, since each READ statement begins reading on a new card:

```
9.08
 .63
```

It is possible to mix REAL and INTEGER fields in READ and PRINT statements. To affix an INTEGER number to indicate the table number at which the meal was served and an INTEGER number to indicate how many people had eaten dinner, we might write the following program:

```
READ,NTABLE,COST,SLSTAX,NPEPLE
CHARGE = COST + SLSTAX
PRINT,NTABLE,CHARGE,NPEPLE
```

The input for this program might be

```
17     9.08     .63     3
```

and the output would be

```
17     0.971000E 01     3
```

The general form of the free-format READ statement is

$$READ, v1, v2, \ldots, vn$$

where $v1, v2, \ldots, vn$ represent variables whose values are to be read in. Constants or expressions are *not* permitted in the list of a READ statement.

If a READ statement requests many fields of data:

```
READ,IDNUM,NHOURS,RATE,OVER,FICA,SOCSEC,UNION,HEALTH
```

the data may not fit on a single data card. In this case the data may be punched on as many cards as are necessary because the READ instruction will keep reading data cards until all locations specified are filled.

The GO TO Statement

In general, the flow of statements in a program is sequential. That is, control passes from each statement to the one below it.

Statement	Order Executed
READ,A,B	1st
C = A✻B	2nd
PRINT,A,B,C	3rd
STOP	4th
END	not executed; indicates last card of program.

However, it is often desirable to alter the normal program flow. This is accomplished by use of a *GO TO* statement. The GO TO statement is simple to construct; it is of the form

GO TO *label*

where label is a statement label. Recall that a statement may have a numeric label in columns 1–5. One use of the label is to serve as an "address" for the GO TO statement. The above program could be written

```
47 READ,A,B
   C = A✻B
   PRINT,A,B,C
   GO TO 47
   END
```

In this revised program, the GO TO statement will be executed after the PRINT and will cause the program to execute statement 47 (the READ) again. The READ will read a new card and the program statements are re-executed. The process terminates when there are no more cards to read. Thus the GO TO statement is the means of constructing program *loops* as discussed in Chapter 1.

The choice of statement label 47 was arbitrary. Any one to five digit number could have been used. Thus, the following program is equivalent:

```
128  READ,A,B
     C = A*B
     PRINT,A,B,C
     GO TO 128
     END
```

The statement labels may appear in any order; any may be skipped. Thus, the following is perfectly correct:

```
         . . .
         . . .
101      . . .
         . . .
 20      . . .
 97      . . .
         . . .
  1      . . .
         END
```

Of course, a given label may only be used to label one statement in the program. Two statements with the same label are not allowed. However, a label may be referenced by many GO TO statements in a program.

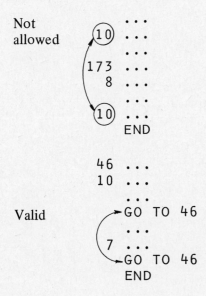

Not allowed

```
  10  . . .
      . . .
      . . .
 173  . . .
   8  . . .
      . . .
  10  . . .
      END
```

```
 46  . . .
 10  . . .
     . . .
     GO TO 46
     . . .
  7  . . .
     GO TO 46
     END
```

Valid

Summary

FORTRAN statements are written according to a set of syntactic rules. Since the most common form of writing a FORTRAN program is on punch cards, the convention arose of reserving columns 1–5 for labels, columns 7–72 for program statements, and columns 73–80 for the programmer's personal use in identifying his program.

FORTRAN variables must be six or fewer letters or numbers in length, with the first character always a letter. Two main types of variables are REAL and INTEGER. INTEGER variables must begin with any of the letters I, J, K, L, M, or N while REAL variables can begin with any letter *except* these. By using assignment statements, one can save, change, or calculate with the value of variables. With INTEGER variables the division operation truncates any fractional remainder.

While input and output statements can be very detailed, there exist easy free-format READ and PRINT statements in WATFOR/WATFIV.

DEBUGGING CLINIC

The rules for constructing simple arithmetic assignment statements are simple enough, but there is still room for error. A common mistake is the failure to recognize the difference between the equals sign in the arithmetic assignment statement and the equals sign as used in algebra. This confusion results in incorrect statements such as

```
B + C = A          Incorrect
```

Such a statement would produce the following error on the WATFOR compiler:

```
C   THIS IS A SPECIAL PROGRAM FOR DETERMINING
C   ERROR MESSAGES
       B = 4.0
       C = 5.0
       B + C = A
***ERROR*** ILLEGAL QUANTITY ON LEFT OF EQUALS SIGN
       PRINT, A, B, C
       STOP
       END
```

The correct form is, of course

```
A = B + C          Correct
```

A few final remarks:

● Don't forget to begin assignment statements after column 6.

● Commas are *not* to be included in numeric values.

Incorrect	*Correct*
4,765.87	4765.87
34,566,000	34566000

● Variable names must adhere to the rules of formation

Incorrect

DISTANCE
7THVAL
HAP.4
JOE'S

REVIEW QUESTIONS

1. What are the uses of the following fields in a FORTRAN statement: *label, continuation, statement,* and *identification?* Which are optional and which must always appear?

2. What is a *comment* card? How is it used? How is it designated? What effect do comments have on the program?

3. What is a *variable*? What is the difference between an INTEGER and a REAL variable? What are the rules for naming INTEGER and REAL variables?

4. What is the function of the assignment statement? How is it evaluated? What operators may be used?

5. How does INTEGER division differ from REAL division?

6. Explain the purpose of the READ statement. How is it similar, in function, to the assignment statement? How is it different? How are data cards set up?

7. What is the function of the PRINT statement? How is it used?

EXERCISES

1. Which of the following are valid arithmetic assignment statements?

a. DIST = RATE✳TIME
b. X = B✳C
c. ABCDEFG = B - C
d. K = 6789
e. 678 = NJH
f. XJ = -7.6
g. A + B = C
h. DENSTY = WEIGHT/VOLUME

i. VOLTS = CURRENT✳RESIST
j. VALUE = 2.71828/TEST
k. PRINC + AMOUNT
l. TOT = SUBTOT
m. TAX = .06 ✳ COST
n. FINAL = TEMP -
o. MMMJ = ✳ KK6

2. Write assignment statements to perform the following calculations:

a. Given the number of feet in a measurement, calculate the number of inches.

b. Calculate the simple interest earned on a principal amount at a rate of 5 percent.

   c. Subtract union dues of $6.00 from a salary figure.

   d. Calculate the area of a square given the length of a side.

   e. Given the number of entries per page of a telephone book and the number of pages, calculate the number of entries in the whole book.

   f. Calculate the term average for a student, assuming that there were two tests.

   g. The current inventory of a local car dealer is 34 cars. He gets a delivery of seven additional cars and sells 11. Write the program fragment to calculate his present inventory of cars.

   h. Given the length, width, and height of a box, calculate the volume.

   i. A salesperson sells three items at $4.50 and six items at $3.98. If the commission rate is 15 percent, calculate his earnings.

   j. The formula for the volume of a sphere is Volume=$(4/3\pi r^3)$, where r is the radius. Calculate the volume if the radius is known.

3. Which of the following WATFOR/WATFIV input/output statements are valid?

   a. `PRINT, MARY`

   b. `READ,VIOLET`

   c. `PRINT,17`

   d. `PRINT,A,A*2.0,Y,KNOT`

   e. `READ,A + 2`

   f. `PRINT,VALUE1,VALUE2`

   g. `READ AND PRINT,X,Y,Z`

   h. `READ,ALPHA,BETA,ALPHABET`

   i. `PRINT,DUNE,SAND,WORM`

   j. `READ A`

4. a. If the number of students initially in a class is 35, four students are added, and two students are dropped, write FORTRAN statements to compute the total class enrollment (all the numbers should be INTEGER values).

   b. Rework exercise 4.a assuming that all the numbers are REAL.

   c. 1) If A = 4.1 and you execute the statement

```
A = A + .5
```

     what will the new value of A be?

    2) If we execute the statement A = A + A?

    3) If we execute the statement A = A?

   d. Which of the following statements will yield the same result if executed?

```
1) A = B + C          7) C = B/B
2) A = B              8) A = (B/2.0)*2.0
3) A = B/(2.0*2.0)    9) A = 1.0
4) A = C + B + 0.0   10) A = B/B
5) A = B**2.0        11) A = B*B
6) C = B + A
```

   e. What values will be *printed out* if the following program is executed?

```
B = 2.0
READ,A,C
B = (B+C)/A          Data Card
PRINT B,C,A        ─────────────
STOP                 2.0 5.0
END
```

5. a. Write a program to read in a distance in feet, convert the results to inches, and print out the results.

   b. Write a program to read in pounds, convert to kilograms (2.2 pounds/kilogram), and print the results and the input.

c. Write a program to read in a principal amount and a yearly rate of interest. Then calculate the interest for one year and print the results.

d. Write a program to read in a value representing the radius of a circle, print the radius, calculate the area of the circle, print the area, calculate the circumference, and print the circumference.

e. Write a program to read two INTEGER numbers and determine how many times the second divides into the first.

SPIRAL PROBLEMS

Note: You should prepare a data card as directed for use in these problems.

A. Student Grading

Write a program to read in two REAL test scores from a single data card of the form

```
/ XXX.X     XXX.X

  Score 1    Score 2
```

Find the average by summing the two scores and dividing by two. Finally, print the scores and the averages.

B. Commercial Application: Salesperson Commissions

Write a program to read in a sales amount and a rate of commission which have been punched on a single data card in the form

```
/ XXXX.XX  X.XX

  Amount    Rate
```

Calculate the amount of commission by multiplying the two values and print the sales amount, rate of commission and amount of commission.

C. Mathematical Application

Write a program to read a single data card with two real values indicating the base radius and the height of a cylinder.

```
/ XXX.X     XX.X

  Base       Height
  radius
```

Calculate and print the volume of the cylinder as given by the formula $V = \pi r^2 h$.

MORE FORTRAN

The Analytical Engine is therefore a machine of the most general nature. Whatever formula it is required to develop, the law of its development must be communicated to it by two sets of cards. When these have been placed, the engine is special for that particular formula.

Charles Babbage, Passages from the Life of a Philosopher (1864)

CHAPTER 4

In Chapter 3 a simple form of the assignment statement was introduced. However, the assignment statement need not be restricted to a single arithmetic operation. When more than one operator is used in an assignment statement, the question of operator precedence (which operator is evaluated first) arises. For example, the statement

A = B + C * D

could conceivably mean

A = B + (C*D) or A = (B+C) * D

To avoid problems of ambiguity, FORTRAN establishes a hierarchy of operators. In FORTRAN, multiplication and division are performed before addition and subtraction. Thus, the first interpretation above is the correct one.

FORTRAN has two modes of arithmetic operations: INTEGER and REAL. INTEGER arithmetic is used for counting and enumerating while REAL arithmetic is used for measurement.

A further extension of the power of the assignment statement is the use of library functions. Library functions are programs which are available for general use. They may be combined with a programmer's code merely by using their names in an arithmetic assignment statement. For example, the library function to calculate a square root may be utilized by coding an expression such as

Y = SQRT(X) + 5.

Library functions are used like arithmetic operators such as + and *.

The input and output statements used until now have used a pre-specified standard format for data. It is sometimes desirable to specify a customized format for a particular READ or PRINT statement. An option allowing you to reference a FORMAT statement is discussed in this chapter.

Introduction

The programming basics presented so far have dealt only with complete programs that performed computations and produced output. In this chapter the power of the arithmetic statement will be extended.

Restricting the assignment statement to a single arithmetic operation makes the statements simple to construct, but it imposes artificial constraints on the programmer. In most programs, it is desirable to create more complex arithmetic statements. What follows in this chapter is a discussion of the rules for forming more complicated expressions.

The simplified READ and PRINT statements are also restrictive. FORTRAN allows one the ability to perform more complex forms of input and output. That flexibility will be dealt with in the discussion of simple FORMAT statements.

Unrestricted Assignment Statements

When the arithmetic assignment statement is restricted to a single operator, it is difficult to write complex expressions. For example, to calculate the volume of a box, one is forced to write statements such as

```
AREA = SIDE1 * SIDE2
VOLUME = AREA * HEIGHT
```

This is perfectly good programming, but it would be more convenient to write

```
VOLUME = SIDE1 * SIDE2 * HEIGHT
```

Such an arithmetic assignment statement is, in fact, quite legal. However, there are some conventions that must be observed when writing arithmetic assignment statements with multiple operators.

A problem develops because it is not possible to use some conventional mathematical notations on a keypunch. For example, the average of four numbers—A, B, C, and D—may be computed by

$$\text{Average} = \frac{A + B + C + D}{4.0}$$

but this cannot be typed on a keypunch. We cannot punch a numerator above a denominator; the entire expression must be stated on a single line. One attempt to do so is the statement

```
AVERAG = A + B + C + D/4.0
```

Unfortunately, this statement would only sum up A, B, C and one-fourth of the value of D. Though this is a valid statement, it certainly does not calculate the average; it is equivalent to the algebraic statement

$$\text{Average} = A + B + C + \frac{D}{4.0}$$

The desired result may be obtained by inserting parentheses:

```
AVERAG = (A + B + C + D)/4.0
```

The parentheses, which guarantee that the entire sum is divided by four, should seem natural to anyone familiar with algebra.

When an arithmetic statement is written on a single line, the corresponding FORTRAN statement is usually quite obvious. For example, the statement

$$A = \frac{B}{C} \times D$$

if written on a single line would be

$$A = (B/C) \times D$$

which in FORTRAN is simply

```
A = (B/C)*D
```

A few more examples should make the process clear.

Example 1

To calculate the number of seconds in a year we need to evaluate this equation:
Seconds per year = 60 seconds per minute
$\times$ 60 minutes per hour $\times$ 24 hours per day
$\times$ 7 days per week $\times$ 52 weeks per year

which could conveniently be written as

```
NSECS = 60*60*24*7*52
```

If you are curious about the answer, try to run a program with this statement (don't forget to include a suitable PRINT statement).

Example 2

A payroll program might calculate the size of the net paycheck by multiplying the pay rate times the number of hours and then subtracting the sum of the union dues and the health insurance costs:

```
WAGES = RATE*HOURS - (UNION + HEALTH)
```

Example 3

Conversion of Fahrenheit to Centigrade is accomplished by using the formula

$$\text{Centigrade} = \frac{5}{9}(\text{Fahrenheit} - 32)$$

which, in FORTRAN, is written as

```
CENT = 5.0/9.0*(FAHREN - 32.0)
```

Example 4

The area of a circle is Area $= \pi r^2$. This could be written as

```
AREA = 3.141592 * RADIUS ** 2
```

In these examples, the order of execution of the computations is intuitively clear. But there are examples which might result in confusion. The statement

```
X = A/B*C
```

could be read to mean

$$X = \frac{A}{BC}$$

or

$$X = \frac{A}{B}C$$

Another confusing statement is

```
Y = D - E - F
```

which has two interpretations:

$$Y = (D - E) - F \quad \text{or} \quad Y = D - (E - F)$$

Each of these produces a different numerical result.

To resolve these ambiguities, FORTRAN is designed around a set of conventions which specify the meaning of arithmetic expressions. The first such convention specifies the hierarchy of evaluations for arithmetic operators:

Level 1 ** Exponentiation
Level 2 * / Multiplication and division
Level 3 + – Addition and subtraction

In evaluating an arithmetic expression, the level 1 operations (exponentiation) are performed first, then level 2 operations (multiplication and division), and finally level 3 operations (addition and subtraction). It is now possible unambiguously to evaluate an arithmetic assignment statement such as

```
X = A ✶ B ✷✷ C - D/E
    ↑   ↑   ↑   ↑
    2   1   4   3        Order of operations
```

According to the conventional hierarchy, it is equivalent to

```
TEMP1 = B✷✷C
TEMP2 = A✷TEMP1
TEMP3 = D/E
X = TEMP2 - TEMP3
```

This is the same as if it had been written

```
X = (A✷(B✷✷C)) - (D/E)
```

The second rule of evaluation is that when there are several operations of the same level to be performed, then the statement is evaluated left to right. Thus, the example given earlier:

```
Y = D - E - F
    ↑   ↑
    1   2        Order of operations
```

is evaluated as

```
TEMP1 = D - E
Y = TEMP1 - F
```

just as if it had been written

```
Y = (D - E) - F
```

In the case of

```
X = A/B✷C
```

the evaluation would correspond to

$$X = \frac{A}{B} C$$

Problem 4.1

Write the evaluation of this last expression as a series of statements, each having one arithmetic operation.

A more complicated example is

    X = A*B/C**D*E- F/G - H*S

which in algebraic notation would be written as

$$X = \frac{AB}{C^D} E - \frac{F}{G} - HS$$

Exponentiation

The third convention allows the insertion of parentheses to resolve ambiguities and to guarantee that the FORTRAN expression computes what the programmer intends it to compute. The last expression could be made clearer by inserting parentheses:

    X = ((((A*B)/(C**D))*E)-(F/G)) - (H*S)

or as

    X = ((A*B)/(C**D))*E - F/G - H*S

or as

    X = (A*B/C**D)*E - F/G - H*S

In fact, it could be done in any of several other valid ways. In every case its value would be the same.

In these examples, the parentheses were optional. But there are occasions when it is necessary to use parentheses to override the usual rules. The formula for converting from Fahrenheit to Centigrade (Centigrade = $\frac{5}{9}$(Fahrenheit – 32)) must be written with parentheses:

    CENT = 5.0/9.0*(FAHREN - 32.0)

in order to insure that 32.0 is subtracted from the Fahrenheit temperature before it is multiplied by 5.0/9.0. When you evaluate an expression involving parentheses, evaluate the expression inside the parentheses first. If parentheses are nested, the deepest (or innermost) expression is evaluated first. In the case of

    K = L*((M+N)*I/J)

the addition is performed first since it is in the deepest pair of parentheses.

Summary

- The hierarchy of arithmetic operators is

    Level 1   **
    Level 2   * /
    Level 3   + −

    Lower level operations are performed before higher level ones.

- When operators of the same level appear in an arithmetic expression, they are executed from left to right.

- Parentheses may be inserted to clarify the order of execution and to override the standard conventions.

Although these rules may seem a bit complicated, they are quite intuitive and, in general, a statement is evaluated as common sense would expect. A few more examples in Table 4.1 should help clarify any questions. In each case the first answer comes from using the minimum number of parentheses.

There are a few other conventions in the hierarchy of operations. The *unary minus* (a minus sign making a number negative) may occur in an arithmetic expression as follows:

$$x = \frac{y}{-3.0}$$

When you write this formula in FORTRAN, the −3.0 must be surrounded by parentheses to prevent the occurrence of two operators in a row:

```
X = Y/(-3.0)
```

Thus, when you write

$$d = r^{-2}$$

the FORTRAN expression must be

```
D = R**(-2.0)
```

Another rule applies to powers of powers. When you evaluate

$$x = a^{b^c}$$

the algebraic interpretation is

$$x = (a)^{(b^c)}$$

Table 4.1

Algebraic representation	FORTRAN arithmetic assignment statement
Volume of a cylinder = $\pi r^2 h$ where r = radius h = height π = 3.141592	VOLUME = 3.141592*RADIUS**2.0*HEIGHT or VOLUME = 3.141592*(RADIUS**2.0)*HEIGHT
$d = \dfrac{1}{2}at^2$ where d = distance a = acceleration t = time	DIST = ACCEL*TIME**2.0/2.0 or DIST = (ACCEL*(TIME**2))/2.0
$F = \dfrac{9}{5}C + 32$ where F = degrees Fahrenheit C = degrees Centigrade	FAHR = 9.0/5.0*CENT + 32.0 or FAHR = (9.0/5.0)*CENT + 32.0
$PX = PO(1 + R)^X$ where PO = initial principal PX = principal after X years R = rate of interest	PX = PO*(1.0 + RATE)**X or PX = PO*((1.0 + RATE)**X)
$M = \dfrac{Y_1 - Y_0}{X_1 - X_0}$ where M = slope of a line through points (X_1, Y_1) and (X_0, Y_0)	SLOPE = (Y1 - Y0)/(X1 - X0)
$F = \dfrac{G\,m_1 m_2}{r^2}$ where F = force between two objects m_1, m_2 = masses of the objects r = distance between them	FORCE = G*XM1*XM2/R**2.0 or FORCE = (G*XM1*XM2)/(R**2.0)
$e = \dfrac{p(\Delta q)}{q(\Delta p)}$ where e = relative elasticity of demand in economics Δp = change in price at price p Δq = change in quantity at quantity q	ELAST = P*DELTAQ/(Q*DELTAP) or ELAST = (P*DELTAQ)/(Q*DELTAP)

In FORTRAN, the expression

X = A**B**C

is also interpreted as

X = A**(B**C)

which is an exception to the rule that when operators of the same level appear, the evaluation is performed from the left to the right.

Problem 4.2

Convert the following algebraic formulas to FORTRAN:

a. $V = \dfrac{4}{3}\pi r^3$

b. $S = 4\pi r^2$

c. $v = v_0 + a^t$

d. $y = x^3 + 2x^2 - 4x - 3$

e. $i = \dfrac{j+k}{j-k}m$

f. $m = (n-1)(n-2)(n-3)$

g. $x = y^{3a}$

h. $d = m/v$

i. $y = (x-2)(x+3)$

j. $k = \dfrac{n^2+1}{2} + 6$

Problem 4.3

a. Convert the following FORTRAN statements to algebraic representation:

1) A = B*(C - D/E)
2) X = Y + W/Z
3) D = D1 + (A*T**2.0)/2.0
4) P = A**2.0*R
5) X = (1.0-X)/(Y-X)
6) Y = X**3 + 5.0*X**2 - 2.5*X + 6.0
7) P = P + P*R*T
8) J = K*L - K+L/(M-N)*(M+N)
9) M = 3/(I/J-K)*M - N+6
10) I = J**(K-3)**L/7

b. Rewrite the statements in fully parenthesized form.

Integer and Real Arithmetic

FORTRAN has two primary types of arithmetic, *integer* and *real*. There are times when it is convenient to select one type of arithmetic over the other. Real arithmetic allows very large or very small numbers to be expressed easily. For example, the real constant 25.E11 represents the number 2,500,000,000,000. However, the number is not stored in the computer as a 13-digit number, but rather as 25×10^{11}. This is because the computer can only carry about seven digits with accuracy. If the statement

```
A = 123456789123456789.
```

were executed, the value stored in A would be 1234567.E 11 or

```
123456700000000000.
```

Actually, this does not present much of a problem in most scientific calculations since experimental results tend to be approximate anyway. Of course, errors may occur in real arithmetic. For example, the FORTRAN statement

```
A = (10.0/3.0)*3.0
```

will produce the result

```
A = 9.999999
```

Though this is usually not too serious, there are certain types of calculations in which this slight imprecision cannot be tolerated. In financial computations, for example, a result that is off by as little as one cent is simply not acceptable. In these cases integer arithmetic is used.

Integer arithmetic is always precise. The real expression

```
A = 2.7 * 100.0
```

may result in a value of

```
269.9999
```

but the integer statement

```
I = 27 * 10
```

will result in a precise answer of 270. Unfortunately, integer values do not have as great a *range* as real values. 5.E60 is a valid real number, but 123456789123456 is too large for an integer. On the IBM 360/370 and similar computers, only numbers with the characteristics shown in Table 4.2 can be manipulated.

Table 4.2

Characteristic	Real	Integer
Maximum magnitude	About 10^{75}	2147483647
Maximum number of digits	About 7	About 10
Smallest fraction	About 10^{-75}	Fractions cannot be represented

Thus, while integer values are more precise than real, they do not have as large a range and they cannot be used to represent numbers with a fractional part.

Real numbers are normally used when measurements are involved, while integers are generally reserved for counting and enumerating. The temperature on a given day may be measured at 75.2 degrees (real); counting the number of people who can be seated in an auditorium, on the other hand, always gives a whole number such as 203 (integer).

Mixed Mode Operations

The arithmetic assignment statements discussed so far have contained either INTEGER or REAL expressions, but not both. Early versions of FORTRAN enforced this convention, but current compilers allow *mixed mode arithmetic*.

Although INTEGER numbers are generally used for counting or enumerating while REAL numbers are used for measuring, the distinction is sometimes blurred. Occasionally, it is desirable to switch from one mode to another. Consider the problem of finding the average of a number of student grades (Chapter 2). Taking the average of two INTEGER values, say 84 and 87, produces a fractional result, 85.5, which is not a permitted value for an INTEGER. In this case it is desirable that the outcome of an operation on integers be stored as a REAL value. *To guarantee that the result of an operation is a REAL value, then at least one of the operands must be a REAL value.* Writing

```
AVERAG = (MARK1 + MARK2)/2.0
```

will cause the computer to calculate the sum of the marks as an INTEGER number. But since the division is by 2.0 (a REAL value, as opposed to the INTEGER value 2), the final result will be REAL and will be stored in the REAL location AVERAG:

```
AVERAG = (MARK1 + MARK2)/2.0
```
$$\underbrace{\text{(MARK1 + MARK2)}}_{\text{integer sum}}$$
$$\underbrace{\text{(MARK1 + MARK2)/2.0}}_{\text{real quotient}}$$

An INTEGER value may be converted into a REAL value by simply assigning the INTEGER value to a REAL location. If the distance between two cities is stored in location MILES as an INTEGER, it can be converted into a REAL value by assigning it to the REAL location XMILES:

```
XMILES = MILES
```

If MILES had the value 226, then XMILES will have the value 226.0.

Conversion from REAL to INTEGER is equally simple. Of course, the fractional part of the REAL value will be truncated. Assigning the REAL value 647.83, stored in location VALUE, to the INTEGER location NVALUE:

```
NVALUE = VALUE
```

will result in NVALUE being set equal to 647.

One use of mixed mode arithmetic is to round off numbers. For example, if the school records of grades are kept as two-digit numbers (perhaps two columns of a punch card containing the student's course record), our computed average of 85.5 must be rounded off to the nearest INTEGER.

Using INTEGER arithmetic, one gets

```
NAVERG = (MARK1 + MARK2)/2
```

which, after the fraction is ignored, is equal to 85. However, it is conventional to round off 85.5 to 86. To correct the error, one can write

```
NAVERG = AVERAG + .5
```

If the REAL number has a fractional part between .5 and .999 . . . , this will increase the INTEGER part of the number by one. If it is less than .5, the INTEGER part of the number will remain the same. Converting this REAL number into an INTEGER truncates the fractional part and produces a correctly rounded number.

A few examples will help clarify this idea. If B = 10.6,

```
N = B + .5
```

results in N = 11, because 10.6 + .5 is 11.1 which is truncated to 11. However, if B = 10.4, the results would be N = 10, because 10.4 + .5 = 10.9 which is truncated to 10. In both cases, the value of N is the correctly rounded off INTEGER of the REAL number.

Summary

To change a single value from INTEGER to REAL, assign the INTEGER value to a REAL variable.

To change a single value from REAL to INTEGER, assign the REAL value to an INTEGER variable but remember that the fractional part will be truncated.

When performing a computation, if one of the operands is REAL, then the results of the operation will be REAL, even if the other operand is INTEGER.

Consider the following program fragments which demonstrate mixed mode arithmetic:

```
1. A = 3.5
   N = 3
   B = A*N
```

B is assigned the value 10.5.

```
2. X = 2.4
   K = 2
   M = K*X
```

The multiplication operation produces a REAL result of 4.8, but when the value is stored in the INTEGER location M the value is truncated to 4.

3. ```
K = 5
L = 2
X = K/L
```

This case is a little bit more tricky. The division is performed in INTEGER mode and the result is 2 (remember the rules for INTEGER division); but when stored in the REAL location X, it has a value of 2.0. In order to have the result 2.5 stored in X, one of the operands in the division must be REAL. This could be accomplished by writing

```
K = 5
L = 2
XL = L
X = K/XL
```

We have used the REAL location XL in order to convert L to REAL and force the division to take place in REAL mode.

4. ```
X = 5.6
Y = 4.1
K = X + Y
```

The sum is evaluated as a REAL value, 9.7, but is truncated and stored as 9 in the INTEGER location K.

Worked Example

The Stingy Rental Car Company charges $12 a day and 10¢ per mile. Write a program to read an INTEGER number up to three digits in length for the number of days and a REAL number of the form XXXX.X for the number of miles (remember, the company is Stingy and measures miles down to tenths of a mile). Calculate the charge and print the number of days, the mileage, and the total charge:

WATFOR/WATFIV   [Standard FORTRAN]

READ, NDAYS, XMILES   [READ(5,1000) NDAYS, XMILES]

These statements put in the number of days (INTEGER) and the number of miles driven (REAL).

CHARGE = NDAYS*12.00 + XMILES*0.10

This statement calculates the charge; notice the mixed mode operation NDAYS*12.00. Since one of the operands is a REAL number, the result will be a REAL value. No parentheses are needed, since the multiplications will be performed before the addition.

```
PRINT, NDAYS, XMILES      [       WRITE(6,1000) NDAYS, XMILES
PRINT, CHARGE                      WRITE(6,1000) CHARGE
                          [1000   FORMAT(5G16.8)            ]
STOP
END
```

Library Functions

Certain mathematical functions turn up frequently in solving problems. For instance, it is often desirable to calculate a square root. Instead of writing a long series of instructions each time, this may be done in FORTRAN by using the *library function* SQRT. To use the function SQRT it is only necessary to include it in an arithmetic assignment statement. In the statement

```
X = SQRT(25.0)
```

the value assigned to X will be 5.0. Note that the number whose square root we want is written within parentheses. Any positive number may be used. Thus, if we write

```
X = SQRT(49.)
```

then X will have a value of 7.0.

The number within parentheses, called the *argument* of the function, may be a variable:

```
Z = 50.26
P = SQRT(Z)
```

A function may be used in an arithmetic assignment statement like any value. Thus,

```
P = 36.0
Q = 2.0 * SQRT(P) + 1.0
```

will result in Q having a value of 13.0. The argument of a function may be an expression as well as a constant or variable. Any variable, constant, or expression that is used as the argument to SQRT must be of REAL mode and must have a value greater than 0.0.

For example, the distance from the origin to a point (x, y) on a coordinate graph is given by the formula

$$\text{distance} = \sqrt{x^2 + y^2}$$

The distance could be calculated by writing

```
DIST = SQRT(X**2 + Y**2)
```

For another example, consider the problem of designing a pendulum clock. The time it takes for a pendulum to make one complete swing and return to the starting point is given by the formula

$$T = 2\pi \sqrt{\frac{L}{g}}$$

where L is the length of the pendulum, g is the acceleration of gravity (32 ft/sec/sec), and π is 3.141592. To build a pendulum clock, one must first determine the time for a full swing of the pendulum. This can be done by writing

```
TIME = 2*3.141593*SQRT(RLEN/32.0)
```

(It is *not* correct to use a library function on the left side of an assignment statement. A statement such as

```
SQRT(25.0) = X
```

would mean "store the value of X in $\sqrt{25}$," which makes no sense.)

Library functions are actually programs used by a program to calculate commonly used values. They are kept available on a reel of magnetic tape or a magnetic disk and are used whenever required. FORTRAN provides a number of these functions; later in this text a method of writing functions will be explained.

SIN and COS

The trigonometric functions *sine* and *cosine* are important enough to be included in the library functions. Given the length of the hypotenuse of a right triangle and one of the angles (in radians), it is a simple matter to calculate the length of the opposing side (Figure 4.1) by

```
OPP = HYPOT*SIN(ANGLE)
```

The length of the adjacent side is

```
ADJ = HYPOT*COS(ANGLE)
```

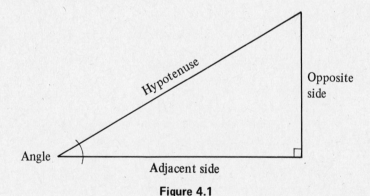

Figure 4.1

Note that the arguments to SIN and COS are REAL numbers and are expressed in radians (rather than degrees). Of course, these two trigonometric functions find their way into many more complex mathematical expressions. The bending of light by a prism is expressed by the formula

$$n = \frac{\sin\frac{1}{2}(D + A)}{\sin\frac{1}{2}A}$$

where n is the index of refraction of the glass, A is the prism angle (Figure 4.2), and D is the minimum deviation. (All angle measurements are given in radians.)

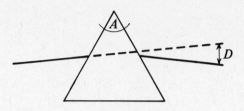

Figure 4.2

In FORTRAN, the index of refraction can be evaluated by writing

```
N = SIN((D + A)/2.0)/SIN(A/2.0)
```

Finally, it might be necessary to find the sine or cosine of a particular angle. This is simply accomplished by

```
COSVAL = COS(ANGLE)
SINVAL = SIN(ANGLE)
```

where the ANGLE must be specified in radians. You may recall from geometry that

$$(\text{angle in radians}) = \frac{\pi}{180} \times (\text{angle in degrees})$$

This translates into FORTRAN as

```
ANGLER = (3.141592/180.)*ANGLE
```

ABS and IABS

Quite often, a researcher will want to know the amount of error in a measurement. To determine this, a library function known as the absolute value function can be used. This function gives the value of a number stripped of its sign. Thus, the absolute value of –3.57 is 3.57; the absolute value of –7849.6 is 7849.6, and the absolute value of +196 is 196. Of course, this library function is used to determine the error of a measurement when one is interested simply in the amount of error—not its direction. One could write

```
ERROR = ABS(TRUE - TEST)
```

A companion library function works with INTEGER arguments:

```
NERROR = IABS(NTRUE - NTEST)
```

FLOAT and IFIX

To convert an INTEGER value to a REAL value, the FLOAT function is used. Returning to the student grade average problem, the sum of two grades might be converted to a REAL value in the following manner:

```
AVERAG = FLOAT(84 + 87)/2.0
```

the INTEGER sum of 84 and 87 would be a REAL value 171.0 and then the division by a REAL value (2.0) can proceed simply in REAL mode.

To convert from REAL to INTEGER mode, the IFIX library function is used. Thus

```
IVALUE = IFIX(5.64)
```

causes the INTEGER value 5 to be stored in the location NVALUE. Since conversion across an equal sign is permitted, the use of IFIX in this case is optional and does not affect the result. When conversion to INTEGER mode is performed in the body of an arithmetic expression, it may be necessary to use the IFIX function. In the next example, two REAL values are converted to INTEGER before they are added:

```
K = IFIX(VAL1) + IFIX(VAL2)
```

The library functions covered in this section are summarized in Table 4.3.

Table 4.3

Function	Argument	Result	Definition
SQRT	REAL > 0.0	REAL	Square root
SIN	REAL	REAL	Sine function
COS	REAL	REAL	Cosine function
ABS	REAL	REAL	Absolute value for REAL numbers
IABS	INTEGER	INTEGER	Absolute value for INTEGER numbers
FLOAT	INTEGER	REAL	Convert from INTEGER to REAL
IFIX	REAL	INTEGER	Convert from REAL to INTEGER

In an assignment statement, functions are evaluated before anything else.

Level 1   library functions
Level 2   **
Level 3   * /
Level 4   + −

Of course, anything within the parentheses of a function is evaluated before the function.

REDUCING PROGRAM COMPUTING TIME

Decreasing the run time of a program is desirable, because computer time is expensive. Unfortunately, it will sometimes increase the storage requirements, and almost certainly the programming effort. In determining the effort which should be devoted to reducing the computing time of a program, the factors to be considered are

- The number of times that the program will be run.
- The savings in computing time which can be realized.
- The development time available.
- The complexity of the program.
- The cost of computer time.
- The cost of programmer time.
- The trade-off with respect to storage.

It may not be reasonable to expend a great deal of effort to achieve a relatively small reduction in computing time, especially in a short program to be run only once. On the other hand, a frequently executed routine such as a library subprogram or a complex, long-running program may benefit from extensive analysis.

Eliminating Redundant Expressions. One of the most frequent causes of computational inefficiency is the calculation of unnecessary expressions. Some compilers are able to detect and correct these faults at the expense of increased compiler time. Since one of the advantages of high-level languages is computer independence, you should not rely upon a sophisticated compiler to optimize your programs; especially as an optimizing compiler may not always be available. Of course, a "smart" compiler should be employed when available.

It is often difficult to determine the extent and nature of the optimization provided by a given compiler. Compilers such as WATFOR, WATFIV, and IBM OS/360 FORTRAN G provide very little optimization; however, the IBM OS/360 FORTRAN H performs extensive optimization. As a rule, it is best to eliminate redundant computations when doing so provides a reasonable return for the effort expended.

Arithmetic Expressions. Consider the familiar formula for solution of a quadratic equation:

$$r_1, r_2 = \frac{-b \pm \sqrt{b^2 - 4ac}}{2a}$$

The two roots of the equation (r_1 and r_2) may be successfully computed by transliterating the formula into the following FORTRAN statements:

```
R1 = (-B + SQRT(B ** 2. - 4.0 * A * C)) / (2.0 * A)
R2 = (-B - SQRT(B ** 2. - 4.0 * A * C)) / (2.0 * A)
```

This transliteration involves a considerable amount of redundancy due to the unnecessary recomputation of common subexpressions. The value

$$b^2 - 4ac$$

(the discriminant) need be computed only once:

```
DISCR = B ** 2. - 4. * A * C
R1 = (-B + SQRT(DISCR)) / ( 2.0 * A)
```

```
    R2 = (-B - SQRT(DISCR)) / ( 2.0 * A)
```

If the value of the discriminant is not required as such elsewhere in the program, the two function calls to SQRT may, similarly, be reduced to one, and the redundant computation of the subexpression 2.0 * A may be eliminated:

```
DENOM = 2.0 * A
SDISCR = SQRT(B ** 2. - 4. * A * C)
R1 = (-B + SDISCR) / DENOM
R2 = (-B - SDISCR) / DENOM
```

The redundant subexpression —B is probably not worth eliminating, since most computers have a fast *negate* command in their instruction set. More subtly, the multiplication in DENOM may be replaced by addition (a faster process), and the exponentiation in SDISCR may be replaced by multiplication (eliminating a possible subroutine call):

```
DENOM = A + A
SDISCR = SQRT(B * B - 4.0 * A * C)
R1 = (-B + SDISCR) / DENOM
R2 = (-B - SDISCR) / DENOM
```

This set of statements is considerably more efficient than the original expression. Note that the increased efficiency has caused a reduction in the clarity of the algorithm. For this reason, it is necessary to document such changes carefully.

Rules for Avoiding Redundancy. The elimination of redundant subexpressions can be summarized by the following rule: *If an expression does not change value between multiple occurrences of that expression, then it should be evaluated only once and its value assigned to a new variable which replaces all subsequent occurrences of the original expression.*

You must be certain that none of the variables in the common subexpression change value between occurrences of the subexpression. A double check should be made of variables which are arguments of subroutines, occur in COMMON, or are declared equivalent to other variables.

Notice that certain arithmetic operators have been replaced by others for increased execution speed. The details of execution times must be gleaned from manufacturer's manuals, but the following general rules apply:

- INTEGER arithmetic is faster than REAL arithmetic, and REAL arithmetic is faster than DOUBLE PRECISION arithmetic.
- Addition and subtraction are faster than multiplication.
- Multiplication is faster than division.
- Exponentiation is very slow and is usually performed by a library subroutine.

As mentioned, functions may be used freely in arithmetic assignment statements. The square root of an INTEGER value can be found by writing

```
SQ = SQRT(FLOAT(INTVAL))
```

If there is a possibility that the argument of the square root function might be negative, then the argument could be made positive by using the absolute value function

```
SQ2 = SQRT(ABS(VALUE))
```

An attempt to obtain the square root of a negative value would result in an error message. Other examples of combinations of library functions are

```
X = COS(SQRT(Y)) - 6.7
Z = FLOAT(KVALUE) + ABS(RESULT)
DONE = IFIX(100.0*SIN(Y))
A = ABS(A) + 1.0
V1 = SQRT(SQRT(V))
RESULT = SQRT(1.0 - SIN(X)**2)
LUCKY = IFIX(50.0*ABS(SIN(Z)))
```

Worked Example

In order to simplify billing, the Hot Shot Electrical Utility Corp. rounds off the number of kilowatt hours used to the nearest kilowatt and then charges 8¢ per kilowatt hour. Write a program to read in the usage information to the nearest tenth of a kilowatt hour, round off, calculate, and print the charges.

WATFOR/WATFIV   [Standard FORTRAN]

```
READ, XKWH                       [READ(5,1000) XKWH]
```

This statement gets the input into the REAL location XKWH.

```
KWH = IFIX(XKWH + 0.5)
BILL = FLOAT(KWH)*0.08
```

The first statement does the rounding off. First add 0.5 and then truncate the fractional part with the IFIX library function. If XKWH had been 45.7, the addition would have produced 46.2 and the truncation would have left 46. If XKWH had been 45.3, the addition would have produced 45.8 and the truncation would have left 45. As an exercise, combine the two statements into one.

```
PRINT, BILL              [        WRITE (6,1000) BILL]
                         [1000 FORMAT (5G16.8)       ]
```

The print statement produces the output.

```
STOP
END
```

These statements make the program complete.

Introduction to FORMAT

Whenever results are printed by means of a PRINT statement, there is no way of controlling the *format* of the printed output. Often, however, the need may arise to specify a format for our printed output. For example, when our restaurant bill was printed, using a PRINT statement the output looked like this:

```
.908000E 01
.630000E 00
.971000E 01
```

It would be better to be able to produce a bill which looks like this:

THE HAPPY HAMBURGER
   CUSTOMER CHECK

DINNER	$9.08
SALES TAX	.63
TOTAL	$9.71

In order to do this, however, the programmer must be able to specify *both* the *values* to be printed and the *format* in which they are to be printed.

It may be desirable to specify the format of input data as well. When the statement

```
READ,A,B
```

is used, it is assumed that the variables will appear on an input card separated by blanks or a comma. However, if there are many values to be squeezed on a card, there may not be room for any commas. Or, perhaps data have been supplied on cards where the numbers are not in standard format. In such cases, it is often useful to specify a custom format both when reading and when printing values.

Suppose a printer were offering business cards in two different styles:

Style 101

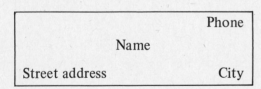

Style 102

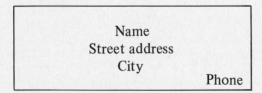

and the printer received the following order:

Print cards in format 101,
Winfred Shloop, 37 Main Street,
New York, 123-4007

He would produce cards as follows:

```
                                   123-4007

              Winfred Shloop

37 Main Street                   New York
```

On the other hand, if the order had specified cards printed using format 102 (everything else being the same), the finished cards would look like this:

```

       Winfred Shloop
       37 Main Street
       New York
                         123-4007
```

There are several points to note:

- The print instruction and the format specification are separate.
- Many print orders could specify the same format. The card that the printer produces depends on *both* the format specified and the data contained in the print order.
- The fact that the printer has specified formats does not cause card printing to begin. Cards will not be printed until a print instruction is received. The print statement should be thought of as an *instruction* whereas the format is only a *specification*.

- The labels "style 101" and "style 102" are arbitrary. The printer could just as well have called the styles "1" and "2" or "76" and "4092." Of course they could not have both the *same* number or the printer would not know which style to use.

Thus, in this example, the print request tells what to print and the format explains how to print it.

The business card analogy serves as an introduction to the techniques of format specification available in FORTRAN. In FORTRAN it is possible to specify the formats of input and output. Without it, a programmer who wished to print the values of variables would be restricted to the print statement of the form

PRINT, *list*

where *list* is a list of variables. For example, to print A, B, and C the programmer could code

```
PRINT,A,B,C
```

This print statement produces output in standard format. But to specify a particular format, a FORMAT statement is needed.

The FORMAT statement is like the printer's style specification—it explains how the data should be displayed. Like the style specifications, the FORMAT statement must have a number; this is accomplished by means of a statement label. An example of a FORMAT statement would be

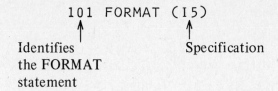

101 FORMAT (I5)

Identifies   Specification
the FORMAT
statement

In this example the specification indicates that an *integer* of *5* (I5) or fewer digits is to be printed.

In the business card printing analogy, the print order specified the style; in FORTRAN, the PRINT statement specifies the FORMAT statement to be used. To indicate that the format labeled 101 is to be used for a print operation, the PRINT statement could be

PRINT 101,I,J,K

In other words, when a format specification is used it is placed between the word PRINT and the first comma in the statement. Following are some examples:

PRINT 7, A
PRINT 1492,NINA,PINTA
PRINT 107,I,A,QR23,Z

We will now consider some simple format specifications. More complex format specifications will be introduced in later chapters. One advantage offered by FORMAT statements is that the specifications allow printed messages to be interspersed with the data output.

FORMAT and PRINT Statements for INTEGER Values

In learning about controlling the output, one must first become familiar with carriage control. The *carriage* on a typewriter (or line printer) holds the paper in position to be printed on. When using a typewriter, it is possible to make the carriage return and skip to the next line or skip two lines; a third option available on a typewriter is to begin the next line on a new page. FORMAT specifications also allow these three options when printing. Associated with each of these three options is a special character called the *carriage control character:*

Carriage Control Character	*Function*
' ' blank	Skip to the next line.
'0' zero	Skip two lines (double space).
'1' one	Start on a new page.

At the beginning of each line of printing, one of these control characters must be used in order to specify whether to space one line, two lines, or to skip to a new page.

After indicating the carriage control, one must also indicate how much space to allow for each of the INTEGER values to be printed. This is accomplished by writing I3 for a three-digit INTEGER number, I8 for an eight-digit INTEGER number, I2 for a two-digit INTEGER number, and so on. The space should never be smaller than the number of digits you expect, but it may be larger.

The following example shows how these instructions are used:

```
      NHRDAY = 24
      NDAYWK = 7
      PRINT 101,NHRDAY,NDAYWK
101   FORMAT('1',I2,I2)
      NHRWK = NHRDAY*NDAYWK
      PRINT 102,NHRWK
102   FORMAT(' ',I3)
      STOP
      END
```

Notice that each of the PRINT statements has a specified label before the first comma; this tells the computer which FORMAT statement to use for printing. This is similar in concept to the "style specification" in the business card analogy.

Each FORMAT statement must have a unique label. This is placed, as usual, in columns 1 to 5 (the *statement number field*) of the FORTRAN program card. A FORMAT statement may be placed anywhere in the program, but generally it is placed immediately following the first (or only) PRINT statement referring to it. The FORMAT statements are not executable instructions; they simply give additional information to direct the operation of the printer when a PRINT instruction is issued. They may be thought of as adverbs which modify the action of printing.

The PRINT 101 statement indicates that the contents of the locations named NHRDAY, NDAYWK are to be printed according to the FORMAT given in statement 101. The FORMAT statement 101 indicates that printing is to begin at the top of a new page (the '1' does this) and that there are two INTEGER numbers, each two digits long, to be printed. On the line printer's output, positions 1 and 2 will contain the digits 24, position 3 will be a blank, and position 4 will be the digit 7. The output is

```
24 7
```

Notice that if the format had been ('1',I2,I1), then the output would have been

```
247
```

This would have been confusing. However, such a specification is perfectly legal. A FORMAT such as ('1',I2,I5) would separate the values even more. This would leave four blanks between the two values:

```
24    7
```

In general, it is good practice to reserve a generous amount of space for printing each value. Not only does this spread the values out, but it leaves room for error in case the size of the value to be printed is underestimated. If the values are negative, an extra space must be available for the printing of a minus sign to the left of the value.

The PRINT 102 statement indicates that the contents of location NHRWK are to be printed according to FORMAT 102 which is (' ',I3). This format calls for skipping to the next line and for the printing of a three-digit INTEGER value. The entire output of this program example is

```
24  7
168
```

In general, then, when printing a series of integer values, the FORMAT specification is of the form

('s',I*a*,I*b*, . . . I*n*)

where *s* is a blank (skip to next line) or a 0 (skip two lines) or a 1 (skip to next page), and *a, b,* and so on are the amount of space to be reserved for each integer.

In general, there will be as many specifications as variables to be printed. For example,

```
      PRINT 417,I
417   FORMAT(' ',I7)

      PRINT 103,INTRST,NUMDAY
103   FORMAT('0',I7,I3)

      PRINT 1009,J,K,L,M
1009 FORMAT('1',I4,I6,I5,I3)
```

The specifications (such as I3) are often called *field specifications* because they may be thought of as defining fields on the printed page. For example, the specification in the FORMAT statement

```
101   FORMAT('0',I8,I5,I7)
```

may be thought of as defining three fields or columns—one eight characters wide, one five characters wide, and one seven characters wide.

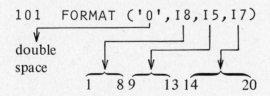

Within a given column or field the numbers printed are *right justified* (that is, positioned against the right end of the field). Leading blanks are inserted to fill out the field.

Suppose a FORMAT statement were defined as follows:

```
1276   FORMAT(' ',I3)
```

This statement specifies that the value to be printed will be right justified within a three-position field. In this case, the field will start in column 1 of the line and extend to column 3. Consider the following program:

```
      I = 5
      J = 27
      K = 193
      L = 4028
      PRINT 1276,I
      PRINT 1276,J
      PRINT 1276,K
      PRINT 1276,L
 1276 FORMAT(' ',I3)
      STOP
      END
```

Note that the FORMAT could have been placed anywhere in the program. Each PRINT statement will start a new line. The output will be

```
Column
1 2 3
───────
    5
  2 7
1 9 3
* * *
```

As usual, the numbers are right justified. In the case of the last number printed, the value was too large to fit in the specified field. To indicate the error, asterisks were printed instead.

Minus signs are printed just before the first digit. They require one column. Thus, if the values

```
I = -5
J = -27
K = -193
L = -4028
```

had been assigned in the previous program, the output would have been

```
Column
1 2 3
───────
  - 5
- 2 7
* * *
* * *
```

FORMAT and PRINT Statements for REAL Values

REAL values can also be printed under FORMAT control. The carriage control mechanism is the same, but the specification of the fields is different. With REAL numbers, space must be saved for a decimal point. The programmer must also indicate how many places to the right and left of the decimal point are to be printed. Unlike the case of INTEGER values, where the letter "I" is used, the letter "F" indicates that a REAL value is to be printed.

"F" stands for *fixed point.* When a REAL value is printed using an F specification, the decimal point appears in the fixed place where it belongs. For example, if you printed the number 100. in F format, you would get

    100.

In the standard format-free output you would have produced

    .100000E 03

F format, therefore, makes it possible to avoid printing the exponent (E 02). In addition, the decimal point does not need to be moved to interpret the number printed.

The F-format specification is similar to the I specification. It is of the form

    F*w*.*d*

where *w* is the *width* of the field and *d* is the number of places to be printed to the right of the decimal point. Some examples of F-format specifications are:

    F10.3   F5.2
    F6.2   F7.4

The first part of the specification indicates the width of the field just as it does in the I specification. Thus

    F10.3   F10.2
    F10.5   F10.1

all require ten print positions. As in the integer case, the number to be printed is right justified and leading blanks are inserted. One print position is required for the decimal point. The specification

    F8.3

means that the number will be printed in the format

    xxxx.xxx

That is, it will show up to seven digits plus a decimal point. In F format, the value is *rounded* to the required number of decimal places before printing.

As examples of how values are printed, consider the values in Table 4.4, all printed by an F8.3 specification.

Table 4.4

Value	Printed Output
.01	.010
100.25	100.250
-50.2	-50.200
-12.1236	-12.124
1123.1236	1123.124
-1123.1236	✕✕✕✕✕✕✕

Note that space in the width specification must be reserved for the decimal point and minus sign if required.

As an improvement on the customer dinner bill, consider the following program:

```
      READ,COST,SLSTAX
      PRINT 106,COST
106 FORMAT('1',F6.2)
      PRINT 107,SLSTAX
107 FORMAT(' ',F6.2)
      CHARGE = COST + SLSTAX
      PRINT 108,CHARGE
108 FORMAT('0',F6.2)
```

In each case, an F6.2 description is used to print the cost. This indicates that the entire field is to be six characters long and that two digits should be printed to the right of the decimal point. The carriage control indicates that the results should begin on a new page, that the sales tax should be printed on the line following the cost, and that we should leave a blank line (skipping two lines is called for in FORMAT 108 by use of the '0') before printing the total charge. Our output for this program is

```
9.08
0.63

9.71
```

This begins to look more like the desired bill. The F6.2 description allows values up to 999.99, which should be sufficient in this case. If larger values are expected, an F8.2 or an F10.2 description might be used. To print out more places to the right of the decimal point, an F6.3 or an F10.5 description could be used. It usually is good practice to reserve more space than is needed in case the number is larger than you expected. This allows the numbers to be spaced apart and it saves place for a possible minus sign.

To print the value -768.215, a description no smaller than F8.3 is required. A few more examples of the minimum description size will help clarify the F-specification technique:

```
7.8679     F6.4        -556748.9    F9.1
2384.86    F7.2        0.73951      F7.5
-2.34      F5.2        99.76        F5.2
```

Producing a business' payroll is a large and complex task for which computers are commonly employed. This is how the basic process works. An employee's identification number (ID), the number of hours he or she worked in the past week (HOURS), and the rate of pay per hour (RATE) are all read in. Then the wages earned (WAGES) are calculated and printed. This simplified procedure can be implemented by the following program:

```
      READ,ID,HOURS,RATE
      PRINT 105,ID,HOURS,RATE
105 FORMAT('1',I8,F5.1,F6.2)
      WAGES = HOURS*RATE
      PRINT 109,WAGES
109 FORMAT(' ',F8.2)
```

If it read a data card with the values

```
74680752, 37.5, 3.52
```

it would produce as output

```
74680752 37.5  3.52
  132.00
```

The spacing is precise. Notice that it is perfectly acceptable to mix I and F descriptions in a FORMAT statement. This follows from the ability to mix INTEGER and REAL fields in the PRINT statement.

The general form of the PRINT statement accompanying a FORMAT statement is

PRINT xxxxx,$f1,f2,\ldots,fn$

where xxxxx is a 1 to 5 digit number indicating the statement number of a FORMAT statement and $f1,f2,\ldots,fn$ represent fields of data that may be printed. A field may be an INTEGER or a REAL variable, constant, or expression.

FORMAT and READ Statements

If you are not using the WATFOR/WATFIV versions of FORTRAN, you must use the FORMATted READ statement. Even if you have WATFOR/WATFIV available, the FORMATted READ may be useful in packing data on input data cards since the intervening blanks or commas are not needed.

When reading with a FORMAT statement, the input data must be placed precisely in the columns specified. This is a tricky affair and many novice programmers (and even some professionals) have trouble getting it right.

If the input for the payroll calculation of the last section had been entered on a data card as

```
74680752 37.5  3.52
```

then the following READ and FORMAT statements could be used:

```
      READ 103,ID,HOURS,RATE
103 FORMAT(I8,F5.1,F6.2)
```

The important point is that the FORMAT must exactly match the way the data appear on the input data card. This means that you must know the pattern of the data that is being read in. The programmer must give precise directions to the person who types up the data cards. If the keypuncher is off by even a single card column, the results will probably come out wrong.

Assume that the width and length of a storage shed have been entered on a data card. This program will read the dimensions, calculate the area it covers, and print the result. Then, the next data card containing the height of the shed will be read in and the volume will be calculated and printed. If the data are punched on cards as follows:

width length
$\overbrace{8.5}$ $\overbrace{10.2}$
$\underbrace{7.50}$
height

the program needed is

```
      READ 205,WIDTH,LENGTH
205 FORMAT(F4.1,F6.1)
      AREA = LENGTH*WIDTH
      PRINT 208,AREA
208 FORMAT('1',F9.1)
      READ 211,HEIGHT
211 FORMAT(F5.2)
      VOLUME = HEIGHT*AREA
      PRINT 220,VOLUME
220 FORMAT(' ',F9.1)
```

and its output is

```
bbbbb86.7
bbbb650.3
```

The general form of the READ statement that refers to a FORMAT is

READ xxxxx,$f1,f2,\ldots,fn$

where xxxxx represents a 1 to 5 digit number indicating the statement number of a FORMAT statement and $f1,f2,\ldots,fn$ represent INTEGER or REAL location names into which data are to be read.

The general form of the FORMAT statement is

xxxxx FORMAT ($d1,d2,\ldots,dn$)

where xxxxx is a 1 to 5 digit statement number and the $d1,d2,\ldots,dn$ are descriptions of the form

    In INTEGER field of length n.

    F$n.d$ REAL fields of total length n and d digits to the right of the decimal point.

A discussion of other descriptor fields follows shortly. On output, the first field ($d1$) must be a carriage control character:

   ' '   Skip to the next line
   '0'   Skip two lines (leave one blank line)
   '1'   Skip to the top of the next page

Let us sum up some important points about specifying a format:

- FORMAT statements associated with PRINT statements must have carriage control information, while the FORMAT statements associated with READ must not.
- The descriptive I (for INTEGER) and F (for REAL) fields may be intermixed in a FORMAT statement, but each descriptor is separated from its neighbor by a comma.
- FORMAT statements may be placed anywhere in the program. It is common practice either to place them immediately following the I/O statement which refers to them, or to place them all at the beginning or all at the end of the program.
- The statement numbers for formats may be any valid statement numbers as long as no two FORMAT statements have the same number. This text will usually keep to the convention that FORMAT statement numbers be in the hundreds and that they be in ascending order in the program.

Skip Fields

Programming considerations may make it necessary or helpful to leave blank spaces on input cards or on output listings. To make this task as simple as possible the X format item is used.

If the input data card appears as

then the following READ and FORMAT statements could be used to describe it

```
      READ 101, IDENT, SCORE, NCODE
  101 FORMAT(I8, 8X, F5.2, 3X, I3)
```

The X format item indicates that the spaces are to be skipped over. The general form is nX where n is an INTEGER number which specifies how many spaces are to be skipped. On output, the X format item indicates how many blank spaces should be left on the output line between printed values. The above information might be printed out with different spacing.

```
      PRINT 102, IDENT, SCORE, NCODE
102 FORMAT('0', 50X, I8, 5X, F5.2, 5X, I3)
```

This format would help to center the output in the page, producing

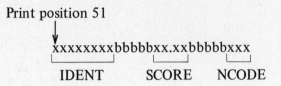

Print position 51

xxxxxxxxbbbbbxx.xxbbbbbxxx

IDENT   SCORE   NCODE

Adding Explanatory Messages to Output

Numbers printed on a page without explanation can be confusing. Therefore, every effort should be made to produce output which is neat and self-explanatory. It is a simple matter to add character information to FORMAT statements. By surrounding the character string to be printed in apostrophes and including it as a field in a FORMAT statement, we can cause the string to be printed. We might print

```
      PRINT 220,VOLUME
220 FORMAT('0','THE VOLUME IS',F9.1)
```

After skipping two lines the line printer would print

```
THE VOLUME IS     650.3
```

A more complicated example might be

```
      PRINT 105,ID,HOURS,RATE
105 FORMAT('1','EMPLOYEE ',I8,' WORKED ',
   1    F5.1,' HRS, AT $', F6.2, ' PER HR.')
```

This FORMAT statement required a continuation card for a total description which yields the output

```
EMPLOYEE 74680752 WORKED  37.5 HRS, AT $  3.52 PER HR.
```

This output is far more meaningful than the simple listing of the values. In fact, we might want to produce a line of output which has only explanatory information such as

```
      PRINT 160
160 FORMAT('1','TAXES HAVE NOT BEEN DEDUCTED FROM WAGES')
```

or

```
    PRINT 143
143 FORMAT('0','FINAL GRADE LISTING FOR COURSE CS 101')
```

You may notice the similarity of the mechanism for carriage control and the mechanism for sending text strings to the printer. In fact, they are really the same. The line printer is built to treat the first character of information sent to it as the instruction for carriage control. Thus, it is possible to combine the carriage control information with a text string immediately following it:

```
    PRINT 160
160 FORMAT('1TAXES HAVE NOT BEEN DEDUCTED FROM WAGES')
```

The line printer would strip off the first character for carriage control purposes and then would print the remaining text. An additional trick allows a page heading to be centered by including an appropriate number of blanks:

```
    PRINT 143
143 FORMAT('1      FINAL GRADE LISTING FOR COURSE CS 101')
```

To return to the restaurant problem, it is now possible to produce a readable bill telling the customer exactly how much is owed and how that figure was calculated:

```
    PRINT 106,COST
106 FORMAT('1MEAL COST        ',F6.2)
    PRINT 107,SLSTAX
107 FORMAT(' SALES TAX        ',F6.2)
    CHARGE = COST + SLSTAX
    PRINT 108,CHARGE
108 FORMAT('0TOTAL           ',F6.2)
```

This program might produce the following output:

```
MEAL COST      9.08
SALES TAX      0.63

TOTAL          9.71
```

If the restaurant demanded a fancier bill, a line of minus signs '---------------------' might be printed just above the total line. The name and address of the restaurant could also be printed. As an exercise, program the format for the Happy Hamburger bill.

Summary

In *free-format I/O*, in WATFOR/WATFIV, the mechanism for I/O is simplified to the point where the user need not worry about the precise positioning of the data. On input, fields of data are separated by one or more blanks or by a comma. On output, the results are printed in a format and a position chosen by the computer. This simplifies the task of the programmer, since FORMAT statements are not needed. It also reduces the possibility of error. Carriage control operations are automatically performed by the computer. Of course, the simplicity of free-format I/O is accomplished at the expense of precise control of the positioning of the data.

When precise positioning of data is required or when WATFOR/WATFIV is not available, FORMAT statements are needed. The FORMAT statement number is placed in the READ or PRINT statement preceding the first comma. This number refers to a FORMAT statement with the matching statement number. FORMAT statements may be placed anywhere in the program.

The INTEGER description is In, where I stands for INTEGER and n is the length of the field. The REAL description is F$n.d$, where F stands for REAL, n is the total length of the field (including a count for the decimal point and a count for the sign), and d is the number of places to the right of the decimal point. The skip description is nX, where n is the number of spaces to be skipped. Output FORMAT statements must have a carriage control character in the first field. Character strings may be included in output by enclosing the string in apostrophes and including it as a field in the FORMAT statement.

Formats for I/O give the user complete control over the placement of data and results. This flexibility and power should be used to maximize the clarity of the printed results.

DEBUGGING CLINIC

The single most common error in the assignment statement is the mismatching of parentheses. For every left parenthesis there should be one and only one right parenthesis. The error is obvious when there is a small number of parentheses:

Incorrect

```
    A = D * (B - C
PRINC = 1.+ RATE) * PRINC
```

Correct

```
    A = D * (B - C)
PRINC = (1.+ RATE) * PRINC
```

But when there are many sets of parentheses, it becomes difficult to tell when there is an error and even more difficult to determine the correct statement:

Incorrect statements

```
A = D * (B - (C + D) + E
X = (((Y** (Z - 2. * (PI/3.0)) + W)
Y = SQRT(7 - Z/(Q -1) * (T * (FLOAT(A) ))))
I = ((J - (K**(K/2))))/(L + 5))/7
```

You can check for this error by counting; there should be the same number of left and right parentheses. If there is a discrepancy, you can find it by checking off pairs of parentheses, from innermost to outermost. (Try it out on the incorrect statements above.)

The compiler will catch an incorrect syntactic statement and will print a diagnostic error message. It is more difficult to locate the *logic* errors which result from the incorrect transcription of a mathematical formula into FORTRAN form:

Math Formula	Incorrect	Correct
$X = \dfrac{b-a}{ab}$	X = (B - A)/A * B	X = (B - A)/(A * B)
$A = x(\sqrt{y} + z)$	A = X * (SQRT(Y + Z))	A = X * (SQRT(Y) + Z)

Input and output statements have long been a source of difficulty for programmers. The rules are complex, often arbitrary, and frequently a result of hardware restrictions. A large fraction of the errors made by programmers, from the novice to the expert level, involve incorrect input/output specification. A few reminders may help to minimize the number and seriousness of your "bugs":

- Make sure that the FORMAT statement number referred to by your READ or PRINT statements actually has been included in your program.
- Check to see that there is a format item in the FORMAT list for every value in the READ or PRINT list. The omission of F7.2 in the FORMAT list would lead to complications:

```
      READ 102, GRAMS, MOLES, VOLUME
102 FORMAT( F9.3, 5X, I3, F7.2 )
```

- Make sure that the type of the variable (REAL or INTEGER) corresponds to an appropriate FORMAT item. Printing a REAL value with an I-format item yields incorrect results.
- Don't forget the carriage control character for printed output.
- Double check that you have counted the card columns or print positions correctly.

It is a good habit to print out every value that has been read in. Each READ statement should be followed by a PRINT statement which "echoes" the input. When the program has been thoroughly debugged, this echo check can be removed to produce a final run with only the desired output.

REVIEW QUESTIONS

1. Arrange the FORTRAN operators, + - * / **, in their order of evaluation.
2. Explain the difference between INTEGER and REAL arithmetic. Why are both types available? In general, when would each be used?
3. Explain the meaning of *mixed mode* expressions. How can conversion across an equals sign be used to round values to the nearest integer?
4. What is a library function? Give five examples.
5. Explain the purpose of a FORMAT statement. How is a FORMAT statement associated with a READ or PRINT statement? Why is a FORMAT statement considered "nonexecutable"?
6. What are the carriage control characters? How are they used?
7. What is a *field* in a FORMAT statement? Explain the use of I and F formats. Why does F format specify F*w.d* while I format specifies I*w*?
8. What do asterisks printed on an output field signify? How can they be eliminated?

1. Convert the following algebraic expressions to FORTRAN notation.

a. $y = \dfrac{ab}{c}$

b. $Z = \dfrac{1}{a^{b^c}}$

c. $ab + c = y$

d. $\dfrac{a^2 + b^2}{2} = x$

e. $Z = 2 \sin X + \cos X$

f. $s = \dfrac{1}{2} + \dfrac{1}{3} + \dfrac{1}{4} + \dfrac{1}{5}$

g. $i^2 = j^2 + Z$

h. $f = \dfrac{1}{\sqrt{pqr}}$

i. $x = \dfrac{a/b}{c/d}$

2. Convert the following FORTRAN expressions to algebraic notation.

a. A = Y + X**2/2.0

b. B = (Y + X**2)/2.0

c. C = Y + X**(2/2.0)

d. Q = D * A + B * C

e. SUM = AB + CD

f. M = 1/I/J + K**2

3. Given the length and width of a rectangle, write a program to calculate the length of the diagonal. The formula is

$$\text{length of diagonal} = \sqrt{(\text{length})^2 + (\text{width})^2}$$

4. One of the roots of the quadratic equation is given by the formula

$$x = \frac{-b + \sqrt{b^2 - 4ac}}{2a}$$

Write this formula in FORTRAN. Given the material presented so far, this problem should prove to be a real challenge.

5. The mean deviation in statistics is given by the formula

$$\text{mean deviation} = \frac{|x_1 - \bar{x}| + |x_2 - \bar{x}| + \cdots + |x_n - \bar{x}|}{n}$$

where $\bar{x}$ is the average of the x's and n is the number of x's. The vertical bars indicate the absolute value function. Assume n is equal to 4. Write a FORTRAN statement to find $\bar{x}$. Then write another FORTRAN statement to find the mean deviation.

6. The velocity of a swinging pendulum is given by the formula

velocity = $rw \cos wt$

The acceleration is

acceleration = $rw^2 \sin wt$

where r is the length of the pendulum, w is the angular velocity, and t is the time elapsed since the pendulum passed through the bottom of its swing. Write FORTRAN statements to calculate the velocity and the acceleration.

7. Write READ and FORMAT statements for the following card images.

a.
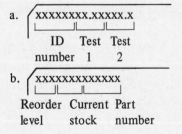

b.

```
/ XXXXXXXXXXXXX
  |___||___||___|
Reorder  Current  Part
level    stock    number
```

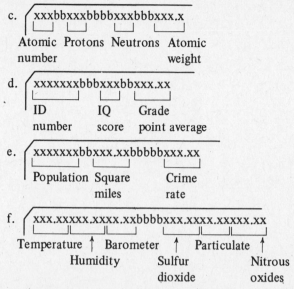

c. xxxbbxxxbbbbxxxbbbxxx.x

Atomic Protons Neutrons Atomic
number   weight

d. xxxxxxxbbbxxxbbxxx.xx

ID   IQ   Grade
number   score   point average

e. xxxxxxxbbxxx.xxbbbbbxxx.xx

Population Square   Crime
            miles   rate

f. xxx.xxxxx.xxxx.xxbbbbbxxx.xxxx.xxxxx.xx

Temperature ↑ Barometer ↑ Particulate ↑
     Humidity   Sulfur   Nitrous
                   dioxide   oxides

8. (a–f) Write PRINT and FORMAT statements to print out the information read in from cards in 7a–f. Each item should be printed on a new page with an explanatory message. For example, for problem 8a the results might be

   ID NUMBER   xxxxxx   TEST1   xx.xx   TEST2   xxx.x

9. Prepare several data cards containing mileage (xxxx.x) and gas consumption (in gallons xxx.x) figures for a group of trips. Use FORMAT statements.

   a. For each trip calculate and print the miles per gallon value.
   b. Convert the miles to kilometers (.621 kilometers per mile) and print the kilometers per gallon value.
   c. Convert the gallons to liters (3.785 liters per gallon) and print the kilometers per liter value.

10. Write complete programs for each of the following problems taken from Chapter 3. Create input data and describe the input and output using FORMAT statements.

   a. Write a program to read in a distance in feet, convert the results to inches, and print out the results.
   b. Write a program to read in pounds, convert to kilograms (2.2 pounds/kilogram), and print the results and the input.
   c. Write a program to read in a principal amount and a rate of interest. Then calculate the interest for one year and print the results.
   d. Write a program to read in a value representing the radius of a circle, print the radius, calculate the area of the circle, print the area, calculate the circumference, and print out the circumference.
   e. Write a program to read two INTEGER numbers, determine how many times the second divides into the first, and print the result.

SPIRAL PROBLEMS

Note: In each of these problems, processing should be continued till there is no more data. This will result in an error message from the system. Don't worry, you will learn how to clear up this difficulty in the next chapter. FORMAT statements are optional. You must prepare 4 of 5 of your own data cards according to the directions in each problem.

A. Student Grading

   Write a program to read and print real test scores from a series of data cards of the form

XXX.X	XXX.X	XXX.X
Score 1	Score 2	Score 3

Find the average by summing the three scores and dividing by three. Print the averages, and keep processing till you run out of data cards.

B. Commercial Application: Salesperson Commissions

Write a program to read and print sales amount, rate of commission and number of items which have been punched on a series of data cards in the form

XXX.XX	X.XX	XXX
Amount per item	Rate	Number of items

Calculate the amount of commission by multiplying the three values and print the amount of commission. Keep processing till you run out of data.

C. Mathematical Application

Write a program to read and print a series of data cards with two real values indicating the base radius and the height of a cylinder.

XXX.X	XX.X
Base radius	Height

Calculate and print the volume of the cylinder by the formula $V = \pi r^2 h$. On a new line, calculate and print the surface area by the formula $A = 2(\pi r^2) + h(2\pi r)$. Keep processing till you run out of data.

DECISIONS, DECISIONS

"I only said 'if'!" poor Alice pleaded in a piteous tone.
The two Queens looked at each other, and the Red Queen
remarked with a little shudder, "she says she only said 'if'—"
"But she said a great deal more than that!" the White Queen
moaned, wringing her hands, "Oh, ever so much more than that!"
Lewis Carroll, Through the Looking Glass (1871)

CHAPTER 5

It is not always desirable to perform precisely the same computations for every possible piece of input data. Special cases often require special computational treatment. For example, in a payroll computation some employees may be eligible for overtime while others may not. In order to provide programs with the ability to select their actions depending upon value variables in the program, the IF statement is used. The IF statement has the general form of "IF (condition) consequent statement". The condition *which is specified is either true or false. A condition asks, for example, if two variables are equal, if an arithmetic expression is within a certain range, and similar constructs. The consequent statement is executed if the condition is true; otherwise, the statement following the IF is executed. If the consequent statement is a GO TO, the program flow may be altered.*

One common use of the IF statement is to determine whether a card, just read, is the last data card. This is done by specifying a special data value which indicates the end of data. For example, in a payroll computation an employee number of 000000 might be used to indicate the end of the input data. The use of an IF statement to detect such an end of file *condition allows the programmer to produce totals and other types of summary results.*

Introduction

In the programs studied so far, the sequence of execution of statements was simple and straightforward. Except for some very simple branching after each statement the *next sequential instruction* was executed. This chapter goes more deeply into the need for, and the methods of altering the flow of control of a program, including the techniques of counting and looping.

Decision-Making and Branching

In the first two chapters we introduced decision-making in programming. The concept of branching should be a familiar one. It is constantly seen in English language instructions, such as the operating directions for a washing machine.

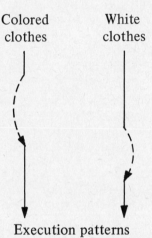

Colored clothes   White clothes

Execution patterns

1. Load clothes loosely into washer.
2. If colored clothes, go to step 6.
3. Add detergent and bleach.
4. Set temperature to hot.
5. Go to step 8.
6. Add mild detergent.
7. Set temperature to warm.
8. Close door.
9. Insert 25¢.
10. Push plunger.

The decision instruction is step 2, in which the user is asked to decide whether or not colored clothes are being laundered. For colored clothes, the user should perform steps 6 and 7; otherwise, the user should perform steps 3 and 4. In any particular wash, only one of the two conditions can prevail. This program has ten instructions, but not all ten instructions will be executed for any given wash. Figure 5.1 represents this program by a flowchart and two execution patterns.

The instructions to "Go to step . . . " do not appear as a box on the flowchart, but the meaning of the "Go to step . . . " is embodied in the lines connecting the boxes. The numbered statements are a one-dimensional representation of the two-dimensional flowchart, and it is necessary to include "Go to step . . . " statements in order to jump over certain instructions. Without the "Go to step 8" instruction at step 5, the user might add detergent and bleach, set the temperature to hot, and then add mild detergent and set the temperature to warm, thus destroying the previous setting and possibly the clothes.

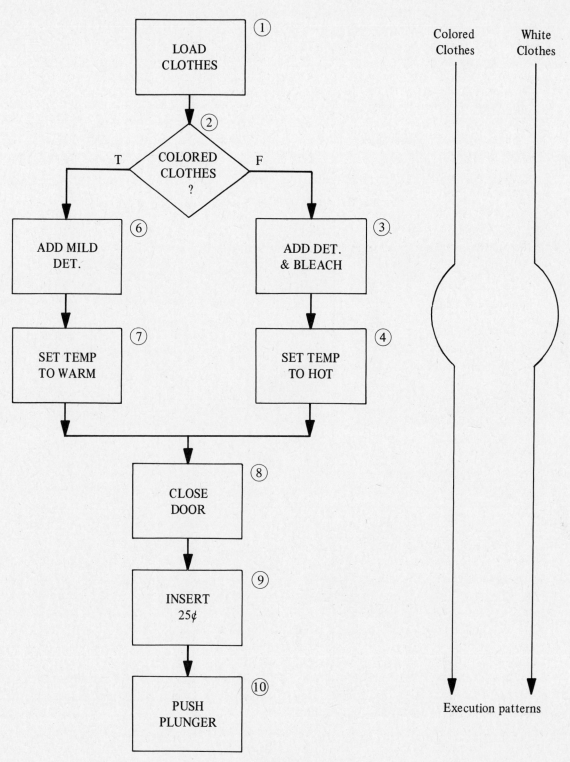

Figure 5.1

The income tax form provides a rich source for examples of decision instructions. If the tax form says that if earnings are less than $10,000.00, then taxation is at a rate of 10 percent, but if earnings are above $10,000.00, then the rate of taxation is 18 percent, the instructions might be

1. If wages are less than $10,000.00, go to step 4.
2. Taxes = 0.18*Wages
3. Go to step 5.
4. Taxes = 0.10*Wages
5. Enter amount of taxes on tax form.

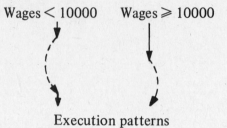

Execution patterns

The flowchart for this simple set of instructions is shown in Figure 5.2.

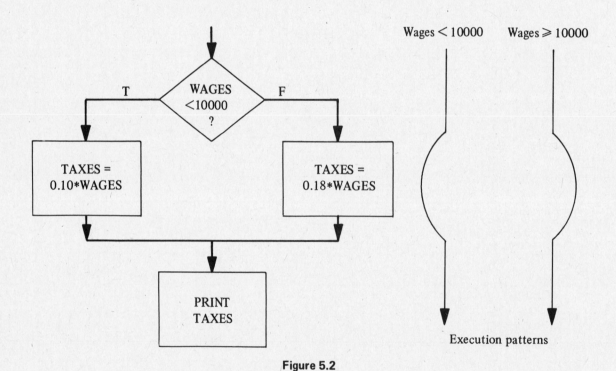

Execution patterns

Figure 5.2

The set of instructions for the washing machine cannot be run on a computer; however, the instructions for calculating income tax do make sense in terms of computer operations. In FORTRAN, this program fragment might appear as

```
      . . .
      IF(WAGES .LT. 10000.) GO TO 4
      TAXES = 0.18*WAGES
      GO TO 5
   4  TAXES = 0.10*WAGES
   5  . . .
```

The IF Statement

In FORTRAN, the IF statement is used to specify a decision. In effect, the IF statement specifies *conditional execution* of a statement. The general form of the IF construct is

IF (*condition*) *consequent statement*

The *condition* specifies a relationship between the values of two or more variables, a relationship which is either *true* or *false* when the IF statement is executed. Some examples of conditions are

```
A .EQ. B
```

(the value of A is equal to that of B) and

```
VAR2 .LT. 32.6
```

(the value of VAR2 is less than 32.6). If the condition is *true* then the consequent statement is executed. Otherwise the consequent will not be executed.

One way of looking at the IF statement is that when a statement is prefixed by the construct

IF (*condition*)

it may or may not be executed depending upon the result (*true* or *false*) of evaluating the condition. Some examples of IF statements follow.

```
IF(RATE .GT. 50.0) GO TO 86
```

If the value of RATE is greater than 50.0, then go to statement 86.

```
IF(NUMBER .EQ. 7) GO TO 43
```

If the value of NUMBER is equal to 7, then go to statement 43.

```
IF(SCORE .GE. 65.0) GO TO 1551
```

If the value of SCORE is greater than or equal to 65.0, then go to statement 1551.

```
IF(SALARY - DEDUCT .LT. 474.0) GO TO 8
```

If the value of SALARY minus the DEDUCTion is less than 474.0, then go to statement 8.

```
IF(NVALUE .EQ. NFINAL) GO TO 30
```

If the value of NVALUE equals the value of NFINAL, then go to statement 30.

The *consequent* of an IF statement may be a READ, WRITE, GO TO, or arithmetic assignment statement. As always, if the condition is true, the consequent statement is executed. Otherwise, the next statement is executed.

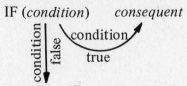

Suppose the consequent of an IF statement is represented by the letter A and the following statement by the letter B:

IF (*condition*) A

B

If *condition* is true, statement A will be executed. Unless A is a GO TO statement, B will be executed next. Thus, if A is a READ, PRINT, or arithmetic assignment statement, the sequence "AB" will be executed when the condition is true and the sequence "B" will be executed when the condition is false.

If the consequent of an IF statement is a GO TO, then when the condition is true the branch will be taken; when the condition is false, statement B is executed.

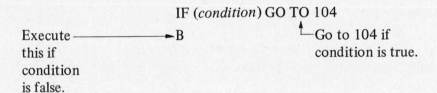

By using a GO TO as the consequent of an IF, it is possible to set up two different sets of instructions, only one of which will be followed, depending upon the circumstances. When this is done, it is necessary to use a GO TO statement to skip over the second set of instructions:

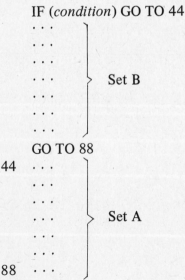

If the condition is *false*, then set B will be executed. If the condition is *true*, then set A will be executed. This arrangement can be understood as: IF the condition is *true* THEN do A ELSE do B.

The flow of control which results from this program structure is illustrated in Figure 5.3.

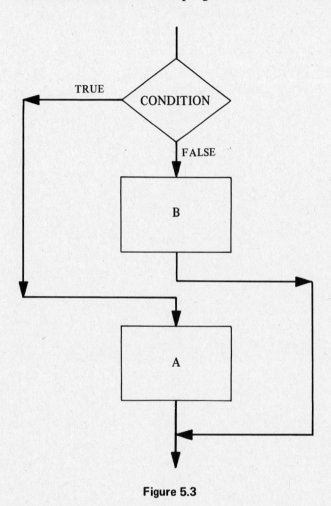

Figure 5.3

Problem 5.1

What sequence of instructions would be executed if the GO TO 88 instruction were not included?

Conditions

The *condition* evaluated is either *true* or *false*. It is composed of *two arithmetic expressions joined by a relational operator*. The permissible relational operators are

.LT.   less than
.LE.   less than or equal

```
.EQ.    equal
.GE.    greater than or equal
.GT.    greater than
.NE.    not equal
```

The expressions used on either side of the relational operator may be of any form: a constant, a variable, or a complicated expression. As an example, consider the following condition:

```
((A + B) .LT. 100.0)
```

The arithmetic expression A + B has a value. The expression (constant) 100.0 has a value. The whole condition will have the value *true* if the value A + B is less than 100.0; otherwise, the condition will have the value *false*. Here are some more examples:

```
IF (I .EQ. 10) GO TO 50
IF (X - .05*Q .GE. Q - SQRT(X)) I = 7
IF (FICA .GT. SALRY) PRINT 101, FICA, SALRY
```

Problem 5.2

Given that A = 2.0, B = 1.0, and C = –2.5, which of the following conditions are true and which are false?

a. A .LT. B

b. A/2.0 .EQ. B

c. A*B .LE. A*C

d. B .LT. A

e. B .GT. C

f. A + C .GT. B

Usually, the statement used as the consequent of an IF is a GO TO statement. The GO TO statement can be used to jump over (that is, skip) program statements or to go back and repeat program statements. In the tax program, presented above, both the GO TO 4 and the GO TO 5 refer to statements further along.

A student grading program might include a statement to print out the difference between a particular student's grade and the class average. Both the case in which the student's grade is less than the average and the case in which it is greater than or equal to the average must be accounted for even though only one of those conditions can occur:

```
      .
      .
      .
    IF(GRADE .GE. AVERAG) GO TO 70
    DIFF = AVERAG — GRADE
    PRINT 101, DIFF
    GO TO 80
101 FORMAT (' THIS STUDENT GRADE WAS', F5.2, 'BELOW AVERAGE')
 70 DIFF = GRADE - AVERAG
    PRINT 102, DIFF
102 FORMAT (' THIS STUDENT GRADE WAS', F5.2, 'ABOVE AVERAGE')
 80
      .
      .
      .
```

The general pattern for this sequence is similar to the "Set A and Set B" example on page 132. It can be represented by the following schema:

$$\vdots$$

IF (B) GO TO n_1
Statements to be executed if B *is not true*
GO TO n_2
n_1 Statements to be executed if B *is true*
n_2 $\vdots$

The execution patterns are displayed in Figure 5.3.

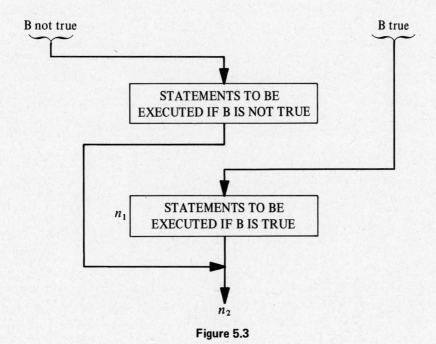

Figure 5.3

Applying the IF statement

A common accounting problem concerns the updating of a bank account. If the old balance is stored in OLDBAL and the amount of the withdrawal is AMOUNT, the program must determine whether there is an overdraft:

```
                    .
                    .
                    .
        BALANC = OLDBAL - AMOUNT
        IF(BALANC .LT. 0.0) GO TO 57
        PRINT 101, BALANC
101 FORMAT (' THE NEW BALANCE IN YOUR ACCOUNT IS', F10.2)
        GO TO 35
 57 PRINT 102, AMOUNT, BALANC
102 FORMAT ('0*** YOUR ATTEMPT TO WITHDRAW $', F10.2,
   1         'HAS RESULTED IN AN OVERDRAFT OF $', F10.2)
 35
                    .
                    .
                    .
```

This program fragment again demonstrates the same kind of program flow that was discussed earlier. But there are some interesting points to observe. Notice that statement numbers 57 and 35 are not in ascending numerical order in the program. Although it is a useful convention that statement numbers should appear in ascending order, this is not necessary and the program is correct as it stands. Though we are using the convention that FORMAT statements are numbered starting with 101 in ascending order, FORMAT statement numbers do not have to be in any specific order. These conventions make it easier for us to pick up a program and easily determine certain features. A final point about this

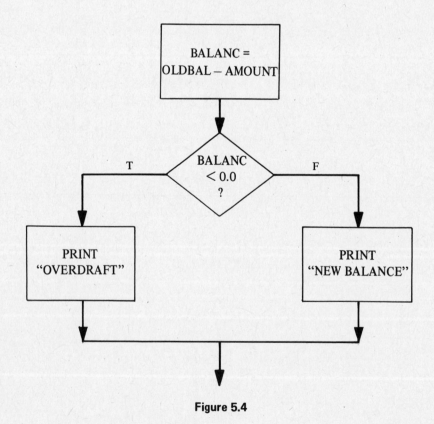

Figure 5.4

program fragment: FORMAT statement 102 did not fit on a single line and a continuation character (the "1") has been used on the following card. The flowchart for this program fragment (Figure 5.4) is similar to the chart for our income tax program.

The banking problem can be expanded to include a section for deposits. Assume that the location NTYPE contains a 1 for deposits and a –1 for withdrawals. Before executing a transaction, the nature of the transaction must be determined. The flowchart should now look like Figure 5.5. The program fragment is

```
         .
         .
         .
      IF(NTYPE .EQ. -1) GO TO 40
      BALANC = OLDBAL + AMOUNT
      PRINT 101, BALANC
      GO TO 35
   40 BALANC = OLDBAL - AMOUNT
      IF(BALANC  .LT. 0.0) GO TO 57
      PRINT 101, BALANC
  101 FORMAT ('0THE NEW BALANCE IN YOUR ACCOUNT IS', F10.2)
      GO TO 35
   57 PRINT 102, AMOUNT, BALANC
  102 FORMAT ('0***YOUR ATTEMPT TO WITHDRAW $', F10.2,
    1        ' HAS RESULTED IN AN OVERDRAFT OF $', F10.2)
   35   .
        .
        .
```

Here we see how a number of IF statements can be compounded to produce a complex flow of control. Notice also that in the third line of the program fragment we have referred to FORMAT statement number 101 which was part of the original program fragment. It is not necessary to create another FORMAT statement since the one that we need already appears somewhere else in the program.

Problem 5.3

Write a program to read in two numbers X and Y and print the appropriate one of these three messages:

X IS GREATER THAN Y
X IS EQUAL TO Y
X IS LESS THAN Y

Another example of this pattern of program structure occurs when trying to determine which of three numbers is the largest. If the numbers are integer values read in and stored in locations I, J, and K then I might be compared to J. If I is larger, then I must be compared to K. On the other hand, if J is larger, then J must be compared to K. Finally the largest is printed. The flow of control is charted in Figure 5.6.

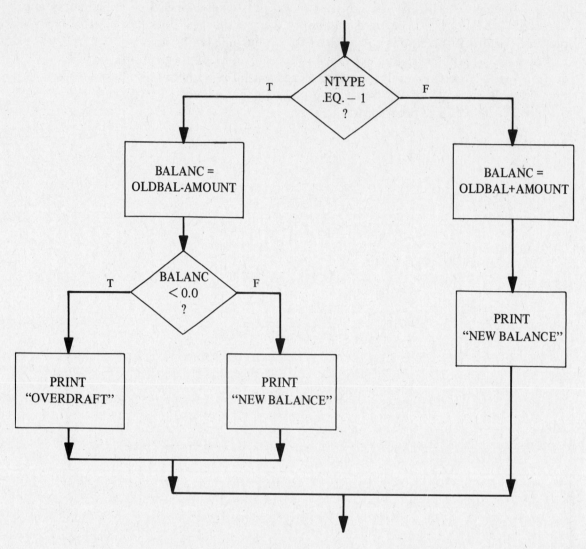

Figure 5.5

The FORTRAN program that implements the following flowchart (Figure 5.6) is

```
      READ 100, I,J,K
  100 FORMAT(I4,I4,I4)
      PRINT 101, I,J,K
  101 FORMAT('1THE INPUT VALUES ARE', I6, I6, I6)
      IF(I .GT. J) GO TO 30
      IF(J .GT. K) GO TO 10
      PRINT 102,K
  102 FORMAT('1THE LARGEST VALUE IS', I5)
      GO TO 50
   10 PRINT 102,J
      GO TO 50
   30 IF(I .GT. K) GO TO 40
      PRINT 102,K
```

```
   GO TO 50
40 PRINT 102,I
50 STOP
   END
```

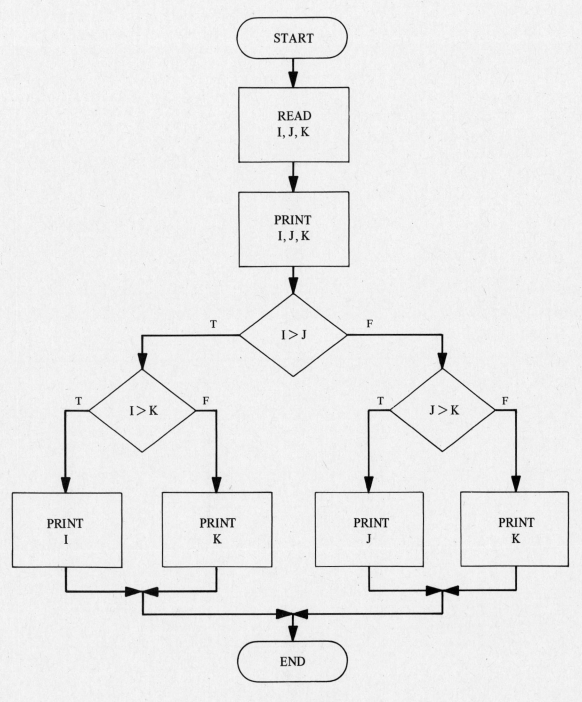

Figure 5.6

This program will solve the problem adequately, but there is a way to shorten it by eliminating two lines and changing one line. Can you figure out the shortened version which produces exactly the same output?

The pattern used in these programs can be found in many programs. Another common sequence involves several series of decisions designed to determine which interval a value belongs to. A classic example of such a sequence occurs when trying to determine what grade a student has earned. Assuming that the final grade is determined strictly by term average and that the classification scheme is

90 or above	A
80 – 90	B
70 – 80	C
less than 70	F

a flowchart might be drawn like Figure 5.7.

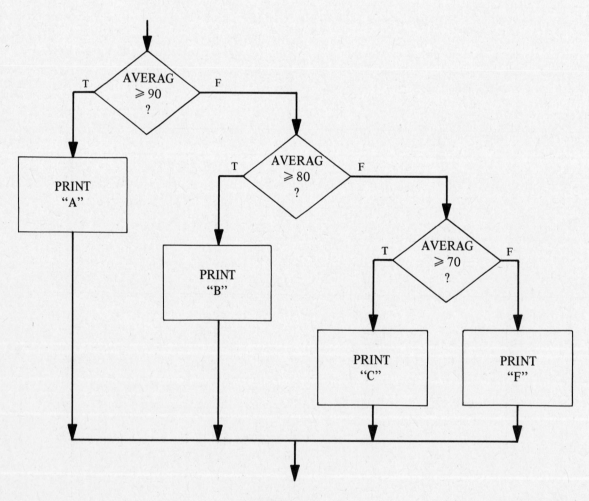

Figure 5.7

INCREASING COMPUTATIONAL ACCURACY

Even computers make mistakes. Although it is extremely rare for a computer to make arithmetic errors such as adding two and two and getting five or to make operational errors such as adding when multiplication was programmed, more subtle errors often occur. These mistakes do not mean that computers are undependable or that we must check all computer calculations by hand; they do mean that care should be taken in writing programs in order to prevent the occurrence of computational inaccuracy.

Inaccuracy results from the way in which computers store and manipulate numbers. Our mathematical training tells us that

$$(1./3.)*3.$$

is precisely and incontestably 1 but a computer is likely to disagree. The result of dividing 1. by 3. is the infinitely repeating decimal .333333333 . . . which cannot be accurately represented in the hardware of a finite computer. When .333333333 . . . is multiplied by 3. the result is a bit less than 1. The difference may seem minute, but the compounding of these minor faults by millions of operations can produce major errors and invalidate the results.

INTEGER Overflow. The range of permissible INTEGER values is determined by the number of binary digits (bits) available in a memory word. This varies from computer to computer: The IBM 360/370 series has a 32-bit word and can store integers ranging from -2147483647 to 2147483647.

If a computation inadvertently exceeds the representable range, a condition known as *overflow* occurs and results will not be correct. The programmer may not even be aware of the error. The greatest danger comes in multiplication of large values and in repeated additions/subtractions.

REAL Overflow, Underflow, and Division by Zero. If the result of a mathematical operation exceeds the permitted range, it is not possible to store the value. If the exponent is too large we have an overflow; if the exponent is too small (too large a negative exponent) we have an underflow. The following program could not be run properly on an IBM 360/370 which accepts numbers ranging in magnitude from 16^{-65} (approximately 10^{-78}) to 16^{63} (approximately 10^{75}):

```
A = 8.0E50
B = 6.0E40
C = A * B
```

Overflow would occur since the expected result, 48.E90, is beyond the acceptable range, and an error message would be printed by the operating system.

In some cases, reordering the operations can prevent overflow or underflow. Consider the following program fragment:

```
      A = 7.0E-65
      B = 6.0E-24
      C = 2.0E+56
C        THE TRUE VALUE OF D IS 42.E-89
      D = A * B
C        THE TRUE VALUE OF E IS 84.E-33
      E = D * C'
```

Underflow will occur when A is multiplied by B and although the result is not beyond the capacity of the hardware this sequence of computations would not be permitted. However, by rearranging the operations, the result 84.E−33 could be arrived at as follows:

```
C          THE TRUE VALUE OF DD IS 14.E09
    DD = A * C
C          THE TRUE VALUE OF EE IS 84.E-33
    EE = DD * B
```

Division by extremely small quantities may result in overflow, or roundoff errors. Division by *zero* produces an error because the operation is not defined. To prevent these errors the division should be tested before it is attempted.

```
    IF (ABS(DIVSOR .LT. 1.0E-50)) GO TO 30
    QUOTNT = DIVDND/DIVSOR
         .
         .
         .
 30 WRITE(3,101) DIVDND,DIVSOR
101 FORMAT (' **** DIVISION ATTEMPTED WITH DIVIDEND =',
   1           E16.8,' AND DIVISOR=',E16.8)
```

It is difficult to suggest what you should do at this point, but at least there is a record of what transpired when this situation arose. One alternative is simply to terminate the run and try to find out why the condition occurred.

Each decision block further limits the possible choices until there is only one left. As soon as the proper classification is determined, the grade may be printed and no more testing is necessary. Converting the flowchart to a program can be tricky, but if the decisions are made in an orderly way then an efficient program can be written:

```
         .
         .
         .
    IF(AVERAG .GE. 90.0) GO TO 10
    IF(AVERAG .GE. 80.0) GO TO 20
    IF(AVERAG .GE. 70.0) GO TO 30
    PRINT 101
101 FORMAT('1YOUR GRADE IS F')
    GO TO 40
 10 PRINT 102
102 FORMAT('1YOUR GRADE IS A')
    GO TO 40
 20 PRINT 103
103 FORMAT('1YOUR GRADE IS B')
    GO TO 40
 30 PRINT 104
104 FORMAT('1YOUR GRADE IS C')
 40    .
         .
         .
```

Even though there are four categories, only three tests are necessary. If the grade is not greater than or equal to 70.0, then it must be less than 70.0 and the message can be printed immediately. The three occurrences of "GO TO 40" are necessary in order to jump over the other messages. This is one of the necessary details that must be remembered when you convert the two-dimensional flowchart to the linear form of the actual program.

When more than one condition is to be tested in an IF statement, the logical operators .AND. and .OR. may be used. For example, to determine if both X and Y are positive, the statement IF (X .GT. 0 .AND. Y .GT. 0) may be used. To determine if either X or Y is positive, the statement IF (X .GT. 0 .OR. Y .GT. 0) may be used. The connectives .AND. and .OR. must always be used between two relations. It is not correct to construct a statement such as IF (X .OR. Y .GT. 0); only the form above is legal. Logical operators will be more fully discussed in Chapter 10.

The Arithmetic IF[1]

There is a second form of the IF statement that is occasionally used, although it does not provide any new features; this statement is the *arithmetic* IF. The format of the arithmetic IF is quite simple:

$$\text{IF}\,(expr)\ l_1, l_2, l_3$$

where *expr* is any arithmetic expression—it can be INTEGER or REAL—and l_1, l_2, l_3 are three statement labels.

The statement is executed as follows:

If the value of *expr* is less than 0, then the program branches to l_1.
If the value of *expr* is equal to 0, then the program branches to l_2.
If the value of *expr* is greater than 0, then the program branches to l_3.

The statement

```
IF(I) 10, 20, 30
```

is the same as

```
IF(I .LT. 0) GO TO 10
IF(I .EQ. 0) GO TO 20
IF(I .GT. 0) GO TO 30
```

It is also the same as

```
IF(I .LT. 0) GO TO 10
IF(I .EQ. 0) GO TO 20
GO TO 30
```

To remember the order of the statement labels following the IF, notice that it spells out the word *leg*. That is:

[1] This section describes a little-used statement. It is included because a few compilers accept it as the only valid form and because it exists in ANSI FORTRAN. It may be omitted without loss of continuity.

```
IF(expr)   L,   E,   G
           e    q    r
           s    u    e
           s    a    a
                l    t
           t         e
           h    t    r
           a    o
           n         t
                0    h
           0         a
                     n

                     0
```

The statement following an arithmetic IF *must* be labeled. Why?

There are times when there is no need to test an expression for less, equal, or greater than zero. Instead, it may be necessary to test an expression for less, equal, or greater than some other number. Thus, to determine if the expression

```
A + .5*B
```

is less, equal, or greater than 50.0, subtract 50.0 from the expression:

```
A + .5*B - 50.0
```

and the resultant expression will have the desired properties; that is

A + .5*B – 50.0 is less than 0 if A + .5*B is less than 50.0
A + .5*B – 50.0 is equal to 0 if A + .5*B is equal to 50.0
A + .5*B – 50.0 is greater than 0 if A + .5*B is greater than 50.0

Thus

```
IF(A + .5*B - 50.0) 10, 75, 90
```

will execute as desired.

The labels that follow the arithmetic IF need not all be different. The following are legal:

```
IF(X - .05) 10, 10, 79
IF(I - J) 150, 98, 98
```

Figure 5.8 shows how the arithmetic IF is represented in a flowchart.

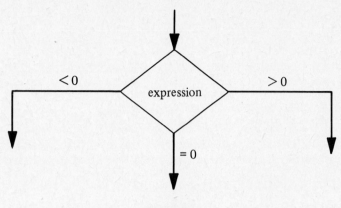

Figure 5.8

Controlling Loops

In every example cited thus far, the GO TO statement referred to a statement below it; that is, every jump has been to a point further down in the program. The cases in which the jump is back to an earlier portion of the program are equally important. By jumping back and repeating a portion of the program we can begin to capitalize on the astounding speed and accuracy of a computer in performing repetitious tasks. Determining a single student's grade or the balance in one person's account is much too simple to warrant writing a program and implementing it on a computer. Only when thousands of student grades or the balances in thousands of accounts are to be calculated does the power and speed of a computer become useful.

The technique of going back to an earlier statement and repeating a sequence of instructions many times is called *looping*. A common kind of *loop* contains an input section, a calculation, and an output section. For example, a program fragment to read in sets of three grades and to print out the average might be

```
 10  READ 100, A,B,C
100  FORMAT(F5.0, F5.0, F5.0)
     AVERAG = (A+B+C)/3.0
     PRINT 101, A,B,C,AVERAG
101  FORMAT('0THE AVERAGE OF', F6.0,F6.0,F6.0, ' IS ', F6.1)
     GO TO 10
```

This program will repeat the sequence of read, calculate, and print until it has exhausted the data in the input device (card reader, tape, disk, or any other). If there is some processing to be done when all the grades have been averaged, it will be necessary to detect the fact that the input device contains no more data. This may be accomplished in several ways. The first method is usually referred to as the *trailer* data technique. Assuming that the data were being put in from cards, then an additional card would be included which contains a special piece of information. In this case, we might assume that the test grades are all positive and that if a negative grade is encountered, it should be taken as a signal that all the data has been processed. If our input data cards appear as

bb−4.bbbb0bbbb0
bb74.bb77.bb91.
bb43.bb84.bb92.

then this set of data produces only two lines of output:

```
THE AVERAGE OF   43.   84.   92. IS   73.0
THE AVERAGE OF   74.   77.   91. IS   80.7
```

One makes use of the trailer data to get out of the loop by inserting a test for the negative value in the program.

```
 10  READ 100, A,B,C
100  FORMAT(F5.0, F5.0, F5.0)
     IF(A .LT. 0.0) GO TO 20
     AVERAG = (A+B+C)/3.0
     PRINT 101, A,B,C,AVERAG
101  FORMAT('0THE AVERAGE OF', F6.0, F6.0, F6.0, ' IS ', F6.1)
     GO TO 10
 20  .
     .
     .
```

The flowchart in Figure 5.9 should clarify the flow of control in this example.

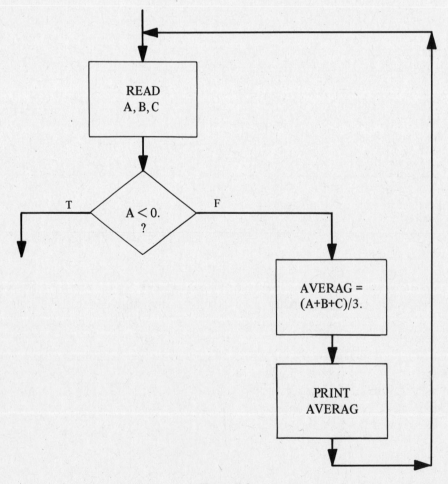

Figure 5.9

Problem 5.4

    Write a program to read a set of numbers, one per card, until a negative number is encountered. Print a message indicating the number of *positive* numbers read and their average.

    Another technique used to control the number of cards processed and to prevent termination by exhaustion of input is to add a special *trailer field* to the data. For example, when converting Fahrenheit temperatures to Centigrade, we might enter a single Fahrenheit temperature on a data card with a trailer field. The trailer fields on each card but the last one would be a single integer position with a value of zero. On the final data card, the trailer field would contain a one. The program should read a data card, perform the conversion, print the results, and test to see if the data card is the final one. The data cards would appear like this:

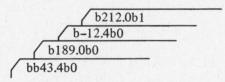

    Blanks in numeric data fields are treated as if they were zeroes, making it possible to omit the keypunching of the zeroes. The "1" on the last card must, of course, be entered. To make the program more elegant, an additional feature can be added to count the number of cards processed and print out the total when all the data have been processed.

```
      NDATA = 0
   10 READ 101, FAHR, NTRAIL
  101 FORMAT(F6.1, 1X, I1)
      CENTIG = (5./9.)*(FAHR - 32.0)
      PRINT 102, FAHR, CENTIG
  102 FORMAT(' FAHRENHEIT ', F6.1, '  CENTIGRADE ', F6.1)
      NDATA = NDATA + 1
      IF(NTRAIL .NE. 1) GO TO 10
      PRINT 103,NDATA
  103 FORMAT(' NUMBER OF DATA CARDS - ', I4)
      STOP
      END
```

Remember that the statement

```
  NDATA = NDATA + 1
```

is read as "Take the current value of NDATA, add one to it, and store the result back in NDATA."

    The output from this program for our sequence of four data cards is

```
FAHRENHEIT    43.4   CENTIGRADE     6.3
FAHRENHEIT   189.0   CENTIGRADE    87.2
FAHRENHEIT   -12.4   CENTIGRADE   -24.7
FAHRENHEIT   212.0   CENTIGRADE   100.0
NUMBER OF DATA CARDS -     4
```

Yet another technique for controlling a loop when there is input data depends on knowing the precise number of sets of data to be processed. Assuming there are seven sets of grades to be averaged, the program would keep a tally of how many sets have been processed and would execute the next part of the program following the loop when the tally reached seven. The computer does not make tally marks, but a counter can be established and incremented by one each time a set of grades is processed. When the counter reaches seven, all the grades have been processed and the next section of the program would be executed. The counting mechanism might be abstracted as in Figure 5.10.

The initialization consists of setting the counter location to zero. The increment adds one to the counter and the test determines if the process is to be repeated. Imagine a box of marbles used for counting purposes. The box is initialized by clearing it out. The incremen-

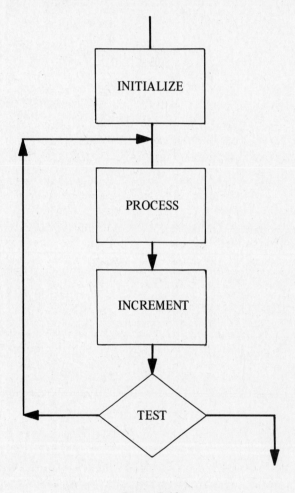

Figure 5.10

tation involves the addition of a single marble and the test is to determine if there are seven marbles. This sequence of initialization, incrementation, and testing is one of the fundamental ideas in computing.

The FORTRAN version of this sequence is

```
      NCOUNT = 0
10
      [Process]
      NCOUNT = NCOUNT + 1
      IF(NCOUNT .LT. 7) GO TO 10
```

To return to the student grading program, it is possible to guarantee that exactly seven sets of student grades are processed by inserting the statements

```
      NCOUNT = 0
  10  READ 100,A,B,C
 100  FORMAT(F5.0, F5.0, F5.0)
      AVERAG = (A+B+C)/3.0
      PRINT 101, AVERAG
 101  FORMAT('0THE AVERAGE IS', F6.1)
      NCOUNT = NCOUNT + 1
      IF(NCOUNT .LT. 7) GO TO 10
        .
        .
        .
```

The ability to repeat the same set of instructions is useful in many situations. The repeated processing of input data is basic to business applications of computers. Employee payroll programs, bank account processing programs, billing programs and the like are based on this procedure. Other applications, such as the construction of a table of numbers including the square and the square root of the number, do not involve the input of new data. In this case, the counter is used for two purposes: (1) to count the number of times through the loop and (2) as the value to be used for the arithmetic calculations. The following program will print a table for the integers from one to fifty:

```
      NCOUNT = 0
  25  NCOUNT = NCOUNT + 1
      NSQ = NCOUNT*NCOUNT
      XSQRT = SQRT(FLOAT(NCOUNT))
      PRINT 101, NCOUNT, NSQ, XSQRT
 101  FORMAT(' NUMBER', I3, ' SQUARE ', I6, ' SQUARE ROOT ', F8.3)
      IF(NCOUNT .LT. 50) GO TO 25
      STOP
      END
```

The DO Statement

Program loops of the sort we have been discussing here are so fundamental that a special statement has been incorporated into the FORTRAN language to facilitate construction of loops. That statement is the DO. The most used DO statement has a form similar to the following

```
      DO 50 I = 1,N

      [Statements]

  50  CONTINUE
```

This statement pair instructs the computer to execute the statements between the DO and the CONTINUE N times.

The first time through, I is assigned the value of 1 and each time through the loop (called an *iteration*) the value of I is increased by 1. The iterations end when $I > N$ and the statement following the CONTINUE is executed. Thus the DO statement provides an automatic counter.

The DO statement has a number of options and is quite flexible. It will be discussed in depth in the next chapter.

Three New Input/Output Statements

Thus far, four input/output statements have been discussed:

```
READ, X, Y, Z
READ 100, X, Y, Z

PRINT, X, Y, Z
PRINT 101, X, Y, Z
```

There is a preferred form of the second and fourth statements:

```
READ(5,100) X, Y, Z
WRITE(6,101) X, Y, Z
```

These statements are executed in exactly the same way as the statements they replace; only the form is different. However, this new form of input/output is considered better by many programmers. There are several reasons for this. The statement

```
READ(5,100) X, Y, Z
```

is similar to

```
READ 100, X, Y, Z
```

except for the additional number 5. The purpose of this number is to specify the device from which the read is to take place. In most computer installations 5 means the card reader. It is possible, of course, that a program which normally reads input from cards will be run with input from some other device; a tape, for example. In this case, it is only necessary to change the number 5 to a number designating a tape drive. In general, the number 5 is used to mean card reader but this may vary from installation to installation.

The same logic is used in the WRITE statement.

```
WRITE(6,101) X, Y, Z
```

is the same as

```
PRINT 101, X, Y, Z
```

with 6 designating the printer. This may also vary from installation to installation. If, for some reason, the output is desired on tape (perhaps for later printing or transcription to microfilm), it is necessary only to change the *unit number* specified. For example,

```
WRITE(10,101) X, Y, Z
```

In general, the unit numbers are allocated as in Table 5.1.

Table 5.1

Number	Device
1–4	Tapes and disks
5	Card reader
6	Printer
7	Card punch
8–99	Tapes and disks

It is even possible to use an INTEGER variable as the unit number in the READ and WRITE statements, as in

```
    IN = 5
    KOUT = 6
    READ(IN,100) X, Y, Z
100 FORMAT(. . .
101 FORMAT(. . .
```

One advantage of the READ(5, format) statement is that it makes it possible to specify a label to which control will be transferred when no more data exist. This is done by specifying END = *nn* in the READ statement where *nn* is a label to which control should be transferred when the READ statement finds no more data. (Recall that in the READ 100, X, Y, Z form, the program will terminate if no more data exist.) The form of this option is

READ(unit, format, END = *nn*) list

Some examples are

```
READ(5, 250, END = 47) X, Q7
READ(5, 102, END = 200) V1, V7
```

The END = option can be extremely useful at times:

```
   N = 0
10 READ(5,110, END = 99) TAX, FICA
   N = N + 1
             .
             .
   GO TO 10
99 WRITE(6,120) N
110 FORMAT(F10.2, F10.2)
120 FORMAT('0A TOTAL OF', I4, ' CARDS WERE READ')
   STOP
   END
```

You may wonder whether it is possible to use the END = option with simplified input. Some FORTRAN compilers (including WATFIV but *not* WATFOR) allow the format number in the READ to be replaced by an asterisk indicating standard simple input. Thus, the following two statements are equivalent:

```
READ(5,*) A,B          READ, A, B
```

and the following is legal:

```
READ(5,*, END = 900) B, A, PAL
```

The PUNCH Statement

It is sometimes desirable to produce data on punch cards for later input to a program. For example, a payroll program might punch a set of cards listing the employee number and the amount contributed to the credit union. These cards might be used later to update the employee's account.

By using the new form of the WRITE statement, output may be directed to the card punch by specifying the appropriate logical device. At many installations this number is 7; thus the statement

```
WRITE(7,101) A,B
```

will direct output to the punch.

The alternate forms of the PRINT statement have their counterparts for producing punched output. The statement

```
PUNCH 101, A,B
```

is the same as the WRITE statement above.

Format-free output may be generated by the statement

```
PUNCH, A,B
```

When specifying a FORMAT statement for punched output you are restricted to a line of 80 or fewer characters because of the size of the card. No carriage control character is used for punched output.

Summary

The IF statement is an extremely powerful statement which provides control over the execution of program statements. With the IF statement it is possible to select from one of two possible execution patterns. This choice is necessary since different actions must be performed if the bank balance is above or below zero, if a student's grade is above or below 60 or if the temperature of a solution goes above 212°. The second function of the IF statement is to provide control over program loops. By the careful use of a counter, an increment statement, and an IF statement it is possible to repeat a group of program statements a precise number of times. IF statements are also used to control the input of data: cards may be read until a trailer or "end of data" card is detected. In the next chapter we will make a careful study of the DO statement which allows a simpler approach to controlling loops.

Several IF statements may be combined to produce very complex execution patterns. These combinations can quickly become complicated and difficult to analyze without the use of flowcharts. When you develop a program, flowcharts are a useful aid to understanding the problem.

The READ and PRINT statements that we have been using till now can be replaced with a more sophisticated input/output statement. For the remaining chapters the

READ(*unit number, format number*) *list*

WRITE(*unit number, format number*) *list*

statements will be used. The unit number indicates which of the many input/output units on the computer will be used (usually 5 for the card reader and 6 for the printer). The format number is the number of a format statement in the program by which the list of variables will be printed.

DEBUGGING CLINIC

Debugging programs with IF and GO TO statements is substantially more difficult than debugging programs without these features. These control structures which permit the repetition of program statements or the selection between two alternative execution patterns permit the construction of extremely complex programs. Additional debugging output can be printed before each IF statement. This information can be helpful in determining the cause of errors. Instead of writing

```
IF(N .LT. 8) GO TO 10
```

insert an additional print statement:

```
PRINT, 'THE VALUE OF N IS ', N
IF(N .LT. 8) GO TO 10
```

If more than one variable participates in an IF statement, both values should be printed:

```
PRINT, ' X = ', X, ' Y = ',Y
IF( X .GT. Y) GO TO 50
```

Whenever information is read in, the values should be immediately "echo printed" or "echoed":

```
    READ(5,101) TEMP,HUMID,BAROM
101 FORMAT(F6.1, F7.2, F5.2)
    PRINT, ' TEMP HUMID BAROM ', TEMP,HUMID,BAROM
```

If the free-format PRINT statement is available, it may be used to check that the values have been read in properly.

The most common typographic errors associated with IF statements are the omission of a parentheses or a period surrounding the relational operator. The following statements are invalid for typographic reasons:

```
IF(K .EQ. M*(I-Z) GO TO 30
IF(BALANC .LT 0.0) GO TO 55
IF( NTYPE = 7)GO TO 60
IF(CODE - 2.0)*(VALUE+TEST) .GT. 78.8)GO TO 70
IF(NUMBER - 7) GO TO 63
IF(K EQ N) GO TO 46
```

Whenever there is a GO TO 30 or a GO TO 46 there must be a statement with a label 30 or 46. Statement labels should be in columns 1–5; they may appear anywhere within these five columns.

An extremely dangerous situation arises when two real values are to be compared for equality. Since roundoff error can cause a mathematical result to be slightly inaccurate, the condition of the following IF statement will not be true and the program will go on to the next instruction—the GO TO will not be executed:

```
AVER=(2.4+2.6)/2.0
IF(AVER .EQ. 2.5) GO TO 50
```

If this test is necessary, then the difference between the two values should be tested:

```
AVER=(2.4+2.6)2.0
DIFF=ABS(AVER -2.5)
IF(DIFF .LT. 0.000001) GO TO 50
```

When the new READ and WRITE statements are used, care must be taken to insure that the unit numbers correspond to proper numbers. This information must be obtained from your computer center. If the unit numbers are incorrect you may be attempting to print on the card reader and read cards from the printer. Make sure that the format number corresponds to a FORMAT statement in the program.

REVIEW QUESTIONS

1. Describe the general form of the IF statement. What is its function? Why is the IF statement called a "conditional execution" statement?

2. What are the six *relational operators*? How are they used?

3. Describe the *arithmetic* IF statement. How is it used? How can it be used to determine if some number is less than, equal to, or greater than some value other than zero.

4. Explain the READ(*u, fmt*) and WRITE(*u, fmt*) forms. How are they used?

EXERCISES

1. Write an IF statement for each of the following conditions.
   a. If x is larger than 25, set x to 25.
   b. If the divisor, D, is zero print the message "The divisor is zero-error".
   c. If $I \leqslant N$ read a card with x, y, and z.
   d. If the deductions (DED) are more than half the wage (WAGE) deduct only half the wage.
   e. If J is even, transfer to statement 99. (Hint: a number is even if it is divisible by 2. Consider the expression $(I/2)*2$ with respect to integer division. What is the result if $I = 7$? If $I = 8$?)

2. Convert the following READ and PRINT statements to logical unit form.
   a. `READ 1000, X,Y,Z`
   b. `PRINT 45, A, VALUE`
   c. `PRINT 14, FICA, TAX`
   d. `READ 1110, X1, X2`
   e. `READ, V8`   (WATFIV only)

3. Rewrite the program to determine the largest of three numbers, using only "less than" tests.

4. Write a program to read in three numbers to determine which is the smallest and print it out.

5. Rewrite the program to determine the student grade using "less than" tests.

6. A professor decided to determine the students' grades on the basis of the highest grade obtained out of three tests (rather than the average). Combine the maximum finding program with the classification program to suit the professor's needs.

7. The property tax rate in the town of Opportunity, Montana was set on an increasing scale (Table 5.2).

Table 5.2

Tax Rate	Assessed Value
3 percent	Less than $20,000
4 percent	$10,000-$30,000
5 percent	$30,000-$60,000
6 percent	Above $60,000

Write a program to read in the assessed value, determine which category the property is in, calculate and print the tax charge.

8. A manufacturing process for resistors requires that they be within 1 percent of the rated value. Write a program to read in a rated value and an actual value. If the actual value differs from the rated value by more than 1 percent, print "DEFECTIVE"; otherwise print "MEETS REQUIREMENTS."

9. An inventory management program fragment contains a variable NAVAIL which indicates how many of a particular part are available. NREQ indicates the number of parts requested. If NREQ is less than or equal to NAVAIL, subtract NREQ from NAVAIL; otherwise print "REQUEST CANNOT BE FILLED."

10. Write a student grading program which reads a term average score and prints out the final grade on the basis of Table 5.3.

Table 5.3

Term Average	Grade
Above 95	A+
90–95	A
85–90	B+
80–85	B
75–80	C+
70–75	C
65–70	D
Less than 65	F

11. Write a program to print out the proper medical advice based on body temperature. If the patient's temperature is within one-half of a degree of normal (98.6°F), then the patient is "NORMAL." If the temperature is more than one-half of a degree from normal but one and one-half degrees or less from normal, the patient should "REST IN BED." If the temperature is more than one and one-half degrees from normal, the patient should "CONTACT DOCTOR."

12. A stockbroker's commission is calculated by the following algorithm: If the price per share is less than $50.00, the stockbroker gets $0.20 per share; otherwise $0.35 per share. If the number of shares is less than 100, the commission is doubled. Write a program to read in an integer number of shares and a real number for the price, calculate, and print the commission.

13. If N is any number greater than 0, the *square root* of N is the unique number y such that $y*y = N$. One method for finding square roots was given by Isaac Newton: If x_n is an approximation to y, then

$$x_{n+1} = \tfrac{1}{2}\left(x_n + \frac{N}{x_n}\right)$$

is a better approximation. You are to write a program which reads a series of numbers and finds their square roots. Use these specifications:

Specifications:
1. Input will be one number per card, in format F10.5. A negative number will indicate the end of file.
2. Find the square root by applying Newton's formula until the difference between consecutive approximations is less than 1.0×10^{-5}.
3. Use $N/2$ as an initial guess.
4. Your output format should show at least the following for each input: the input number, each approximation, and the final answer. Additional data may be shown, so long as the required items are not obscured. All data should be well spaced and labeled using FORMAT statements.
5. Run your program with five numbers between 0. and 100.

(This problem was supplied by Mitchell Wand.)

SPIRAL PROBLEMS

Note: In each of these problems some form of end of data (last card) test should be used to avoid the error message printed by the system in the Spiral Problems in Chapter 4. FORMAT statements must be used to describe the input and the output. You must prepare 4 or 5 of your own data cards according to the directions in each problem.

A. Student Grading

Read a series of student test grades and print the grade and the word "PASSING" if the grade was 60 or above and "FAILING" otherwise. Keep processing until you run out of cards. The input cards have a three-digit integer grade punched in columns 1-3.

B. Commercial Application: Salesperson Commissions

For sales of less than $100.00 a commission of 4 percent is paid, while only 3 percent is paid on sales of $100.00 or more. Write a program to read data cards with sales amounts punched in columns 1-7 in the form XXXX.XX and to calculate and print the amount of the commission for each sale. Keep reading, calculating, and printing until you run out of cards.

C. Mathematical Applications

Data cards containing the base radius and the height of various cylinders have been prepared in the form

XXX.X XX.X

base   height
radius

Write a program to read a data card, calculate the volume ($V = \pi r^2 h$), and print the volume with the message "BIG" if the volume is more than 100.0 and "SMALL" otherwise. Your program should process all the cards.

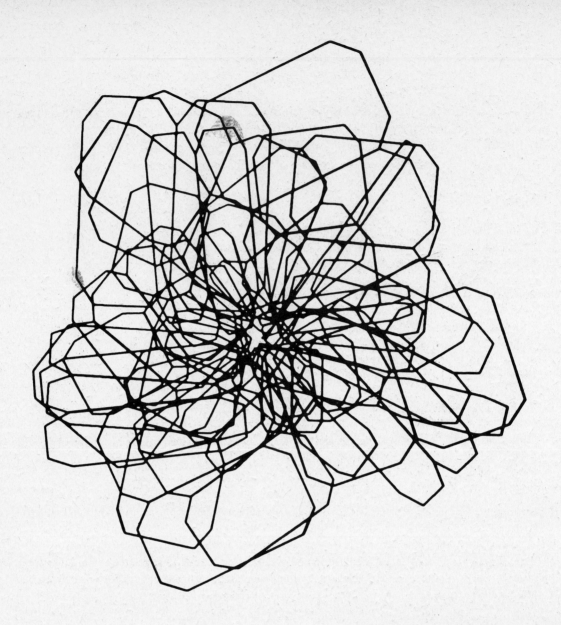

PROGRAM LOOPING

Doing is the great thing. For if, resolutely, people do what is right, in time they come to like doing it.

John Ruskin

CHAPTER 6

The DO statement (introduced in Chapter 5) is an extremely power-ful FORTRAN construct which permits a group of statements to be repeated a predetermined number of times. This statement is thus a means for creating loops within the body of a program. One important use of the DO statement is to repeat a READ statement so that an entire set of data may be read in by means of a single statement repeated the appropriate number of times. In order to count the number of times that the statements in a DO loop have been repeated, the DO statement util-izes a variable known as the index. The index of the DO is an integer var-iable which is given an initial value the first time through the loop and is incremented each subsequent time that the loop is executed. The index may be used in arithmetic statements within the loop.

A special statement, the CONTINUE statement, may be used to in-dicate the end of the DO loop. The CONTINUE statement is optional but provides a useful device for indicating the extent of the DO loop. In effect, the DO-CONTINUE statements serve as a parenthesis around the group of statements which are to be repeated.

Within a DO loop it is possible to include another DO loop. When DO loops are enclosed, one within the other, they are known as nested DO loops. Nested DO loops allow extremely elaborate computational procedures to be compressed into a very few statements.

Introduction

The power of the computer is most evident when an algorithm requires that a group of statements be repeated a number of times. Program loops, which were discussed in Chapter 5, use an IF and a GO TO to branch back to the beginning of the program in order to process multiple sets of data. FORTRAN provides a special statement, the DO statement, for creating loops. The DO is an extremely powerful statement which can be used for a multiplicity of purposes.

The DO statement causes the group of statements within the body of the loop to be repeated a number of times. The statement that delimits the body of the DO is usually a CONTINUE statement. This special statement is a useful place to hang a label:

```
DO 11 KK = M, N, I
.
.
.
11 CONTINUE
```

but it causes no other action.

The DO statement is extremely important to the FORTRAN programmer. This chapter will begin with a discussion of the simplest DO form and then go on to consider the options it makes available to the programmer.

The Basic DO

One example where programmed repetition is necessary is the following program to print business cards:

```
      WRITE(6,101)
      WRITE(6,102)
      WRITE(6,103)
      WRITE(6,104)
      WRITE(6,105)
      WRITE(6,106)
      WRITE(6,107)
      WRITE(6,108)
      WRITE(6,109)
101 FORMAT('0********************************')
102 FORMAT(' *                              *')
103 FORMAT(' *                              *')
104 FORMAT(' *    GEORGE MONEYMAKER         *')
105 FORMAT(' *    143 SOUTH EAST STREET     *')
106 FORMAT(' *    BLOOMINGTON, IN   47401   *')
107 FORMAT(' *                              *')
108 FORMAT(' *                              *')
109 FORMAT(' ********************************')
      STOP
      END
```

This program produces only one business card per run. If more than one business card is desired (as is usually the case), the operator is left with the tedious and wasteful job of submitting the program over and over again.[1]

There are a number of techniques that could be used to correct this problem, but the most direct method is to use a DO statement. By surrounding a group of statements with a pair of DO and CONTINUE statements, it is possible to specify that the group of statements is to be repeated. To repeat the WRITE statements to generate three business cards, surround the executable WRITE statements with a DO and CONTINUE pair:

```
      DO 50 I = 1,3
      WRITE(6,101)
      WRITE(6,102)
      WRITE(6,103)
      WRITE(6,104)
      WRITE(6,105)
      WRITE(6,106)
      WRITE(6,107)
      WRITE(6,108)
      WRITE(6,109)
   50 CONTINUE
  101 FORMAT('0*********************************')
  102 FORMAT(' *                               *')
  103 FORMAT(' *                               *')
  104 FORMAT(' *      GEORGE MONEYMAKER         *')
  105 FORMAT(' *      143 SOUTH EAST STREET     *')
  106 FORMAT(' *      BLOOMINGTON, IN   47401   *')
  107 FORMAT(' *                               *')
  108 FORMAT(' *                               *')
  109 FORMAT('  *******************************')
      STOP
      END
```

(Since the FORMAT statements are not executable, it would make no difference if the CONTINUE statement were moved down to the position after the FORMAT statements.)

The output of this program is

```
*********************************
*                               *
*                               *
*                               *
*      GEORGE MONEYMAKER         *
*      143 SOUTH EAST STREET     *
*      BLOOMINGTON, IN   47401   *
*                               *
*                               *
*********************************
```

---

[1] A simple loop using a GO TO statement cannot be used to produce repetition by branching to the first statement, since the program would never terminate. It would print business cards until the printer ran out of paper. A loop like this which never terminates is called an *infinite loop* and often occurs as a result of programmer errors.

```
xxxxxxxxxxxxxxxxxxxxxxxxxxxxx
x                           x
x                           x
x    GEORGE  MONEYMAKER      x
x    143  SOUTH  EAST  STREET x
x    BLOOMINGTON,  IN    47401 x
x                           x
x                           x
xxxxxxxxxxxxxxxxxxxxxxxxxxxxx


xxxxxxxxxxxxxxxxxxxxxxxxxxxxx
x                           x
x                           x
x    GEORGE  MONEYMAKER      x
x    143  SOUTH  EAST  STREET x
x    BLOOMINGTON,  IN    47401 x
x                           x
x                           x
xxxxxxxxxxxxxxxxxxxxxxxxxxxxx
```

To produce 20 business cards the DO statement would read

```
DO 50 I = 1,20
```

and for 200 business cards

```
DO 50 I = 1,200
```

The 50 indicates that all statements up to the statement labeled 50 are to be repeated. This statement is usually a CONTINUE statement that serves only to delimit the extent (*scope*) of the loop. The I = 1,200 indicates that the statements are to be repeated while the INTEGER variable I is used as a counter ranging from 1 to 200. The location I acts as an *index* to keep track of how many times the loop has been executed. Any INTEGER variable would serve as well:

```
DO  50  INDEX = 1,200
DO  50  MCOUNT = 1,200
DO  50  K27 = 1,200
DO  50  J = 1,200
```

The value of the index could be printed out after each run-through by using the appropriate printing command following the DO statement:

```
    DO 19 J = 1,6
    WRITE(6,110) J
110 FORMAT(' ',I5)
 19 CONTINUE
```

This enables us to watch the counter as it counts up from 1 to 6. The DO statement in the program means, "Repeat all the statements up to and including statement number 19,

USING OVERLAYS

A frequent problem in programming is that the computer's main storage is not able to contain the entire program. There is a corollary to Murphy's law[2] which states that "programs expand to exceed the available memory." When a program cannot fit into the available main storage, it is necessary to store parts of the program on secondary storage (disks and drums) and transfer the program segments to main storage as they are needed. The segments transferred to main storage will "overlay" some of the segments already in main storage; therefore this process is known as *overlaying.*

Overlaying may be accomplished in two ways: *virtual memory overlays* and *planned overlays.* Virtual memory overlays are available only on computers with very sophisticated operating systems. In a virtual memory overlay, the program is arbitrarily divided into fixed length segments (*pages*) by the operating system. These pages are then automatically transferred by the operating system to main storage as required. Virtual memory overlays are very convenient for the programmer since they are totally automatic; unfortunately very few computers provide this service to the programmer.

Far more common is the planned overlay. In a planned overlay, the programmer is responsible for designating the segments to be transferred to main storage; the operating system performs the actual loading of the segment. Programs are naturally structured into subprograms, which serve as the units of transfer. That is, the smallest program segment which can be transferred to main storage at any time is a subprogram.

A small fraction of the program, called the *main overlay* or *root phase*, must remain in the processor storage throughout execution in order to call in the appropriate overlays or *phases.* At the start of execution, the processor storage could be represented as

After one overlay is brought in, the processor storage contains

After some computations are performed in OVERLAY 1, a second overlay might completely replace the first:

A third and fourth overlay could be then brought in:

And finally, a fifth overlay might replace the fourth one:

---

[2]Murphy's law states that "if anything can go wrong, it will."

Main	Overlay 3	Overlay 5	

In order to accomplish planned overlay, it is necessary to inform the operating system of the overlay structure. This is usually done quite simply by means of control cards. Since the details vary considerably among various computers, the appropriate programming manual should be consulted for specific details.

changing the INTEGER variable from an initial value of 1 to a final value of 6 in steps of 1."

The DO-CONTINUE statements, thus, serve to indicate which group of statements is to be repeated and how many times. The DO-CONTINUE pair is executed as follows:

```
        Label      Index    Starting value
          ↓          ↗          ↙
DO       43        MM    =    1,        7  ←—— End value
   ⋮
43 CONTINUE
```

1. The *index* is set to the *starting value* (MM=1).
2. The statements up to the CONTINUE are executed.
3. When the CONTINUE is reached, the index is incremented by 1 (MM=MM+1). If the index is greater than the *end value*, the statement after the CONTINUE is executed. Otherwise, an automatic branch back to the statement following the DO occurs. Processing continues as in step 2.

For a concrete example, consider the statements

```
        •
        •
        •
     DO 127 K = 1,2
     L = K + 3
     WRITE(6,500) L
127 CONTINUE
        •
        •
        •
```

These will execute as follows:

1. When the DO statement is first executed, the value of K is set to 1.
2. L is set equal to K + 3, which is 4. The value 4 is printed.
3. When the CONTINUE statement is reached, the value of K is incremented by 1 and the program goes to the statement following the DO; that is, the assignment statement.
4. L is set equal to the value of K (which is now 2) + 3 so L now has a value of 5. The value 5 is printed.

5. When the CONTINUE statement is reached, the value of K is now 2, which was specified as the last value that K was to take on; instead of branching back to the assignment statement, control passes to the statement following the CONTINUE.

Thus, in this program fragment the DO-CONTINUE pair (also called a "DO loop") is equivalent to the following sequence of statements:

```
K = 1
L = K + 3
WRITE(6,500) L
K = 2
L = K + 3
WRITE(6,500) L
```

One value of the DO statement is that it can be used to turn a potentially formidable programming problem into a trivial one; consider a program to produce a table of the squares and cubes of the integers from 1 to 50. Basically, for a given value of I we need to calculate the square:

```
ISQ = I*I                 (or I**2)
```

and the cube:

```
ICUBE = I*I*I             (or I**3)
```

and to print the results:

```
      WRITE(6,101) I,ISQ,ICUBE
101 FORMAT(' ', I3, I6, I9)
```

Still, a mechanism is needed to change the INTEGER variable I from an initial value of 1 to a final value of 50 in steps of 1; the DO statement, of course, is designed to perform just this function:

```
      DO 90 I = 1,50
      ISQ = I*I
      ICUBE = I*I*I
      WRITE(6,101) I,ISQ,ICUBE
101 FORMAT(' ',I3,I6,I9)
 90 CONTINUE
      STOP
      END
```

The CONTINUE statement sets the limit on how many statements are to be repeated; the 90 in the DO statement matches the 90 in the CONTINUE statement. The output of this program is three columns of numbers, shown in Figure 6.1.

1	1	1
2	4	8
3	9	27
4	16	64
5	25	125
6	36	216
7	49	343
8	64	512
9	81	729
10	100	1000
11	121	1331
12	144	1728
13	169	2197
14	196	2744
15	225	3375
16	256	4096
17	289	4913
18	324	5832
19	361	6859
20	400	8000
21	441	9261
22	484	10648
23	529	12167
24	576	13824
25	625	15625
26	676	17576
27	729	19683
28	784	21952
29	841	24389
30	900	27000
31	961	29791
32	1024	32768
33	1089	35937
34	1156	39304
35	1225	42875
36	1296	46656
37	1369	50653
38	1444	54872
39	1521	59319
40	1600	64000
41	1681	68921
42	1764	74088
43	1849	79507
44	1936	85184
45	2025	91125
46	2116	97336
47	2209	103823
48	2304	110592
49	2401	117649
50	2500	125000

Figure 6.1

Of course, a similar program can be obtained by using an IF statement to create a loop. But this forces the programmer to take care of the tedious details of initializing the counter, incrementing it, and testing it. The previous program could be written as

```
      I = 1
   30 ISQ = I*I
      ICUBE = I*I*I
      WRITE(6,101) I,ISQ,ICUBE
  101 FORMAT(' ',I3, I6, I9)
      I = I + 1
      IF(I .LE. 50) GO TO 30
      STOP
      END
```

The results would be the same, but the extra complications provide additional opportunities for error and reduce the clarity of the program. Stated in a positive sense, the DO statement is a higher-level concept which combines a number of operations into a single powerful statement. The flowchart in Figure 6.2 describes the functions of the DO statement.

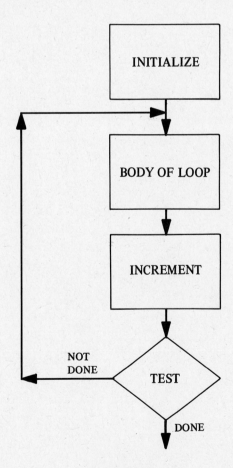

Figure 6.2

While there is no standard notation for drawing a flowchart involving a DO statement, we shall adopt the convention shown in Figure 6.3.

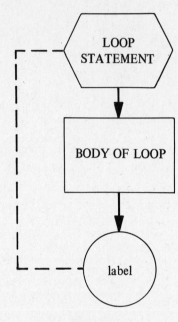

Figure 6.3

The flowchart for the square and cube program is shown in Figure 6.4.

Problem 6.1

Draw a flowchart and specify the output values for each of the following program fragments.

```
a.      DO 10 J = 1,5
        WRITE(6,100) J
    10  CONTINUE


b.      I = 1
        DO 43 K = 1,4
        WRITE(6,100) I
    43  CONTINUE


c.      DO 94 I = 1,7
        J = I + 2
    94  CONTINUE
        WRITE(6,100) J
```

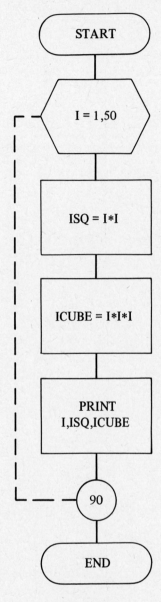

Figure 6.4

Loop Control with Increments of 1

Returning to the problem of converting from Fahrenheit to Centigrade, one might wish to construct a table of temperature conversions. Consider the problem of writing a program to create the table for Fahrenheit temperatures from 1.0 degrees to 40.0 degrees. Unfortunately, the DO statement operates only on INTEGER variables, so we must convert to REAL values inside the body of the loop:

```
      DO 70 I = 1,40
      FAHR = FLOAT(I)
      CENT = (5./9.)*(FAHR - 32.)
      WRITE(6,101) FAHR,CENT
  101 FORMAT(' ', F6.1, F6.1)
   70 CONTINUE
```

A more useful table would include 0.0 degrees and would range up to 40.0 degrees, for a total of 41 values. Since in most versions of FORTRAN the starting value of a DO cannot be zero, we write

```
      DO 70 I = 1,41
      J = I - 1
      FAHR = FLOAT(J)
      CENT = (5./9.)*(FAHR - 32.)
      WRITE(6,101) FAHR, CENT
  101 FORMAT(' ', F6.1, F6.1)
   70 CONTINUE
```

By subtracting 1 from I, we force the variable J to range from 0 to 40 in steps of 1 and FAHR ranges from 0.0 to 40.0 in steps of 1.0. (Note that the use of the FLOAT function is optional.)

A variation of this idea makes it possible to produce a table of conversions ranging from −20.0 to +20.0 in steps of 1.0:

```
      DO 70 I = 1,41
      J = I - 21
      FAHR = FLOAT(J)
      CENT = (5./9.)*(FAHR - 32)
      WRITE(6,101) FAHR,CENT
  101 FORMAT(' ', F6.1, F6.1)
   70 CONTINUE
```

To create a table which ranges from 0.0 to 4.0 in steps of 0.1, 41 values are still needed, but a transformation of the loop index is needed to produce steps of 0.1. This can be accomplished by dividing by 10.0:

```
      DO 70 I = 1,41
      J = I - 1
      FAHR = FLOAT(J)/10.0
      CENT = (5./9.)*(FAHR - 32.)
      WRITE(6,101) FAHR,CENT
  101 FORMAT(' ',F6.1, F6.1)
   70 CONTINUE
```

Suppose the table were desired in reverse format; that is, from 4.0 to 0.0 in steps of 0.1. Since it is *not* legal to write DO 70 I = 41,1, the programmer must provide the additional statements. The solution is a common programming "trick":

```
      DO 70 I = 1,41
      J = 41 - I
      FAHR = FLOAT(J)/10.0
      CENT = (5./9.)*(FAHR - 32.)
      WRITE(6,101) FAHR,CENT
  101 FORMAT(' ', F6.1, F6.1)
   70 CONTINUE
```

When we subtract I from 41 the value of J ranges from 40 down to 0 in steps of 1 and the value of FAHR ranges from 4.0 to 0.0 in steps of 0.1—just what was needed.

Finally, the last program can be cleaned up by adding some identification on the output and comment cards:

```
C PROGRAM TO PRODUCE TABLE OF FAHRENHEIT TO CENTIGRADE
C CONVERSION FOR 4.0 TO 0.0 DEGREES IN STEPS OF 0.1 DEGREES
C
C
C PRINT HEADING
C
      WRITE(6,100)
  100 FORMAT('1 FAHRENHEIT CENTIGRADE')
      DO 70 I = 1,41
C
C TRANSFORM
C
      J = 41 - I
      FAHR = FLOAT(J)/10.0
C
C CONVERT
C
      CENT = (5./9.)*(FAHR - 32)
C
C PRINT CONVERTED VALUE
C
      WRITE(6,101) FAHR,CENT
  101 FORMAT(' ', F11.1, F11.1)
   70 CONTINUE
C
C PRINT FOOTING
C
      WRITE(6,102)
  102 FORMAT('0END OF LIST')
      STOP
      END
```

Summary

The DO statement may be used to cause a group of statements to be repeated. The form of the basic DO is

DO < label > < index > = 1, < end value >

⋮
⋮

< label >   CONTINUE

Using a starting value of 1 and incrementing until the end value is reached causes the index, an INTEGER variable, to assume the values

1, 2, . . . , < end value >

as the loop is repeated. If a range other than 1 to < end value > is desired or REAL (rather than INTEGER) values are required, appropriate transformations are employed

DO Statements with Starting Values Other than 1

Although the loops which have been shown all utilized starting values of 1, any positive integer may be used as a starting value, as long as it is smaller than the ending value.

If it is necessary to count from 100 to 200 in steps of 1, then a DO statement similar to one of the following could be employed:

```
DO 50 I = 100,200
```

or

```
DO 50 INDEX = 100,200
```

or

```
DO 65 K = 100,200
```

To count from 64 to 188 in steps of 1, any of the following statements could be used:

```
DO 34 LL = 64,188
DO 700 I = 64,188
DO 100 MCOUNT = 64,188
DO 3 JJJJ = 64,188
```

Worked Example

A wholesaler of the new sensational SuperSlipSkis will distribute a minimum of 10 pairs and a maximum of 50 pairs of skis to each ski store. The skis cost $65.00 per pair if less than 30 pairs are purchased, and $62.00 if 30 to 50 pairs are purchased. Write a program to print out the total cost of orders for 10 to 50 pairs.

Solution 1

In this solution, only one DO statement is needed, but an IF statement must be used to determine whether the value of the index is less than 30. The flowchart for this solution is shown in Figure 6.5.

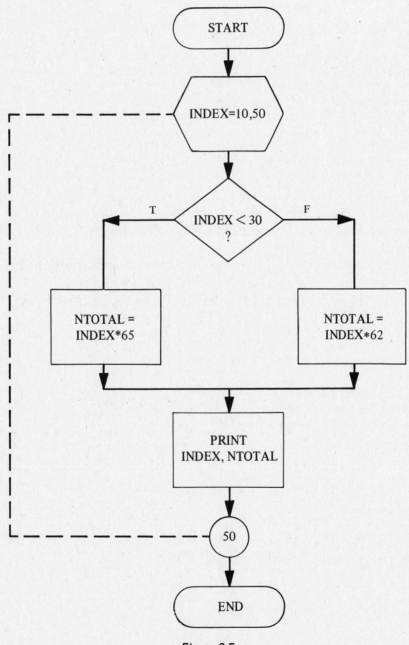

Figure 6.5

This flowchart can be converted to a FORTRAN program in a straightforward manner.

```
      DO 50 INDEX = 10,50
      IF(INDEX .LT. 30) GO TO 40

C
C  HANDLE 30-50 PAIR AT $62 PER PAIR
C
      NTOTAL = INDEX*62
      GO TO 45
C
C  HANDLE 10-29 PAIR AT $65 PER PAIR
C
   40 NTOTAL = INDEX*65
C
C  PRINT RESULTS
C
   45 WRITE(6,101) INDEX,NTOTAL
  101 FORMAT('0FOR ', I2, ' PAIRS THE TOTAL COST IS $ ', I4)
   50 CONTINUE
      STOP
      END
```

Solution 2

The second solution involves two DO loops. The first handles the case of 10–29 pairs and the second handles the case of 30–50 pairs. The flowchart for this solution is shown in Figure 6.6.

Two DO loops eliminate the need for an IF statement, but two WRITE statements must be used, although only a single FORMAT statement is necessary. This second solution will run slightly faster than the first since the instruction for making a decision has been eliminated.

```
C
C  HANDLE 10-29 PAIRS AT $65 PER PAIR
C
      DO 30 INDEX = 10,29
      NTOTAL = INDEX*65
      WRITE(6,101) INDEX, NTOTAL
  101 FORMAT('0FOR ', I2, ' PAIRS THE TOTAL COST IS $ ', I4)
   30 CONTINUE
C
C  HANDLE 30-50 PAIRS AT $62 PER PAIR
C
      DO 40 INDEX = 30,50
      NTOTAL = INDEX*62
      WRITE(6,101) INDEX, NTOTAL
   40 CONTINUE
      STOP
      END
```

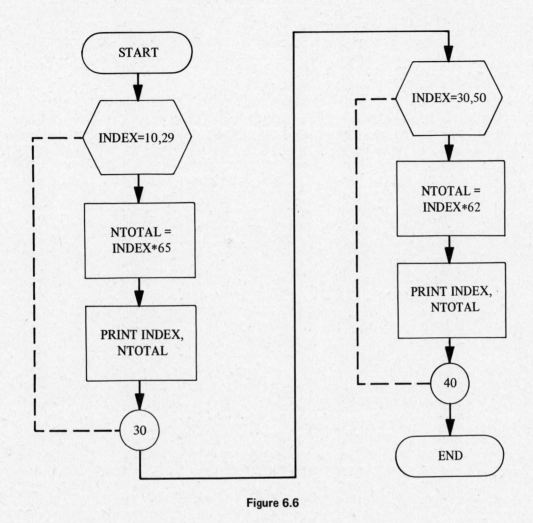

Figure 6.6

Either technique produces the same output, shown in Figure 6.7.

Loop Control with Increments Greater Than 1

In all of the examples thus far, the index value or the counter was incremented by 1. Often it is necessary to have increments greater than 1. If the manager at the SuperSlipSki plant discovered that it was convenient to crate and ship his skis in cartons containing two pairs of skis, he might require that all orders be in multiples of two. A DO statement may specify the increment by which the index is to be increased each time the loop is repeated. The increment is placed following the end value:

DO < label > < index > = < start value > , < end value > , < increment >

```
FOR 10 PAIRS THE TOTAL COST IS $  650
FOR 11 PAIRS THE TOTAL COST IS $  715
FOR 12 PAIRS THE TOTAL COST IS $  780
FOR 13 PAIRS THE TOTAL COST IS $  845
FOR 14 PAIRS THE TOTAL COST IS $  910
FOR 15 PAIRS THE TOTAL COST IS $  975
FOR 16 PAIRS THE TOTAL COST IS $ 1040
FOR 17 PAIRS THE TOTAL COST IS $ 1105
FOR 18 PAIRS THE TOTAL COST IS $ 1170
FOR 19 PAIRS THE TOTAL COST IS $ 1235
FOR 20 PAIRS THE TOTAL COST IS $ 1300
FOR 21 PAIRS THE TOTAL COST IS $ 1365
FOR 22 PAIRS THE TOTAL COST IS $ 1430
FOR 23 PAIRS THE TOTAL COST IS $ 1495
FOR 24 PAIRS THE TOTAL COST IS $ 1560
FOR 25 PAIRS THE TOTAL COST IS $ 1625
FOR 26 PAIRS THE TOTAL COST IS $ 1690
FOR 27 PAIRS THE TOTAL COST IS $ 1755
FOR 28 PAIRS THE TOTAL COST IS $ 1820
FOR 29 PAIRS THE TOTAL COST IS $ 1885
FOR 30 PAIRS THE TOTAL COST IS $ 1860
FOR 31 PAIRS THE TOTAL COST IS $ 1922
FOR 32 PAIRS THE TOTAL COST IS $ 1984
FOR 33 PAIRS THE TOTAL COST IS $ 2046
FOR 34 PAIRS THE TOTAL COST IS $ 2108
FOR 35 PAIRS THE TOTAL COST IS $ 2170
FOR 36 PAIRS THE TOTAL COST IS $ 2232
FOR 37 PAIRS THE TOTAL COST IS $ 2294
FOR 38 PAIRS THE TOTAL COST IS $ 2356
FOR 39 PAIRS THE TOTAL COST IS $ 2418
FOR 40 PAIRS THE TOTAL COST IS $ 2480
FOR 41 PAIRS THE TOTAL COST IS $ 2542
FOR 42 PAIRS THE TOTAL COST IS $ 2604
FOR 43 PAIRS THE TOTAL COST IS $ 2666
FOR 44 PAIRS THE TOTAL COST IS $ 2728
FOR 45 PAIRS THE TOTAL COST IS $ 2790
FOR 46 PAIRS THE TOTAL COST IS $ 2852
FOR 47 PAIRS THE TOTAL COST IS $ 2914
FOR 48 PAIRS THE TOTAL COST IS $ 2976
FOR 49 PAIRS THE TOTAL COST IS $ 3038
FOR 50 PAIRS THE TOTAL COST IS $ 3100
```

Figure 6.7

If an increment is not specified, then it is assumed to be 1. Thus, the following pairs of DO statements are equivalent:

```
DO 10 I = 1,17          DO 10 I = 1,17,1
DO 47 KK = 43,981       DO 47 KK = 43,981,1
```

Specifying an increment causes the index to increase by the amount specified. Thus, either of the DO statements

```
DO 10 I = 1,5
```

```
DO 10 I = 1,5,1
```

causes the index to assume the values

1,2,3,4,5

while the DO statement

```
DO 10 I = 1,5,2
```

causes the index to assume the values

1,3,5

The DO loop terminates when the result of adding the increment to the index would *exceed* the end value. Some further examples follow:

DO statement	Values of the Index
`DO 14 K = 1,5,3`	1,4
`DO 52 MVAL = 4,12,2`	4,6,8,10,12
`DO 19 N = 4,13,2`	4,6,8,10,12
`DO 7 NI = 2,25,5`	2,7,12,17,22

Problem 6.2

List the values assumed by the index during execution of the DO.

a. DO 10 J = 1,7   d. DO 11 MM = 14,27,3
b. DO 10 J = 1,7,2   e. DO 47 L = 2,20,2
c. DO 141 K = 5,18,1   f. DO 199 L4 = 1,30,4

If the ski manufacturer wishes to ship skis only in units of two, the program for determining the total cost of an order has to be rewritten to produce total costs for 2 to 28 in steps of 2 and from 30 to 50 in steps of 2. By adding a comma and the increment value of 2 to the end of the DO statement, the manager can easily obtain a new price list:

```
C
C   ASSUME SHIPMENTS OF SKIS IN MULTIPLES OF 2
C   HANDLE 10-28 PAIRS AT $65 PER PAIR
C
      DO 30 INDEX = 10,28,2
      NTOTAL = INDEX*65
      WRITE(6,101) INDEX,NTOTAL
  101 FORMAT('0FOR ', I2, ' PAIRS THE TOTAL COST IS $ ', I4)
   30 CONTINUE
C
C   HANDLE 30-50 PAIRS AT $62 PER PAIR
C
      DO 40 INDEX = 30,50,2
      NTOTAL = INDEX*62
      WRITE(6,101) NTOTAL,INDEX
   40 CONTINUE
      STOP
      END
```

By the same token, one might wish to count by threes. To count from 1 up to 31 in steps of 3 we write

```
DO 90 NCOUNT = 1,31,3
```

The values of NCOUNT will be

```
1,4,7,10,13,16,19,22,25,28,31
```

a total of *11* times through the loop. If the programmer typed

```
DO 90 NCOUNT = 1,30,3
```

then the loop would be executed only *10* times with NCOUNT equal to 28 during the last execution of the loop.

Counting from 10 to 100 in steps of 10 is accomplished by

```
DO 40 I = 10,100,10
```

If counting is begun at 1 and goes to a final value of 101 in steps of 10, the loop is executed 11 times:

```
DO 60 KKKKK = 1,101,10
```

Loop Control with Variable Parameters

The programs to do temperature conversion or calculate total cost for skis are rigid. To produce a new table of conversions for a different range would require a new program. For the ski pricing program, a new packing scheme that allowed for five pairs of skis per carton would necessitate the writing of a new program. If production were increased so that the upper limit on the number of pairs of skis per order could be raised, then a new program would have to be written and tested. To eliminate this rigidity, one or more of the INTEGER constants in the DO statement can be replaced with INTEGER variables which could be set by reading in a value or by a calculation in a different part of the program.

For example, recall the program to print business cards earlier in this chapter. One technique for producing several copies of the card was demonstrated. But it is also possible to make the number of repetitions a variable, which is read in. The importance of this flexibility is obvious. It is made possible by having a single data card with the number of copies required punched on it. Assuming there will not be a need for more than 999 business cards at one time, a three-digit INTEGER field in columns 1–3 will suffice. To get 85 business cards printed, the data card will look like this:

```
b85
```

A READ statement would place the input value in location NCARDS:

```
       Basic FORTRAN           ⎡ WATFOR/WATFIV ⎤
       READ(5,100) NCARDS      ⎣   READ,NCARDS ⎦
 100   FORMAT(I3)
```

The DO statement would then be

```
       DO 50 I = 1,NCARDS

         Body of loop

  50   CONTINUE
```

This might be read as "DO all the statements up to statement number 50, changing the INTEGER variable I from an initial value of 1 to a final value equal to the contents of location NCARDS, in steps of 1." The effect of all this is to execute the body of the loop NCARDS times, where the value of NCARDS has been established by reading it in from a data card.

To produce a temperature conversion chart which ranges from one degree up to a variable called NHIGH, one could write

```
       READ(5,100) NHIGH
 100   FORMAT(I3)
       DO 70 I = 1,NHIGH

         Body of loop

  70   CONTINUE
```

To produce a temperature conversion chart which ranges from NLOW to NHIGH degrees in steps of one degree one could write

```
      READ(5,100) NLOW,NHIGH
100   FORMAT(I3, I3)
      DO 70 I = NLOW, NHIGH
   ┌
   │        Body of loop
   └
 70   CONTINUE
```

Problem 6.3

What would the input data card look like if a temperature conversion chart for the range 10 to 80 degrees were required? How many lines of output would be produced?

Finally, it is possible to make all three parameters of the DO statement variables. To get a temperature conversion chart for 10 to 500 degrees in steps of 10 degrees a data card could be prepared as follows:

b10500b10

and the program would be

```
      READ(5,100) NLOW,NHIGH,NSTEP
100   FORMAT(I3, I3, I3)
      DO 70 I = NLOW,NHIGH,NSTEP
   ┌
   │        Body of loop
   └
 70   CONTINUE
```

How many lines of output would be produced in this case?

Using Loops in Computing Values

Most of the examples of loops presented thus far used the loop to cause a group of statements to be repeated a number of times. Each iteration of the loop has produced a complete result. For example, in the business card printing program, each iteration causes the printing of a complete card.

Often, however, each iteration of the loop performs part of a computation and the values computed during one iteration are used in the next. The simplest example of such a computation is the summation of a series of numbers.

Consider the problem of summing three numbers, each of which has been punched onto a single data card:

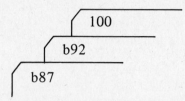

The numbers might indicate student grades on three tests. A program will be designed to clear an accumulator location called NSUM and then to perform the summation in a sequential manner. The body of the loop will contain an instruction to read a single data card, to add the input value to the current value of NSUM, and to store the result back in NSUM. By repeating the body of the loop three times, the program will perform the summation:

```
      NSUM = 0
      DO 25 I = 1,3
      READ(5,101) MARK
  101 FORMAT(I3)
      NSUM = NSUM + MARK
   25 CONTINUE
```

Tracing through the execution of this program fragment, Table 6.1 gives values for the variables after execution of each of the statements.

Table 6.1

Statement	I	NSUM	MARK
NSUM = 0	?	0	?
READ(5,101) MARK	1	0	87
NSUM = NSUM + MARK	1	87	87
READ(5,101) MARK	2	87	92
NSUM = NSUM + MARK	2	179	92
READ(5,101) MARK	3	179	100
NSUM = NSUM + MARK	3	279	100

In the statement NSUM = NSUM + MARK, the occurrence variable NSUM on the right side of the equals sign indicates that the old value of NSUM is to be added to the current value of MARK to produce the new value for NSUM. This sequence might be diagrammed as

```
NSUM = NSUM + MARK

NSUM = NSUM + MARK

NSUM = NSUM + MARK
```

The arrows show that the value established on the previous iteration is used during the current iteration.

The program to sum three values can easily be generalized to perform the summation of any number of values. If eight values were to be summed, then the number 8 could be read from a data card to control the number of repetitions of the loop:

```
    READ(5,100) N
    NSUM = 0
    DO 25 I = 1,N
    READ(5,101) MARK
    NSUM = NSUM + MARK
 25 CONTINUE
    WRITE(6,102) NSUM
102 FORMAT('0 THE SUM IS ', I6)
101 FORMAT(I4)
100 FORMAT(I3)
    STOP
    END
```

Successive summations form the basis for a well-known mathematical curiosity called the Fibonacci sequence of numbers. Named after a thirteenth century Italian mathematician, this sequence exhibits numerous mathematical, biological and natural properties.[2]

The Fibonacci series is generated as follows. The first and second terms are both 1. Each succeeding term is generated by summing the two preceding terms. Thus, the third term is 1 + 1 or 2, the fourth term is 1 + 2 or 3, the fifth term is 2 + 3 or 5, and so on. The first ten terms are

```
           1+1  1+2 2+3 3+5 5+8   8+13  13+21  21+34
            ↓    ↓   ↓   ↓   ↓      ↓      ↓      ↓
    1    1  2    3   5   8   13     21     34     55
```

One curious result is that the quotient of successive terms converges to a common value:

2/3	.666
3/5	.600
5/8	.625
8/13	.615
13/21	.619
21/34	.618
34/55	.618

This common value was known to the Greeks as the golden section or ratio and was considered the ideal ratio of length and width that gave splendid proportions to buildings and sculpture. Artists still use this ratio in paintings and room designs because of its aesthetic appeal.

To use the computer to produce a list of the Fibonacci numbers requires that the previous two terms be summed to produce the next value. If the starting point is established as

---

[2] For a discussion of the Fibonacci series, read Kramer, Edna, *The Mainstream of Mathematics*. New York: Fawcett Premier Books, 1961.

```
      LAST = 1
      NOW = 1
```

then we can calculate the next value and print it:

```
      NEXT = NOW + LAST
      WRITE(6,101) NEXT
101 FORMAT(' ', I6)
```

Before we calculate the fourth value, the values of NOW and LAST have to be reset to reflect the current status and to prepare for the new NEXT value:

```
      LAST = NOW
      NOW = NEXT
```

To produce eight more Fibonacci numbers, a DO loop is introduced; the complete program is

```
      LAST = 1
      NOW = 1
      DO 85 I = 1,8
      NEXT = NOW + LAST
      WRITE(6,101) NEXT
101 FORMAT(' ', I6)
      LAST = NOW
      NOW = NEXT
 85 CONTINUE
      STOP
      END
```

Understanding this program requires careful attention to the details of the assignment statement. Follow through the execution of this program to make sure you see how it generates the Fibonacci sequence.

Another classic example of computation utilizing a DO loop is the "Indian problem." The story goes that Peter Minuit purchased the island of Manhattan in 1624 for $24.00 worth of trinkets and blankets. What would the $24.00 be worth if it had been deposited in a savings bank at 4 percent interest per year compounded annually? The first few years can be done by hand:

```
.04 * 24.00 = .96      24.00 +  .96 = 24.96
.04 * 24.96 = 1.00     24.96 + 1.00 = 25.96
.04 * 25.96 = 1.04     25.96 + 1.04 = 27.00
.04 * 27.00 = 1.08     27.00 + 1.08 = 28.08
```

It is relatively simple but it is rather tedious to repeat this calculation for 350 years and you would have little confidence in the accuracy of the result. But since the sequence of operations is simple to follow, it can be easily programmed. The process might be generalized to taking the principal, multiplying by the rate of interest, adding the interest to the principal, and then repeating this process 350 times. The FORTRAN statement for a single year's calculation might be

```
PRINC = PRINC + PRINC * RATE
```

All that is necessary is to include the DO loop to repeat the process 350 times:

```
    DO 45 I = 1,350
    PRINC = PRINC + PRINC * RATE
45 CONTINUE
```

This program fragment does not establish initial values for PRINC or RATE nor does it print the results. To complete the program,

```
     PRINC = 24.00
     RATE = .04
     DO 45 I = 1,350
     PRINC = PRINC + PRINC * RATE
  45 CONTINUE
     WRITE(6,101) PRINC
 101 FORMAT('1$24,00 AT 4 PERCENT INTEREST PER YEAR',
   1 ' FOR 350 YEARS YIELDS ', F16.2)
     STOP
     END
```

The PRINT statement appears outside the body of the loop and therefore only one line of output is produced. By including another PRINT statement in the body of the loop, we could have the value of the principal printed out for each of the 350 years (350 lines of output) and the pattern of growth could be studied.

Nested Loops

A statement within a DO loop will be executed once each time the loop is repeated. Thus, the PRINT statement in the loop below will be executed 25 times.[3]

```
    DO 14 I = 1,25
    PRINT, 'XXXX'
14 CONTINUE
```

If a DO loop is itself enclosed within an outer DO, it will be executed once each time the loop is repeated. The following program:

---

[3] The PRINT statements used in this example and the next are WATFOR/WATFIV language extensions.

```
┌──   DO 5 I = 1,2
│      PRINT, 'XXXX'
│  ┌   DO 10 J = 1,3
│  │   PRINT, 'YYYY'
│  └10 CONTINUE
│      PRINT, 'ZZZZ'
└──  5 CONTINUE
```

will produce the following output:

```
XXXX
YYYY
YYYY
YYYY
ZZZZ
XXXX
YYYY
YYYY
YYYY
ZZZZ
```

When an outer loop contains one or more inner loops, the loops are said to be *nested*. Nested loops are very powerful computational devices.

Nested loops may be used in the Indian problem. As previously stated, the problem concerned $24.00 compounded at an annual rate of 4 percent. But what if it had been 5 percent or 6 percent or 7 percent? Conceptually, the problem is to repeat the previous program for rates of interest varying from 4 percent to 7 percent in steps of 1 percent.

```
     DO 55 J = 4,7
     RATE = FLOAT(J)/100.
     PRINC = 24.00

     ┌   Calculate principal after
     │   350 years and print result
     └

 55  CONTINUE
```

The body of the DO 55 loop should contain the calculation of the principal after 350 years of compounding interest at the specified rate. This calculation is performed by the DO 45 loop of the previous program and the DO 45 loop can be directly inserted into the body of the DO 55 loop:

```
     DO 55 J = 4,7
     RATE = FLOAT(J)/100.
     PRINC = 24.00
     DO 45 I = 1,350
     PRINC = PRINC + PRINC * RATE
 45  CONTINUE
     WRITE(6,101) J,PRINC
101  FORMAT('0$24.00 AT ', I2, ' PERCENT INTEREST PER YEAR ',
    1  ' FOR 350 YEARS YIELDS ', F16.2)
```

```
55 CONTINUE
   STOP
   END
```

The WRITE and FORMAT statements have been modified to include information about the varying rate of interest. The body of the inner DO 45 loop is executed 350 times for *each of the four values* of the outer DO 55 loop for a total of 1400 executions. This example demonstrates quite dramatically how the DO statement can be used to amplify the power of the program. This program produces only four lines of output, since the WRITE statement is part of the body of the outer loop but is *not* part of the body of the inner loop. A WRITE statement in the body of the inner loop would produce 1400 lines of output.

As a further variation of this problem, it might be interesting to see how the results would change had the initial principal been $22.00, $24.00, $26.00, $28.00 or $30.00 for each of the four percentages. This variation requires a third level of nesting of loops. A little careful thought should lead to the realization that the change in the initial principal has a less dramatic effect on the result than does the change in the interest rate. The rate of growth is a much more significant factor than the initial amount.

The effect of nesting DO loops is to hold the index of the outer loop constant while utilizing every value of the inner loop. For example, in the nested loops below:

```
┌──────── DO 10 I = 1,2
│ ┌────── DO 5 J = 1,3
│ │            .
│ │            .
│ │            .
│ └─  5 CONTINUE
└── 10 CONTINUE
```

the inner loop will be executed a total of six times. The indexes will have the following values:

I	J
1	1
	2
	3
2	1
	2
	3

To demonstrate the actions of nested loops further, consider the following problems.

Students in a lecture class are often assigned numbers reflecting their chair position. It might be helpful to have the computer to prepare a blank attendance form to be filled in with student names. If a classroom has six rows with eight seats each, the desired output would be

```
1    1
1    2
1    3
1    4
1    5
1    6
1    7
1    8
2    1
2    2
2    3
2    4
2    5
2    6
2    7
2    8
3    1
3    2
3    3
     .
     .
     .
6    7
6    8
```

To produce this kind of output, it is necessary to count seats from one to eight for rows one to six. Once again this calls for a pair of DO loops, one nested in the other:

```
      DO 30 NROWS = 1,6
      DO 20 NSEATS = 1,8
      WRITE(6,101) NROWS, NSEATS
101   FORMAT(' ',I3, I3)
  20  CONTINUE
  30  CONTINUE
      STOP
      END
```

If for some reason (such as a broken seat), it is necessary to skip seat four in row five, a test could be inserted to skip the WRITE statement.

```
      DO 30 NROWS = 1,6
      DO 20 NSEATS = 1,8
      IF(NSEATS .EQ. 4 .AND. NROWS .EQ. 5) GO TO 20
      WRITE(6,101) NROW,NSEATS
  20  CONTINUE
  30  CONTINUE
```

The GO TO is directed to the CONTINUE statement at 20 which represents the bottom of the loop. A GO TO 30 would have been erroneous and would have caused the omission of entries for seats 4, 5, 6, 7, and 8 in row five. The placement of GO TO statements in loops can be tricky and, if the programmer is not careful, can lead to surprising results.

Two or more nested loops may end on the same CONTINUE statement. Therefore, the following program fragments are equivalent:

```
┌─    DO 10 I = 1,5
│           ·
│           ·
│  ┌─ DO 15 J = 1,7
│  │        ·
│  │        ·
│  └─15 CONTINUE
└──10 CONTINUE
```

```
┌─    DO 10 I = 1,5
│           ·
│           ·
│  ┌─ DO 10 J = 1,7
│  │        ·
│  │        ·
└──└─10 CONTINUE
```

There are certain nestings of loops and transfers of control that are simply not permitted because they have no logical meaning; for example,

```
    DO 20
    DO 30

20  CONTINUE
30  CONTINUE
```

Invalid

Neither loop is properly nested within the other and it is impossible to determine what is to be done. Transfers of control into a loop bypassing the DO are also invalid, since an initial value for the loop index has not been established:

```
    GO TO 40
    DO 50 I = 1,N

40  ...
50  CONTINUE
```

Invalid

The restrictions on transfers of control within nested loops can be summarized by two diagrams. The first shows *valid* transfers of control:

```
DO
DO

CONTINUE
CONTINUE
```

Valid

and the second shows *invalid* transfers of control:

```
DO
DO

CONTINUE
CONTINUE
```

Invalid

Essentially, a DO loop must always be entered from the top and never from anywhere else.

```
 Valid entry
 DO 10  I = 14,32,3
       .
       .                 ———————— Invalid entry
       .
10 CONTINUE
```

If this restriction were not observed the DO loop would never be initialized. It is valid, however, to transfer *out* of a DO loop before its normal end.

When a DO loop terminates normally by "falling through" a CONTINUE statement the value of the index becomes undefined. The following program will print an indeterminate result:

```
DO 14 JJ = 4,11
      .
      .
      .
14 CONTINUE
   PRINT, JJ
```

The proper value of the index can only be printed while the loop is in progress.

Omitting the CONTINUE Statement

It is not actually necessary to end a loop on a CONTINUE statement; if the last statement of a loop is not a GO TO statement, an arithmetic IF or another DO statement, the label may be placed on the last statement of the loop. The following are equivalent:

```
   DO 70 I = 1,7          DO 70 I = 1,7
   X = I + .05            X = I + .05
70 WRITE(6,101) X            WRITE(6,101) X
                        70 CONTINUE
```

Summary

The following rules summarize the use of the DO loop.

The DO loop has the general form

DO < label > < index > = < start value > , < end value > , < incr >

where < label > must appear below the DO and defines the loop's scope.

< index > must be an INTEGER variable.

< start value > , < end value > , and < incr > may be integer constants or INTEGER variables.

The < incr > is optional and if missing is assumed to be 1.

The < start value > , < end value > , and < incr > may not be changed within the DO loop.

When "falling through" a DO loop the index value becomes undefined and should not be used (although it may be used as a variable elsewhere in the program). However, if the program should transfer out of the DO before the end value is reached (as, for example, via an IF) the index value remains at its current value and may be used.

The only valid way to enter a DO loop is "from the top." You must execute the DO statement itself.

In most versions of FORTRAN (including WATFOR and WATFIV) a DO loop is always executed once even if the start value exceeds the end value when the loop is entered. Thus the following loop will be executed once:

```
N = 4
M = 5
DO 10 I = M,N
```

A DO loop should usually end on a CONTINUE statement. It may never end on a GO TO, DO, or arithmetic IF.

DEBUGGING CLINIC

The power and relative complexity of the DO-CONTINUE combination leads to a substantial number of debugging problems.

Syntactic problems are relatively easy to clear up with the aid of good diagnostic output from the compiler. Errors in this category frequently result from the severe restrictions that have been placed on the DO statement. The loop variable must be an INTEGER variable. The initial value, the final value, and the increment must all be *positive* INTEGER constants or INTEGER variables. Each of the following examples is INVALID:

```
DO 55 X = 1,0,5.0
DO 55 J = 1,5,0.5
DO 75 K = 1,10.5
DO 150 INDEX = 1,LIMIT+1
DO 72 I = 10,1,-1          Invalid
DO 333 IVALUE = 0,10
DO 45 I = 1,N-1
DO 7 M = 1,N*2
```

Remember also that if the program contains a DO 80, then there must be a statement labeled 80 later in the program. In addition, the rules described in the last section about nesting of loops must always be followed.

The loop variable in the body of the loop should not be altered. The following program is typical of the kind of mistake that leads to disaster:

```
DO 25 I = 1,50
    .
    .
    .
I = 2
    .
    .
    .
25 CONTINUE
```

In this loop, the value of the loop variable is reset to 2 each time that the body of the loop is executed. The value of I never reaches 50 and the execution of the loop never terminates—the program is in an *infinite loop*. It is because of the potential for this kind of mistake that most operating systems impose a fixed time limit on the length of the program execution. If the time limit is exceeded, the program is automatically terminated.

For the same reason, it is invalid to use the same index in two nested loops. The following will produce indeterminate results:

```
DO 111 KK = 1,8
DO 123 KK = 1,5
    .
    .
    .
123 CONTINUE
111 CONTINUE
```

Since a DO loop may cause thousands of instructions to be executed, it is useful to print out the value of the index and other significant variables each time the loop is executed. This additional debugging output may then be eliminated once the program is working properly. Programs do not always perform the way that they are expected to perform and it is good programming practice to produce additional output during debugging.

REVIEW QUESTIONS

1. What is the general form of the DO statement? How is it used?

2. What forms may the parameters of the DO assume? What restrictions are placed on their values?

3. What is the function of the CONTINUE statement? When may it be omitted? Under what circumstances may two or more DO statements specify the same statement label as the end of their scope?

4. What are the restrictions on transfers into and out of DO loops?

1. Which of the following statements are valid and which are invalid?

  a. DO 7 I = 1.8
  b. DO 777 III = 10,20
  c. DO I 5 = 1,5
  d. DO 5 IDO = 8,9
  e. DO 17 = I,3
  f. DO 17 II = I,3,-1
  g. DO 90 KVALUES = 1,80
  h. DO 90 I90 = 90,9090,90
  i. DONT OP I = 1,657
  j. DO 75 I = 1,NFINAL,3
  k. DO 55, I = 1,NTEST
  l. DO 70 X = 1,0,5.0
  m. DO 100 I = 1,5,0.5
  n. DO 14 K = 1,N
  o. DO 9 NINE = 1,I*9

2. What is the output of each of the following program fragments?

a.
```
      DO 70 I = 1,4
      WRITE(6,101) I
101 FORMAT(' ',I3)
 70 CONTINUE
```

b.
```
      NSUM = 0
      DO 25 J = 1,8
      K = J/2
      NSUM = NSUM + K
 25 CONTINUE
      WRITE(6,101) NSUM
101 FORMAT(' ', I5)
```

c.
```
      K = 5
      J = 3
      DO 6 I = J,K
      WRITE(6,101) I,J,K
  6 CONTINUE
101 FORMAT(' ', I3, I3, I3)
```

d.
```
      K = 5
      DO 5 I = 1,4
      J = 7
      WRITE(6,101) I,J,K
  5 CONTINUE
101 FORMAT(' ', I3, I3, I3)
```

e.
```
      KVAL = 9
      DO 70 I = 3,KVAL,2
      WRITE(6,101) I
 70 CONTINUE
101 FORMAT(' ', I3)
```

f.
```
      N = 36
      NN = 7
      DO 76 M = 1,N,NN
      WRITE(6,101) M
101 FORMAT(' ', I3)
 76 CONTINUE
```

g.
```
      DO 90 I = 1,51,10
      X = FLOAT(I-1)
      Y = X**2 + 3.0*X - 4.0
      WRITE(6,101) X,Y
101 FORMAT(' ', F8.1, F8.1)
 90 CONTINUE
```

h.
```
      DO 60 I = 1,4
      DO 50 J = 2,5
      WRITE(6,101) I,J
101 FORMAT(' ', I3, I3)
 50 CONTINUE
 60 CONTINUE
```

```
i. 101 FORMAT(' ', I3)              j. DO 1115 I = 5,9
      DO 77 I = 1,8                       IF(I .EQ. 8) GO TO 1115
      IF(I .EQ. 4) GO TO 77              DO 1114 J = 1,4
      WRITE(6,101) I                     WRITE(6,101) I,J
   77 CONTINUE                   1114 CONTINUE
                                 1115 CONTINUE
                                  101 FORMAT(' ', I3, I3)
```

PROGRAMMING EXERCISES

3. Write a program to print your name exactly 25 times.

4. Write a program which will read in a REAL value, square it, and print the result for exactly 17 data cards.

5. Print a table to convert from inches to centimeters (2.54 centimeters = 1 inch):
   a. From 1 to 36 inches in steps of 1 inch.
   b. From 37 to 72 inches in steps of 1 inch.
   c. From 6 to 36 inches in steps of 6 inches.
   d. From 1 to 36 inches in steps of 1/2 inch.
   e. From INCH1 to INCH2 in steps of INCH3, where each variable is a positive INTEGER.

6. Computer time is sold by a service bureau at the following rates:
   $100.00 fee per month plus
   $5.00 per hour for the first 10 hours
   $4.00 per hour for each hour above 10 hours
   Write a program to print out a table of total charges for one to 20 hours of use.

7. Find the sum of the integers from 1 to N, where the value of N is read in.

8. Write a program to calculate and print the value of N factorial (N!). Factorials are obtained this way:

   $3! = 1*2*3$
   $4! = 1*2*3*4$
   $5! = 1*2*3*4*5$
   $\vdots$

   $N! = 1*2* \cdots * (N-1)*N$

9. Print a table of x and $f(x)$ where $f(x) = 3x^2 + 5x + 2$. The range of x values is from 0.0 to 3.0 in steps of 0.1.

10. a. Calculate the value of π (3.141592 . . .), summing the first 100 terms of the following series:

    $$\frac{\pi^2}{6} = \frac{1}{1^2} + \frac{1}{2^2} + \frac{1}{3^2} + \frac{1}{4^2} + \cdots$$

    b. Try summing the first 1000 terms.
    c. Try summing in reverse order; that is, smallest term first. Compare the results.

11. A colony of 1200 ants increases by 8 percent every week. Print a table to show the growth of the colony for ten weeks.

12. A university was designed to accommodate 15,000 students. At present, there are 9000 students and the growth rate is 6 percent per year. If the present growth rate is maintained, in how many years will capacity be reached?

13. A mathematician who is the victim of a hit-and-run accident claims to have seen the license plate but remembers only that there were two letters—GX—followed by four numbers which were the

same backwards as they were forwards (such as 1221 or 9559). Write a program to find all the numbers between 0000 and 9999 which are the same backwards and forwards. Hint:

Method 1—Use one DO loop and the INT function division to separate the numbers and compare them.

Method 2—Use four nested DO loops.

Method 3—There is a clever short-cut—think!

14. Write a program to generate and print all of the prime numbers from 1 to 1000. A prime number is one which is divisible only by 1 and itself.

15. Write a program to test Goldbach's conjecture which suggests that every even number above 6 can be represented by the sum of two prime numbers. C. Goldbach (1690–1764) made his conjecture more than three hundred years ago, yet no one has been able to prove or disprove it until now. The conjecture has been tested and found to be valid for even numbers up to 100 million but no one is sure that there is not a counterexample for larger values.

16. In the range 2 to 1000 find all the prime numbers which are also Fibonacci numbers.

17. Once upon a time, a king in a far-off land requested the wise man of the court to devise some game to entertain the king. The response to this request was the invention of the game of chess. The king was so overjoyed with this new game that he called the wise man before him and informed him that whatever reasonable reward he desired would be granted. The wise man replied, "My needs are simple. Give me one grain of rice for the first square of the chess board, two grains for the second square, four grains for the third square, eight grains for the fourth square, and so on until all of the sixty-four squares are accounted for." The king, impressed with the seeming modesty of the request, ordered that it be satisfied. Of course, all of the wealth of the kingdom came into the hands of the wise man.

Write a program to determine how many grains of rice were needed to satisfy the wise man's request.

18. A Pythagorean triple is a set of three numbers, a, b, and c, such that

$$a^2 + b^2 = c^2$$

Write an efficient program to print out all of the Pythagorean triples where each of the numbers is less than 100. Watch out! An inefficient version of this program could consume a great deal of machine time.

19. *Plane Geometry.* During a solar eclipse the moon moves across the face of the sun, obscuring the light. Assume that the size of the disk of the sun is equal in size to the disk of the moon. The moon moves past the sun at a rate of one-tenth of the diameter per minute (the eclipse lasts 20 minutes). Print a table indicating the percent of the sun's disk which is obscured for each of the 20 minutes.

20. *Ecology.* A natural resource is being consumed at a rate of 1000 units per year and the rate of growth of consumption is 5 percent per year. The total known sources are 20,000 units and an additional 800 units are discovered each year.

a. Print out the usage and available sources left at the end of each year till the demand exceeds the available resource. How long will it take? Modify the program to compute the resource use under the following conditions:

b. If 2000 units are discovered each year?

c. If 10 percent of each year's consumption were recycled for use in the next year?

21. *Mathematics.* Define the "super-Fibonacci" numbers as the sequence where the first three values are ones and successive values are the sum of the three most recent values.

SF(i) = SF(i−1) + SF(i−2) + SF(i−3)
SF(1) = SF(2) = SF(3) = 1

The series begins

1, 1, 1, 3, 5, 9, 17, 31 · · ·

a. Write a program to generate and print the first 100 super-Fibonacci numbers.

b. Does the ratio of successive terms converge? To what value?

22. A mathematically inclined child named Danny enjoys counting his marbles. When he counts by two, threes, fours, fives and sixes he always has one left over, but when he counts by sevens he has none left over. How many marbles does Danny have? Write a program to find the answer (less than 1000).

SPIRAL PROBLEMS

A. Student Grading

Read a data card with a three-digit INTEGER number, N, punched in columns 1-3. The next data cards contain REAL test scores for a single student in the form XXX.X in columns 1-5. Using a DO loop, read, print, and sum these N scores. Compute and print the average with an appropriate message. Then print "PASSING" if the average was 60.0 or greater, and "FAILING" otherwise.

B. Bank Interest

The island of Manhattan was bought in 1624 for $24.00. If this amount had been placed in a bank at 5 percent interest compounded annually, what would the account contain today? Show the growth of the money in ten year intervals and print the final amount with appropriate messages.

C. Mathematical Application: Prime numbers

A prime number is an integer divisible only by one and itself. Thus 2, 3, 5, 7, 11, 13, 17 are all prime numbers. Write a program to read in data cards containing a three-digit integer value punched in columns 1-3. The last data card contains a −1 to indicate the end of the data. After each card has been read in, determine if the value is a prime number or not. Print out the value and an appropriate message indicating whether or not it is prime. When all the data cards have been processed, print a message to indicate how many data cards were processed. Typical output might be

```
 17  IS A PRIME NUMBER
845  IS NOT A PRIME NUMBER
 23  IS A PRIME NUMBER
352  IS NOT A PRIME NUMBER
  4  IS NOT A PRIME NUMBER

  5 DATA CARDS HAVE BEEN PROCESSED
```

SUBSCRIPTED VARIABLES

Reading maketh a full man; conference a ready man; and writing an exact man; and therefore, if a man write little, he had need have a great memory.

Francis Bacon

CHAPTER 7

The variables considered in the previous chapters have each contained a single value. Such variables are known technically as scalar variables. Sometimes it is convenient to group variables together because they contain related information. For example, it might be desirable to store the population of each state in the United States. Although the population for each state could be stored in a separate variable, such as STAT01, STAT02, . . . STAT50 it is more convenient to group them into a single variable which can store 50 distinct values. Such a variable is called an array. An array allows the programmer to store multiple values under a single name. The number of values to be stored is specified by means of a DIMENSION statement. The power of an array is that a specific value (in this example, the population of a given state) to be used or stored may be determined at execution time. If STATE contained the population of the 50 states, then the value of STATE(I) would depend on the current value of I. If I=1, then the population of the first state would be indicated; whereas if I=25, then the population of the 25th state would be utilized. Arrays may be used within DO loops to manipulate quantities of data in very few statements.

If the scalar variable is visualized conceptually as a "box" containing a value, an array might be considered to be a string of "boxes" laid end to end. Each box is similar to a scalar variable in that it can store a single value. Arrays also can be structured in two-dimensional form. The squares on a checkerboard are similar in structure to a two-dimensional array. Two-dimensional arrays are more convenient than one-dimensional arrays for certain applications.

Introduction

The DO loop, discussed in the previous chapter, provides a structure that allows groups of statements to be repeated while the *index* of the DO is varied.

Another feature of FORTRAN, *subscripted variables,* permits the programmer to perform a set of computations on groups of variables. It is often coupled with a DO loop to create powerful program constructs.

Consider the problem of calculating the total annual rainfall for a state when all that is known is the monthly accumulated rainfall. Typical input data are represented in Table 7.1.

Table 7.1

**NORMAL MONTHLY RAINFALL
IN NEW YORK STATE
(THE 1973 WORLD ALMANAC)**

Month	*Precipitation in Inches*
January	2.5
February	2.2
March	2.7
April	2.8
May	3.5
June	3.3
July	3.5
August	3.1
September	3.6
October	2.8
November	2.7
December	2.8

If each month's data are punched in columns 1–3 of a separate data card, a program to read in the 12 data cards and calculate the annual rainfall could be written as follows:

```
      RTOTAL = 0.0
      DO 50 I = 1,12
      READ(5,101) AMOUNT
      RTOTAL = RTOTAL + AMOUNT
   50 CONTINUE
      WRITE(6,102) RTOTAL
      STOP
  101 FORMAT(F3.1)
  102 FORMAT(' THE TOTAL RAINFALL WAS', F7.1)
      END
```

In this program, the DO loop is used first, to repeat the operation of reading in a value into the location AMOUNT and then to add the AMOUNT to the single location RTOTAL.

DO looping enables the programmer to avoid repeating the read and summation statements 12 times (once for each of the 12 months).

If it were necessary to compute the annual rainfall statistics for each of the 50 states and the data were organized by *month* (that is, there are 50 data cards for January, followed by 50 data cards for February and so on through December), the 50 summations would require 50 variables, each of which must be initially set to zero.

It is desirable to avoid writing groups of statements such as

```
STAT01 = 0.0
STAT02 = 0.0
STAT03 = 0.0
        .
        .
        .
STAT49 = 0.0
STAT50 = 0.0
```

Otherwise, one would be left with a most unwieldy program. To get around this problem, a *subscripted variable* can be used.

The familiar nonsubscripted, or *scalar,* variable we have used so far is represented symbolically as a box in which a single value may be stored. A variable, STATE, could be represented as follows:

A subscripted variable or *array* (also called a *vector*[1]) is like a collection of boxes, each of which may contain a value. For example, STATE may be constructed (or declared) to be a subscripted variable with 50 boxes:

STATE	STATE	STATE		STATE	STATE
			...		
1	2	3		49	50

Each box or *element* of the array can contain a value independent of any other element. In order to utilize part of an array in an arithmetic expression, the element referred to must be specified by enclosing its position in parentheses. Thus,

```
STATE(1)
```

refers to the first element

```
STATE(2)
```

---

[1] A vector is a special class of array. The arrays discussed in the first part of this chapter are all vectors.

refers to the second element and

```
STATE(50)
```

refers to the last element. The specification of the position is called the *subscript*. Note that the subscript is not included in the six-letter limit on the length of a variable's name.

```
STATE(29)
```
      subscript

Each element of the array is like a scalar variable in that it may be assigned a value:

```
STATE(14) = 0.0
STATE(19) = B*2.5
```

Also, it may participate in an arithmetic expression:

```
Y = STATE(17)*5.0 + Q
```

Whenever an array element is used in an arithmetic expression, it must appear with a subscript.

You may be wondering why subscripted variables are used, since they seem to function just like scalar variables. There is an important difference between an array and a group of scalar variables.

Elements of an array	Individual scalar variables
STATE(1)	STAT01
STATE(2)	STAT02
.	.
.	.
.	.
STATE(50)	STAT50

The difference lies in the fact that the subscript of a vector need not be a constant. It may be an integer variable or even an integer expression. Thus in the program fragment

```
I = 4
STATE(I) = 27.0
```

the value '27.0' will be assigned to STATE(4):

STATE(1)	STATE(2)	STATE(3)	STATE(4)		STATE(50)
				...	

                    27.0

whereas in the program fragment

```
I = 11
STATE(I) = 27.0
```

the value '27.0' will be assigned to STATE(11).

This ability to compute the subscript in the program is extremely important. While setting 50 scalar variables to zero requires 50 separate assignment statements, the STATE array may be set to zero simply by using a DO loop:

```
   DO 14 K = 1,50
   STATE(K) = 0.0
14 CONTINUE
```

As the value of K changes from 1 to 50 in steps of 1, each of the 50 locations in the STATE array is set to zero.

Using a DO loop, it is as easy to set a 500-element array to zero as it is to set a 50-element array to zero. Thus, the combination of subscripted variables with DO loops can be very powerful. An array can be of REAL or INTEGER mode; the rules for naming vectors are the same as for naming scalars. However, a variable name may not be used both as a vector and a scalar in the same program.

Problem 7.1

Write a DO loop to perform the following operations.
a. Set a 14-element REAL vector named X to zero.
b. Set a 5-element INTEGER vector named N7 to 11.
c. Set a 250-element INTEGER vector named NUMBER such that the value of each element is equal to its subscript. That is, NUMBER(1) should have the value 1, NUMBER(2) should have the value 2, and so on.

The DIMENSION Statement

The number of elements in a vector is specified in a special FORTRAN statement, the DIMENSION statement. To declare the vector STATE as having 50 elements, write

```
DIMENSION STATE(50)
```

More than one variable may be declared in a single DIMENSION statement:

```
DIMENSION X(79), N3(100), A(2)
```

Use of the DIMENSION statement allows the rainfall program to be concisely written to compute the annual rainfall for all 50 states.

```
      DIMENSION STATE(50)
      DO 30 I = 1,50
      STATE(I) = 0.0
   30 CONTINUE
      DO 50 I = 1,12
      DO 40 J = 1,50
      READ(5,101) AMOUNT
      STATE(J) = STATE(J) + AMOUNT
   40 CONTINUE
   50 CONTINUE
      DO 60 I = 1,50
      WRITE(6,102) I, STATE(I)
   60 CONTINUE
      STOP
  101 FORMAT(F6.2)
  102 FORMAT('0FOR STATE NUMBER ',I2, ' TOTAL RAINFALL WAS ',
     1F9.2)
      END
```

Note the use of the nested DO loops and the DIMENSION statement. The subscript specified in the DIMENSION statement *must be an integer constant.* The following are valid DIMENSION statements:

```
DIMENSION A(15)
DIMENSION ALPHA(675)
DIMENSION IVAL(70)                            VALID
DIMENSION TABLE(100),KTABLE(100)
DIMENSION A(50), Y(50), Z(50), KBAR(15)
```

The following are *invalid* DIMENSION statements:

```
DIMENSION TABLE(8.5)
DIMENSION VALUE(NUM + 5)
DIMENSION LIST(80),LIST(50)
DIMENSION VARIABLE(100)                       INVALID
DIMENSION X(50) - Z(50)
DIMENSION ALPHA(50 + 30)
```

As these examples show, the DIMENSION statement has a basically simple structure. It is used to reserve space for an array having subscripts ranging from 1 to the maximum value specified in the DIMENSION statement.

Problem 7.2

Write a DIMENSION statement to
a. Declare the array YY having subscripts 1–49.
b. Declare arrays, A4, I, and F having subscripts of 1–7, 1–15, and 1–1000, respectively.

Arrays are a common device used in many programs. The rainfall problem is typical. But though common, they do take some getting used to. The following example may facilitate that.

In order to declare a 50-element INTEGER array, IVALUE, one writes

```
DIMENSION IVALUE(50)
```

To set this array to zero the following code could be used:

```
    DO 20 K = 1,50
    IVALUE(K) = 0
 20 CONTINUE
```

If it is necessary to fill the array by reading in a set of values, the statements below can be used:

```
    DO 30 J = 1,50
    READ(5,101) IVALUE(J)
 30 CONTINUE
```

To write out the contents of only the first 20 values of the array, the following is used:

```
    DO 40 I = 1,20
    WRITE(6,102) IVALUE(I)
 40 CONTINUE
```

Individual elements of the array can be referred to by providing the appropriate subscript. To assign the value 1 to the third element:

```
    IVALUE(3) = 1
```

To set the Kth element to 7:

```
    IVALUE(K) = 7
```

To increment the 5th position by 1:

```
    IVALUE(5) = IVALUE(5) + 1
```

and to increment every element by 1:

```
    DO 80 I = 1,50
    IVALUE(I) = IVALUE(I) + 1
 80 CONTINUE
```

A subscripted variable may appear as part of an arithmetic expression in much the same manner as scalar variables; you could write

```
RESULT = PI*RADIUS(I)**2
```

or

```
PRINC(KACCT) = PRINC(KACCT) + RATE*PRINC(KACCT)
```

or

```
IRES = IBAR(K)**2 + 3*IBAR(1)
```

More than one array may be declared in a single program. In addition, operations between elements of different arrays are valid. Assume that there are 20 students in a class and that three tests have been given, the results of which are stored in three arrays. The DIMENSION statement to reserve place for the data as well as each student's average score might be

```
DIMENSION TEST1(20),TEST2(20),TEST3(20),AVER(20)
```

Filling the AVER array with each student's average could be done by

```
     DO 30 I = 1,20
     AVER(I) = (TEST1(I) + TEST2(I) + TEST3(I))/3.0
30 CONTINUE
```

Worked Example 1

The Slinky Sweater Corporation has twelve different sweater designs. In order to produce the weekly sales report, the price of each sweater design is read into an array named PRICE and the number sold is read into an array named NUMBER. Then, an array called AMOUNT, containing the value of the sales, is filled by multiplying the price by the quantity. Finally, the total sales are calculated by summing up the elements of the AMOUNT array.

The arrays to be declared are

```
DIMENSION PRICE(12),NUMBER(12),AMOUNT(12)
```

Assuming that a price and a number are on each of twelve cards, both values may be read in at once:

```
     DO 10 I = 1,12
     READ(5,101) PRICE(I),NUMBER(I)
101 FORMAT(F5.2,I6)
 10 CONTINUE
```

Once the values are established it is possible to fill the AMOUNT array with the required values. The multiplication of a PRICE by a NUMBER requires a mixed mode calculation; the INTEGER value in NUMBER is converted to REAL before the computation is performed:

```
     DO 20 I = 1,12
     AMOUNT(I) = PRICE(I)*NUMBER(I)
20 CONTINUE
```

To calculate the total sales for the week, the elements of the AMOUNT array are summed in a scalar variable called TOTAL, which must first be set to zero:

```
    TOTAL = 0.0
    DO 30 I = 1,12
    TOTAL = TOTAL + AMOUNT(I)
30 CONTINUE
```

Finally, a neatly arranged output sheet can be printed. First, a general heading can be set up:

```
    WRITE(6,102)
102 FORMAT('1   WEEKLY SALES REPORT FOR SLINKY SWEATERS')
```

then, suitable column headings:

```
    WRITE(6,103)
103 FORMAT('0 PRICE      NUMBER        AMOUNT')
```

and a loop to print the twelve rows:

```
    DO 40 I = 1,12
    WRITE(6,104) PRICE(I),NUMBER(I),AMOUNT(I)
104 FORMAT(' ', F6.2, 5X,I6,6X,F8.2)
 40 CONTINUE
```

At the bottom of the sheet, the total sales should be printed:

```
    WRITE(6,105) TOTAL
105 FORMAT('0TOTAL SALES FOR THE WEEK $',F10.2)
    STOP
    END
```

This program is not the most efficient program that could be written for this problem; another could have been written using only one DO loop. This presentation separated the problem into a series of simple, clear steps. A good programmer has the ability to subdivide complicated problems into a series of smaller, simpler segments that can be dealt with one at a time.

Worked Example 2

Another aspect of the Slinky Sweater Corporation's accounting system requires the accumulation of the sales of the twelve sweater products from each of the different salespeople. For each sale, a single data card is prepared containing a product number from 1 to 12 that indicates which sweater was sold. It also contains an INTEGER value indicating how many were sold in this transaction. The data cards appear as:

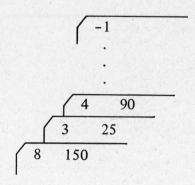

The last data card contains a product number of –1 to indicate that it is the end of the input data. The program must read a data card, and add the number sold to the proper array element to accumulate the number of sweaters sold. Finally, a report is printed.

The first step is to make the data declaration for an array, NUMBER, with 12 elements:

```
DIMENSION NUMBER(12)
```

and to set the entire array to zero:

```
      DO 10 I = 1,12
      NUMBER(I) = 0
10 CONTINUE
```

Next, it is necessary to read in a data card with IPROD(the product number) and IQTY(the quantity sold). Also, we must test to see if the card is the last card (in which case the control should be transferred to another point). In addition, we must add IQTY to the IPROD element of the NUMBER array:

```
 20 READ(5,101) IPROD,IQTY
101 FORMAT(I2,I6)
     IF(IPROD .EQ.-1) GO TO 30
     NUMBER(IPROD) = NUMBER(IPROD) + IQTY
     GO TO 20
```

The key statement here is the assignment of NUMBER(IPROD) + IQTY to NUMBER (IPROD). IPROD, which is a design number between 1 to 12, is used as a subscript to refer to the proper element of the NUMBER array. If IPROD were 7 and IQTY were 150 (indicating that 150 sweaters of type 7 were sold), it would be necessary to increment NUMBER(7) by 150. The assignment performs just this function. Only *one* of the 12 accumulators is incremented for each READ statement.

The report printout is similar to that in Worked Example 1. First a page heading is printed:

```
 30 WRITE(6,102)
102 FORMAT('1 TOTAL SWEATER SALES')
```

then, column headings:

```
    WRITE(6,103)
103 FORMAT('0 DESIGN      NUMBER')
```

and, finally, a loop to print the twelve rows of data:

```
    DO 40 I = 1,12
    WRITE(6,103) I,NUMBER(I)
103 FORMAT(' ', I7, 5X,I7)
 40 CONTINUE
    STOP
    END
```

The problem would become more elaborate, if the even-numbered designs were women's sweaters and the odd-numbered designs were men's sweaters. To print the women's sweater amounts:

```
    DO 50 IEVEN = 2,12,2
    WRITE(6,103) IEVEN,NUMBER(IEVEN)
 50 CONTINUE
```

Similarly, to print the men's sweater amounts:

```
    DO 60 IODD = 1,11,2
    WRITE(6,103) IODD,NUMBER(IODD)
 60 CONTINUE
```

Access to Arrays

An array may be thought of as a table of values. For example, the STATE array, used in the rainfall program, can be considered a table of values, each line of which contains the annual rainfall for one state (Table 7.2).

Unlike a printed table, however, the array has no labels to help a reader locate information. It is often necessary in a program to fill an array with values and then locate a specific element of the array. Questions such as, "What state had the most rainfall?", must be answered by searching the array for the largest number.

In order to answer questions about the data contained in an array, it is essential to know what state corresponds to each element of the array. This depends, of course, on the way in which the program has been designed and run. If the data for the rainfall program were organized so that the states were in alphabetical order, it would be clear that

STATE(1)   is Alabama
STATE(2)   is Alaska

.

.

.

STATE(50) is Wyoming

Table 7.2

(1)	68.13
(2)	54.62
(3)	7.20
(4)	48.66
(5)	14.68
(6)	18.69
(7)	14.81

.
.
.

(46)	17.19
(47)	38.77
(48)	30.16
(49)	29.51
(50)	15.06

The question, "What was the annual rainfall in Arkansas?", is the same as the question, "What is the value of STATE(3)?"

It is sometimes possible to convert a name or ID number directly to a subscript. In a class of 32 students, each student could be assigned an ID number from 1 to 32. If an array MARKS were used to hold the students' marks, the grade for the fifth student (who has ID #5) can be found in MARKS(5). In the sweater example, the number of sweaters sold for a given design can also be obtained easily. The number of design 9's sold is in NUMBER(9) and so on.

This technique works because the design number can be used as the subscript of the array. But many situations are not quite that simple. Design numbers, part numbers, student identification numbers, bank account numbers, or serial numbers do not always (or often) range from 1 to some constant without any gaps. When they are arbitrarily assigned, a two-level retrieval scheme is required for access. For example, if the sweater design numbers were

IDESGN
 43   108   85   75   95   106   185   164   54   13   91   87

with corresponding sales quantities:

NUMBER
 150   1800   600   750   860   100   1700   1500   800   600   50   100

the subscript will not immediately identify which NUMBER corresponds to, say, design 106. To find out how many design 106's were sold, one must first find the position in the IDESGN array and then look up the corresponding position in the NUMBER array. Design

106 appears in position 6 in IDESGN and, thus, position 6 in NUMBER reveals the result, 100. The FORTRAN program to do this requires that the "target key" 106 be stored in a position that we call ITARG. Then the array can be scanned from position 1 to position 12 in steps of one, testing in each position to see if the target key is matched. When a match occurs, the answer can be found by transferring to statement 50 and looking in the NUMBER array, using the loop index as the subscript. If no match occurs (that is, if 106 is not a valid design number) an error message is printed:

```
C   LOCATE A TARGET KEY
C
      ITARG = 106
      DO 30 INDEX = 1,12
      IF(ITARG .EQ. IDESGN(INDEX)) GO TO 50
   30 CONTINUE
      WRITE(6,101) ITARG
  101 FORMAT('0******THE TARGET KEY IS NOT FOUND******',I12)
      GO TO 60
          .
          .
          .
   50 NUM = NUMBER(INDEX)
          .
          .
   60     .
```

This sequential search technique is not the most efficient, but it is simple to understand and program. The flowchart in Figure 7.1 shows how it works. In effect, the program searches an array in order to determine whether it contains a specific value.

Problem 7.3

Write a program to read a two-digit integer from a card and determine whether it is in an array named NUMS. Assume that NUMS has been filled in an earlier segment of the program and that the size of the array is 1000.

If the number is found, write the message
THE VALUE xx IS IN POSITION yyyy

If the number is not in the array, write the message

THE VALUE xx IS NOT FOUND.

How will your program operate if the number occurs more than once? Can you extend it to locate *every* occurrence of the value read in?

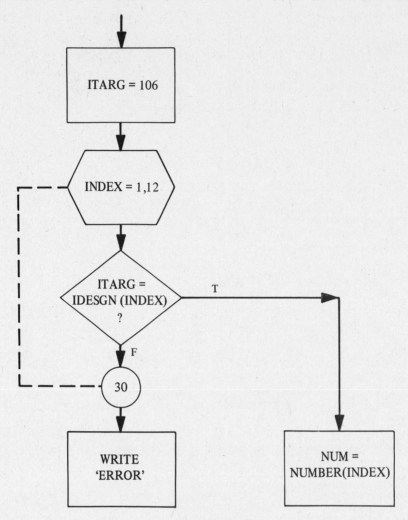

Figure 7.1

Finding the Maximum Value of an Array

A further elaboration of Worked Example 2 might be to find and print the position in the array that contains the largest value. In this case, it would represent the best-selling sweater design for the company and would no doubt be of interest to company executives. Similarly, the smallest element, representing the poorest-selling design, would also be of interest.

Given a printout showing how many of each design were sold, a clerk could pick out the best-selling design merely by looking over the list. Computers do not have the ability to scan an entire list at once. Rather, they must perform simple operations on one data item at a time. As an analogy, suppose one is presented with a list of numbers by having them flashed on a screen one at a time and is asked to report which value is the largest. A simple way of solving this problem would be to write down the first number on a slip of paper, then compare it to the numbers that follow as they are flashed on the screen. When a number is displayed that is larger than the number already written down, it should be written down in place of the old value. When all the numbers have been displayed, the largest value will be written down on the slip of paper.

LOOP OPTIMIZATION

In FORTRAN the most direct technique for looping is the DO statement. Since a large proportion of the program's time is usually spent in loops, the loops should be optimized. The speed of the computer should not be abused by careless programming of loops. Operations which can be performed before entering a loop should be removed from the scope of the loop; redundant calculations should be avoided.

Removing Loop-Independent Expressions. Expressions in DO loops that involve variables which are independent of the loop variable should be evaluated outside the loop and, if necessary, stored in a temporary location. This technique avoids unnecessary and repetitious calculation. In the example below, the expression (X*X + 3.0*X + 2.0) is independent of the loop variable J, but will be calculated 50 times:

```
    X = 3.4
    DO 9 J = 1,50
9   Y = Y + A(J)*(X*X + 3.0*X +2.0)
```

The expression can be calculated once outside the loop and stored in location Z. Then the occurrence of the expression in the DO loop is replaced by Z:

```
    X = 3.4
    Z = X*X + 3.0*X + 2.0
    DO 9 J=1,50
9   Y = Y + A(J) * Z
```

In the following program:

```
    X = .4739
    DO 7 I = 1,100
7   A(I) = 3.0 * X * SIN(X)
```

the expression (3.0*X*SIN(X)) may be removed from the loop. As a result the expression need be evaluated only once, instead of 100 times:

```
    X = .4739
    Y = 3.0 * X * SIN(X)
    DO 7 I=1,100
7   A(I) = Y
```

Expressions involving subscripted variables in which subscripts are independent of the DO loop variable should also precede the loop. This avoids the calculation of a subscripting function each time the expression is evaluated. Thus,

```
    I = K + 1
    DO 6 J = 1,30
6   A(J) = B(J) * C(I)
```

should be replaced by

```
      I = K + 1
      TEMP = C(I)
      DO 6 J = 1,30
6 A(J) = B(J) * TEMP
```

"Jamming." If two adjacent DO loops have the same limits on the loop variable, it may be possible to combine the two loops. This operation not only reduces the size of the program, but also substantially reduces the execution time.

In the following example, two 600-word arrays are set to zero by two separate DO loops:

```
      DO 20 I = 1,600
20 A(I) = 0.0
      DO 30 I = 1,600
30 B(I) = 0.0
```

However, only one loop is necessary:

```
      DO 40 I = 1,600
      A(I) = 0.0
40 B(I) = 0.0
```

This technique, known as *loop jamming,* reduces overhead in the loop by 50 percent.

Unswitching. If a test inside a DO loop is not influenced by any of the variables in the loop then it may be possible to remove the test from the loop. For example, in

```
      DO 50 K = 1,1000
      IF ( T .GT. 0.0) GO TO 40
      A(K) = B(K) + C(K)
      GO TO 50
40 A(K) = B(K) - C(K)
50 CONTINUE
```

the variable T is unaffected by the loop, but the IF statement is executed 1000 times. The program could be restructured to decrease the execution time by coding

```
      IF (T .GT. 0.0) GO TO 40
      DO 30 K = 1,1000
30 A(K) = B(K) + C(K)
      GO TO 60
40 DO 50 K = 1,1000
50 A(K) = B(K) - C(K)
60 CONTINUE
```

Although the second program is more complicated, the IF statement is executed only once.

This procedure can be used to locate the largest value in an array. Assume that the numbers are stored in an array, A, of length N and that a variable ABIG will be used to store the largest value. The value of A(1) is copied into ABIG. Then, the second thru the Nth location are compared to ABIG. Whenever a larger value is found, it replaces the previous content of ABIG. When the entire array has been scanned, the largest value will be in ABIG. A flowchart in Figure 7.2 represents this procedure.

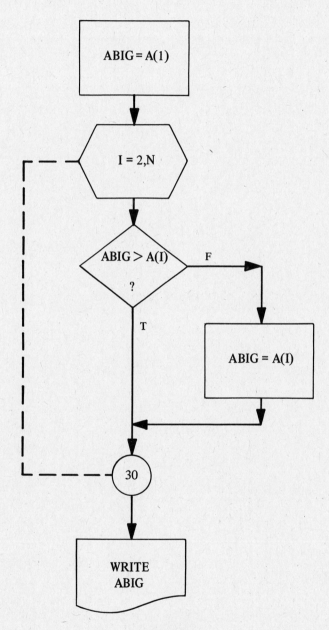

Figure 7.2

Converting the flowchart to a program fragment, we get

```
C       FIND THE LARGEST VALUE
C
        ABIG = A(1)
        DO 30 I = 2,N
        IF(ABIG .GT. A(I)) GO TO 30
        ABIG = A(I)
     30 CONTINUE
        WRITE(6,102) ABIG
    102 FORMAT ('1THE LARGEST VALUE IS', F10.2)
```

A concrete example of this might arise in which the array A contains student term averages and N, the number of students, is 8. The array A might have the values

78.6   74.5   88.7   86.1   81.0   93.4   90.2   89.8

Just how the program is executed provides an insight into the algorithm:

```
ABIG←78.6
        78.6 > 75.5
        78.6 < 88.7
ABIG←88.7
        88.7 > 86.1
        88.7 > 81.0
        88.4 < 93.4
ABIG←93.4
        93.4 > 90.2
        93.4 > 89.8
```

When the loop is completed, the value of ABIG is 93.4, the largest element of the array.

In many cases, it is important to find not only the largest value, but also *the position of the largest value*. In order to do this it is necessary to record the array position (that is, the loop index) whenever the value of ABIG is changed.

```
C       FIND THE LARGEST VALUE AND ITS POSITION
C
        ABIG = A(1)
        IPT = 1
        DO 30 I = 2,N
        IF(ABIG .GT. A(I)) GO TO 30
        ABIG = A(I)
        IPT = I
     30 CONTINUE
        WRITE(6,102) ABIG, IPT
    102 FORMAT('1THE LARGEST VALUE IS ', F10.2, ' POSITION ', I3)
```

Problem 7.4

Write a program to locate the *smallest* value of a ten-element vector, X, and print the message

THE SMALLEST VALUE IS nnnn.n IN LOCATION xx.

An interesting variation on the problem of locating the largest element of an array is the problem of locating the second largest element. This can be done simply: first find the largest element and eliminate it, then find the largest of the remaining elements. (This algorithm is not the most efficient, but it is easy to understand.) If all the values in the array are positive, the elimination can be done by setting at zero the location which contains the largest element. To do this, the location of the largest value is found just as it was in the previous example. The procedure is then performed a second time. The number of *iterations* (times through the loop) is stored in a variable called NCOUNT. Figure 7.3 shows the flowchart for this algorithm. The program is

```
C       FIND THE SECOND LARGEST AND ITS POSITION
C
        NCOUNT = 0
   20   ABIG = A(1)
        IPT = 1
        DO 30 I = 2,N
        IF(ABIG .GT. A(I)) GO TO 30
        ABIG = A(I)
        IPT = I
   30   CONTINUE
        NCOUNT = NCOUNT + 1
        A(IPT) = 0.0
        IF(NCOUNT .LT. 2) GO TO 20
        WRITE(6,102) ABIG, IPT
  102   FORMAT('1THE SECOND LARGEST IS', F10.2,' POSITION',I3)
```

In the previous array, the largest value was 93.4, occurring in position 6. Thus, when NCOUNT was set equal to 1, the contents of the array were

78.6   74.5   88.7   86.1   81.0   0.0   90.2   89.8

When the DO 30 loop is completed for the second time, the second largest value is obtained. The printed results would be

```
THE SECOND LARGEST IS        90.20 POSITION   7
```

By changing the test statement IF(NCOUNT .LT. 2) GO TO 20 to IF(NCOUNT .LT. 3) GO TO 20, it is possible to find the third largest element of the array. What would the result be in this example? The fourth, fifth, and sixth largest elements and so on can also be found using this program.

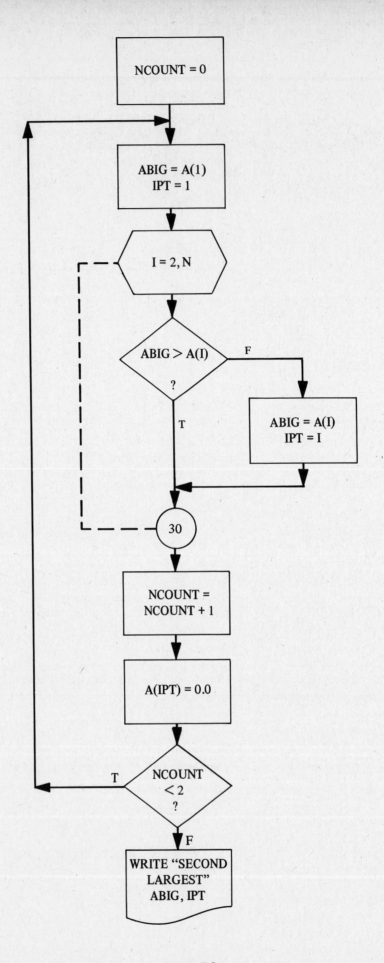

Figure 7.3

This program has number of sophisticated and important applications. If the elements can be ordered, then a list of the values in descending order can be printed. To do this, a DO loop can be used to replace the setting and to test the NCOUNT. This program should clarify the meaning of the nested DO loops:

```
      DO 40 NCOUNT = 1,N
      ABIG = A(1)
      IPT = 1
      DO 30 I = 2,N
      IF(ABIG .GT. A(I)) GO TO 30
      ABIG = A(I)
      IPT = I
   30 CONTINUE
      WRITE(6,103) NCOUNT,ABIG
  103 FORMAT(' ',I3,F10.2)
      A(IPT) = 0.0
   40 CONTINUE
```

For the set of data used in the problem of student averages, the output is

```
   1      93.40
   2      90.20
   3      89.80
   4      88.70
   5      86.10
   6      81.00
   7      78.60
   8      74.50
```

When the execution of this program fragment is complete, all eight locations of the A array contain 0.0, since one element was set to zero during each execution of the DO 40 loop.

Once at the stage where it is possible to print out an array in decreasing order, it is only a short step to performing an internal sort during which the values can be reordered to produce an array in which they are in descending order.

A simple way to perform the sort is to create a new array, B, in which the sorted list will be built as the A array is set to zero. The previous program is modified merely by replacing the WRITE statement with the proper assignment statement.

```
      DO 40 NCOUNT = 1,N
      ABIG = A(1)
      IPT = 1
      DO 30 I = 2,N
      IF(ABIG .GT. A(I)) GO TO 30
      ABIG = A(I)
      IPT = I
   30 CONTINUE
      B(NCOUNT) = ABIG
      A(IPT) = 0
   40 CONTINUE
```

After this program fragment is executed, the contents of the arrays are

Array A

| 0.0 | 0.0 | 0.0 | 0.0 | 0.0 | 0.0 | 0.0 | 0.0 |

Array B

| 93.40 | 90.20 | 89.80 | 88.70 | 86.10 | 81.00 | 78.60 | 74.50 |

This algorithm is a natural outgrowth of the previous series of programs. As has been noted, though easy to understand, it is not efficient. There are many sorting algorithms in the literature of computer science and much discussion as to the merits of various schemes. Different conditions make one algorithm more convenient or more efficient than another. Sorting theory is one of those peculiar research areas that are at once accessible to the beginner and interesting to leading researchers and mathematicians.[2]

Sorting in a Single Array

The main problem with the sorting algorithm above is that it requires two arrays of length n. Since storage is limited in many computers, an algorithm that uses only a single array is preferable to one that uses two. This sorting algorithm operates by comparing the first and second elements of the array, and interchanging them if the first element happens to be smaller than the second. Then the second and third are compared and, if necessary, another interchange is performed to ensure that the smaller element is moved down. This process is repeated, forcing the smallest element to "bubble up" at the end of the array. The process is then repeated, forcing the second smallest element to the second from the end position. Repeating the process $n-1$ times sorts the array until it is in descending order. This algorithm can be implemented with only a few FORTRAN statements:

```
      NM = N - 1
      DO 30 I = 1,NM
      JM = N - I
      DO 20 J = 1,JM
      IF(A(J) .GT. A(J+1))GO TO 20
      TEMP = A(J)
      A(J) = A(J+1)
      A(J+1) = TEMP
   20 CONTINUE
   30 CONTINUE
```

The three assignment statements after the IF statement perform the interchange of values. That interchange might be represented by Figure 7.4. A temporary location, TEMP, is used during the interchange.

---

[2] For additional information on this topic see Ivan Flores, *Computer Sorting* (Englewood Cliffs, N. J.: Prentice-Hall, 1969) or Donald Knuth, *The Art of Computer Programming: Sorting and Searching,* Vol. 3 (Reading, Mass: Addison-Wesley, 1973).

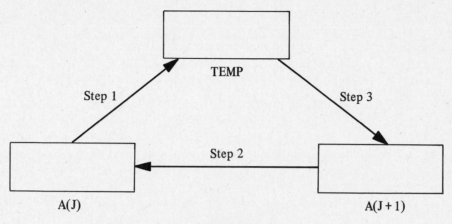

Figure 7.4

Table 7.3 follows the execution of this program for the case of N = 4, where the array A contains (8.5, 4.2, 6.9, 9.1). NM is set to 3.

TABLE 7.3

I	JM	J	J + 1	A	(1)	(2)	(3)	(4)	
1	3	1	2		8.5	4.2	6.9	9.1	Array contents
		2	3		8.5	6.9	4.2	9.1	at statement 20
		3	4		8.5	6.9	9.1	4.2	
2	2	1	2		8.5	6.9	9.1	4.2	
		2	3		8.5	9.1	6.9	4.2	
3	1	1	2		9.1	8.5	6.9	4.2	

Problem 7.5

Write a program fragment to sort an array, A, into *ascending* order.

Permissible Subscript Forms

In the above sorting example, the statement

```
A(J) = A(J+1)
```

was used. This was the first example where a subscript was something other than a positive integer constant or an unsubscripted integer variable.

In many FORTRAN compilers, including WATFOR and WATFIV, any expression at all may be used as a subscript. If the expression is of *real* mode it will be converted to *integer* according to the standard rules. However, in standard FORTRAN there are restrictions on the form that subscripts may assume. To run a program on any compiler (or on a compiler that has restrictions on the form of subscripts), subscripts that conform to one of the following standard forms should be used:

$$c_1$$
$$v$$
$$v + c_1$$
$$v - c_1$$
$$c_1 * v$$
$$c_1 * v + c_2$$
$$c_1 * v - c_2$$

where v is an unsubscripted INTEGER variable and c_1 and c_2 are positive INTEGER constants. Thus, the following are valid standard subscript forms

```
A(7) = A(I)
BETA(2*J) = GAMMA(2*J-1) + DELTA(2*J+1)
IVAL(INDEX) = IVAL(INDEX2-47)/2
N(186) = N(187) + IFIX(ARRAY(IK-4))
```

These, on the other hand, contain *invalid* standard subscript references (although they are valid in WATFOR/WATFIV)

```
A(3) = A(2+J)
ALPHA(I-J) = 7.1
DEMAND(N(I)) = SUPPLY(8)
TEMP = TEST(NVAL/2)
Q(2+J+K+L) = A(2+J+K+L)
```

If it is necessary to use a nonstandard subscript form, the programmer can circumvent the restrictions with a construction like

```
JJ = 2+J+K+L
Q(JJ)= A(JJ)
```

Two-Dimensional Arrays

A singly subscripted variable has been compared to a linear string of scalar variables:

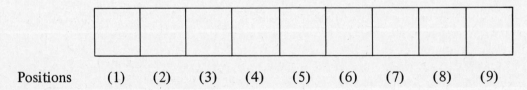

It is sometimes convenient to arrange variables in two dimensions:

	Column 1	Column 2	Column 3
Row 1	(1,1)	(1,2)	(1,3)
Row 2	(2,1)	(2,2)	(2,3)
Row 3	(3,1)	(3,2)	(3,3)

In such an arrangement, an element of the array can be referred to by specifying its row and its column. Table 7.4 shows the way in which each element can be specified. The two-dimensional boxes are often called *cells,* and a two-dimensional array is called a *matrix.*

Cell	Row	Column
(1,1)	1	1
(2,1)	2	1
(3,1)	3	1
(1,2)	1	2
(2,2)	2	2
(3,2)	3	2
(1,3)	1	3
(2,3)	2	3
(3,3)	3	3

Such a two-dimensional structure can be very convenient for certain applications.

A two-dimensional matrix can be used for storing data with major and minor subdivisions. For example, a company with three salespeople and four products could create a 3 x 4 (read "three by four") matrix, called SALES. It would have three rows and four columns in which to store the amount of each product sold by each salesperson:

SALES	Prod 1	Prod 2	Prod 3	Prod 4
Salesperson 1				
Salesperson 2				
Salesperson 3				

When referring to an element of the array, two subscripts are needed. Thus, the amount of product 2 sold by salesperson 3 is stored in SALES (3,2). The subscripts are always given in the order (*row, column*).

In order to declare a two-dimensional array, the DIMENSION statement must specify the number of rows and the number of columns. DIMENSION A(4,3), I(3,4) declares two arrays—a REAL array with four rows and three columns and an INTEGER array with three rows and four columns.

A seating-arrangement chart for a room with four rows and six seats per row can be represented by a two-dimensional array. Each element of the array might contain the student's ID number. To declare a 4 x 6 array the following DIMENSION statement might be used:

```
DIMENSION IDNOS (4,6)
```

A total of 24 locations will be reserved by this statement. The array will have the structure shown in Table 7.4.

TABLE 7.4

	Column 1	Column 2	Column 3	Column 4	Column 5	Column 6
Row 1	(1,1)	(1,2)	(1,3)	(1,4)	(1,5)	(1,6)
Row 2	(2,1)	(2,2)	(2,3)	(2,4)	(2,5)	(2,6)
Row 3	(3,1)	(3,2)	(3,3)	(3,4)	(3,5)	(3,6)
Row 4	(4,1)	(4,2)	(4,3)	(4,4)	(4,5)	(4,6)

Assume that ID numbers for the 48 students have been entered on data cards. A program is desired to read the cards and assign the students seats by rows. The input data cards contain the following list of ID numbers

```
65786
45738
67219
60018
48298
88910
67841
22301
33589
56183
94864
  .
  .
  .
69486
```

The declaration and input sections of the program are

```
      DIMENSION IDNOS(4,6)
      DO 20 IROW = 1,4
      DO 10 JCOL = 1,6
      READ(5,101) IDNOS(IROW,JCOL)
  101 FORMAT(I5)
   10 CONTINUE
   20 CONTINUE
```

When this program fragment is executed, the READ statement is executed 24 times and the 24 elements of the array are filled one row at a time. The results appear in Table 7.5.

TABLE 7.5

	Column 1	Column 2	Column 3	Column 4	Column 5	Column 6
Row 1	65786	45738	67219	60018	48298	88910
Row 2	67841	22301	33589	56183	94864	94864
Row 3	68492	40003	76289	10704	10463	68211
Row 4	72841	10001	47401	32821	19144	69486

In general, two-dimensional arrays are filled by using nested DO loops. To set an N X M array to zeroes, a program such as the following could be used:

```
      DO 20 I = 1,N
      DO 10 J = 1,M
      A(I,J) = 0.0
   10 CONTINUE
   20 CONTINUE
```

This program will set the elements to zero in row order. If one wants access to the matrix in column order, a program such as the following could be used:

```
      DO 20 J = 1,M
      DO 10 I = 1,N
      A(I,J) = 0.0
   10 CONTINUE
   20 CONTINUE
```

The techniques of getting access to a matrix by row or by column may be used for input and output. To print out a matrix by rows, we could write

```
C   PRINTING BY ROWS
      DO 40 IROW = 1,4
      DO 30 JCOL = 1,6
      WRITE(6,102) IDNOS(IROW,JCOL)
  102 FORMAT (' ',I5)
   30 CONTINUE
   40 CONTINUE
```

or to print the matrix by columns,

```
C    PRINTING BY COLUMNS
     DO 40 JCOL = 1,6
     DO 30 IROW = 1,4
     WRITE(6,102) IDNOS(IROW,JCOL)
102  FORMAT(' ',I5)
 30  CONTINUE
 40  CONTINUE
```

It is also possible to print a single row, such as row 3:

```
C    PRINT ROW 3
     DO 50 I = 1,6
     WRITE(6,102) IDNOS(3,I)
 50  CONTINUE
```

or to print a single column, such as column 5:

```
C    PRINT COLUMN 5
     DO 60 I = 1,4
     WRITE(6,102) IDNOS(I,5)
 60  CONTINUE
```

or to print a particular element, such as row 2 column 3:

```
C    PRINT A SINGLE ELEMENT
     WRITE(6,102) IDNOS(2,3)
```

A more interesting problem is to determine in which seat a particular student is sitting. To do this, a target identification number should be read in. Then the entire array must be scanned to locate the target identification number. If it is found, the row and column position in which the match was made should be printed. If it is not found, an appropriate error message could be issued.

```
C LOCATING A TARGET IDENTIFICATION NUMBER
     READ(5,101) ITARGT
101  FORMAT(I5)
     DO 45 IROW = 1,4
     DO 35 JCOL = 1,6
     IF(ITARGT .EQ. IDNOS(IROW,JCOL)) GO TO 55
 35  CONTINUE
 45  CONTINUE
     WRITE(6,102) ITARGT
102  FORMAT('0****TARGET NOT FOUND****',I12)
     GO TO 65
       .
       .
       .
```

```
 55 WRITE(6,103) ITARGT,IROW,JCOL
103 FORMAT('0TARGET ',I5,' FOUND IN ROW ',I2,'COLUMN ',I2)
       .
       .
 65    .
```

Problem 7.6

Write a program fragment to search a 4 X 7 array; locate the largest and smallest values in it.

Arrays with More Than Two Dimensions[3]

It is possible to specify arrays with three or even more dimensions. Most FORTRAN compilers permit up to seven dimensions. The declaration

```
DIMENSION A(2,3,4), B(3,5,2,7)
```

declares a three-dimensional array and a four-dimensional array. It is difficult, of course, to visualize arrays of more than three dimensions; a three-dimensional array may be visualized as a cube-shaped structure.

How are such multidimensional arrays used? Consider the problem of producing a tri-annual report for a company with four salesmen and five products. A three-dimensional array can be used to hold the sales data. The first subscript can represent the report periods (ranging from one to three), the second subscript can represent the salesmen (ranging from one to four), and the third subscript can represent the products (ranging from one to five). The visual representation of the data requires three levels, four rows and five columns. The content of each element is the amount of a particular product sold by a particular sales-person in a particular trimester. The three-dimensional matrix is illustrated in Figure 7.5.

The DIMENSION statement for this array might be

```
DIMENSION IPROD(3,4,5)
```

Access to three-dimensional arrays may be obtained in many ways. Input or output can be done one row at a time or one column at a time (as with two-dimensional arrays). But now operations can also be done across the levels. For example, to determine how many product 3's were sold by salesman 2 during the entire year would require the summation of

```
IPROD(1,2,3)  +  IPROD(2,2,3)  +  IPROD(3,2,3)
```

which could be accomplished by a DO loop:

```
    ITOTAL = 0
    DO 20 LEVEL = 1,3
    ITOTAL = ITOTAL + IPROD(LEVEL,2,3)
 20 CONTINUE
```

---

[3] This section contains advanced material which may be omitted without loss of continuity.

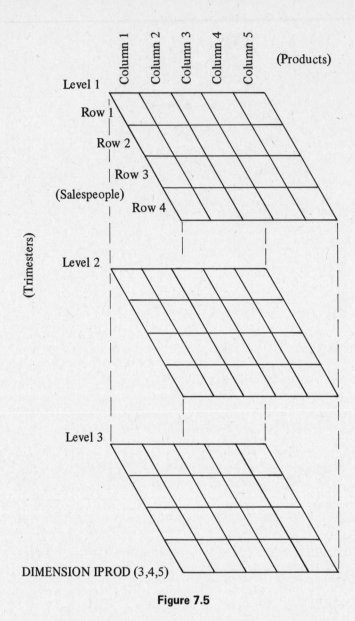

Figure 7.5

Operations on the entire array require three nested DO loops. For example, the entire array may be set to zero by the following instructions:

```
    DO 30 LEVEL = 1,3
    DO 20 IROW = 1,4
    DO 10 JCOL = 1,5
    IPROD(LEVEL,IROW,JCOL) = 0
10  CONTINUE
20  CONTINUE
30  CONTINUE
```

The assignment statement will be executed a total of 3*4*5 times or 60 times, once for each element.

Complete Array Input/Output

To read or print the entire contents of an array the name of the array (without any subscripting) may be used in the list of the READ or WRITE statement:

```
    DIMENSION ARRAY(4)
    WRITE(6,102) ARRAY
102 FORMAT(' ',F5.2,F5.2,F5.2,F5.2)
```

This format statement prints all four values of the array on the same line. The format statement associated with complete array input/output must reflect the number of data items in the array. If items remain in the input/output list when the end of the FORMAT is reached, a new card is read (input) or a new line is started (output) and the format is reused. The statements

```
    DIMENSION INVTRY(50)
    READ(5,103) INVTRY
103 FORMAT(I6,I4)
```

will cause 25 cards to be read; two values will be obtained from each card. The input/output list associated with a complete array operation may also contain scalar variables. Assume that two integer values, a real array of length 8 and another real value were to be read. The program might be

```
    DIMENSION ACCEL(8)
    READ(5,104) IDENT,ITIME,ACCEL,DIST
104 FORMAT(I3,I6,8F5.2,F10.3)
```

and the input data card might be

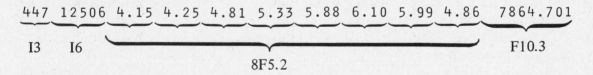

Two-dimensional arrays can also be processed by this technique. However, the data are read in, in column order for most versions of FORTRAN. Thus, if an array has been declared as

```
DIMENSION A(3,4)
```

the order of the data must be

A(1,1)
A(2,1)
A(3,1)
A(1,2)
A(2,2)
A(3,2)
A(1,3)
A(2,3)
A(3,3)
A(1,4)
A(2,4)
A(3,4)

If we assume that the first subscript is the row and the second is the column, the tabular format is

A(1,1)	A(1,2)	A(1,3)	A(1,4)
A(2,1)	A(2,2)	A(2,3)	A(2,4)
A(3,1)	A(3,2)	A(3,3)	A(3,4)

and the input or output sequence is then said to be down the columns and across the rows. This order is sometimes confusing and care should be taken to make sure that the data for an entire column are read in before data appear for the next column.

This technique of array input/output is less flexible and more error-prone than the *implied DO* which will be discussed in the next chapter.

Type Declarations

The DIMENSION statement is a special type of statement known as a *declaration*. A declaration differs from other executable statements in that it does not cause any action to take place at execution time. Rather, it is an instruction to the compiler which helps determine how the program is to be translated.

To help clarify the difference, consider the following sign which might appear in a building corridor:

IN CASE OF FIRE
1. TURN IN ALARM AT BOX BELOW

2. WALK TO NEAREST EXIT

POST THIS SIGN IN A
   CONSPICUOUS PLACE

The first two instructions are to be executed in case of a fire. But the third statement is different; it does not instruct the reader to do something when a fire occurs. Rather, this instruction refers to the sign itself and must be carried out when the sign is received.

Similarly, the statement

```
A(4) = 0.0
```

is executed in its turn when the program is *run*. But the statement

```
DIMENSION A(10)
```

takes effect when the program is *compiled*.

In general, declarations appear at the beginning of the program. Since declarations are nonexecutable statements (with the exception of the FORMAT statement), *they can never have a statement label.* For the same reason, it is not possible to perform computations within a declaration. A statement such as

```
DIMENSION A(N+10)
```

is not valid.

In addition to the DIMENSION statement, there are several other declarations in FORTRAN. Two of the most common are the INTEGER statement and the REAL statement. These statements are used to declare that a variable is of a type *other* than the type implicitly declared by the first letter of its name.

For example, the variables I, J, and MONEY would normally be of INTEGER type. If the programmer desired to use these names as REAL variables, he could add the declaration

```
REAL I, J, MONEY
```

Similarly, the variables A, B, and X could be used as INTEGER variables if so declared

```
INTEGER A, B, X
```

It is unnecessary, although not incorrect, to write declarations such as

```
INTEGER I,J
```

and

```
REAL A,B
```

When a variable is declared in a REAL or INTEGER statement, any dimension information can be included. Thus the DIMENSION statement is optional. The following declarations are equivalent:

```
DIMENSION I(10)        INTEGER I(10)

DIMENSION J(2,3)       REAL J(2,3)
REAL J
```

As in the DIMENSION statement, more than one variable may be declared in a REAL or INTEGER statement:

```
REAL KOUT, JJ(2), A(10,3,5)
```

It is not valid to DIMENSION a variable in both a type statement and a DIMENSION statement. Thus if they appear together the statements

```
INTEGER BOB(5)
DIMENSION BOB(5)
```

are invalid, Valid constructions are

```
INTEGER BOB(5)
```

```
INTEGER BOB
DIMENSION BOB(5)
```

Type declarations will be, explored in greater depth in Chapter 10.

Summary

The ability to deal with a large collection of data items enhances our computational power. With arrays of subscripted variables it is possible to utilize the extreme speed and accuracy of the computer. By using variable array subscripts which are altered by DO loops, entire arrays of data can be processed with almost the ease with which single data items were processed. One- or two-dimensional arrays can be read in and printed out under loop control or with the complete array technique. Important tasks such as finding the largest element of an array, sorting an array, locating a particular element of an array, adding two arrays, or copying an array become the building blocks of more sophisticated programs. It is not enough to learn the rules of use for subscripted variables; the concepts behind these basic operations must be thoroughly understood.

The basic principles are simple enough. The DIMENSION statement, which must appear before any executable statement, saves space for one or more arrays. Individual elements of the array can be referred to by using integer constants for subscripts. When integer variable subscripts are used, a DO loop serves to alter the value of the variable.

DEBUGGING CLINIC

At this point the programs you are writing are of such complexity that it may be difficult to follow the flow of control or the values of certain variables in loops. At the early stages of debugging a program, it is good practice to print a line of output at crucial points in the program. The values of the variables to be tested in an IF statement should be printed before the IF statement. The value of critical variables in a DO loop and the values of subscripts should be printed in order to check that they are as they were intended to be.

Although this debugging step may cause a few more pages of output to be printed, the information contained in the output may help to reduce the total number of runs necessary to produce the final program. The debugging output also serves as an educational aid to reinforce the notions that you have about how the execution of your program is proceeding. Once the program is working satisfactorily, the debugging output may be deleted and a clean version of the program's execution can be produced.

Working with subscripted variables provides extra power of expression and additional opportunities for error. Don't forget the DIMENSION statement! This may seem obvious, but missing DIMENSION statements are a major source of errors. Remember to put the DIMENSION statement at the beginning of your program before any executable statements. If the compiler that you are using restricts the form of the subscripts to the seven basic forms, make sure that your program adheres to this restriction. The value of subscripts must always be greater than zero and less than or equal to the size of the array as given in the DIMENSION statement. The WATFOR/WATFIV compilers will provide execution time error messages if the array boundaries are exceeded. The result with other compilers is unpredictable.

REVIEW QUESTIONS

1. What is a subscripted variable? How is it declared?
2. How does a singly subscripted variable differ in use from a collection of scalar variables?
3. How does a two-dimensional array differ from a one-dimensional array?
4. Explain how an array may be searched for the largest or smallest element. How may a one-dimensional vector be sorted?
5. Explain the use and format of the REAL and INTEGER declarations.

EXERCISES

1. Which of the following are valid and which are invalid DIMENSION statements?

a. DIMENSION ALPHA (10)

b. DIMENSION BETA (20)

c. DIMENSION TEST(20), MARK(30), GRADE(10)

d. DIMENSION PRESSR(20, VOLUME(20))

e. DIMENSION POPULN(40, AREA940),DENSTY(40)

f. `AREA(50) DIMENSION`

g. `DIMENSION = AREA(50)`

h. `DIMENSION PRICE(100.5)`

i. `DIMENSION A(2)`

j. `DIMENSION SUPPLY(20),DEMAND(10+10)`

2. Write a program fragment to declare a REAL array of size 200 and to zero out the first 50 locations. Then alter the program to zero out the last 40 locations as well.

3. Declare an INTEGER array of size 100 and fill each of its locations with its array position (that is, fill the first location with 1, second location with 2, ... and the 100th location with 100).

4. Declare an INTEGER array of size 50 and fill all the even-numbered positions with +1 and the odd-numbered positions with -1.

5. Declare a REAL array of size 20 and fill each position with the square root of the position number. Such a table might be used in programs which frequently require square roots of the numbers from 1 to 20. By using the table instead of calculating the value each time, it may be possible to save execution time.

6. a. Write a program to read in two integer arrays of length N and M respectively. Assume that the arrays have been sorted in ascending order.

   b. Merge the two arrays into a single array of length N+M which is sorted in ascending order.

7. *Computer Math.* a. Write a program to read in an integer quantity and convert it to binary. Print out the integer and its binary equivalent.

   b. Read in a binary number which has been punched in columns 20–39 (right justified) into an integer array of length 20. Convert to a decimal integer and print the result.

8. a. Write a program to determine the second largest element of an array of integers.

   b. Change the program to obtain the third largest element.

9. Write a program to find the median of an array of REAL values of length N. For arrays of odd length the median is the $(N/2 + 1)$th value. For arrays of even length the median is the average of the $(N/2)$th and the $(N/2 + 1)$th values. The median may be determined by sorting the entire array and then selecting the proper value or values. There is a somewhat faster way if you are clever.

ADVANCED EXERCISES

10. It is frequently necessary to store extremely large integer numbers. This may be accomplished by storing an 80-digit integer value in an integer array of length 80. Thus one decimal digit ($n ... 9$) is stored in each location.

    Write a program to read in two 80-digit numbers, store them in two arrays, and generate the sum in another 80-location array. Be sure to check for possible overflow.

    a. Print the input values and the result.

    b. Rewrite the program to perform subtraction.

   c. Rewrite the program to perform multiplication. The result should be stored in a 160-digit array.

   d. Rewrite the program to perform division. Divide a 160-digit dividend by an 80-digit divisor to produce an 80-digit quotient.

11. Write a program to print the permutations of the digits 1 to N, where N is read in. Thus for $N=3$ the output should be

```
123
132
213
231
312
321
```

or 3! = 6. For $N=4$ there are 4!=24 possibilities:

```
1234    2134    3124    4123
1243    2143    3142    4132
1324    2314    3214    4213
1342    2341    3241    4231
1423    2413    3412    4312
1432    2431    3421    4321
```

and for $N=k$ there $k!$ possibilities.

12. One technique for generating random numbers is the center-squared method. Choose a starting value, called the seed, which is four digits long. Square it, producing an eight-digit result. Select out the middle four digits and this is your first random number. Repeat the process to generate a series of random numbers.

    For example, take 8317 as the seed. Square it to produce 69172589. The first random number is 1725. Square and select the inner four digits to get the next random number.

    Write a program to perform this process 1000 times and print the results on a single sheet of output. Devise a test to determine if the results are random. After experimenting with different seeds give suggestions for good seed selection.

13. *Post Tag Problem.* Take an initial string of 0's and 1's of length four or greater. If the left-most digit is a 0, delete the first three digits and append 00 to the right. If the leftmost digit is a 1, delete the first three digits and append 1101 on the right. Repeat the operation as long as the string is not wiped out by the deletion of three digits. For example, these strings are wiped out:

```
0110→
   000→nothing

001011→
   01100→
      0000→
         000→nothing
```

while this string produces a repeating sequence which never terminates:

```
001101→
   10100→
      001101→
```

$$10100 \rightarrow$$
$$001101 \rightarrow$$
$$10100$$

There are these possibilities

- The process terminates.

- The process goes into a loop.

- The string keeps getting longer and longer.

Write a program to study this process by performing the operations and printing values. You might develop a technique to detect looping.[4]

14. A little probability theory demonstrates that it is a fair bet that in a room filled with 23 people there are at least two people who were born on the same day of the year. Write a program to read in an arbitrary number of data cards containing the month and date of birth of a group of people. Keep track of all of the birthdays in a 12 by 31 array. Print out a list of all the dates on which two or more people were born. Take into account the possibility that there are no such dates.

15. *Chess Knight's Tour.* A knight is placed on an empty chessboard and begins marching around the board.[5] It is possible for the knight to land on each of the 64 positions once and only once. Write a program which keeps jumping the knight and keeps track of the path. Finally print out the path when there are no available moves. Make sure that the knight does not fall off the board and does not land in the same space twice. The jumps may be selected randomly or by an algorithm. After 20 moves the board might resemble Figure 7.6.

1	12				14		
		2	13				15
11				3	16		
		20				4	
	10					17	
			19				5
9				7	18		
		8				6	

Figure 7.6

Try changing the move-generating algorithm to see how far you can get.

---

[4] The striking result of a computer science analysis is that it is not possible to determine the outcome as a function of the initial string. For more see Marvin Minsky, *Computation: Finite and Infinite Machines* (Englewood Cliffs, N. J.: Prentice-Hall, 1967).

[5] A knight moves two squares in a straight line then moves one square to the right or left.

16. *Eight Queens.* Write a program which tries to find a way to place eight queens on a chessboard so that none of the queens is attacking any of the other queens.[6]

In this attempt five queens, represented by 1's(assume 0's are in all the other locations), have been successfully placed, but there is no safe place in the sixth column. There are several solutions.

SPIRAL PROBLEMS

Choose one spiral problem from A, B, and C and one from D, E, and F.

A. Student Grading

Read a data card with a two-digit integer number, N, punched in columns 1-2. The next N data cards contain real test scores in the form XXX.X in columns 1-5. Read the scores into an array and print out the scores. Find the highest and the lowest scores and print them with appropriate messages. Print the range, the difference between the highest and the lowest scores, with an appropriate message.

B. Stock Portfolio Analysis

Data cards containing the purchase price (columns 1-7 in the form XXX.XXX) and the number of shares (columns 10-15 in the form XXXXXX) have been prepared. The last data card contains a -1.0 in the first field. Read a data card, print the information, compute the value (price times number of shares) and store it in an array. When all the data cards have been read, compute and print the total value of the portfolio.

C. Prime numbers—The Seive of Eratosthenes

A prime number is an integer divisible only by one and itself. Thus 2, 3, 5, 7, 11, 13, and 17 are all prime numbers. Use the technique called the seive of Eratosthenes to find all the prime numbers up to 200. Fill an array of 200 locations with ones. Then to eliminate multiples of 2, sweep through the array, setting locations 4, 6, 8, . . . ,200 to zero. Then set locations 6, 9, 12, . . .; 10, 15, 20, . . .; 14, 21, 28, . . .; and so on to zero. When done, print out the prime numbers by scanning the array to find positions which have ones in them. Keep track of and print the number of primes.

---

[6] Queens may move any number of squares horizontally, vertically or diagonally.

D. Student Grading

A series of four tests has been given to six students and the results have been punched onto data cards in the form

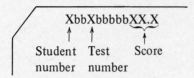

The students are numbered from 1 to 6 and the tests from 1 to 4. The input cards are not ordered. Read each card till a card comes up with student number equal to zero, entering each test score into an array. Print the array in a neat form with proper headings. Label the rows and columns. Print the average for each student and for each test with appropriate and meaningful messages.

E. Commercial Application: Salesperson Commissions

Read 15 data cards with salesperson numbers (from 1 to 5), region numbers (from 1 to 3) and amounts in the form

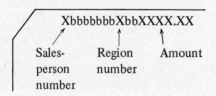

Keep reading data cards until a card with a salesperson number equal to zero is encountered. As each card is read, enter the amount in an array. Print the array in a neat form with proper headings. Label the rows and columns. Print the sums by region and by salesperson with appropriate and meaningful messages.

F. Mathematical Applications—Magic Square Tester

A magic square is an $n \times n$ array of integers which has the same sum across the rows, down the columns and across the two major diagonals. Seven input cards, each with seven two-digit integer numbers are to be prepared. The 49 data items are the numbers 1 to 49. The first card contains row one items for a 7 by 7 array. Cards 2 through 7 contain the data items for rows 2 through 7 respectively. Read in the data and print it out in tabular form, labeling the rows and columns. Finally test the array to determine if it is a magic square. Print a message to indicate the result.

Here is a valid 7 by 7 magic square to assist in testing your program.

	1	2	3	4	5	6	7
1	30	39	48	1	10	19	28
2	38	47	7	9	18	27	29
3	46	6	8	17	26	35	37
4	5	14	16	25	34	36	45
5	13	15	24	33	42	44	4
6	21	23	32	41	43	3	12
7	22	31	40	49	2	11	20

Advanced Project: Write a program to generate magic squares.

MORE INPUT/OUTPUT

We should bring the whole force of our minds to bear upon the most minute and simple details and to dwell upon them for a long time so that we become accustomed to perceive the truth clearly and distinctly.

René Descartes, Rules for the Direction of the Mind *(1628)*

CHAPTER 8

There are additional features to FORTRAN input/output which simplify the work of the programmer. In addition to the format items which have already been discussed (I, F, X, and E), two new format items (G for general numeric input and output, and T, which permits going to a specific column) are discussed in this chapter. Since it is often necessary to be able to read and print character information, an A-format item (for alphanumeric input/output) is also introduced.

Use of arrays requires special consideration in input/output because a programmer may want to print all the elements of an array or only specified elements. An entire array may be printed by specifying its name, without subscripts, in the data list of a READ, PRINT, or WRITE statement. A special modification of the DO statement known as an implied DO is utilized to permit selective input or output of elements of an array. At times, it may be desirable to defer specifications of the FORMAT statement until the program is actually run, and the technique allowing the FORMAT statement to be read into an array at execution time is presented here.

Introduction

The input/output statements used so far have been relatively simple in form. But the FORMAT statement has considerable flexibility, much of which we have not yet explored. The general form of the FORMAT statement as we have studied it so far is

$$nn \quad \text{FORMAT}(f_1, f_2, \ldots f_n)$$

where nn is a statement label and $f_1, \ldots, f_n$ are specification fields.

After a review of several familiar FORMAT items, some new specifications will be introduced.

I Format

The I-format specification is used to describe fields of integer data. Its form is I_w, where w indicates the numbers of positions in the field, including a position for the sign if the value may be negative. On input, the field is assumed to be right-justified, that is, leading blanks (to the left of the leftmost digit or sign) are ignored while trailing blanks (to the right of the digit) are considered zeroes. Input of several six-position fields with an I6 specification produces the internal values shown in Table 8.1.

TABLE 8.1

Input Data	Internal Value Assigned
bbb645	645
bb645b	6450
bb–645	–645
b–b645	–645
645bbb	645000

When an I specification is used for output, the value printed is right-justified in the field, and a minus sign is printed if the value is negative. If the value of the field to be printed is too large to fit in the specified field, asterisks are printed instead of the digits. To correct this error, it is necessary to alter the format specification and rerun the program. Output of the several internal values with an I4-format specification produces the results shown in Table 8.2.

TABLE 8.2

Internal Value	Characters Printed
863	b863
–863	–863
–8634	****
7	bbb7
75698	****
0	bbb0

F Format

The F-format item is used to describe fields of real data. Its form is F$w.d$ where w indicates the total number of positions in the field and d indicates the number of positions to the right of the decimal point. On input, the decimal point need not be punched; if it is omitted, the decimal point is assumed to be d positions from the right-hand side of the field. If the decimal point is punched, it overrides the FORMAT specification. Input of some six-position fields with an F6.2 specification produces the internal values shown in Table 8.3.

TABLE 8.3

Input Data	Internal Value Assigned
b25.63	25.63
bb2563	25.63
25.63b	25.63
2563bb	2563.00
–b2563	–25.63

On output, the value printed is right-justified in the w position field. Exactly d positions appear to the right of the decimal point, which is always printed on output. (The lower-order digit is rounded off before printing.) If the value to be printed is negative, a minus sign occupies the leading position; if it is positive, no sign is necessary. If the field is too small to contain the value, all positions are filled with asterisks, as is the case with the I specification. Writing internal real values with an F7.3 format item produces printed results like those shown in Table 8.4.

TABLE 8.4

Internal Value	Characters Printed
56.832	b56.832
56.8327	b56.833
.7	bb0.700
–78.	–78.000
–786.6	*******
786.6	786.600
6497.65	*******
.00004	bb0.000

Since the output field must always contain a decimal point, w must be at least one larger than d.

X Format

The X-format item is used to skip positions on input and to insert blanks on output. The X-format item differs from all other format items in that the width of the field is placed *before* the X. On input, the X-format item is used to skip over unwanted data items or over unused positions. For example, if a data card contains two I6 fields followed by an F7.2 field, the second integer field could be skipped if the card is read as

```
    READ(5,101) KVAL,TEST
101 FORMAT(I6,6X,F7.2)
```

On output, the X-format item is used to position output fields in order to make them easier to read. To print two columns of integer data separated by five spaces one can write

```
    WRITE(6,102) IVAL,JVAL
102 FORMAT(' ',I7,5X,I4)
```

Note the use of the carriage control character.

H Format and Literal Output

The H(Hollerith)[1] format item is used for printing strings of characters, called *literals*. The string of characters to be printed follows the H; the length of the string precedes the H. Thus, the general form of the H specification is wHxxx . . . xx. The following examples demonstrate the use of Hollerith fields:

```
5HHELLO
1H1
26HTHE QUICK BROWN FOX JUMPED
5H TEST
5H1TEST
17H THE VALUE OF X =
```

Care must be taken to ensure that the literal string is the right length. To guard against the possibility of error, many FORTRAN compilers (including WATFOR/WATFIV) allow the literal string to be enclosed in apostrophes. When this form is used, the wH is omitted. Using this form, the items above would be specified as follows:

---

[1] This item is named in honor of Herman Hollerith, the inventor of the punch card.

```
'HELLO'
'1'
'THE QUICK BROWN FOX JUMPED'
' TEST'
'1TEST'
' THE VALUE OF X ='
```

This form of the Hollerith specification has been used in previous chapters to insert carriage control characters in the output line. If it is necessary to print a single apostrophe, two single apostrophes are used. The following are equivalent:

```
5HDON'T        'DON''T'
```

Note that two single apostrophes (' '), not the double quote ("), are used.

Data that contains both literals and numerical values is called *alphanumeric*. We shall return to it later in the chapter.

Carriage Control

Literal data are often used to specify the carriage control character that appears at the beginning of every line to be printed. The carriage control character specifies line spacing and page control. The following codes are used:

'1' Skip to the top of a new page before printing.
'0' Skip two lines (leaving one blank line) before printing.
' ' Skip to the next line before printing.
'+' Print on the same line as the previous PRINT statement.

Carriage control information may be combined with characters to be printed:

```
    WRITE(6,101) X
101 FORMAT('1THE VALUE OF THE VARIABLE X IS ', F6.2)
```

This produces the following output on the top of a new page (assuming X had a value of 13.31):

```
THE VALUE OF THE VARIABLE IS   13.31
```

Note that there are two blanks between IS and the value; one blank was included in the literal string, the other resulted because the leading position of the F6.2 field was not needed.

E Format

The F-format item is used to print real data, but it is not recommended when the magnitude of the values becomes very large (for example, 78000000000000.0) or very small (for example, 0.000000000000000000034). In these cases, the E-format item should be used for input and output of real values expressed in power-of-ten notation (for example, 0.78E14 or 0.34E–19). Although some compilers will permit an F-specification wider than 8, it is not a good practice on the IBM 360/370 series and similar computers. This is because the IBM 360/370 can only retain about seven or eight digits. For example, consider the following statement:

```
A = 50000.*500000.
```

The result (mathematically, 25 billion) is stored as $.2500000 \times 10^{11}$, that is, .2500000E 11. Only seven digits are kept. The statement

```
A = (50000. * 500000.) + 1.
```

will also result in .2500000E 11, *not* 25000000001. Again only the seven most significant digits are kept.[2]

The E-format item appears as E*w.d,* where *w* is the total length of the field and *d* is the number of digits to the *right* of the decimal point. The value of *w* must be large enough to contain the exponent (which requires four places), the decimal point, the leading zero and the sign (if needed).

$$
\overset{\displaystyle w}{\overbrace{\pm 0.\underbrace{xxxxxx}_{\displaystyle d}E\pm xx}}
$$

This format item is somewhat tricky to use and there is much room for error. The examples in Table 8.5 may help to clarify how it works.

TABLE 8.5

Value	E Notation	E-Format Item
4500.0	0.45E 04	E9.2
–4500.0	-0.45E 04	E9.2
7681070000.	0.768107E 10	E13.6
7681070000.	0.76811E 10	E12.5
–0.000675	-0.675E–03	E10.3
0.0000	0.0000E 00	E11.4
–1.0000	-0.10000E 01	E12.5

---

[2] The number of digits which can be kept is dependent upon the specific computer. The manufacturer's manual will contain details.

If the decimal point is omitted on input, it will be inserted so that d digits appear to the right of the decimal point. In addition, the leading zero and the blank in the exponent may be eliminated on input. An example of output would be

```
      TOSUN = 93.0E6
      WRITE(6,101) TOSUN,TOSUN
  101 FORMAT('0', E9.2, E15.3)
```

This prints the distance to the sun in miles in two formats:

b0.93E 08bbbbbb0.930E 08

The d specification should not be longer than the number of decimal digits of accuracy that the computer can provide. For the IBM 360/370 series, d should never be greater than 7.

G Format

The G-format item (G stands for General) is a special designation which may be used in place of I-, F-, or E-format designations. This format is not available on all compilers. The form of the value is determined by the type of variable in the input/output list and by the magnitude of the value. The G-format item is specified as $Gw.d$ where w is total width and d is the number of places to the right of the decimal point. For integer values, the d is ignored and Gw functions precisely as if Iw had been specified. For real values, the input may be in either E or F form and, on output, E or F form is selected, depending on the value's magnitude. If the value to be printed is in the range $0.1 \leqslant n \leqslant 10^d$, then the value is printed as if the format had been $Fw.d$; otherwise, the value is printed as if the format had been $Ew.d$. Again, care must be taken to ensure that the total field width w is sufficiently large to accomodate the value and the exponent.

T Format

The T-format item is used to *tabulate* (move the printing over) to the next field of data to be printed. Its form is Tw, where w indicates the actual column or print position desired. (The tabulation may be toward either the right or the left.) Thus, if an input deck of cards contains a three-digit integer field in columns 11–13 and an F5.2 field in columns 30–34, this card might be read as

```
      READ(5,101) IFIELD,FFIELD
  101 FORMAT(T11,I3,T30,F5.2)
```

This system is often simpler than using an X field. An equivalent format would be (10X,I3, 15X,F5.2). The T-format item eliminates the need to count columns. Since the T format allows tabulation either left or right, fields may be read in a different order from that punched on the data card:

```
     READ(5,102) FFIELD, IFIELD
102 FORMAT(T30,F5.2, T11, I3)
```

It is even possible to read a single item of data twice, possibly by using two different format item specifications. For example, a three-digit integer field could be read as a single value and then each digit could be read individually into three integer locations:

```
     READ(5,103) IFIELD, N1, N2, N3
103 FORMAT(T11, I3, T11, I1, I1, I1)
```

On output, the T-format item specifies in which print position the next field is to be printed. This control is useful for creating neat columnar output as well as for placing data in precise positions for elegant output, without having to use the X-format item. Column one of the page is located at T2 because of the carriage control character.

Problem 8.1

Write a program to calculate the square of the numbers from 1 to 25. Print the number in columns 19–20 and the square in columns 50–54.

A Format

It is sometimes desirable to read input as *characters*. For example, one could read two names from a data card and compare them to see if they are the same. In order to read data as characters, an A-format specification is used.

A variable that is to contain character (or literal) data may be of integer or real mode. Each variable may contain up to four characters[3]:

A	B	C	D

These characters, however, are always processed as a unit. For example, two four-letter names may be read by the following program fragment:

```
     READ(5,101) CHARS1,CHARS2
101 FORMAT(A4,A4)
```

If the data card contained

BILLJOE

---

[3] The four-character limitation is for the IBM 360/370 computers. Check the manufacturer's manual for the limitation on your local machine. In chapter 10, we will discuss REAL *8 variables which may contain up to eight characters.

the variable CHARS1 would contain the letters | B | I | L | L | and the variable CHARS2 would contain the letters | J | O | E | | . Note that the blank is treated as a character in A format and occupies one position.

TABLE 8.6

FORMAT ITEMS

Format Item	Form	Use
I	Iw	On input the next w columns of data are assigned to the corresponding integer variable in the READ statement. On output, up to w digits are printed or, if the value is negative, a minue sign and up to w–1 digits are printed.
F	Fw.d	On input the next w columns are assigned to the corresponding REAL variable. If a decimal point is not punched, it is assumed to be in front of the dth digit from the right. On output, up to w–1 digits are printed w d digits after the decimal point. A minus sign, if needed, occupies one position.
X	wX	On input, this item skips w columns. On output, this item causes w blanks to be inserted.
H	nH ...	The n characters following the H or the characters between the quotes are printed.
E	Ew.d	On input this specification operates exactly as the F item. Input data may contain an E exponent. On output, an optional sign, (if neg) a leading zero (if there is room), a decimal point followed by d digits and a four digit E exponent is printed.
G	Gw.d or Gw	If the variable in the list is integer, the format Gw [or Gw.d] is treated as if it were Iw. If the variable is real the specification Gw.d (the d must be specified) operates as if it were Fw.d or Ew.d. On output, a value in the range of $0.1 \leq n \leq 10^d$ is printed without an exponent. Otherwise a four position exponent is printed.
T	Tw	This item will skip to position w to obtain (input) or put (output) the next item. On a printed page, a specification of w will cause the next item to begin in position w–1.
A	Aw	On input the next w columns of data are assigned to the corresponding variable as alphanumeric characters. On output, w characters are printed.

Data which have been read with an A-format item can also be printed with an A-format item. Since most versions of FORTRAN do not have special variables for storing literal data, real or integer variable locations may be used. To read a four-digit word such as

WORD

the following READ and FORMAT statements would be used:

```
    READ(5,101) LITERL
101 FORMAT(A4)
```

To write out the word "WORD," we would use

```
    WRITE(6,102) LITERL
102 FORMAT('1THIS IS THE WORD - ', A4)
```

In this case, the output on the top of a new page would be

```
        THIS IS THE WORD - WORD
```

Of course, not all literal data are of length 4, as in this case. A1, A2 and A3 fields may be used as well. If data are read with a field smaller than A4, the rightmost positions of the variable are filled with blanks.

If more than four characters are to be read or printed, several variables must be used. For example, to read the name

```
        GEORGE WASHINGTON
```

five separate variables must be used:

```
    READ(5,103)NAME1,NAME2,NAME3,NAME4,NAME5
103 FORMAT(A4,A4,A4,A4,A4)
```

Problem 8.2

Write a program fragment to read a card containing characters and print the data centered at the top of a page as a heading.

So far, we have dealt with eight formats. Table 8.6 sums and compares them.

Repetition Factors

As the previous example illustrates, it is sometimes necessary to repeat a format item several times. A shorthand form exists which simplifies such constructions. In this case, the format can be abbreviated to read

```
103 FORMAT(5A4)
```

The same technique can be applied to all format items except H-format and X-format items. If three I5 fields are to be read, followed by two F6.3 fields, the READ and FORMAT statements might be written as

```
    READ(5,104) IVAL,NCOUNT,NK, RF3,TOTAL
104 FORMAT(3I5,2F6.3)
```

This natural shorthand conveniently solves the tedious problem of specifying formats when many data values of the same form are to be read or written.

Problem 8.3

Simplify each of the following FORMAT statements wherever possible by using repetition factors.

```
(I3,I3,I3)
(F4.3,F5.4,F4.3)
(F10.2,A4,A4,A3,I2,F6.2,F6.2)
(I1,I1,F2.1,E12.6,E12.6)
```

Group-Format Specifications

If a group of format specifications occurs more than once, the entire group may be repeated by enclosing it in parentheses and prefixing the number of repetitions. For example, a data card may contain an I3 field followed by an F6.2 field, repeating three times across the card. The data might look like this:

$$b12b34.54b66bb3.01b99b87.62$$

The unabbreviated READ and FORMAT statements might be written as

```
    READ(5,105) N1,RA,N2,RB,N3,RC
105 FORMAT(I3,F6.2,I3,F6.2,I3,F6.2)
```

but the format can be abbreviated as

```
105 FORMAT( 3(I3,F6.2))
```

To print six I4 fields with three spaces between each of the fields, the following format might be used:

```
107 FORMAT(' OTHER VALUES ARE ',  6(I4, 3X) )
```

Several group-format specifications may be used in a single FORMAT statement:

```
108 FORMAT(' RAW DATA ', 6(F6.1,2X), ' VALUES ', 6(I4,2X) )
```

but, in most implementations of FORTRAN (including WATFOR/WATFIV and IBM 360/370 FORTRAN), group-format items can only be nested to a depth of two:

```
109 FORMAT('1OUTPUT ', 3(F6.2,3X, 2(I2,I4)) )
```

Slash Character

When data items appear on more than one data card, the information can be read in using as many READ and FORMAT statements as there are cards. For example, the data cards

```
   789

85.3
```

can be read by the following two sets of statements:

```
      READ(5,110) RDATA
110   FORMAT(F4.1)
      READ(5,111) IDATA
111   FORMAT(I3)
```

It is more convenient to indicate within a single FORMAT statement that the next data card is to be read in. This function is performed by use of the slash (/) character. When the slash is encountered in a FORMAT statement, a new card is read—even if the present card contains further information. The above example can be rewritten as

```
      READ(5,112) RDATA, IDATA
112 FORMAT(F4.1 / I3)
```

With this technique, data from several cards may be read using a single FORMAT statement.

On output, the slash character can be used to indicate that the next item is to be placed on a new line. When the slash is used to skip to a new line, a new carriage control character must be issued. For example, consider this program fragment:

```
      WRITE(6,113) NPAGE
  113 FORMAT('1PAGE ', I3/ '0THIS IS A HEADING')
```

The first carriage control character causes printing on a new page, the slash causes the printer to skip to a new line, and the carriage control character '0' causes double spacing, leaving a single blank line between the two lines of output

```
              PAGE   17
              THIS  IS  A  HEADING
```

By placing several slashes in a row, it is possible to leave blank lines between lines of printed output. The rule is that n slashes leave $n-1$ blank lines. The statements

```
      WRITE(6,114)
  114 FORMAT('1HELLO'////' GOODBYE')
```

cause three blank lines to be left between the messages.

Implied DO Loops

Although the complete array input/output technique discussed in Chapter 7 is simple, an entire array must always be read or written. In addition, the order of input and output for multidimensional arrays is fixed. The implied DO loop overcomes these limitations by "embedding" a DO loop within the input/output list itself. For example, in order to print the contents of all of the twenty locations in an array called TOTAL we can use an implied DO:

```
      DIMENSION TOTAL(20)
      WRITE(6,101) (TOTAL(I), I = 1,20)
                                  implied DO
  101 FORMAT(' ', 20F6.2)
```

This is equivalent to

```
WRITE(6,101) TOTAL
```

With the implied DO loop it is possible to specify that only the first ten elements of the array are to be written:

```
WRITE(6,102) (TOTAL(I), I = 1,10)
```

or that the first four elements are to be written:

```
WRITE(6,103) (TOTAL(I), I = 1,4)
```

Similarly, the DO loop's flexibility makes it possible to specify that the last ten elements of the array are to be printed:

```
WRITE(6,104) (TOTAL(K), K = 11,20)
```

It can also specify even-numbered locations:

```
WRITE(6,105) (TOTAL(IEVEN), IEVEN = 2,20,2)
```

or the first N locations of the array:

```
WRITE(6,106) (TOTAL(I), I = 1,N)
```

(assuming that N has been set earlier).

The form of the implied DO is similar to the DO:

$$(array\ (\ index\ ),\ index = m1,m2,m3)$$

where

array is an array of declared dimensions;

index is an unsubscripted integer variable;

$m1$ is an unsubscripted integer variable or constant representing the initial value;

$m2$ is an unsubscripted integer variable or constant representing the final value; ·

$m3$ is an unsubscripted integer variable or constant representing the increment (optional).

The accompanying format statement must match the data that are being processed.

A single implied DO loop can process more than one array. Thus, if arrays A, B, and C are to be printed out in parallel, that is, A(1), B(1), C(1),A(2),B(2),C(2),A(3),B(3),C(3), . . . then the statement would be

```
WRITE(6,107) (A(I),B(I),C(I), I = 1,10)
```

In fact, any list of variables may precede the implied DO loop. The general form is

$$(list,\ index = m1,m2,m3)$$

This form is allowed where list is any list of variable names with or without subscripts and index, $m1,m2$, and $m3$ are as above.

One useful application of the generalized form allows the index variable to be printed along with the array location:

```
WRITE(6,108) (I,A(I), I = 1,15)
108 FORMAT(15(' POSITION ', I3, ' CONTAINS ', F6.3/))
```

Several implied DO loops may appear as part of an input/output list:

```
WRITE(6,109) (A(I), I = 1,N), (B(I), I = 1,N)
```

This statement causes the first N locations of the A array to be printed preceding the first N locations of the B array.

The same techniques apply to input as well. An entire array or just a portion of an array may be read using the implied DO loop. WATFOR/WATFIV users may use the implied DO loop as a component of an input/output list for format-free READ and PRINT statements:

```
READ,X,Y,(A(K), K = 1,18),(B(K), K = 1 ,18)
PRINT,(TEST(I),RESULT(I), I = 1,N), TOTAL
```

A more complex case arises when dealing with multidimensional arrays. Implied DO loops can be nested for more flexible control of the processing of the rows and columns in a two-dimensional array than was possible with the complete array technique. The data may be displayed row by row. To print a three-row, five-column array of integers, we might write

```
      DIMENSION NCELL(3,5)
      WRITE(6,110) ((NCELL(I,J), J = 1,5), I = 1,3)
110 FORMAT( 3( ' ', 5I4/) )
```

These instructions could produce the following result:

```
67   78   56   70   56
45   16    9    4   77
83   74   47   88   16
```

In the case of nested implied DO loops, the inner loop (that is, the loop with index J) is enclosed in the outer loop (the loop with index I). Thus I is set to one and J goes from one to five. Then I is set to two and J goes from one to five. Finally, I is set to three and J goes from one to five. The sequence of values printed is

```
NCELL(1,1)
NCELL(1,2)
NCELL(1,3)
NCELL(1,4)
NCELL(1,5)
NCELL(2,1)
NCELL(2,2)
NCELL(2,3)
NCELL(2,4)
NCELL(2,5)
NCELL(3,1)
NCELL(3,2)
NCELL(3,3)
NCELL(3,4)
NCELL(3,5)
```

Several arrays may be processed with nested implied DO loops. The following syntax can be used if the first row of two different arrays has been punched on a single card, while the second, third and fourth rows follow:

```
DIMENSION APPLES(4,3), PEARS(4,6)
  READ(5,111) ( (APPLES(I,J), J = 1,3), (PEARS(I,J),J = 1,6),
1                    I = 1,4)
```

Three-dimensional arrays require even more delicate handling:

```
DIMENSION X(3,4,5)
READ(5,112) (((X(I,J,K), K = 1,5), J = 1,4), I = 1,3)
```

Problem 8.4

Write implied DO and FORMAT statements to print an 8 x 20 array in row order.

Reuse of FORMAT statements

In all examples used so far, the number of elements in the input/output list of a READ or WRITE statement has corresponded with the number of elements in the FORMAT statement. This makes good sense and it is a good way to write programs. However, since the number of elements processed is determined by the number of items in the input/output list (and *not* by the number of elements in the format statement), it may be necessary to reuse all or part of the format list. When the input/output list is shorter than the format list, a portion of the format list remains unused.

The ability to reuse a format statement can be helpful when the exact number of items in the input/output list is not known. Consider the case of the WRITE statement for the arrays X and Y which contain N elements:

```
    WRITE(6,101) (I,X(I),Y(I), I = 1,N)
101 FORMAT( ' ', I3, 3X, 2F12.2)
```

The first time through the implied DO loop, I (equal to 1), X(1) and Y(1) are sent to the printer according to the FORMAT statement 101. At this point, the entire FORMAT statement has been scanned once. Still, there are additional values to be printed. At the end of the FORMAT statement (indicated by the right parenthesis), a command is sent to the printer to skip to a new line and the FORMAT statement is rescanned, starting with the carriage control character. On input, a new card is read when the end of the FORMAT statement is reached.

If a group of format items is repeated by use of a repetition specification:

```
FORMAT (F5.2, 4(F4.3, 1X))
```

and items remain in the input/output list, control returns to the last repeat item. This item is repeated until the list is exhausted. Thus, the statement above would be processed as if it had been written

```
F5.2, 4(F4.3,1X)/4(F4.3,1X)/...
```

More about Alphanumeric Data

Characters can be read and written in groups of four by the use of an A4-format item. But it is often useful to read or write characters one at a time, using A1-format items. A student grade report might be based on the following scheme:

Grade	Average
A	Over 90.0
B	Over 80.0
C	Over 70.0
F	70.0 or less

The four grades could be entered on a data card in columns 1 to 4 and read as

```
    DIMENSION NGRADE(4)        ABCF
    READ(5,101) NGRADE
101 FORMAT(4A1)
```

After calculating the average, the grade can be assigned by

```
NFINAL = NGRADE(4)
IF(AVERAG .GT. 70.0) NFINAL = NGRADE(3)
IF(AVERAG .GT. 80.0) NFINAL = NGRADE(2)
IF(AVERAG .GT. 90.0) NFINAL = NGRADE(1)
```

and the result would be printed as

```
    WRITE(6,102) NFINAL
102 FORMAT('0THE FINAL GRADE IS ', A1)
```

In this program, character data assigned to a location are used in assignment statements—care should be taken to see that mixed mode assignment statements are not used.

The equality of two locations containing characters may also be tested. If an input data card contains a letter grade for a student, the grade can be determined by comparing it to each of the stored letter grades:

```
    READ(5,103) IGRADE
103 FORMAT(A1)
    DO 40 I = 1,4
    IF(IGRADE .EQ. NGRADE(I)) GO TO 50
```

```
 40 CONTINUE
        .
        .
        .
 50
```

If mixed mode is used inadvertently:

```
(GRADE .EQ. NGRADE)
```

the statement will not work as desired. To avoid possible errors, it is good practice to decide which mode will be used—REAL or INTEGER variables—for character data and use only that mode. In WATFOR/WATFIV, a special CHARACTER mode is available. Its use will be discussed in a later chapter.

Using these techniques, one can write a program to read and print a set of data cards containing this letter:

```
****
DEAR FRIENDS:
        I HOPE THAT YOU WILL EXCUSE THE USE OF A COMPUTER-
WRITTEN FORM LETTER BUT IT WAS THE SIMPLEST WAY TO LET YOU
ALL KNOW WE HAVE MOVED AND ARE NOW LIVING AT THE FOLLOWING
ADDRESS:


                MR. AND MS. JACK SMITH
                43 WEST SOUTH STREET
                BLOOMINGTON, INDIANA 47401


DROP BY WHEN YOU HAVE THE CHANCE.
****
```

The four asterisks serve as delimiters for the letter.

The letter could be read and written out by the following program, employing the complete array technique for specifying an entire array:

```
        DIMENSION LINE(20)
C
C       READ LEADING ASTERISKS
C
        READ(5,101) NASTER
    101 FORMAT(A4)
C
C          SKIP TO THE TOP OF NEXT PAGE
        WRITE(6,102)
    102 FORMAT('1')
C          READ AND PRINT LETTER, TESTING FOR TERMINATING
C          ASTERISKS
C
     10 READ(5,103) LINE
    103 FORMAT(20A4)
        IF(LINE(1) .EQ. NASTER) GO TO 20
        WRITE(6,104) LINE
```

```
104 FORMAT( ' ', 20A4)
    GO TO 10
 20 STOP
    END
```

Notice that an IF statement was used to compare four-character fields for equality in order to determine if the letter was complete. This program produces a single copy of the input letter. To produce multiple copies it would be necessary to store the letter in a two-dimensional array where each row of the array contained a single line of the letter.

The technique for reading and writing a letter can also be used to produce a form of "computer art." By punching specified characters in the correct positions on input data cards and then listing the cards, graphic printouts can be obtained. Examples may be found scattered throughout the text. As an aid to the keypunching task, it might be helpful to print out a sheet containing fifty lines where each line contains 80 X's. The drawing may be made on this worksheet and the proper data cards can then be more easily prepared. With a little thought you should be able to figure out how to use two data cards to describe the printout for a full printer line of 132 characters.

Another form of graphic output is a plot of a mathematical function. Although there are many sophisticated ways to print a graph we will show one of the simplest and crudest. Figure 8.1 gives the program, the worksheet, and the output for a simple sine curve.

```
C
C            PROGRAM TO PRINT A SIMPLE GRAPH
C
      DIMENSION LINE(100)
C            INPUT CHARACTERS ASTERISK AND BLANK
C
      READ (5,101) NASTER,NBLANK
  101 FORMAT(2A1)
C            BLANK OUT LINE
C
      DO 10 I = 1,100
      LINE(I) = NBLANK
   10 CONTINUE
C
C            PRODUCE GRAPH
C
      WRITE(6,102)
  102 FORMAT('1  GRAPH PROGRAM')
      DO 20 I = 1,50
      X = FLOAT(I)/4.0
      Y = 30.0*SIN(X)  + 50.0
      J = IFIX(Y)
      LINE(J) = NASTER
      WRITE(6,103) X,Y,LINE
  103 FORMAT(' X =', F6.2, ' Y =',F7.3,'  I', 100A1)
      LINE(J) = NBLANK
   20 CONTINUE
      STOP
      END
```

Figure 8.1

```
GRAPH PROGRAM
X =  0.25  Y = 57.422   I
X =  0.50  Y = 64.383   I
X =  0.75  Y = 70.449   I
X =  1.00  Y = 75.244   I
X =  1.25  Y = 78.470   I
X =  1.50  Y = 79.925   I
X =  1.75  Y = 79.520   I
X =  2.00  Y = 77.279   I
X =  2.25  Y = 73.342   I
X =  2.50  Y = 67.954   I
X =  2.75  Y = 61.450   I
X =  3.00  Y = 54.234   I
X =  3.25  Y = 46.754   I
X =  3.50  Y = 39.477   I
X =  3.75  Y = 32.853   I
X =  4.00  Y = 27.296   I
X =  4.25  Y = 23.150   I
X =  4.50  Y = 20.674   I
X =  4.75  Y = 20.021   I
X =  5.00  Y = 21.232   I
X =  5.25  Y = 24.232   I
X =  5.50  Y = 28.834   I
X =  5.75  Y = 34.752   I
X =  6.00  Y = 41.618   I
X =  6.25  Y = 49.005   I
X =  6.50  Y = 56.454   I
X =  6.75  Y = 63.501   I
X =  7.00  Y = 69.710   I
X =  7.25  Y = 74.692   I
X =  7.50  Y = 78.140   I
X =  7.75  Y = 79.838   I
X =  8.00  Y = 79.681   I
X =  8.25  Y = 77.678   I
X =  8.50  Y = 73.955   I
X =  8.75  Y = 68.742   I
X =  9.00  Y = 62.364   I
X =  9.25  Y = 55.217   I
X =  9.50  Y = 47.745   I
X =  9.75  Y = 40.414   I
X = 10.00  Y = 33.679   I
X = 10.25  Y = 27.959   I
X = 10.50  Y = 23.609   I
X = 10.75  Y = 20.900   I
X = 11.00  Y = 20.000   I
X = 11.25  Y = 20.966   I
X = 11.50  Y = 23.736   I
X = 11.75  Y = 28.140   I
X = 12.00  Y = 33.903   I
X = 12.25  Y = 40.666   I
X = 12.50  Y = 48.010   I
```

Figure 8.1 (continued)

Execution-Time Format Statements

The FORMAT statement can be considered restricting because it must be defined at the time that the program is written. It may sometimes be desirable to alter formats during execution of a program. If three sets of four data cards have been prepared by different research groups, the program to process the data would have to be run three separate times with three separate format statements if different input formats have been used. Execution-time formats can make life far more simple for the programmer. Before the data are read in, a single card describing the format of the input is read in. It is used to perform the input. Thus, the data might appear as

```
(3F4.1)
 4.1  5.3  4.5
 5.2  5.3  6.0
 4.4  2.2  2.0
 0.0  0.3  9.1
```

```
(3F7.2)
    4.66     4.56     3.67
    3.54     9.78     5.09
    6.22     7.67     4.09
    0.88     7.67     1.48
(F4.1,2F6.2)
  5.6   7.66   7.54
  3.5   8.78   8.21
  5.1   3.89   0.23
  0.1   7.23   1.77
```

The format is read into an array under A-format control and then the array is referred to in the program as the source of the format statement:

```
        DIMENSION FMTX(20), A(4), B(4), C(4)
C
C           LOOP CONTROL FOR SETS OF DATA
C
        DO 70 IDATA = 1,3
C
C           READ IN THE FORMAT
C
        READ(5,101) FMTX
  101 FORMAT(20A4)
C
C           NOW READ IN THE DATA ACCORDING TO FMTX
C
        READ(5,FMTX) (A(I),B(I),C(I), I = 1,4)
C
C           PROCESS THE DATA
C
          .
          .
          .
   70 CONTINUE
```

This case demonstrates the reuse of a FORMAT statement.

The clever programmer can discover numerous ways to make use of the execution-time format technique. By reading in or altering parts of the format statement, the program itself can be made to select or modify the format statement that is used. Furthermore, through calculations performed during execution, a format statement may be created to suit the needs of the data that is generated.

Summary

The complexity and variety of the operations that are permitted when performing input and output operations is staggering. The number of possibilities is limited only by the skill and imagination of the programmer. Unfortunately, there is no shortcut to learning the techniques and, as usual, experience is the best teacher. This chapter reviewed the integer(I), floating point(F), skip(X), and Hollerith(H) format items. It covered the exponential notation(E), general(G), tab(T), and character(A) format items in their general form. It covered the slash character for terminating a line within a format list and presented the techniques for specifying repetition within a format list (repetition factors, group-format specification and reuse) and repetition within an input/output list (complete array, implied DO loops). Finally, the use of execution-time formats to provide greater generality was explained in its most basic form. The skilled programmer knows not only how to use each of these techniques, but also how to combine them to produce the most lucid and efficient program.

DEBUGGING CLINIC

Because the rules for input and output processing are so complex, they provide many opportunities for error. No other component of programming is as difficult and intricate as the writing of READ, WRITE, and FORMAT statements.

As a first step, check to see that the number of elements in the input/output list of the READ or WRITE statement matches the number of elements in the FORMAT list. Be sure to account for complete array or implied DO loop specifications in the input/output list. In the FORMAT list, check the repetition factors, group-format items and possible reuse of FORMAT statements.

As items are counted, make sure that integer variables are specified by I- or A-format items and that real variables are specified by F-, E-, or A-format items. Alphameric data should be described by A-format items. If H format is being used for output of literal data, make sure that the count preceding the H matches the length of the literal data. A carriage control character must be specified for each line of printed information. If a carriage control character is omitted the first character of the line will be stripped off and used. After a slash character or a group of slashes in a FORMAT list a carriage control character must be specified.

When using the complete array or the implied DO loop technique, the number of items in the format list must correspond to the length of the array. For two-dimensional arrays, double-check to ensure that the input data are in the order specified by the input/output list.

Within a format list, each item must be separated from the others by commas. When using the apostrophe notation for literal data, make sure that apostrophes are matched. Consider this violation:

```
101 FORMAT('1', F6.2,'TEST DATA, I5,3X,I5)
```

Since there is no matching apostrophe on the right, the rest of the statement is considered as literal data and at least one error message will be produced.

REVIEW QUESTIONS

1. How are the format codes I, F, X, H, E, A, G, and T used? How are slashes, group repeat, and repitition factors used?

2. What is an implied DO loop? How is it coded? How are implied DO loops nested?

3. How is "execution time" format used?

4. What are the limitations on the length specifications of A-format items. Why is it necessary to be careful in assigning or comparing characters in mixed-mode expressions?

EXERCISES

1. Create READ and FORMAT statements for each of the following input descriptions.

   a. bbbXXXbbbXX.XX

      K   X

   b. XXbbXXbbXXbbXXbb

      N(1) N(2) N(3) N(4)

   c. XXX.XXbbXXXXXX.XbbbbX.XXXXbbXXXX

      SOUP   VEGE   TABLE   MEAT

   d. XXXXXXXXXXXX

      NEGGS(1)...NEGGS(12)

   e. bXX.XbXX.XbXX.XbXX.X

      bXX.XbXX.XbXX.XbXX.X   TABLE (4,4)

      bXX.XbXX.XbXX.XbXX.X

      bXX.XbXX.XbXX.XbXX.X

2. Create WRITE and FORMAT statements to print data for each of the descriptions in exercise 1.

3. Show what output would be produced by each of the following program fragments. Use 'b's to indicate blanks.

   a.
   ```
         ALPHA = 78.346
         BETA = 88643.14
         GAMMA = 1.00
         WRITE(6,101) ALPHA, BETA, GAMMA
   101 FORMAT('1', 3F10.2)
   ```

   b.
   ```
         DIMENSION A(6), B(6)
         DO 10 I = 1,4
         A(I) = FLOAT(I)
         B(I) = 2.0 *A(I)
    10 CONTINUE
         WRITE(6,102) (A(I),B(I), I = 1,4)
   102 FORMAT('1', 4(2F6.1/' ') )
   ```

```
c.      I = 483421
        WRITE(6,103) I,I,I
    103 FORMAT ('0TEST', I7, I10, 3X, I6)
d.      FLAKE = 84.57346
        WRITE(6,104) FLAKE, FLAKE, FLAKE
    104 FORMAT(' DEMONSTRATION- ', F10.5, '/', F8.3, '/', F6.5)
e.      PLANE = 707.747
        WRITE(6,105) PLANE, PLANE, PLANE
    105 FORMAT(' AIR ', F8.3, T20, E12.5, T35, E10.6)
```

PROGRAMMING EXERCISES

4. a. Write a program to read in a string of up to 15 characters which represent a number in Roman numeral form; for example:

MCLXII	1162
LXXIV	74
MMDCCLXVIII	2768
CIX	109

The character values are

M	1000
D	500
C	100
L	50
X	10
V	5
I	1

Print the Roman numeral form and then convert to standard integer form (Arabic numbers) and print the result.

b. Write a program to convert a read-in integer quantity to a Roman numeral quantity and print the result.

5. *Psychology.* Data cards with names of length 28 and IQ scores (three-digit integers) have been prepared. Read and store the names and IQ scores. Sort the IQ scores with the names and produce a listing with names and IQ scores in descending order. Print meaningful headings.

6. *Graphics—Snowflake designs.* It is possible to produce elegant designs similar to snowflake or kaleidoscopic patterns by a simple mathematical trick.

Use a random number generator to produce an *x* and a *y* value in the range 0 to 25. Declare an array to be 50 by 50 and fill all the locations with character blanks. Then, assuming that the center of the array is the origin, make the proper translation to fill the following locations with asterisks.

(x,y)	*(x,-y)*
(y,x)	*(-y,x)*
(-x,y)	*(-x,-y)*
(y,-x)	*(-y,-x)*

Repeat this process 15 times. Finally, print the array, centered on a fresh sheet of output.

7. Print a neat table of values with $i, i^2, i^3, \sqrt{i},$ and $\sqrt[3]{i},$ where i ranges from 1 to 200. Print 50 values per page and begin each page with a neat heading line and page number.

8. *The Printer Turtle*. (Mitchell Wand). Imagine a "turtle" under computer control. The turtle can walk forward and turn under the control of the computer. The turtle carries (in his tail) a pen which he lifts or drops, again under program control. (Such devices have actually been constructed for use in teaching programming in elementary schools.) Imagine the turtle is crawling around a page on the line printer. Your program should take a series of commands, like

```
PENDOWN
FORWARD 10
RIGHT
FORWARD 10
RIGHT
FORWARD 10
RIGHT
FORWARD 10
PENUP
STOP
```

and produce the right thing: in this case, a square.

You should include at least the following commands: FORWARD, RIGHT, LEFT, PENUP, PENDOWN, STOP, and NEWPAGE. You may make any conventions you like, or modify the syntax of these commands if you prefer.

9. *Pattern Matching* (Mitchell Wand). Write a program which accepts two strings of characters, one called "STRING" and one called "PATTERN" and find every occurrence of PATTERN in STRING. For example, if

> STRING   is   AABCAAADA
> PATTERN   is   AA

there are occurrences of PATTERN at positions 1, 5, and 6 in STRING, as follows:

> Position   1 2 3 4 5 6 7 8 9
> STRING   AABCAAADA
> $\Big\{$ AA
> Occurrences of PATTERN   AA
>   AA

Follow these specifications:

- Your input will be pairs of cards consisting of the STRING followed by the PATTERN. You should read them into 80-place arrays, using 80A1 format

- The STRING will consist of everything on the first card; the PATTERN will consist of everything on the second card, starting with column one, up to but not including the first blank. So STRING is always 80 characters long, but PATTERN may be (and usually will be) shorter.

- Your output should include the STRING, the PATTERN, and the locations at which the PATTERN appears in the STRING.

- A blank in column 1 of STRING signifies end of file. Thus, there will always be an *odd* number of data cards.

ADVANCED EXERCISES

10. *Random English* (Mitchell Wand). Consider the following grammar for a subset of English:

SENT→NP VP	SENT stands for Sentence
NP→N	NP stands for Noun Phrase
NP→the N	VP stands for Verb Phrase
NP→a N	N stands for Noun
N→boy, girl, John, dog	
VP→sees, runs, cried	

One can apply these rules to get sentences, such as SENT→NP VP→the N VP→the boy NP→the boy cries. This scheme is called a "phrase-structure grammar"; the partial sentences are called "sentential forms," and the capitalized symbols are called "nonterminals."

Write a program to generate English sentences according to this scheme. You will probably want to represent a sentential form as an integer array; positive integers would stand for words, and negative integers for nonterminals. You will also probably want to store the rules in an array so that you can change the rules without changing the program too much.

Your algorithm should then follow this reasoning:

1. Are there any nonterminals in the current sentential form? If no, convert each number to the word and print it out.

2. Take the first nonterminal and pick a rule which is applicable to it (using a random number generator).

3. Rewrite the sentential form with the right-hand side of the rule inserted.

4. Go to 1.

First get the program going with these simple set of rules; then alter the rules to improve the quality and complexity of the sentences generated. Possible new features are transitive verbs, plurals, adjectives, and adverbs. See whether you can avoid grammatical but nonsensical output like

```
THE GREAT GREEN MACHINE SLEEPS FURIOUSLY.
THE ORANGE SKY STEALS A DARK THOUGHT.
```

Finally, the program could be made to produce several lines which might resemble a short poem.

11. *Evaluating Expressions* (Mitchell Wand). Write a program which accepts cards punched with simple arithmetic expressions involving +, *, and −, and evalutes them. For example:

Input	Output
37 + 5	42
127 − 14	113
4 * 80	320

Follow these specifications:

- Your input will be a sequence of cards. Each card will consist of the following: a number (starting in column 1), a single blank, an operator (+,*,or –), a single blank, and the second number, followed by blanks. There is one and only one blank between portions. A blank in column 1 indicates end of file.

- Here a "number" means an unsigned integer constant, in standard decimal notation; that is, a sequence of characters, each of which is one of 0,1, . . . , 9.

- You do not know the number of characters in advance, hence you cannot use FORTRAN I format.

- Your output should include an input echo, the operands and operator found, and the answer.

- You need not check for illegal input.

The key step in the problem is finding the three blanks in the card; these determine the operands. You will probably want to write a conversion subprogram to change from characters to integers. Additional features might include:

- Checking for illegal input.

- Signed numbers.

- Input in a base other than 10.

- Input in Roman numerals.

- An arbitrary number of blanks between fields instead of just one.

SPIRAL PROBLEMS

A. *Student Grading*

A class with 15 students has student grade records of the form: Name (alphabetic characters, columns 1–30), ten integer exam grades (each in the range 0–100, columns 31–70), pass/fail option (character 'A' indicates pass/fail grade, character 'B' indicates letter grade, column 80). Skip to a new page and print a heading. Read each card, print the name, term average in the form xxx.x and the final grade on a single line. If the student has selected the pass/fail option, the final grade is a 'PASS' for a term average above 70.0 and a "FAIL" otherwise. If the student has selected a letter grade, then the final grade is 'A' for a term average above 90.0, 'B' for a term average above 80.0, 'C' for a term average above 70.0 and an 'F' otherwise. Finally, print the class average. For extra credit, print the name of the student with the highest average.

B. The Art Guild Craft Co-op Shop pays its members by the number of each item produced. Each week the data are collected and you are supposed to write a program to do the accounting. The input data contain a series of groups. Each group contains a single master card followed by one or more detail cards, followed by a trailer card. The master card contains the name of the artist in columns 1–40. The detail cards contain an eight-character description of the item in columns 1–8 and a three-digit integer number indicating the number of this item produced in columns 18–20. The trailer card contains the character '*' in column 1 and the rest of the card is blank. The last group of data is followed by a '**' card. The payment per item goes by the following table:

BELT	CANDLE	VASE	BOWL	MUG	HAT	SCARF	EARRINGS
2.5	1.50	6.00	4.05	1.20	3.75	5.65	1.00

For each detail card, look up the value in the table and multiply by the number produced. Accumulate the amount for each artist and print the name and the amount in the form of a check. Finally, print the total amount of money paid out.

For the following input:

```
MARY  ELLEN  DOOLITTLE
BELT             13
CANDLE            4
HAT               3
X

JOHN  POTTERSWHEEL
MUG              27
VASE              8
X
XX
```

the output should be

```
PAY  TO  THE  ORDER  OF  MARY  ELLEN  DOOLITTLE      43.90

PAY  TO  THE  ORDER  OF  JOHN  POTTERSWHEEL          80.40

THE  TOTAL  AMOUNT  OF  MONEY  IS  124.30
```

For extra credit, print out the total number of each item produced.

C. *Game of Life*

Invented by mathematician John H. Conway (*Scientific American*, October 1970, p. 120), this game models the growth and changes in a complex collection of living organisms. The model can be interpreted as applying to a collection of microorganisms, an ecologically closed system of animals or plants, or an urban development.

Start with a clear 50 x 50 checkerboard on which "counters" are to be placed. Each location has eight neighbors. The counters are born, survive or die during a "generation" according to the following rules:

- Survival: Counters with two or three neighboring counters survive to the next generation.

- Death: Counters with four or more neighbors die from overcrowding and are removed for the next generation. Counters with zero or one neighbors die from isolation and are removed for the next generation.

- Birth: Each empty location which has exactly three counters in the eight neighboring locations is a birth location. A counter is placed in the location for the next generation.

    For example, on a 6 x 6 space, the pattern on the left would look like the one on the right in the next generation:

Certain patterns are stable:

Other patterns repeat a sequence:

Set up initial conditions by clearing the board and reading in coordinates of at least 15 counters. Print out the board on a single sheet of paper. Then calculate the next generation in another array and print. Repeat for ten generations. Your output should be an 'X' for live cells and a blank otherwise. Hints: 1) use two 50 x 50 arrays. Establish the initial conditions in one array and produce the new generation in the second array. Print the second array, copy into the first array, and repeat for as many generations as desired. 2) assume that rows 1 and 50, and columns 1 and 50 are "infertile regions" where nothing survives and nothing is born. The examples of output in Figures 8.2 and 8.3 give an idea of some of the possibilities.

Figure 8.2

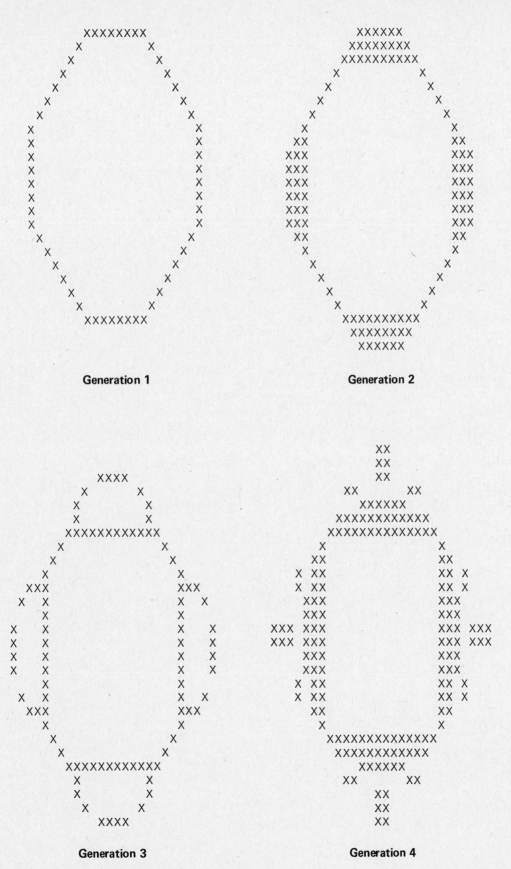

Figure 8.3

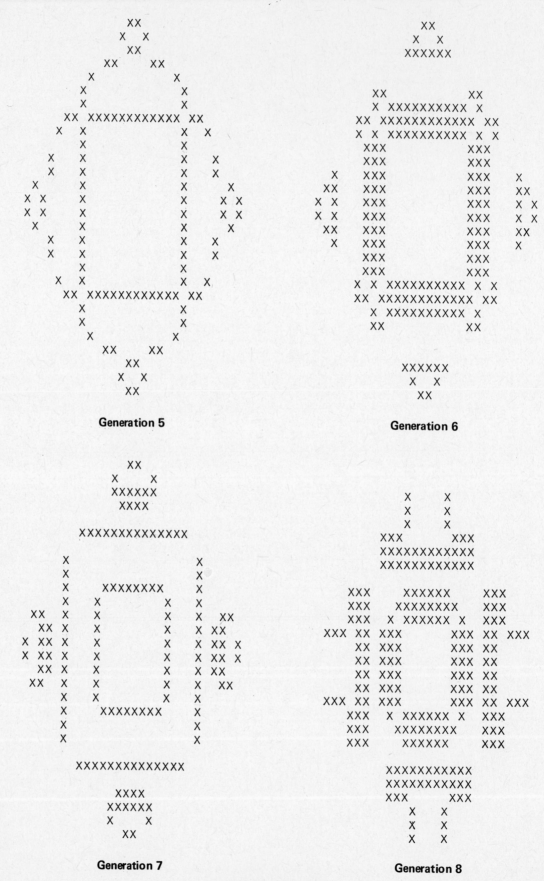

Generation 5

Generation 6

Generation 7

Generation 8

Figure 8.3 (continued)

SUBPROGRAMS

*Order and simplification are the first steps toward the mastery of
a subject—the actual enemy is the unknown.*

Thomas Mann, The Magic Mountain

CHAPTER 9

When a program is large or when a segment of code is used a number of times, it is desirable to create modules (separate units) known as subprograms. There are two kinds of subprograms, subroutines and functions. You have already encountered library functions such as SQRT, SIN, and COS. These subprograms are segments of code which have been written and stored in a library for use by other programmers. Subprograms such as SQRT, SIN, and COS are classified as functions because they return a value. For example, SQRT(25.) returns a value of 5. Some subprograms do not return a value and, hence, cannot be referred to in an arithmetic assignment statement. These subprograms are used either for convenience or to provide a means of dividing a large program into manageable units. Such subprograms are called subroutines and are invoked by means of a CALL statement.

A subprogram may be used many times in a program but need be coded only once. Therefore, subprograms provide an efficient way of reducing repetitive coding chores.

A subprogram may have one or more arguments. In the expression

$$A = SQRT(B)$$

B is an argument (or parameter) of the function. Similarly, a subroutine may require arguments in the CALL statement that refers to it.

$$CALL\ SUB(A,X,I)$$

Arguments allow the calling program to pass a variable or a constant to the subprogram so that the subprogram can use it in its computations.

Introduction

The use of subprograms, independent program modules, is one of the basic ideas of computer programming. Subprograms enable the programmer to apply the principle of "divide and conquer" in the coding of large and complicated problems. This chapter describes the two types of subprograms, *functions* and *subroutines*, and explains how they are combined with a *main program.* One goal of this chapter is to help the reader identify situations in which the use of subprograms is desirable.

You have already encountered the subprograms known as *functions*. SQRT, a function to compute the square root of an expression, is one example. In Chapter 4 we discussed *library functions* which are supplied by the computer manufacturer. In this chapter you will learn how to write your own functions.

Consider the arithmetic assignment statement

```
S = SQRT (25.)
```

The function SQRT is actually a program which computes the square root of a real number. The value 25. which appears within parentheses is called the *argument* or *parameter* of the function. The argument of the function may be considered as the data on which the function operates.

For statements such as

```
A = SQRT(X)
A = SQRT(26.)
A = SQRT(X/Y + Z/2.3)
```

and the SQRT function will compute the appropriate result. Of course, it is possible to provide a function with "bad data" such as a negative argument[1]

```
A = SQRT(-1.)
```

and the routine will not return useful results.

A subprogram like SQRT is actually a complete program which is combined with the user's program prior to execution. For example, a program might be written which calls (*invokes*) the SQRT function in two places.

---

[1]The square root of a negative number is undefined in the real number system.

```
    .
    .
    .
A = SQRT(X+1.) * 4.0
    .
    .
    .
B = 50. + SQRT(Y)
    .
    .
    .
END
```

The program which invokes the SQRT function is known as the *main* or the *calling program*. The function is a *subprogram*. When the programmer refers to a function in his program, the compiler generates instructions to pass the arguments to the subprogram and then go to the subprogram. When the subprogram has completed its calculations, it returns the result and control to the calling program.

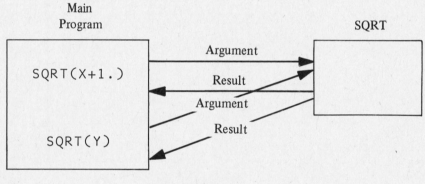

Figure 9.1

From Figure 9.1, you can see that only one copy of the SQRT program is used even though it is invoked in more than one location. This is efficient in terms of storage.

This same efficiency is reflected in the other type of subprogram—the *subroutine*. The only difference between a function and a subroutine is that the function returns a single value and, hence, may be used in arithmetic expressions. Subroutines do not return a single value and cannot be used in arithmetic expressions. They may, however, modify their arguments to new values. Thus, subroutines are used where no value or many values are to be returned. Since subroutines cannot be invoked by means of an arithmetic assignment statement, a special statement, CALL, is used to invoke subroutines.

Subroutines and functions are useful in dealing with a large program. Without subprograms, if a single program statement were to be altered the entire program would have to be recompiled. A more convenient strategy is to divide the program into a number of

INDEPENDENCE, GENERALITY, AND INTEGRITY: THREE DESIGN GOALS

Independence. The independence of a program is a measure of how easily it may be run under a different compiler, operating system, or computer. The more independent a program is, the easier it is to transfer it to a new environment. Certainly, a program or subroutine destined for wide distribution should have a high degree of independence.

Creating a program which is independent requires a detailed knowledge of the compilers, operating systems, and hardware in use and increases the programmer's burden. A program ought not to rely on the advantages of a particular environment since they may not be available under other conditions.

The techniques of creating an independent program are difficult to isolate. A good starting point is to adhere to the ANSI definition of Basic FORTRAN IV (Report X3.10-1966) which most manufacturers specify will be accepted by their production compilers. The subset is restrictive, but it should be possible to code all FORTRAN IV programs within the bounds of this language definition.

Generality. Generality is a measure of how easily a program may be modified to perform a slightly different but closely related task. The major concern is the facility with which different input data sets may be accommodated. A plotting program would have a high degree of generality if it could

Produce any number of plots on the same set of axes.

Handle any number of data points in any input format.

Accept data over any range of values.

Interpret INTEGER or REAL values.

Accept positive or negative values.

Scale axes (possibly even logarithmic scaling).

Optionally print titles or label axes.

Optionally calculate and print interpolated points.

Produce output for a line printer, or cathode ray display, or pen plotter.

Including all of the above items would require an immense program, most of whose facilities might never be used.

Once again, it is the programmer's professional responsibility to decide on the basis of his working environment which options to include. Is the extra effort warranted or is it wasted time spent in pursuit of the elusive perfect program? Do the extra features result in an excessively large, complex, and slow program?

A basic technique for creating a general program is to use parameters or control cards as flags or switches to determine the operation of the program for a particular run. Different operations, inputs, or outputs can be determined by statements preceding a set of data items.

Integrity. Integrity is a measure of the ability of a program to perform correctly on different sets of input. In a sense, integrity is a measure of how thoroughly a program has been tested and debugged. A program to sort numbers in ascending order which works fine for positive values but "bombs" for negative values, or which loops infinitely if there are only one or two numbers to sort lacks integrity. Programs which exceed the declared size of an array for certain cases or do not test for division by zero also lack integrity.

If we could enumerate all the rules for building integrity into a program, we might be able to automate the debugging and program checkout stages. The best we can hope for is to suggest potentially dangerous situations and hope that programmers will carefully evaluate program areas.

Some compilers can help the programmer by inserting code which checks whether array subscripts are exceeded or whether storage locations are referred to before they are set, but not all compilers provide such facilities. In any case, compilers cannot provide intelligible explanations of the cause of the failure. Furthermore, there may be errors which do not violate programming semantics but which produce incorrect results. A keypunching mistake could turn a bank deposit of 30.00 dollars into a 3000.00 windfall. A program with a high degree of integrity should check input values to determine if they are within realistic bounds. For example, a student grading program should screen out all grades that are not in the range of 0 to 100. If an array manipulating subroutine is designed to handle up to 10 by 10 square arrays, then the input argument which specifies the size of the array should be tested to see that it is less than or equal to ten and greater than one.

In debugging a program you should try to create combinations of input so that every branch of the program is tested. A large program such as a compiler or a complex simulation can never be fully tested and it is common to find bugs in such programs years after they have been released.

subprograms so that an alteration affects only one module. Most FORTRAN compilers allow the programmer to save the compiled version of the program so that it need not be re-compiled for every execution. Unfortunately WATFOR/WATFIV does not permit this.

Another advantage in dividing the program into subprograms is that a number of people may work more or less independently on their sections of the program. Each section can be developed and tested separately and then all can be run together.

A third important advantage, which is sometimes the overriding consideration, is that a particular computation may be required in several places in the program. Instead of repeating the same statements, a subprogram is written and invoked wherever it is needed. Typical subprograms would cover sorting, input/output, matrix operations, statistical procedures (finding means, variance, correlation coefficients, and so on), character manipulation (see Chapter 13), and graphing or histogramming.

Since so many of the same procedures are required by large numbers of programmers, libraries of subprograms are available at most installations. They enable a programmer to use pretested and dependable subprograms and avoid reinventing them every time a program is written. The Scientific Subroutine Package provided by IBM, Symmetric List Processor, GASP Simulation System, and the BMD statistical package are widely distributed libraries of FORTRAN subprograms.

The design of a program is a difficult task and the choice of the particular subprograms to be written is often not obvious. In many commercial data processing organizations, the design of the program is the responsibility of a highly skilled *systems analyst.* In Chapter 11 we will consider the problems of program design in greater depth.

Problem 9.1

Classify each of the following subprograms as a function or subroutine according to your estimate of which is the more appropriate way to write it. The criterion is whether the subprogram returns a single value.

a. Find the square root of a number.
b. Find the tangent of an angle.
c. Set an array to zeroes.
d. Compute the largest integer of an array of numbers.
e. Sort an array into ascending sequence.
f. Locate the subscript of the first (or only) occurrence of a value in the array.
g. Locate the largest value in an array.

The Basic Structure of Functions

We have said that subprograms are complete programs which are "linked" with the main program. Library functions such as SQRT, SIN, and COS are available to the programmer. However, there may be cases in which it is advantageous to write a subprogram which does not already exist or even write one to be added to the subprogram library for the use of other programmers. Before we discuss the details of subprogram construction, a simple example of a user-written function will be presented.

A Simple Function

As a simple example of a user-written function consider the following program:

```
FUNCTION AVERAG(A,B)
SUM = A + B
AVERAG = SUM/2.0
RETURN
END
```

This function is similar to programs you have written. Its most distinctive features are the FUNCTION statement which heads the subprogram and the RETURN statement which is the last executable statement before the END. This function computes the average of the variables A and B, which appear surrounded by parentheses in the FUNCTION statement.

The variables A and B are called arguments (or *parameters*) of the function. They indicate that when the function is referred to in a calling program it will have two arguments of *real* mode. Valid ways of referring to this function are

```
X = AVERAG(VAL1,VAL2)
Y = AVERAG(10.0,20.3) + Z/2
Z = AVERAG(D(I,J),34.3+P)
```

Note that in each reference there are two real arguments separated by a comma. The arguments may be variables, subscripted variables, expressions, constants, or any mixture of these. The only requirement is that the arguments be of the form

AVERAG(*real argument, real argument*)

It would be invalid to reference the function AVERAG in the following ways:

```
AVERAG(I,J)
AVERAG(1,2)                    } INVALID
AVERAG(3.4,52.0,6.1)
```

The rule is that there must be a correspondence between the arguments in the function reference and the arguments in the FUNCTION statement with respect to *number of arguments* and *mode of arguments*. Thus the function declaration

```
FUNCTION SAM(I,A,J,B)
```

indicates that every time the function is referred to there will be a list of four arguments: an integer argument, a real argument, an integer argument, and a real argument.

The variables which appear in the FUNCTION statement as arguments are special variables known as dummy variables. They are called dummy variables because when the function is referred to they will be assigned the values of the arguments in the statement which refers to the function. If the function above is referred to by the following statement:

```
A = AVERAG(X,Y)
```

it will execute as though written

```
SUM = X + Y
AVERAG = SUM/2.0
```

On the other hand, if the function is referred to by the statement

```
F3 = AVERAG(W,Z)
```

then the function will execute as if it were written

```
SUM = W + Z
AVERAG = SUM/2.0
```

Thus, the arguments which appear in the FUNCTION statement are dummy arguments in that they will be replaced by the appropriate *calling arguments*.

Since a function (or subroutine) is a separate compilation, the variables used in it bear no *relation to variables of the same names used in a main program.* If the variables A,B, or SUM appear in a calling program they are different from the variables in the function. The only communication between the function and the calling program is by way of the arguments and the value returned. (In Chapter 10, however, another means of communication with a subprogram—COMMON—will be introduced.)

The name of the function, AVERAG, is used as a variable on the left-hand side of an assignment statement in the FUNCTION definition. Thus AVERAG is assigned a value and can be used as a variable in an arithmetic expression within the calling program. It is not enough, however, simply to assign a value to AVERAG; control must be returned to the main program. This action is accomplished by the RETURN statement.

To review the program statements defining a function subprogram, an example of a simple, but complete program using the AVERAG function is

```
C
C            READ PAIR OF GRADES FOR FIRST STUDENT
C
      READ(5,101) GRADE1, GRADE2
  101 FORMAT(2F6.2)
C
C            FIND THE AVERAGE BY CALLING A FUNCTION
C
      STUD1 = AVERAG(GRADE1, GRADE2)
C
C            READ PAIR OF GRADES FOR SECOND STUDENT
C
      READ(5,101) GRADE1, GRADE2
C
C            FIND AVERAGE
C
      STUD2 = AVERAG(GRADE1, GRADE2)
C
C            FIND CLASS AVERAGE
C
      CLASS = AVERAG(STUD1, STUD2)
C
C            PRINT OUT RESULT
C
      WRITE(6,102) CLASS
  102 FORMAT('1CLASS AVERAGE FOR TWO STUDENTS ',F6.2)
      STOP
      END
C     ※※※※※※※※※※※※※※※※※※※※※※※※※※※※※※※※※※※※※※
C     ※  DEFINITION OF THE AVERAGE FUNCTION  ※
C     ※※※※※※※※※※※※※※※※※※※※※※※※※※※※※※※※※※※※※※
      FUNCTION AVERAG(A,B)
      SUM = A + B
      AVERAG = SUM/2.0
      RETURN
      END
```

The function AVERAG is a *real function*, that is, it returns a real value. If a function is to return an integer value, the function name must begin with the letters I–N. (Chapter 10 will discuss a means of circumventing this requirement.) Thus the function

```
FUNCTION IADD(I,J)
IADD = I + J
RETURN
END
```

will return an integer value in arithmetic expressions such as

```
KK = IADD(5,L) + 2
```

It is perfectly valid to use either integer or real arguments (or both) in any function regardless of the mode of the value returned, as long as the arguments are properly declared in the FUNCTION statement.

Problem 9.2

a. Write a function to add +1.0 to a real argument and return the new value.
b. Write a function as in (a) but return the result as an integer.

A Function to Find the Largest of Three Values

As another example of how to write and how to call a function we will write a function to return the largest of three arguments. Such a subprogram would be useful to an instructor who wanted to assign final grades on the basis of the highest of three test grades, to a business executive who would like to know which of three product lines was selling best, to a chemist who wanted to know which of three reactions was proceeding most rapidly, or to a literary style analyst who wanted to know which of three sentences had the most words. If such a function were available in the subprogram library, it could be used by all these people.

What is needed is a generalized program to take three arguments and determine which of the three values is the largest. The function would then return the largest value to the main program. Such a function, to locate the largest of three *integer* arguments, can be written as follows:

```
      FUNCTION LARGE (I,J,K)
      IF(I .GT. J) GO TO 20
      IF(J .GT. K) GO TO 30
10    LARGE = K
      RETURN
20    IF(I .LT. K) GO TO 10
      LARGE = I
      RETURN
30    LARGE = J
      RETURN
      END
```

An appropriate main program might be

```
        READ(5,101)MARK1,MARK2,MARK3
101     FORMAT(3I4)
        MBIG = LARGE(MARK1,MARK2,MARK3)
        WRITE(6,102) MBIG
102     FORMAT('0THE HIGHEST SCORE WAS',I4)
                        .
                        .
                        .
```

Notice that in the reference to the function the order of the arguments

```
MBIG = LARGE(MARK1,MARK2,MARK3)
```

matches the order of the dummy arguments declared in the FUNCTION statement

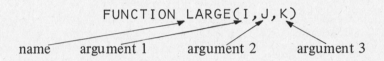

The function name in the definition and in the calling program *must* match; the order, number, and mode of the arguments must agree with the function declaration although the names of the arguments may be different.

Since the names used in the main program have no relationship to the names used in the subprogram, the names may also be identical. Thus all of the following invocations of the function LARGE would be valid:

```
I4 = LARGE(MARK1,MARK2,MARK3)
M = LARGE(M,N,K)
IBIG = LARGE(78,K4,M)
NUMBER = LARGE(6,5,4)
```

In the last two cases, constants were passed to the function. In fact, the arguments may be any valid arithmetic expression, as long as the mode (integer or real) of the expression agrees with the declarations for that argument. The following examples demonstrate more elaborate function calls:

```
IB = LARGE (M,3,I*J)
IC = LARGE (INT(X), I, L/J + 14)
ID = LARGE(NARRAY(14),NARRAY(19),NARRAY(54))
```

In the last case subscripted variables were passed to the subprogram. When this is done the entire array is not passed, only three individual values. Passing of entire arrays will be considered later in the chapter.

Although our function LARGE used three RETURN statements, only one was necessary. An equivalent routine could have been written

```
    FUNCTION LARGE(I,J,K)
    IF(I .GT. J) GO TO 20
    IF(J .GT. K) GO TO 30
 10 LARGE = K
    GO TO 40
 20 IF(I .LT. K) GO TO 10
    LARGE = I
    GO TO 40
 30 LARGE = J
 40 RETURN
    END
```

Many programmers prefer to use a single RETURN because the flow of the resultant routine is "cleaner."

Another example of a function is one to find the area of a circle given the radius. We might invoke the function AREA in attempting to find the volume of a cylinder:

```
    .
    .
    .
READ(5,101) RADIUS,HEIGHT
VOLUME = HEIGHT*AREA(RADIUS)
WRITE(6,102) VOLUME
    .
    .
    .
```

A function to compute the area of the base could be written

```
FUNCTION AREA(R)
PI = 3.141593
AREA = PI*R*R
RETURN
END
```

This very simple but useful function subprogram made it possible to simplify and improve on the clarity of the main program.

Summary—Functions

In general, the structure of a function subprogram is

FUNCTION *fname(arg1,arg2, . . .)*
  ⋮   body of function

fname = value to be returned
RETURN
END

where *fname* is the name of the function and *arg1, arg2, . . .* are the arguments used in the body of the function. There must be at least one argument. The function name must adhere to the conventions for naming real and integer variables. If the first letter of the function name is I,J,K,L,M, or N then the function will return an integer value; otherwise it will return a real value.

Modifying the Function Arguments

The value of arguments to a function may be modified within the function. For example, the following function:

```
FUNCTION SUM(A,B)
SUM = A+B
B = 0.0
RETURN
END
```

adds the two arguments and then sets the second value to zero. Thus, the following program:

```
      X = 2.0
      Y = 3.0
      Z = SUM(X,Y)
      WRITE(5,101) X,Y,Z
101   FORMAT('0',3(F3.1,4X))
      STOP
      END
```

will print the result

```
2.0     0.0     5.0
```

In the SUM function, the second argument is used for input and is modified. It is also possible to use arguments for output from the function only. The variable BOTH in the following function will contain the sum of variables A and B; the variable PROD will contain the product of A and B.

```
FUNCTION FF(A,B,BOTH,PROD)
BOTH = A+B
PROD = A*B
      .
      .
      .
RETURN
END
```

Note that A and B are used only as input arguments while BOTH and PROD are used solely for returning values.

Subroutines

It is often useful to write subprograms in which *all* values are returned by modification of the arguments. Similarly, it is often desirable to write subprograms which return *no* values but instead perform some operation such as printing a result. Since functions are treated as values, they are not appropriate for these two cases. Therefore, another form of subprogram—the *subroutine*— is used.

A subroutine, unlike a function, does not take on a value. Therefore it does not have a mode (*real* or *integer*) nor can it be used in an arithmetic statement. Instead, a special statement—the CALL statement—is used to call a subroutine. The form of the CALL statement is simply

CALL *sname(arg1, arg2, . . .)*

Unlike a function, a subroutine need not have any arguments. The following are all valid subroutine calls:

```
CALL SUB1(A,I,X(4))
CALL ME
CALL X4(3.0,X+2.0,J5)
```

A subroutine is constructed almost exactly like a function. It is headed by a SUBROUTINE statement and terminates by executing a RETURN. Since the subroutine does not take on a value, its name (unlike that of a function) may not appear on the left side of an arithmetic assignment statement.

As an example, consider this trivial but complete program:

```
C
C         SET AND PRINT THE VALUE OF I
C
      I = 3
      WRITE(6,101) I
  101 FORMAT(' I = ', I2)
C
C         CALL THE SUBROUTINE AND PRINT
C
      CALL ADDONE(I)
      WRITE(6,101) I
      STOP
      END
C
C     ××××××××××××××××××××××××××××××××××
C     ×  ADDONE SUBROUTINE DEFINITION  ×
C     ××××××××××××××××××××××××××××××××××
C
      SUBROUTINE ADDONE(N)
      N = N + 1
      RETURN
      END
```

The output of this program is

```
I  =  3
I  =  4
```

Worked Examples

The following subroutine computes the average of the first two (REAL) arguments, returns the average in the third argument and places an INTEGER code in the fourth argument.

The code is assigned according to the following scheme:

Code	Average
3	Greater than or equal to 80.0
2	Greater than or equal to 65.0
1	Less than 65.0

Subroutine

```
    SUBROUTINE MARK(T1,T2,AVER,N)
    AVER = (T1 + T2)/2.0
    IF(AVER .GE. 80.0) GO TO 10
    IF(AVER .GE. 65.0) GO TO 20
    N = 1
    GO TO 30
10  N = 3
    GO TO 30
20  N = 2
30  RETURN
    END
```

This subroutine uses two input values and returns two values. A main program to call this subroutine might be

```
    .
    .
    .
    READ(5,101) TEST1,TEST2
    CALL MARK(TEST1,TEST2,AV,ICODE)
    WRITE(6,102) AV,ICODE
102 FORMAT(' AVERAGE = ', F6.2,' SCORE CODE = ', I1)
    .
    .
    .
```

It is also possible to write a subroutine that has no arguments. A useful example of such a subroutine is one to cause the printer to skip to the top of a new page:

```
      SUBROUTINE PAGE
      WRITE(6,101)
101   FORMAT('1')
      RETURN
      END
```

This subroutine might be invoked at several points in the main program:

```
      .
      .
      .
CALL  PAGE
      .
      .
      .
CALL  PAGE
      .
      .
      .
CALL  PAGE
      .
      .
      .
```

Although it would be hard to argue that this improved the efficiency of the program, it does enhance the readability and the understandibility of the main program.

Summary—Subroutines

The general form of a subroutine is:

$$\text{SUBROUTINE } sname \ (arg1, arg2, \ldots)$$

$$.$$
$$.$$
$$.$$

$$\text{RETURN}$$
$$\text{END}$$

where *sname* is the subroutine's name, and *arg1, arg2, . . .* are the dummy arguments.

A Comparison of Subroutines and Functions

Students often wonder whether a subroutine or a function is appropriate for a particular situation. The advantage of a function is that it can be invoked as part of an arithmetic expression—that is, if only one value is to be returned. On the other hand, many programmers find that a CALL statement is easier to understand. To clarify the problem (and to compare the passing of arguments) here is a computation of factorials by a subroutine and by a function subprogram. The factorial of a positive integer (written $n!$) is the product of the integers from one up to that integer:

$$4! = factorial(4) = 1*2*3*4$$
$$5! = factorial(5) = 1*2*3*4*5$$
$$n! = factorial(n) = 1*2* \ldots (n-1)*n$$

A main program and a subroutine to perform the calculation could be written

```
      READ(5,101) N
101 FORMAT(I2)
      CALL NFACTR(N,NF)
      WRITE(6,102)N,NF
102 FORMAT('1THE FACTORIAL OF',I3, ' IS ', I10)
      STOP
      END
      SUBROUTINE NFACTR(K,KK)
      KK = 1
      DO 10 I = 1,K
      KK = KK*I
  10 CONTINUE
      RETURN
      END
```

A main program and a function for the same calculation could be written

```
      READ(5,101)N
101 FORMAT(I2)
      NF = NFACTR(N)
      WRITE(6,102) N,NF
102 FORMAT('1THE FACTORIAL OF', I3, ' IS ', I10)
      STOP
      END
      FUNCTION NFACTR(K)
      NFACTR = 1
      DO 10 I = 1,K
      NFACTR = NFACTR*I
  10 CONTINUE
      RETURN
      END
```

In this case, the choice between the two methods is largely a question of taste. The function call requires only one argument while the subroutine requires two. Since the value returned from the function is an integer, the name of the function *must* be an integer name. The name of a subroutine does not have to match the mode of the computation.

There are situations in which the function method is simpler to use. In determining the number of ways that k items may be chosen from a group of n items, we must evaluate

$$\text{combinations} = \frac{n!}{k!(n-k)!}$$

If NFACTR is a function subprogram, the combinations could be calculated by

```
NCOMB = NFACTR(N)/(NFACTR(K)*NFACTR(N-K))
```

This is simpler than using subroutine calls, such as

```
CALL NFACTR(N,NF)
CALL NFACTR(K,KF)
CALL NFACTR(N - K, NKF)
NCOMB = NF/(KF*NKF)
```

Conversely, there are occasions when subroutines seem more appropriate. Subroutines may appear with no arguments, but functions must have at least one argument. In the earlier example of a subroutine to skip to the top of a page, it would be unwieldy to use a function, since an artificial argument would have to be used. Most programmers find that if the subprogram returns only a single value, then a function is more convenient. If more than one value is returned or if an array is altered by the subprogram, then a subroutine is more convenient.

Table 9.1
A COMPARISON OF FUNCTIONS AND SUBROUTINES

Function	*Subroutine*
Invoked by means of an occurrence in an expression.	Invoked by means of a CALL statement.
Takes on a value and may be used in an expression. Arguments may be modified if more than one value is to be returned.	Does not take on a value, *per se*, but arguments may be modified.
Function name is assigned a value within the function.	Subroutine name is never assigned a value.
Must have at least one argument.	Need not have any arguments.
The type of the function, integer or real, depends on the function name.	Subroutines are not typed.

Problem 9.3

Extend a subroutine PAGE to print a title at the top of the page. Keep a counter so that you can include a page number in the heading. This counter should be incremented by 1 every time a page is skipped. (How will you set this value initially?)

Passing Arrays as Arguments to Subprograms

It is often necessary to manipulate an array within a subprogram. To do this, a dummy array argument may be defined in the subprogram. In the example below, an array called MARK has been declared in the main program and is passed to the subroutine, MAXARY, which locates the largest element. The largest value in the array will be returned in the second argument.

```
DIMENSION MARK(100)
      .
      .
      .
CALL MAXARY(MARK, MBIG)
      .
      .
      .
```

In this case, we are assuming that all of the 100 locations of the MAXARY contain values; thus the subroutine will examine all 100 locations. The subroutine arguments are an integer array and an integer variable

```
      SUBROUTINE MAXARY(INARY,INBIG)
      DIMENSION INARY(100)
      INBIG = INARY(1)
      DO 10 I = 2,100
      IF(INBIG .GE. INARY(I)) GO TO 10
      INBIG = INARY(I)
 10   CONTINUE
      RETURN
      END
```

The DIMENSION statement in the subroutine is used to let the subroutine "know" that the first argument, INARY, is really the name of an array. Since INBIG has no DIMENSION statement, it is defined as a scalar integer variable. The value of INBIG is determined by the subroutine and is returned to the main routine, which uses the result under the name MBIG. Again, the names of the actual arguments in the main program are independent from the names of dummy arguments in the subroutine. They may match or they may be different.

This subroutine can be modified to make it more general by giving it the capability to examine up to one hundred data items. The subroutine must of course be informed of the number of data items to be inspected. To accomplish this, another argument is added to the argument list to indicate the number of data items in the MAXARY array:

Main Program

```
      DIMENSION MARK(100)
      READ(5,101) N,(MARK(I),I = 1,N)
      CALL MAXARY(MARK,N,MBIG)
      WRITE(6,102) MBIG
      .
      .
      .
```

Subroutine

```
    SUBROUTINE MAXARY(INARY,N,INBIG)
    DIMENSION INARY(100)
    INBIG = INARY(1)
    DO 10 I = 2,N
    IF(INBIG .GE. INARY(I)) GO TO 10
    INBIG = INARY(I)
 10 CONTINUE
    RETURN
    END
```

This modification leads to a subtle but important point. The DIMENSION MARK(100) statement in the main program reserves 100 storage locations. The DIMENSION INARY(100) statement in the subroutine does *not* reserve an additional 100 locations. It is used to indicate that the dummy argument INARY is an array rather than a scalar. Thus the DIMENSION statement in the subroutine could be

```
DIMENSION INARY(500) or DIMENSION INARY(1)
```

Any of these forms would have the same effect in the subroutine; to indicate that the argument INARY is a one-dimensional array whose "true" length was declared in the main program. In fact, most compilers allow the special form

```
DIMENSION INARY(N)
```

to be used in subprograms where N is an argument to the subroutine. This "execution-time dimensioning" or "variable dimensioning" is *only* permitted for arrays that are arguments to a subprogram. If an array is defined within a subprogram—that is, not passed as an argument—then an integer constant *must* be used in the DIMENSION statement.

Converting the MAXARY subroutine to a function requires only minor modifications. The result of the function, in this case, the maximum value in the array, may be used directly in an arithmetic assignment statement.

Main Program

```
DIMENSION MARK(100)
READ(5,101) N,(MARK(I),I = 1,N)
MBIG = MAXARY(MARK,N)
WRITE(6,102) MBIG
        .
        .
        .
```

Subroutine

```
    FUNCTION MAXARY(INARY,N)
    DIMENSION INARY(N)
    MAXARY = INARY(1)
    DO 10 I = 2,N
    IF(MAXARY .GE. INARY(I))
  1     GO TO 10
    MAXARY = INARY(I)
 10 CONTINUE
    RETURN
    END
```

The function name is used as if it were a variable name. It is set to the value that is to be returned. Note that "execution-time dimensioning" was used for the INARY array.

Passing Multidimensional Arrays[2]

When two-dimensional arrays are used as arguments in a subprogram, the first subscript of the dummy array must have the same dimensions as the corresponding declaration in the main program. However, the number of columns declared in the main program for a double subscripted array need not agree with the number of columns declared in the subprogram. In the following example, the number of columns in the DIMENSION statement of the subroutine has been set to 1, but the number of rows is fixed at 20.

Main Program	*Subroutine*

```
DIMENSION ARRAY(20,10)              SUBROUTINE ZERO(X,NR,NC)
       .                            DIMENSION X(20,1)
       .                            DO 20 I = 1,NR
       .                            DO 10 J = 1,NC
CALL ZERO(ARRAY,NROWS,NCOLS)        X(I,J) = 0.0
       .                         10 CONTINUE
       .                         20 CONTINUE
       .                            RETURN
                                    END
```

The ZERO subroutine could be used to zero out arrays which have been *declared* to have 20 rows and any number of columns. By setting NR less than 20, however, it is possible to cause fewer than 20 rows to be zeroed out. For three-dimensional arrays, the first two subscripts in the DIMENSION statement of the main program must match the first two subscripts in the DIMENSION statement of the subprogram. The general rule for n-dimensional arrays is that the first $n-1$ subscripts of the DIMENSION statements in the subprogram must correspond to the declaration in the main program. The rule of corresponding dimensions also applies to "execution-time dimensioning." For a two-dimensional array with "execution-time dimensioning," the *exact* number of rows declared in the main program must be transmitted to the subprogram:

Main Program	*Subroutine*

```
DIMENSION ARRAY(20,10)              SUBROUTINE ZERO(N,X,NR,NC)
       .                            DIMENSION X(N,1)
       .                            DO 20 I = 1,NR
       .                            DO 10 J = 1,NC
CALL ZERO(20,ARRAY,NROWS,NCOLS)     X(I,J) = 0.0
       .                         10 CONTINUE
       .                         20 CONTINUE
       .                            RETURN
                                    END
```

---

[2] This section contains advanced material, which is optional.

This version of the ZERO subroutine could be used to zero out arrays which have been declared to have any number of rows. For n-dimensional arrays, the first $n-1$ subscripts of the DIMENSION statement must be passed as arguments.

It should be noted that the dimensions of an array passed to a subroutine should not be altered in the subroutine.

Statement Functions

Some function subprograms are extremely short. A function to find the average of three numbers might be written

Main Program   *Subprogram*

```
                                  FUNCTION AVER(X,Y,Z)
    .                             AVER = (X + Y + Z)/3.0
    .                             RETURN
Y = AVER(A,B,C)                   END
    .
    .
    .
FINAL = AVER(XINIT,XMID,XLAST)
    .
    .
    .
```

This function is only four lines long and there is really only one line of computation. When a function can be computed on a single line, an abbreviated form of the function definition, called the *arithmetic statement function* may be used. Arithmetic statement functions are defined *in* the main program rather than as separate compilations. An example of an arithmetic statement function is

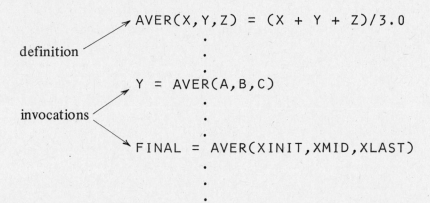

The arithmetic statement function must be defined before any executable statements of the program. The name of the single statement function must reflect the type of the result (real or integer). The arguments in the definitions are dummy arguments and the names used are

independent of names used elsewhere in the program. The actual arguments in the invocation must reflect the type of the dummy arguments. Subscripted variables may *not* appear in the single statement function definition (except in the WATFIV implementation). The definition (on the right-hand side of the equals sign) may contain constants or variable names that appear in other parts of the program.

Further examples of valid statement function definitions include

```
POLY(X) = A*X**2 + B*X + C
```

where A, B and C have been defined in the program, and

```
DIST(X,Y) = SQRT(X*X + Y*Y)

IREMDR(I,J) = I - I/J*J

NRANDM(K) = IREMDR(437*K + 83 ,1000)
```

assuming that IREMDR has been defined earlier.

Valid invocations of these arithmetic statement functions would be

```
FUNC = POLY(4.56)
XVAL = DIST(X1,Y1) + CONST
VAL = FLOAT(NRANDM(K))
IF(IREMDR(N,M) .EQ. 0) GO TO 10
DIFF = DIST(X2 - X1, Y2 - Y1)
```

Summary

The modularization of a program is a useful and sometimes necessary step in the development of large programs. Subroutines and functions are the techniques that allow the FORTRAN programmer to do this. (Similar techniques exist in other programming languages.) The subprogram is called or invoked in the main program, where actual arguments are presented to be passed to the subprogram. Subprogram definitions are models for the computation to be performed. Arguments passed in replace the dummy arguments given in the subprogram definition. The actual arguments must match the dummy arguments in type and order of presentation, but the names in the subprogram are independent of the names in the main program.

When a function can be defined with a single arithmetic assignment statement, it is possible to use a single statement function whose definition and invocation appear in the main program.

DEBUGGING CLINIC

As the complexity of the control structure increases, additional efforts must be applied to ensure that the program is performing as expected. During the debugging of a program containing subprograms, the values of each of the arguments should be printed each time a subprogram is entered. Thus, the first executable statement in a subroutine should be a PRINT statement. Later, when the subprogram is working satisfactorily, the printout statements may be removed. The first function at the bottom of page 281 could have begun

```
      FUNCTION LARGE(I,J,K)
      WRITE(6,101) I,J,K
101 FORMAT('0**FUNCTION LARGE',3I12)
          .
          .
          .
```

As programs become more complex, the indicator FUNCTION LARGE can help to trace the execution of the program. The printout of the values of the arguments will serve to assist in the detection of bugs.

Argument printouts help to detect the most common problem in using subprograms—incorrect argument passing. In desk checking a program, it is important to make sure that the invocation and the definition of the subprogram or statement function have the same number of arguments and the same mode (real or integer), and that when an array is passed in, an array is received. It is important to be extra careful when using multidimensional arrays as arguments.

REVIEW QUESTIONS

1. Why are subprograms important? Under what circumstances would you consider coding part of a program as a subprogram?

2. What are the differences between *subroutines* and *functions*? Where do you use each? How does a function take on a value?

3. What are dummy arguments? How do they relate to the actual arguments used in a subroutine or function reference?

4. How are arrays passed to a subprogram? How is the special form of the DIMENSION statement

DIMENSION X(N)

used? What are the restrictions on its use?

5. How is the CALL statement used? Why must subprograms with no arguments be written as subroutines rather than functions?

EXERCISES

1. Write two different CALL statements and a SUBROUTINE statement for these subroutines.
   a. FUNCT with two real arguments followed by one integer argument.
   b. NUMBER with four integer arguments.
   c. MINVAL with five integer arguments.
   d. XMIN with four real arguments.
   e. XMINAR with a real one-dimensional array, an integer and a real argument. (Make appropriate DIMENSION statements.)
   f. MERGE with two integer one-dimensional arrays and two integer arguments. (Make appropriate DIMENSION statements.)
   g. COMPAR with two real one-dimensional arrays and two integer arguments. (Make appropriate DIMENSION statements.)
   h. CONST with a real two-dimensional array and three integer arguments. (Make appropriate DIMENSION statements.)
   i. MATMUL with three real two-dimensional arrays and three integer arguments. (Make appropriate DIMENSION statements.)
   j. PAGE with no arguments.
2. Repeat Exercise 1 using two function invocations and a FUNCTION statement throughout.

PROGRAMMING EXERCISES

3. a. Write a main program and a subroutine to find the sum of the integers from 1 to N where N is passed as an argument. Make sure to check that N is greater than 0.
   b. Rewrite using a function subprogram.

4. Write a subroutine to set every element of a one-dimensional real array to a constant which has been passed in as an argument.

5. a. Write a subroutine to calculate bank interest. The principal, interest rate and number of years are passed in as arguments. Return the final amount.
   b. Rewrite as a function subprogram.

6. Write a main program and subroutine to find the smallest value of an array of integers. The array and the length of the array are passed in and the value and position of the smallest value are returned.

7. Write a function subprogram named SUM which takes as arguments a real array name and the length of the array. The value of the function is the sum of the values in the array.

8. a. Write a function to evaluate
   $$X_1 = \frac{-b + \sqrt{b^2 - 4ac}}{2a}$$
   b. Write a single statement function to do the evaluation.

9. Write a single statement function to evaluate these expressions.
   a. $q = cv\, e^{-t/RC}$
   b. $i = n(n+1)/2$
   c. $d = \dfrac{at^2}{2}$

10. Create a subroutine to sort an array of real data of length N. Write a main program to input the unsorted data, print it, call the subroutine, and print the sorted array. The array name and length N are passed as arguments.

11. Write a subroutine to sort values in place in ascending order for a real array of arbitrary length. Create a main program to read data values, print the data, call the sort, and print the sorted data.

SPIRAL PROBLEMS

Many programming projects are a team effort: A large project is divided into a main program and a number of subprograms so that each team member writes and debugs part of the project. The Spiral Problem for this chapter is such a team effort, with students working in groups of three, each person responsible for one part of the problem: A, B, or C. When each team member has written his or her portion, the main program is to be combined with the subprograms and the entire project debugged and run.

A. *The main program.*

Write a program to read a data card for each state in the U.S. The data card should contain the monthly rainfall for each of the twelve months of the year. (An example of rainfall data appears in Table 7.1, page 198.) Obtain the data from an almanac, or make up a test data deck of 20 cards.

The twelve numbers should be stored in a REAL array. Call a function AVE to calculate the average rainfall for the year for each state. Call a subroutine HILO to find the largest and smallest values in the array. Call a subroutine PLINE to print the twelve monthly values, the average rainfall, and the highest and lowest values for the year, on a single line, then loop back to read and process another card. When the last card has been processed, print the line: RAINFALL HAS BEEN PRINTED FOR *nn* STATES where *nn* is the number of cards processed. Test your program by using dummy subroutines.

B. *The highest, lowest, and average.*

Write a function AVE which has as its argument a REAL array of length N. AVE should compute the average of the numbers in the array by summing the first N elements of the array and dividing by N. Examples of calls to AVE are

```
Y = AVE(X,N)              and              FMEAN = AVE(ARRAY,K)
```

where X and ARRAY are REAL arrays, and N and K are INTEGER variables indicating the dimension of the array.

Write a subroutine HILO with four arguments. The first two arguments are a REAL array and an INTEGER array size as in the AVE routine. The last two arguments are REAL variables in which the largest and smallest elements of the array are to be returned. An example of a call to this routine is CALL HILO(X,N,BIG,SMALL).

Test your function and subroutine by writing a dummy main program.

C. *The print subroutine.*

Write a subroutine called PLINE with five arguments: X, A, B, S, and NCODE. NCODE should be set to 1 the first time PLINE is called and should be set to greater than 1 thereafter. X is a twelve element REAL array containing the rainfall for the twelve months of the year. A, B, and S are REAL variables containing the average, greatest, and least rainfall for the year. Print the 15 items of information neatly on a single line. The first time the subroutine is called it should print appropriate headings to label the 15 columns. After the first call, print only the data line. Test your subroutine by using a dummy main program.

Note: When the three sections—A, B, and C—are completed independently, each team member is to remove the dummy programs and the team is to combine the main program with the three subprograms. Finally, the entire project is to be run and debugged.

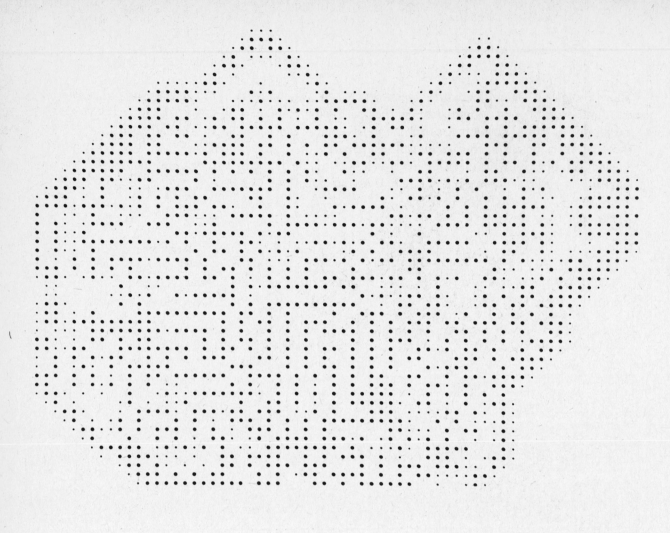

DECLARATIONS

We have a plan when we know, or at least know in outline, which calculations, computations, or constructions, we have to perform in order to obtain the unknown. The way from understanding the problem to conceiving a plan may be long and tortuous. In fact, the main achievement in the solution of a problem is to conceive the idea of a plan.

Polya, How To Solve It

CHAPTER 10

In Chapter 7, type declarations were introduced as a means of overriding the normal variable name – mode conventions. Thus, while A is normally a REAL variable it can be declared INTEGER by the statement INTEGER A while REAL I will declare I as a REAL variable.

This kind of statement also can be utilized to declare other variable types. DOUBLE PRECISION variables have the same range as REAL variables but they allow twice as many digits of accuracy. DOUBLE PRECISION data may be read or written using a D-format item.

Another variable type that can be declared is LOGICAL. LOGICAL variables may assume values "true" and "false." They can be combined with logical operators to create complex condition tests. Logical variables can be assigned the results of a comparison. Thus, L = A.NE.B will assume the value "true" or "false" depending on the data values. More complex conditions may be evaluated using the operators .AND. and .OR. Thus, logical expressions such as A.GT.X .OR. A.LT.Y can be constructed. Such expressions may be used in logical assignment statements as well as IF statements.

It is sometimes desirable to make a variable or array available to a subprogram but to avoid specifying it in the argument list. This may be the case, for example, when there is a large number of variables to be passed to the subprogram. A long calling sequence might be error-prone. A method of sharing variables between programs is the COMMON statement. It allows a variable to be used in more than one routine. Thus, COMMON A might be declared in a main program and several subprograms. The variable A then may be used in both. If the COMMON statement were not used, two separate A's would be created.

Introduction

The first nine chapters were primarily concerned with operations that could be performed in FORTRAN: arithmetic assignment, control structures, input/output, and subprograms. This chapter will turn to the objects of the operations and provide more thorough coverage of the types of data and the techniques that conveniently define data areas. These techniques enhance control of INTEGER and REAL variables. DOUBLE PRECISION, COMPLEX and LOGICAL data types will also be introduced.

Integer and Real Declarations

Thus far, great emphasis has been placed on adhering to the rules for the selection of INTEGER and REAL variable names: INTEGER variable names began with an I,J,K,L,M,N and REAL variable names began with A–H or O–Z. On occasion, however, it may be convenient to ignore these rules. REAL variable names such as MASS, INTRST, MONEY or NUMBER might be desired. An INTEGER variable name such as CONST, SCORE, AMOUNT, or TOTAL might also be useful.

In Chapter 7, it was noted that by using a *type declaration* it is possible to override the usual rules for variable names:

```
REAL INTRST,MONEY
REAL MASS
REAL NUMBER
INTEGER SCORE
INTEGER CONST, AMOUNT, TOTAL
```

These declarations must appear at the beginning of the main program or subprogram before any executable statements. Since these statements are simply declarations and are not executable statements, a variable must remain its declared type through the entire program.

Although these declarations permit the usual convention to be overridden, they should be used with care, since it is easier to follow and debug a program if the standard conventions are adhered to.

It is possible to supply dimension information in a type declaration statement:

```
REAL MARKS(50), NUMBER(100)
```

This statement is equivalent to

```
REAL MARKS, NUMBER
DIMENSION MARKS(50), NUMBER(100)
```

MODULARITY

When should you write a segment of code as a subroutine? There are two cases:

- When the segment performs a well-defined sequence of operations which is repeated several times in the program.

- When the segment performs a well-defined function, but the code is potentially less or more stable than other parts of the program.

In designing a program you always create a flowchart. Perhaps you only do this mentally, but before you write a line of code you must consider the sequence of operations. As you design a program, the blocks of the macro-flowchart (or system flowchart) are expanded as the details become better defined. Finally, the blocks of the micro-flowchart are clarified and converted into program code. The blocks of the macro-flowchart should be considered subroutines. Subroutines represent a higher level logical organization of your program.

To give meaning to these abstract considerations, consider this example. A program is to be written to compare two files of data and determine if specific fields of corresponding records of each file are equal. If the fields do not match, then both records are to be printed. The logic of this program is extremely simple, yet this type of program can be expanded to include a variety of special cases and exceptions. It is the type of utility program which often has a long lifetime and a wide distribution and is susceptible to a wide range of modifications. At the outset the following design goals should be set:

- The program should be as general as possible, using control or parameter cards to determine the number and position of the fields to be compared.

- The program should be as modular as possible to simplify modification and expansion.

Accordingly, the following macro-flowchart is reasonable:

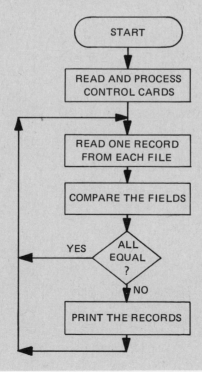

Each of the boxes in the macro-flowchart can be written as a subroutine. Communication among the various routines should be accomplished via a labeled COMMON. The main program of the comparison program is then almost trivial:

```
      COMMON/COMP/...,UNEQ,...
      LOGICAL UNEQ
C
C         READ CONTROL CARDS
      CALL CNTRLS
C
C         READ A RECORD FROM EACH FILE
C
   10 CALL READ12
C
C     CHECK IF ALL FIELDS ARE EQUAL. IF NOT, PRINT RECORDS.
C
      CALL COMPAR
      IF (UNEQ) CALL PRINT
      GO TO 10
      END
```

This program is a good example of modularity. Note the following points:

- The control card analysis and record printout are not critical to the logic of the program; however, both require considerable code. They are also quite likely to change in time. During the initial debugging, they can be written as minimal routines and later replaced by more sophisticated subprograms.

- Although many fields might have to be compared and even one failure is sufficient to cause a record to be rejected, only one condition, UNEQ, causes the information to be transmitted.

- The main program conveys the logic of the overall program. A person who wishes to modify a segment of the program need not be concerned with more than one routine since all changes are isolated.

- The work in developing the program could be split among several programmers, each working separately. They would have to agree only on the order and the contents of variables in the COMMON field.

- If overlaying were necessary, it would be easy to perform.

Large sophisticated programs are not built in a day — they evolve through many versions and modifications. A well-designed modular program can easily grow and be improved.

Double Precision

Approximately seven significant decimal digits are used when performing arithmetic operations using real values on an IBM 360/370. For situations that require a greater degree of precision, it is possible to specify that the accuracy should be increased to approximately

16 significant decimal digits. The magnitude of the largest value that can be stored generally remains unchanged; only the number of significant digits stored is increased. Double precision should be used in situations requiring a high degree of accuracy as well as in algorithms in which the accumulated roundoff error may be large. Roundoff error may occur every time an arithmetic operation is performed. Usually roundoff errors are small, but in some problems these errors are additive and the final result may be substantially off if single precision arithmetic is used. Though double precision arithmetic is more accurate than single precision arithmetic it still does not guarantee complete accuracy; it only reduces the amount of the error. Unfortunately, double precision constants require twice as much storage as single precision constants and double precision operations take two to ten times as long to execute as do single precision arithmetic operations. Double precision should be used only when extreme accuracy is required. Texts in the field of numerical analysis should be consulted for a more thorough discussion of roundoff errors and accuracy.

Since there are no special naming conventions for double precision variable names, they must be explicitly declared at the beginning of the program module by the use of the DOUBLE PRECISION statement. To remind yourself that you have specified double precision for a variable, it is helpful to begin all double precision variable names with the letter "D." The following declarations are typical:

```
DOUBLE PRECISION DGRAMS, DSPEED,DELTA
DOUBLE PRECISION DVALUE, DFINAL
DOUBLE PRECISION DOGGIE
```

Dimension information can also be given in the declaration:

```
DOUBLE PRECISION DTABLE(100), DMATRX(30,30,10)
DOUBLE PRECISION DEW(85), DROP,D(5)
DOUBLE PRECISION DETERM(10,10,10)
```

Double precision constants can have up to 16 decimal places of accuracy (when using the IBM 360/370) and may be suffixed by the letter D as well as a valid exponent:

```
1.0D0
3.141592653589793
4.67D24
 .27182818284590452D1
678.5786873D06
 .166666666666666
4.6D5
4.6D05
4.6D+05
 .46D06
```

In double precision arithmetic the usual operators (+, -, *, /, **) apply. Mixed mode operations should usually be avoided; that is, all variables and constants in an arithmetic assignment statement should be double precision.

If, however, mixed mode is used, conversion will occur according to Table 10.1.

TABLE 10.1

		Mode of b		
		INTEGER	*REAL*	*DOUBLE PRECISION*
	INTEGER	integer	real	double precision
Mode of *a*	REAL	real	real	double precision
	DOUBLE PRECISION	double prec.	double prec.	double precision

This table applies to the mode of the results of the operations

$a + b$ $a - b$

$a * b$ a / b

Along with the FLOAT function, that converts INTEGER variables to REAL, there exists a DFLOAT function to convert INTEGER to DOUBLE PRECISION. This function will be discussed in the next section.

An example of the use of double precision is the following code to find the area of a circle from its radius:

```
DOUBLE PRECISION DRAD,DAREA
   .
   .
   .
DAREA = 3.141592653589793D0 * DRAD * DRAD
   .
   .
   .
```

Library Functions DFLOAT and DBLE

If an integer value is to be used in a double precision expression, the library function DFLOAT can be used to perform the conversion. For example, to sum up the first 30 terms of the series

$$\frac{1}{1} + \frac{1}{2} + \frac{1}{3} + \frac{1}{4} \cdots$$

we might write

```
DOUBLE PRECISION DSUM
DSUM = 0.0D0
DO 10 I = 1,30
DSUM = DSUM + 1.0D0/DFLOAT(I)
```

```
10 CONTINUE
      .
      .
      .
```

The argument of the DFLOAT library function may be any integer expression.
To convert real values to double precision, the DBLE library function can be invoked.

```
DOUBLE PRECISION DELTA
REAL TABLE(100)
   .
   .
   .
DELTA = DBLE(TABLE(I)) - DBLE(TABLE(I-1))
   .
   .
   .
```

As Table 10.1 shows, if one of the two operands of an arithmetic operation is double precision, then the other operand will automatically be converted to double precision. It is helpful to use the library conversion functions in order to make the conversion explicit to the reader of the program.

Input and Output of Double Precision Values

A special format item, the D-format item, is used to process double precision values. The D-format item is similar to the E-format item except that it allows a greater number of decimal digits to be processed. On input, the double precision constant is read in and stored in a double precision location. A data card containing

```
45.78596784105D04bbb5.167D0
```

$$\underbrace{\underbrace{\text{45.78596784105D04}}_{\overset{11}{}}\underbrace{\text{bbb}\underbrace{\text{5.167D0}}_{\overset{3}{}}}_{}}$$

| 11 | 3 |
| 17 | 7 |

might be read by

```
      DOUBLE PRECISION DONE,DTWO
      READ(5,101) DONE, DTWO
101 FORMAT(D17.11,3X, D7.3)
```

The general form of the D-format item is D$w.d$, where w is the total width of the field and d is the number of places to the right of the decimal point. If the decimal point is not punched, then it will be inserted so that there will be d places to the right of the decimal point.

On output, the D-format item is similar to the E-format item except that the maximum value of d is 16 (for IBM 360/370). The difference $(w - d)$ should still be a minimum of seven to allow enough space for the printed output. For example,

```
      DOUBLE PRECISION DTHIRD
      DTHIRD = 0.3333333333333333D0
      WRITE(5,101) DTHIRD,DTHIRD,DTHIRD
  101 FORMAT(' ', D23.16, D20.10, D10.3)
```

produces the following output:

```
0.3333333333333333D 00        0.3333333333D 00  0.333D 00
```

In general, a D$w.d$-format item produces

$$\pm 0.xxx \ldots xD \pm nn$$

where $xxx. . .x$ is a string of w decimal digits;

a minus sign is printed if the value is negative or a blank is printed if it is positive;

nn is the exponent.

Worked Example

The foreign exchange rate is $621\frac{1}{3}$ Italian lire for one American dollar. How many lire will one get for \$3.5 million?

```
      DOUBLE PRECISION DXCHNG,DOLLAR,DLIRE
      DXCHNG = 621.333333333333D0
      DOLLAR = 3.5D6
      DLIRE = DXCHNG*DOLLAR
      WRITE(5,101) DLIRE
  101 FORMAT('1THE AMOUNT IS ', D20.13)
      STOP
      END
```

This program prints

```
THE AMOUNT IS  0.2174666666667D 10
```

An alternate FORMAT for the output would have been F17.2, which would have printed

```
21746666666.67
```

Note

The IBM 360/370 FORTRAN compilers and WATFOR/WATFIV permit an alternative notation when making declarations of single and double precision variables. "REAL*4" is equivalent to "REAL" and "REAL*8" is equivalent to "DOUBLE PRECISION". When using integer variables it is possible to specify "INTEGER*4" or "INTEGER*2". The former is the standard integer location declaration while the latter specifies that only half as much space is to be reserved for an integer value. If the integer values will never exceed 32767 in magnitude, then "INTEGER*2" may be used in the declaration statement. Examples are

```
REAL*4 ALPHA(50), MESS, JOKER(5,10,10)
REAL*8 DUBVAL,DTABLE(500)
INTEGER*2 TINY, SMALLS(65)
INTEGER*4 USUAL(10,10),CARS
```

Logical Data

In situations requiring true-false, yes-no or on-off responses, logical data may be a convenient way of representing the information. (It may, however, also be inefficient in terms of storage space.) The primary advantage of using logical data is that the logical operators .OR. , .AND. , and .NOT. can be used.

Logical Constants and Variables

There are only two logical constants that can appear in a program. They are

```
.TRUE.
.FALSE.
```

All other values are invalid.

Logical variables are declared by the use of a type declaration statement which lists the logical variables and, if necessary, gives dimension information:

```
LOGICAL,LTEST,LTABLE(100),LMAT(20,20)
LOGICAL LOGIC
LOGICAL BOOL1,BOOL2, SWITCH(10)
```

When selecting logical variable names, it may be a mnemonic aid to use variable names that begin with "L." As with other declaration statements, the LOGICAL declaration statement must precede any executable statement.

A logical constant is assigned to a logical variable by the use of the usual assignment statement:

```
LOGICAL LA,LB
LA = .TRUE.
LB = LA
```

In this case, the value .TRUE. will be assigned to both LA and LB.

A logical variable may also be assigned the result of a comparison. For example, suppose we specify

```
LOGICAL LL
REAL DEBT, PAYMNT
   .
   .
   .
LL = DEBT .GT. PAYMNT
```

If A is greater than B, the value of LL will be .TRUE.; otherwise LL will be .FALSE. The construct A .GT. B is called a *logical expression*. It is evaluated as true or false. Since logical variables may assume the same values as logical expressions, they can also be used in IF statements. The following two sequences will produce identical results:

```
LOGICAL L1                  REAL DEBT, PAYMENT
REAL DEBT, PAYMNT           IF (DEBT.LE.PAYMNT) GO TO 50
   .
   .
   .
L1 = DEBT .LE. PAYMNT
IF (L1) GO TO 50
```

Logical Operators

The utility of logical data is evident when one examines the logical operators. The .AND. operation takes two logical operands and produces the result .TRUE. only if the value of both operands is .TRUE. Thus, in the program:

```
LOGICAL L1,L2,LRESLT
   .
   .
   .
LRESLT = L1 .AND. L2
```

LRESLT will have the value .TRUE. only if both L1 and L2 are true. The operation table is

	.AND.	*Operand 2*	
		.TRUE.	.FALSE.
Operand 1	.TRUE.	.TRUE.	.FALSE.
	.FALSE.	.FALSE.	.FALSE.

The logical operator .OR. takes two logical operands and produces the result .TRUE. if either or both of the operands have the value .TRUE. The operation table is

	.OR.	*Operand 2*	
		.TRUE.	.FALSE.
Operand 1	.TRUE.	.TRUE.	.TRUE.
	.FALSE.	.TRUE.	.FALSE.

The third logical operator is .NOT. It takes only a single operand and inverts its value:

Operand	*.NOT. Operand*
.TRUE.	.FALSE.
.FALSE.	.TRUE.

To understand more fully how logical variables are used, assume that three logical variables LGERMN,LFRNCH and LSPAN have been set to indicate whether a student is studying German, French, and Spanish. A value of .TRUE. for any of the variables indicates that the student is studying that language. A value of .FALSE. indicates that the student is not studying that language. To determine which students are taking both French and German, a programmer might set

```
LFAG = LFRNCH .AND. LGERMN
```

For those studying French or German, the following might be set:

```
LFOG = LFRNCH .OR. LGERMN
```

Later these values can be tested in order to alter the flow of control:

```
IF(LFAG) GO TO 40
   .
   .
   .
IF(LFOG) GO TO 60
```

If the value of the variable that is being tested is .TRUE., then the transfer of control will take place; otherwise, the next sequential statement will be executed.

More complex logical assignment statements can be constructed. To locate all students studying all three languages, one can write

```
LALL = LFRNCH .AND. LGERMN .AND. LSPAN
```

To identify students taking one or more of these languages one can write

```
LSOME = LFRNCH .OR. LGERMN .OR. LSPAN
```

The .NOT. operator can be used to identify students not taking Spanish:

```
LNSPAN = .NOT. LSPAN
```

To identify students taking either or both of French and Spanish but not taking German, the following can be written:

```
LCOMBO = (LFRNCH .OR. LSPAN) .AND. .NOT. LGERMN
```

The complexity of this operation demands the inclusion of parentheses in order to make clear just what was intended. As with arithmetic operations, parentheses can be inserted to clarify the intention of the programmer. If parentheses are not inserted, then the hierarchy of operations for logical operators is

Level 1	.NOT.
Level 2	.AND.
Level 3	.OR.

Level 1 operations would be performed first; thus, in the previous statement, the parentheses were not optional. They were required to insure that the order of execution would occur as desired.

Problem 10.1

Convert the following verbal descriptions to logical expressions.

a. A is greater than B.
b. A is between B and C in magnitude.
c. Both A and B are greater than C.
d. Either A or B is greater than C.
e. A is less than either B or C.

Logical operators may be used within IF statements as well:

```
IF (X .LT. 20 .AND. X .GT. 10) GO TO 73
IF (LL .AND. I .NE. J) X = 4.
IF ((A .GT. 1.0.OR. B.GT.1.0) .OR. C .GT. 1.0) GO TO 95
```

Problem 10.2

Convert the IF statements below to a logical assignment statement followed by an IF with a single logical variable.

a. IF (X .GT. Y) GO TO 70
b. IF (A .LT. 1.0 .OR. A .GT. B) X = 17.2

Input and Output of Logical Values

To read or print the logical values .TRUE. and .FALSE. the single letters T and F are used. Thus a data card containing 80 logical values could be prepared

TTTFFTFTFTTFTFTFTF...

and could be read into a logical array with the use of the LOGICAL format item L:

```
      LOGICAL LARRAY(80)
      READ(5,101) LARRAY
  101 FORMAT(80L1)
```

The complete array input feature was used in describing the entire array and the 80L1 field indicates that 80 logical values of length 1 are to be read. The general form of the L-format item is Lw, where w is the length of the field. If w is larger than one then the first T or F that is encountered during a left-to-right scan will be assigned to the specified location.

Data cards may contain a mixture of real, integer, alphabetic, double precision or logical data. A medical information data card might contain the results of true-false questions about medical history, real values indicating weight and height, a pair of integer values indicating blood pressure, and a 20-character name:

TTFTTTFFTF112.568.25 120 80DONALD H. SMITH

This card might be read by

```
      LOGICAL LHIST(10)
      INTEGER NAME(10)
      READ(5,101) LHIST,WEIGHT,HEIGHT,IBPSYS,IBPDIA,NAME
  101 FORMAT(10L1,F5.1,F5.2,I4,I3,5A4)
```

On output, a T or an F is printed to indicate the values .TRUE. or .FALSE. If w is greater than one, T or F is right justified in the field and $(w - 1)$ blanks are inserted to the left of the character. To print the values of the true-false questions about medical history with two blanks between each value, write

```
      WRITE(5,102) LHIST
  102 FORMAT(' ', 10L3)
```

These statements produce:

```
  T  T  F  T  T  T  F  F  T  F
```

The first two medical history questions could have been

- Does your family have a history of heart trouble?   T   F
- Does your family have a history of hypertension?   T   F

The information on the medical information data card might now be used to screen potential heart attack victims. The criteria might concern whether the patient's family has had a history of both heart trouble and hypertension:

```
IF(LHIST(1) .AND. LHIST(2)) GO TO 30
```

Alternatively there might be interest in patients with high blood pressure, say, over 140/90. The blood pressure information has two components: the systolic (IBPSYS) and the diastolic (IBPDIA). We can now test to see whether IBPSYS goes above 140 or IBPDIA goes above 90:

```
IF(IBPSYS .GT. 140 .OR. IBPDIA .GT. 90) GO TO 75
```

Combinations of tests can also be constructed:

```
LTEST = LHIST(2) .AND. (IBPSYS .GT. 140 .OR. IBPDIA .GT. 90)
IF(LTEST) GO TO 85
```

This assumes that the declaration LOGICAL LTEST was included at the beginning of the program. The parentheses resolve ambiguity in the programmer's mind, since by

```
A .AND. B .OR. C
```

one might intend to convey

```
(A .AND. B) .OR. C
```

or

```
A .AND. (B .OR. C)
```

According to our listed hierarchy of logical operations the computer will choose the first interpretation. The complete hierarchy of operations is given in Table 10.2.

TABLE 10.2

Operation	Hierarchy
function evaluation	1
**	2
* and /	3
+ and −	4
.LT. .LE. .EQ. .NE. .GT. .GE.	5
.NOT.	6
.AND.	7
.OR.	8

As noted in Chapter 4, if several operations of the same level appear in the same expression, they are performed from left to right (except for exponentiation operations, which are performed from right to left). In the expression below, the effective order of execution is indicated by the numbers under the expression.

```
A .GT. B - C**D .OR. E .AND. F .LE. G/H
   ↑     ↑  ↑      ↑         ↑      ↑    ↑
   4     3  1      7         6      5    2
```

The variable E must be LOGICAL and the other variables must be REAL. This expression could be rewritten with parentheses to make the meaning clearer:

```
((A .GT. (B - (C**D))) .OR. (E .AND. (F .LE. (G/H))
```

Parentheses can also be used to override the standard interpretation.

Note

The IBM 360/370 FORTRAN compilers and WATFOR/WATFIV permit an alternative notation when making declarations of logical variables. "LOGICAL*4" is equivalent to "LOGICAL." It is also correct to use "LOGICAL*1." This reduces the amount of storage space reserved for logical values. This saving can be significant if large logical arrays are used, for example:

```
LOGICAL*4 LVALUE, BOOL(60)
LOGICAL*1 LARRAY(50,50), LONG(500)
```

Complex data[1]

Many versions of FORTRAN provide the user with a specialized facility for dealing with complex data of the form

$$a + bi$$

where a is the real part of the value;
    b is the imaginary part;
    i is the square root of -1.

To declare a variable to be complex, write

```
COMPLEX ALPHA, COMP(15)
COMPLEX C(10,10)
```

---

[1] This section is optional and need be studied only if operations on imaginary numbers will be programmed.

Complex constants have real and imaginary components, each of which is a real value. The pair of values is enclosed in parentheses:

Written Form	Interpretation
(5.4,6.0)	5.4 + 6i
(6.7E6,7.869)	6.7E6 + 7.869i
(0.0,-1.0)	0 - 1i

Complex assignment statements are similar to real assignment statements:

```
COMPLEX A,B,C
A = (2.0,-7.9)
B = (10.0,0.0) * A
C = A - B
```

There are a number of library functions that are useful for converting from or to complex data as well as for operating on complex data. For more information on complex data, see the manufacturer's guide for FORTRAN on your computer.

Function Typing

The type of the value returned by a function subprogram is determined by the name of the function. The convention is the same for assigning types to variable names. SIN,COS, SQRT,FLOAT are library functions that return real values. IABS, IFIX and INT return integer values. User-defined function subprograms (Chapter 9) usually follow this naming convention. A function that sums three real values might be named SUM, while a function that sums three integer values might be named ISUM. The standard type convention specifies that variables and function subprograms whose names begin with I,J,K,L,M,N are integer; all others are real. To override this standard convention and to create DOUBLE PRECISION, LOGICAL, COMPLEX functions, it is necessary to use a function type declaration. This is done by adding the type information to the FUNCTION declaration and providing a corresponding declaration in the calling program:

Example 1

```
INTEGER PLUS1                    Calling Program
   :
L = PLUS1(M)
   :
INTEGER FUNCTION PLUS1(K)        Function Subprogram
PLUS1 = K + 1
RETURN
END
```

Example 2

```
      DOUBLE PRECISION DERROR,X,Y,DELTA              Calling Program
      ·
      ·
      DELTA = DERROR(X,Y)
      ·
      ·

      DOUBLE PRECISION FUNCTION DERROR(X,Y)   Function Subprogram
      DOUBLE PRECISION DIFF,X,Y
      DIFF = DABS(X - Y)
      DERROR = DIFF/Y
      RETURN
      END
```

The general form of the function typing statement is

> *Type* FUNCTION *name* (*argument list*)

where *Type* is one of INTEGER, REAL, DOUBLE PRECISION, LOGICAL, COMPLEX;
>   *name* is a valid variable name;
>   *argument list* is the list of dummy arguments separated by commas.

Common Storage Areas

So far only one method of passing information between a calling program and a subprogram has been studied. This method, which requires that each item be specified in the argument list of the calling program and the subprogram, can become complicated if there are a large number of variables to be shared by the programs. An alternative is the use of COMMON storage areas. It is possible to specify that an area of the storage be set aside, so that two or more subprograms have access to this COMMON area. Each of the routines having access to this area must have a description of the information stored there.

A payroll program may have many routines that refer to tax table data. The main program might contain a declaration to indicate which tables appear in the COMMON area.

Main Program

```
COMMON DEDUCT(50,20), SOCSEC(50), STTAX(40), FEDTAX(40)
   ·
   ·
   ·
CALL ONE(IDENT,WAGES)
   ·
   ·
   ·
CALL TWO(AMOUNT)
   ·
   ·
   ·
```

This COMMON statement sets aside space for a tax deduction array (DEDUCT) containing 1000 locations, a social security array (SOCSEC) containing 50 locations, a State tax array (STTAX) containing 40 locations and a Federal tax array containing 40 locations. In all, there are 1130 locations in the COMMON area. The COMMON declaration must appear at the beginning of the program before any executable statements. Type declaration information may appear separately following the COMMON statement. To keep matters simple, subprograms should use precisely the same COMMON statement as the calling program:

Subprogram 1

```
SUBROUTINE ONE(ID,SALARY)
COMMON DEDUCT(50,20), SOCSEC(50),STTAX(40),FEDTAX(40)
      .
      .
      .
RETURN
END
```

Subprogram 2

```
SUBROUTINE TWO(VALUE)
COMMON DEDUCT(50,20), SOCSEC(50),STTAX(40),FEDTAX(40)
      .
      .
      .
RETURN
END
```

Any of the routines that have the COMMON declaration may have access to and alter the values that have been stored. Although declarations have appeared in three places, only one set of 1130 locations is allocated.

The use of the COMMON statement simplifies subprogram calls by reducing the number of arguments. As a result, execution is generally faster.

Named COMMON Storage Areas

It may be desirable to have two or more COMMON areas in a large program. Information in the first of two COMMON areas might be shared by a main program and subprogram, while information in the second area might be differently shared. The main program and the subprograms that are to share the data should have COMMON areas with matching names. It is possible to assign a name to a COMMON area by following the key word COMMON with the name enclosed in slashes. Thus, validly named COMMON declarations would include

```
COMMON/MYDATA/TEST(100), VARINC(20), RESULT(100), NTEST
COMMON/ALPHA/MATRIX(50,50)
COMMON/SAVE/ACCT(1000), NEWBAL(1000), I,J, RATE
COMMON/X/XVAL,YVAL,ZVAL,TIME
```

The name of a COMMON area is any valid variable name. Any number of named COMMON areas may be created.

Our payroll program might be modified so that SUBROUTINE ONE shared only the DEDUCT array, while SUBROUTINE TWO shared the SOCSEC, STTAX and FEDTAX tables. The main program would now have two named COMMON declarations:

Main Program

```
COMMON/DED/DEDUCT(50,20)
COMMON/TAXES/SOCSEC(50), STTAX(40), FEDTAX(40)
      .
      .
      .
CALL ONE(IDENT,WAGES)
      .
      .
      .
CALL TWO(AMOUNT)
      .
      .
      .
```

Subprogram 1

```
SUBROUTINE ONE(ID,SALARY)
COMMON/DED/DEDUCT(50,20)
      .
      .
      .
RETURN
END
```

Subprogram 2

```
SUBROUTINE TWO(VALUE)
COMMON/TAXES/SOCSEC(50), STTAX(40), FEDTAX(40)
      .
      .
      .
RETURN
END
```

The most general forms of usage for these types of statements can be extremely complicated and confusing. Incorrect use of COMMON can be disastrous. Only an experienced programmer should try to go beyond the simplified forms given in these sections. A FORTRAN reference guide provides information on more intricate forms.

Problem 10.3

Write the declaration statements needed to allow two subroutines, SUB1 and SUB2, to share a 1000-element real array, A, with a main program. SUB1 and SUB2 should also share a 1000-element integer array, B, which is not part of the main program.

EQUIVALENCE Statement

The EQUIVALENCE statement is another declaration statement whose function is simply to reduce the number of storage spaces necessary in a program. It is entirely possible to do without this statement, but some programmers find it useful in performing a wide variety of clever programming tricks.

The initial portion of a program may contain a large table—say 80 x 100, into which data are to be read. Later, two 50 x 50 arrays may be needed for statistical analysis. Experience shows that the following DIMENSION statement will be needed:

```
DIMENSION INPUT(80,100), STAT1(50,50), STAT2(50,50)
```

This statement causes 13,000 storage locations to be allocated for the arrays. This is a substantial amount of storage and the user may not have so much storage available. By using an EQUIVALENCE statement, it is possible to share the storage space—that is, if the logic of the program does not require the INPUT array at the same time as the STAT1 and STAT2 arrays. This sharing can be created by adding the following EQUIVALENCE statement:

```
EQUIVALENCE (INPUT(1), STAT1(1)), (INPUT(2501), STAT2(1))
```

This statement indicates that the first location of the INPUT array corresponds to the first location of the STAT1 array and that the 2501st position of the INPUT array corresponds to the first location of the STAT2 array. The storage names now overlap and only 8000 locations need be allocated:

INPUT   (8000 locations)

STAT1   STAT2
(2500 locations)   (2500 locations)

In writing a long program, a programmer may inadvertently switch the names of variables. In the first part of the program, the programmer may have used the variable name SUM and later used the name TOTSUM to indicate the same quantity. Instead of punching the program cards, the two names may be made equivalent by adding the following declaration statement to the beginning of the program:

```
EQUIVALENCE (SUM,TOTSUM)
```

This kind of patchwork should be discouraged. In the long run, it is probably better to re-punch the program cards than to contribute to the creation of a program that is difficult to understand.

The general form of the EQUIVALENCE statement is

$$\text{EQUIVALENCE } (v1, v2, \ldots), \quad (w1, w2, \ldots), \ldots$$

where $v1, v2, w1$, and $w2$ are variable names. Two or more names may be assigned to the same location. The names need not be in the same mode. Any number of parenthesized groups may appear in a single EQUIVALENCE statement. There may be more than one EQUIVALENCE statement in a program, but they must appear before any executable statement.

Using EQUIVALENCE statements can become extremely complicated, particularly if the variables appear in COMMON statements. Great care must be taken when using this statement. If possible, avoid the use of the EQUIVALENCE.

Problem 10.4

Write the statements to allow a real array X with 1500 locations to share storage with three integer arrays, IA, IB, and IC, each 500 locations long.

DATA Declaration Statement

An alternative to the assignment statement, the DATA declaration statement provides a convenient and concise technique for establishing the value of a variable. The DATA declaration statement is most commonly used to establish values which are not altered during execution or to initialize variables. In its simplest form a list of variable names is followed by a list of constants which are assigned to corresponding elements in the list of variable names. Thus

```
DATA PI, FREEZE, MAXIM, MINUM/ 3.141593,32.0, 31, 28/
```

establishes two real values and two integer values. Corresponding elements in the two lists must be of the same type, that is, integer variable names must relate to integer constants, real variable names must correspond to real constants, etc.

Any number of DATA statements may be included in a program but like other declaration statements, the preferred placement of DATA statements is before any executable statement. The opening lines of a program with other declarations might begin as:

```
DIMENSION SCORES(4), NGRADE(4)
DATA SCORES/ 65.0, 70.0, 80.0, 90.0/
DATA NGRADE/ 'D', 'C', 'B', 'A'/
READ(5,101) ID,TEST1,TEST2,TEST3
    .
    .
    .
```

Notice that when an entire array is to be filled, only the name of the array need be given in the list of variable names. Make sure that the number of elements in the list of constants is enough to precisely fill the array.

If the array is large and is to be filled with the same value in every location an abbreviated form can be used:

```
DIMENSION ARRAY(150)
DATA ARRAY/ 150*0.0/
```

The same abbreviation can be used for portions of an array or for several separate variables:

```
DIMENSION ARRAY(150)
LOGICAL LGATEA, LGATEB, LTOTAL
DATA ARRAY, LGATEA, LGATEB, LTOTAL/ 100*0.0, 50*1.0,
1      3*  .TRUE./
              .
              .
              .
```

Some versions of FORTRAN, including WATFOR/WATFIV permit implied DO loops in the DATA statement:

```
DIMENSION ODDEVN(100)
DATA (ODDEVN(I), I = 1,99,2), (ODDEVN(I), I = 2,100,2)
1    / 50*0, 50*1/
```

Summary

The additional flexibility provided by the statements introduced in this chapter can simplify certain programming tasks. However, with additional power comes additional complexity and a greater chance of error. Extreme care must be taken when using these sophisticated instructions.

The variety of data types provided by FORTRAN is meager compared to some programming languages. Still, the selection and use of INTEGER, REAL, DOUBLE PRECISION, LOGICAL, or COMPLEX data types is filled with pitfalls. Each of these types should be studied carefully before it is used. DOUBLE PRECISION is useful for improving the accuracy of computations, but by no means does it provide a guarantee of perfect accuracy. LOGICAL data are extremely useful when true-false information is specified. COMPLEX data simplify manipulation of complex numbers—but it is somewhat confusing to the novice.

The storage allocation facilities provided by the COMMON, named COMMON, and EQUIVALENCE statements are powerful. They also can prove to be a deadly trap for the novice. Great care must be exercised in attempting to use these statements. Programmers should experiment with these techniques before using them in large programs. The wise programmer will make sure to produce additional debugging output when implementing these statements.

DEBUGGING CLINIC

When you provide data type information, each variable name should be separated from the others by a comma. It should be remembered that a variable name can only be of one data type throughout the program—the type cannot be altered during the program. All declarations appear at the beginning of the program, before any executable statement. Here are examples of correct use:

```
INTEGER MICRO(50),ALPHA,XBAR,TABLE(20,20)
REAL INPUT(30,40), NEWVAL
DOUBLE PRECISION DVALUE, DTABLE(100)
LOGICAL LTF, LARRAY(10,50), LONE, LTWO
COMPLEX CVALUE, COMEGA(70)

COMMON MALE(500), FEMALE(500)
REAL MALE

COMMON/BUG/ANT(50), SPIDER(50), FLY(50), YESNO(3,50)
COMMON/RODENT/MOUSE(50), CHPMNK(50), YESNO2(2,50)
REAL MOUSE
LOGICAL YESNO, YESNO2

INTEGER FUNCTION THREAT(I)
COMMON/BUG/ANT(50), SPIDER(50), FLY(50), YESNO(3,50)
LOGICAL YESNO
```

Remember these pointers:

- A variable may appear in only one named COMMON area.

- Variables appearing in COMMON should not be used as arguments for subprograms.

- Danger—the EQUIVALENCE statement must be used with great care, especially when variables appear in COMMON.

REVIEW QUESTIONS

1. How can the use of double precision variables be specified? What means are available for input and output of double precision values.

2. How are logical variables declared? What values may they take on? How do the logical operators .AND. , .OR., and .NOT. work? How is a logical expression evaluated?

3. What is program COMMON? Why is COMMON used? How can different COMMON sections be established within the sam program?

4. How can the EQUIVALENCE statement be used to reduce program size? What precautions should the programmer observe when using EQUIVALENCE?

1. What is printed by each of the following programs?

a.
```
      LOGICAL L1,L2
      L1 = .TRUE.
      L2 = .FALSE.
      L1 = L1 .AND. L2 .OR. L2
      WRITE(6,101) L1,L2
  101 FORMAT(' RESULT-', 2L3)
      STOP
      END
```

b.
```
      LOGICAL LOGIC
      LOGIC = .TRUE. .OR. .NOT. .TRUE.
      WRITE(6,101) LOGIC
  101 FORMAT(' LOGIC=',L1)
      STOP
      END
```

c.
```
      TABLE = 4.3
      CHAIR = 2.4
      IF(TABLE .GT. 4.0 .AND. .NOT. CHAIR .EQ. 0.0)
     1    GO TO 10

      WRITE(6,101)
  101 FORMAT('1OAK')
      STOP
   10 WRITE(6,102)
  102 FORMAT('1MAPLE')
      STOP
      END
```

d.
```
      LOGICAL EQUIV, LONE, LTWO, LRES
      LONE = .TRUE.
      LTWO = .FALSE.
      IF(EQUIV(LONE,LTWO)) GO TO 30
      WRITE(6,101) LONE,LTWO
  101 FORMAT(' ', L1, ' NOT EQUAL',L1)
      GO TO 40
   30 WRITE(6,102) LONE,LTWO
  102 FORMAT(' ', L1, ' EQUALS ', L1)
   40 STOP
      END

      LOGICAL FUNCTION EQUIV(LA,LB)
      LOGICAL LA,LB
      IF(LA .AND. LB) GO TO 10
      IF(.NOT. LA .AND. .NOT. LB) GO TO 10
      EQUIV = .FALSE.
```

```
  10 EQUIV = .TRUE.
     RETURN
     END

e.     LOGICAL LIST(10)
       READ(5,101)LIST
 101 FORMAT(10L1)
       DO 10 I = 1,10
       IF (.NOT. LIST(I)) GO TO 20
  10 CONTINUE
       WRITE(6,102)
 102 FORMAT('1ALL TRUE')
       STOP
  20 WRITE(6,103)
 103 FORMAT('1 NOT ALL TRUE')
       STOP
       END

DATA: TTTTFFTFT
```

PROGRAMMING EXERCISES

2. Data cards have been prepared which describe the goods sold by sporting goods stores. Columns 1–40 contain the name of the store. Columns 41–47 contain logical constants T or F to indicate whether the store stocks supplies for particular sport, according to the following list:

Column	Sport
41	tennis
42	skiing
43	camping & hiking
44	mountain climbing
45	archery
46	canoeing
47	scuba diving

a. Write a program to read the data cards and print the names of the stores which carry supplies for

1. Mountain climbing.
2. Canoeing and scuba diving.
3. Tennis or skiing.
4. Either (archery and tennis) or (skiing and mountain climbing).

b. Produce a listing by sports of stores which supply materials for that sport. That is, produce seven listings.

3. Write a logical function called EVEN which has one integer argument. The function returns .TRUE. if the value of the argument is even, .FALSE. otherwise. Test this function by creating a main program to call the function and print the result for ten values read in from data cards.

4. *Logical Expression Evaluation.* Let + represent 'or' and let '*' represent 'and.' Data cards are prepared in the form

Column 1	41
(A+B)	ATBF
(A+(B*C))	ATBTCF
(A+B)*(C+D))	AFBFCFDT
((A*B)+(A*C))	ATBTCF

The logical expressions beginning in column 1 are to be evaluated with the logical values assigned beginning in column 41. In the first example A is assigned the value T and B is assigned the value F. The expression (A+B) is evaluated as T. The logical expressions can be of great complexity: write a program to accommodate all valid expressions.

SPIRAL PROBLEMS

A. Student Grading

Write a logical function subprogram called LPASS which returns the value .TRUE. if a student's term average is above 65, and .FALSE. otherwise. A 100 x 3 array, GRADES, containing the three test grades for each of the 100 students, is passed in the named COMMON block called TESTS. The function has one argument, N, the number (range 1 to 100) of the student being graded.

Write a main program to test the function.

B. Commercial Application

Write a logical function subprogram called LBONUS which returns the value .TRUE. if an employee is entitled to a bonus, and .FALSE. otherwise. A bonus is given if number of absences, IABSC, is less than three days, or productivity, PROD, is above 15.5 or the number of years employed, NYRS, exceeds 10. The function has the three arguments IABSC, PROD, and NYRS.

Write a main program to test the function.

C. Mathematical

Write a double precision function subprogram, DAVER, to return the average of the values stored in the double precision array, DVALS. The array contains 500 elements and is passed as the first argument. The second argument, an integer, indicates how many of the array positions have been filled.

Write a main program to test the function.

AN INTRODUCTION
TO PROGRAM DESIGN

If we understand a problem perfectly, it should be considered apart from all superfluous concepts, reduced to its simplest form, and divided by enumeration into the smallest possible parts.

René Descartes, Rules for the Direction of the Mind

CHAPTER 11

Good program design is an art well worth acquiring. Well-designed programs are efficient, easy to debug, clear, and easily modifiable.

One of the most important elements of program design is modularity. A modular program, rather than being one long intricate block of code, is divided into subprograms. This makes the logic easy to follow and simplifies debugging. Subprograms may be tested independently and later combined to form a complete program.

In a top-down approach to program design, the major facets (macrostructure) are defined and then details are filled in. A bottom-up approach, on the other hand, begins with the details and works upward to the overall program structure. Many programmers use a mixed design strategy which has elements of both.

Design of a program or set of programs is called system development. As an example of the system development process, this chapter demonstrates the construction of a simple computer graphics system.

Introduction

When writing short programs, perhaps 50 to 60 statements in length, the question of program organization is not critical. But as programs become longer, they become increasingly difficult to understand and modify. For this reason, program modularity is an important component of the well-designed program. By dividing a program into a number of subprograms, coding, debugging, modification, and documenting are considerably simplified. The construction of programs with large segments of complicated logic is not good practice.

Often, a well-written main program will consist of very few statements. The bulk of the program is written as a series of subprograms, each of which performs a well-defined process. For example, a payroll program might read employee records, calculate wages, calculate deductions, and print a check. If such a program were written as a single module, it would be both large and complex. Such a program might be better written as a series of modules linked together by a main program such as the following:

```
C       OBTAIN EMPLOYEE RECORD
   10   CALL INPUT
C       CALCULATE WAGES
        CALL WAGE
C       SUBTRACT DEDUCTIONS
        CALL DEDUCT
C       PRINT CHECK
        CALL PCHECK
C       BACK FOR NEXT EMPLOYEE
        GO TO 10
        END
```

Such a main program makes the flow of control quite clear. In fact, it corresponds to the "macro-flowchart" for the program (Figure 11.1)—a chart showing only the largest logical units into which it can be broken.

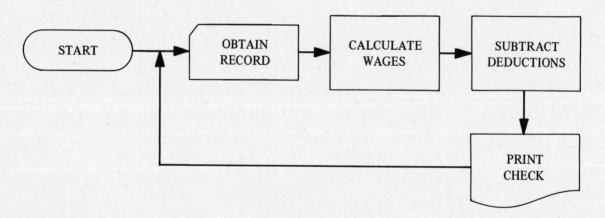

Figure 11.1

DOCUMENTATION

Documentation refers to explanatory material which accompanies a program and explains how it functions. Documentation may be part to the program itself (e.g., meaningful variable names and comments) but it may include program manuals as well.

The amount of documentation which should be included with a program depends on the program's expected life, complexity, and distribution. Each case is unique but here are some guidelines:

- Always provide more documentation than you think you need.
- Document as much of the program within the code as possible.
- Make your program unambiguous and understandable.
- Be neat.

Identifying FORTRAN Statements. The identification field of the FORTRAN card (columns 73–80) may be used for three purposes:

To identify the program.
To keep the cards in sequence.
To flag modifications or special insertions.

Columns 73–76 are available for use in identifying a particular subroutine or program. We suggest that sequence numbering be restricted to columns 77–80. This procedure allows for decks of up to 1000 cards with sequence numbers incremented by 10. Numbering by tens permits insertions to be made without resequencing the entire deck. For example, a FUNCTION subprogram to find the average of an array of values could be identified as follows:

```
      FUNCTION AVERAG(X,N)                          AVER0010
      DIMENSION X(N)                                AVER0020
      SUM = 0.0                                     AVER0030
      DO 10 I = 1,N                                 AVER0040
      SUM = SUM + X(I)                              AVER0050
   10 CONTINUE                                      AVER0060
      AVERAG = SUM/N                                AVER0070
      RETURN                                        AVER0080
      END                                           AVER0090
```

Inserting Comments. The comment card is one of the most powerful documentation tools available. *Meaningful* comments, strategically placed, can remove all doubt about the programmer's intentions. Carefully written comments enhance a program's usefulness and its ability to be modified. Consider the following comment in the context of the statement which it explains:

```
C
C            INCREMENT I BY J
C
      I = I + J
```

Such a comment might just as well not have been written. A more meaningful comment is

```
C
C            SET I TO THE MAXIMUM ALLOWABLE SUBSCRIPT
C
       I = I + J
```

Notice that the second comment is valid only in the context of a specific program, whereas the first comment is valid in any context. The first comment tells the reader nothing that is not obvious from the syntax of the following statement; the second comment tells the reader the meaning of that statement.

Comments are free in format with the exception of the identifying "C" which always appears in column one. The comment should not extend beyond column 72 to avoid interfering with card sequencing.

Some programmers always begin in columns 3, 4, or 5 so that the comments stand out. Others prefer to begin in columns 10, 11, or 12 so that the comments don't interfere with a quick scan of the statement labels or the statements. Some begin with comments in column 7 with their FORTRAN statements. Still other programmers are irregular and begin comments in different columns each time—a sloppy technique. Select a rule that suits you and stick to it.

Another useful technique is to enclose headings and titles in a frame of asterisks:

```
C
C        XXXXXXXXXXXXXXXXXXXXXXXX
C        X                      X
C        X  PROGRAM INITIALIZATION  X
C        X                      X
C        XXXXXXXXXXXXXXXXXXXXXXXX
C
```

This makes it very easy for the reader to locate relevant segments of code in a large program.

Prologue. Just as the prologue of a book introduces the reader to the content which follows, each program and subroutine should contain a prologue to introduce the reader to the routine which follows. COBOL, the business-oriented programming language, has a mandatory prologue called the *identification division.* The concept may be extended to FORTRAN by use of comment cards. The most important sections of the prologue are shown in Table 11.1.

Table 11.1

Section	Information
Program id	What program is this?
Author	Who wrote it?
Date or revision date	When was it written?
Description	What does it do and how does it do it?
Subroutines required	What other subroutines are needed?

Consider the following example:

```
C
C   PROGRAM - SIMEQ
C
C   PROGRAMMER - N.E. NAIM
C   DATE - JULY 1975
C
C   DESCRIPTION - THIS PROGRAM SOLVES A MATRIX OF SIMULTANEOUS
C   LINEAR EQUATIONS UP TO 20 BY 20. THE METHOD USED IS GAUSS
C   ELIMINATION WITH MAXIMIZATION OF THE PIVOTAL COEFFICIENT.
C
C   SUBROUTINES - THIS PROGRAM USES SUBROUTINE RCIN TO FIND THE
C   MAXIMUM COEFFICIENT AND INTERCHANGE THE ROWS AND COLUMNS.
C
```

This prologue provides a good idea of what the program does, what routines are called, who wrote the program, and what technique is used—a tremendous amount of information in fewer than 20 lines.

Listing Variable Names. Programmers may use a number of mnemonic variable names which are difficult to keep track of or may not be obvious to others. To make clear exactly what each variable stands for and its function, the programmer can list each variable used with the problem-related description at the beginning of the program. Consider this brief example:

```
C
C   AVG      AVERAGE OF THE VALUES
C   N        NUMBER OF VALUES IN ARRAY XVAL
C   STDDEV   STANDARD DEVIATION OF THE VALUES
C   XVAL     ARRAY OF VALUES FROM EXPERIMENT
C
```

If a change in the tax laws made it necessary to modify the deduction algorithm, the programmer would have to deal only with that subroutine. The task is thus simplified and the danger of introducing errors into other parts of the program is minimized. The design of programs and of systems of programs is an important task which is often delegated to specialists called *systems analysts*. The effective systems analyst cuts down the system's cost and increases its efficiency and integrity.

Program design is more a matter of experience and aesthetics than a matter of simple rule application, since multiple program structures are possible. While a simple program may consist only of a main program or of a main program and a single subprogram, complex systems may require tens or hundreds of subprograms. Some tasks seem especially appropriate for implementation as subprograms. Procedures such as printing arrays, computing a set of numbers, sorting an array, searching data for a specified value, and input of data values are typical candidates for implementation as subprograms.

A subprogram itself may call upon other subprograms. For example, a main program might call a subprogram to print the contents of an array. The print subroutine might, in turn, call a subroutine to skip to a new page and print a page heading and page number.

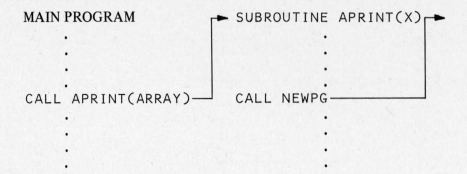

This sequence might be represented graphically by the following diagram:

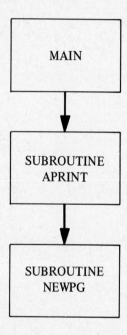

Isolation of the page heading routine eliminates the need to clutter up the program with page counter arithmetic and WRITE statements. The array printing subroutine, APRINT, might also be used in several places in the program. For example, the main program might call an input routine to initialize an array. The input routine in turn could call the array print subroutine to verify that the input has been performed properly. The main program might also call a subroutine to clear an array to zeroes, a function to sum the elements of the array, and the array print subroutine for output of results (Figure 11.2). Program design strategies may become quite complex, involving several levels of subroutines, as in Figure 11.3. However, three limitations must be observed:

- There can only be one main program.
- Subprograms cannot call the main program.
- A subprogram cannot call itself; nor can a subprogram call subprograms which indirectly result in a circular call.[1]

---

[1] Such calls, known as *recursive calls*, are permitted in some other programming languages.

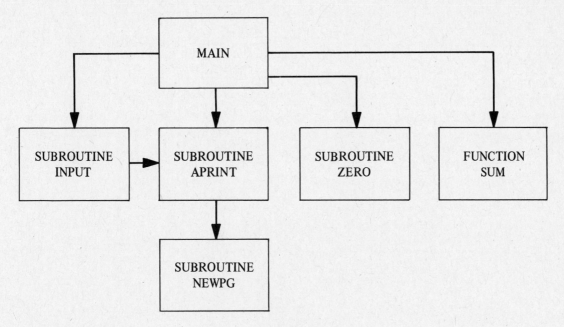

Figure 11.2

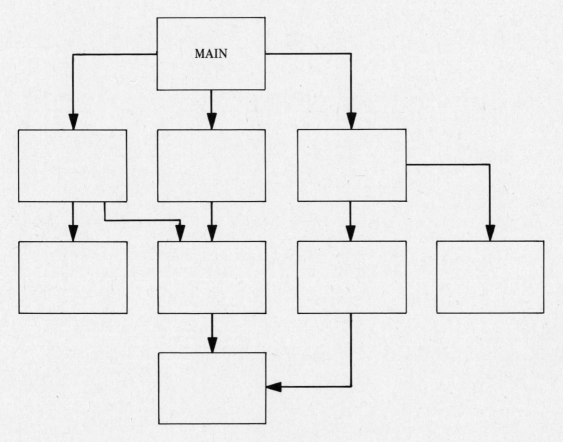

Figure 11.3

Problem 11.1

Which of the following are invalid subprogram calling structures? Why?

a.

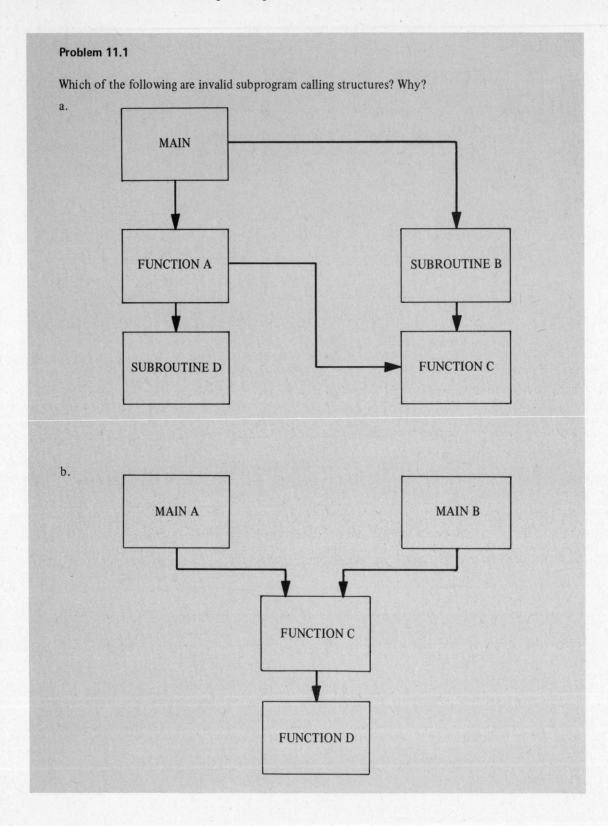

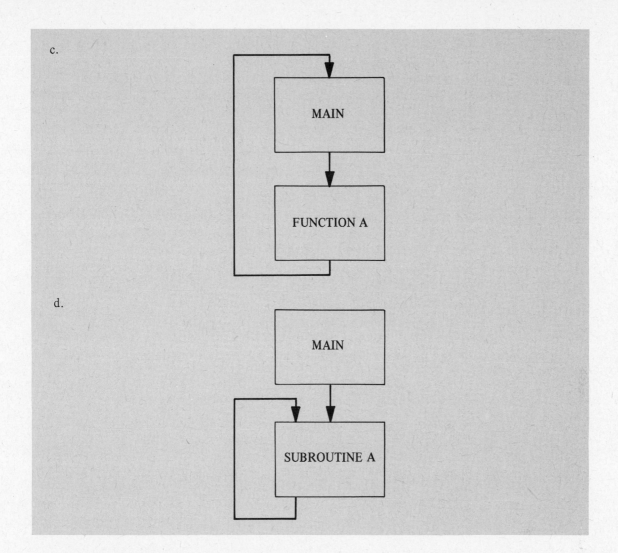

c.

d.

Design Philosophies

There has been considerable discussion in recent years about the best way to design a program. The importance of modularity is generally agreed upon. Experienced programmers find that it is easier to write, debug, understand, and modify programs which have been subdivided into units which perform meaningful operations. The programmer's experience and thorough understanding of the problem are important factors in the quality of the program structure and the particular procedures chosen for implementation as subprograms.

Program designers use various guidelines for determining the optimum length of a program module. If the modules are too large, they will be difficult to understand; but if they are too small, the proliferation of modules may be confusing. A number of arbitrary rules of thumb have been suggested:

- Program modules should be no longer than one page.
- Program modules should have no more than 30 lines.
- Program modules should contain no more than two IF statements.
- Program modules should contain no more than five variables.

Research is currently proceeding to help determine what makes a program module "intellectually manageable."

Another philosophical debate ranges between advocates of the "top-down approach" and the "bottom-up approach." The top-downers claim that the main program should be written first and then the lower and lower levels of subprograms should be written. The bottom-uppers suggest that the low-level subprograms should be thoroughly tested and debugged, and then higher and higher levels should be written. Programmers with an eclectic style claim that they follow both strategies at once. You will have to develop your own style of programming and adapt it to each particular problem. Your own knowledge of the problem and your experience are the best guides.

Some useful techniques for program design are:

- Consider the macrostructure of your program first. Draw a very general flowchart. This may often serve as a design for the main program. For example, many programs follow a

    ⊢► read → process → print⌐   sequence. A main program such as

    ```
    10   CALL READX
         CALL PROCES
         CALL PRINTX
         GO TO 10
         END
    ```

    is a "natural" way to divide such a program.
- Decide what service routines would be useful. For example, printing routines, debugging routines, page heading routines, array clearing routines, array sorting routines, and data validation (such as editing for valid range) routines are often useful in simplifying coding. They may often be used in future programs.
- Isolate *volatile code*—that is, code subject to change—in subprograms to minimize the danger of introducing program errors when the code is modified.
- Make the subroutines as general as possible. Rather than write a subroutine to clear arrays to zero and another routine to set arrays to some other value, write one routine and specify the value to be used as a parameter.
- Consider the use of COMMON declarations to avoid passing many parameters to subprograms.

A Computer Graphics System

As an example of the design of a modular program, we will apply these techniques to the development of a set of subprograms for producing graphic output on the line printer. This set of subprograms could be used to produce graphs, histograms, or pieces of computer "art." The central data structure used in this program is an array IPICT, which has 51 rows and 101 columns. IPICT (which we shall call the "board") is diagrammed in Figure 11.4.

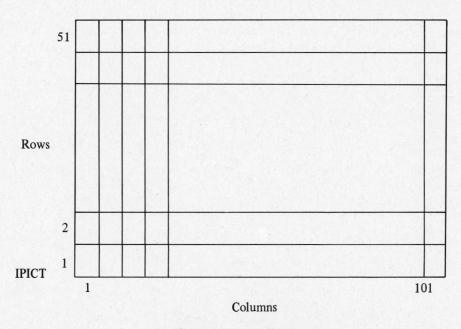

Figure 11.4. The IPICT array.

To translate this board into the more familiar terms of x and y coordinates, we think of the board as if the rows and columns were labeled as in Figure 11.5. The origin board position $(0,0)$ is the array location IPICT(26,51), while board position $(50,25)$ refers to array location IPICT(51,101) which is at the upper right-hand corner of the array. To convert board position (x,y) to IPICT (r,c), use the formulas $r = y+26$ and $c = x+51$. A few more examples are given in Table 11.1.

Table 11.1

Board Position	Array location
(10,10)	IPICT(36,61)
(−10,10)	IPICT(36,41)
(−10,−10)	IPICT(16,41)
(−50,−25)	IPICT(1,1)
(20,−5)	IPICT(21,71)

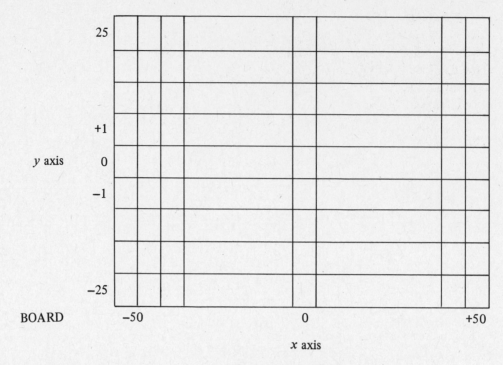

Figure 11.5 The board.

Problem 11.2

In terms of the IPICT array, where are these board positions?

a. (−50,25)
b. (50,−25)
c. (17,15)
d. (−18,−22)

The Subprograms

Initially, the entire board area must be filled with blanks. Then points will be filled in with single characters, one at a time. Finally, the entire board must be printed, starting at the top of a page. Initializing the board to blanks is accomplished by the subroutine CLEAR; storing a single character in the board is the task of subroutine POINT; and delivering output is performed by the subroutine DRAW. All three of these subprograms are linked together and called by a suitable main program. The IPICT array is shared by the subprograms by placing the array in COMMON and providing each subprogram with a copy of the COMMON declaration. Note how the division of the tasks into three subprograms corresponds to the macro-flowchart (Figure 11.6).

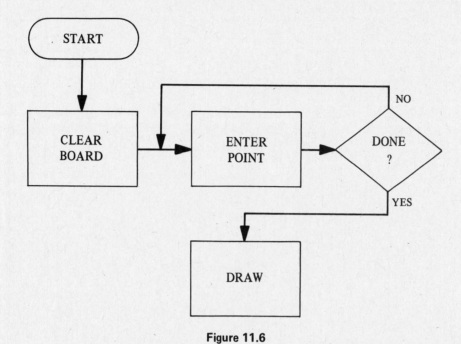

Figure 11.6

The subroutine CLEAR simply sweeps through the entire IPICT array and stores a blank in each of the 5151 locations. The internal representation of the character blank is established by the use of a DATA statement. Debugging output will help in the localization of errors and can be removed when the program is operating properly. Notice that there are no arguments in this subprogram.

```
      SUBROUTINE CLEAR
C
C         THIS SUBROUTINE CLEARS THE PICTURE SPACE
C
      COMMON IPICT(51,101)
      DATA NBLANK/' '/
C
C         DEBUG OUTPUT
C
      WRITE(6,101)
  101 FORMAT(' *DEBUG*CLEAR*')
C
      DO 20 I = 1,51
      DO 10 J = 1,101
      IPICT(I,J) = NBLANK
   10 CONTINUE
   20 CONTINUE
      RETURN
      END
```

The subroutine POINT stores a single character in a given position of the array. Three pieces of information are passed to the subroutine: the *x* and *y* coordinates on the board and the character that is to be stored there. The subroutine prints a debugging line and then tests to see whether the point is on the board. If it is, the proper location in the IPICT array is set to the character specified by the third argument. The conversion of *x* and *y* coordinates to row and column position in the array is performed according to the formulas given earlier. The debugging line should be eliminated when the program is operating properly.

```
        SUBROUTINE POINT(IX,IY,NCHAR)
C
C           THIS SUBROUTINE ENTERS A SINGLE POINT
C
        COMMON IPICT(51,101)
        WRITE(6,100) IX,IY,NCHAR
    100 FORMAT(' *DEBUG*POINT*', 2I12, 5X, A1)
C
C           TEST IF THE POINT IS IN RANGE
C
        IF(IABS(IX) .GT. 50) GO TO 99
        IF(IABS(IY) .GT. 25) GO TO 99
C
C           ENTER POINT
C           NOTICE THE COORDINATE INTERCHANGE
C
        IPICT(IY+26, IX+51) = NCHAR
        RETURN
     99 WRITE(6,101) IX, IY
    101 FORMAT('0***INVALID POINT***', 2I12)
        RETURN
        END
```

The subroutine DRAW causes the printout of the entire array. The printer is first positioned to a new page. Then the output is printed, one line at a time, beginning with the 51st row and working backwards. The first row is printed last. The debugging output should be eliminated when the program is operating properly.

```
        SUBROUTINE DRAW
C
C           THIS SUBROUTINE DOES THE PRINTOUT
C
        COMMON IPICT(51,101)
C
C           DEBUG OUTPUT
C
        WRITE(6,100)
    100 FORMAT(' *DEBUG*DRAW*')
C
C           SKIP TO THE TOP OF A PAGE
C
```

```
      WRITE(6,101)
  101 FORMAT('1')
C
C         PRINT THE PICTURE FROM THE TOP DOWN
C
      DO 10 I = 1,51
      II = 52 - I
      WRITE(6,102) (IPICT(II,J), J = 1,101)
  102 FORMAT(' ', 15X, 101A1)
   10 CONTINUE
      RETURN
      END
```

The Main Program

The three subroutines, CLEAR, POINT, and DRAW must be invoked by a suitable main program. First, look at this main program designed to allow the programmer carefully to study the effect of the various subroutine calls and thus test out the subroutines.

```
C
C         THIS TESTS SUBROUTINES CLEAR, POINT, AND DRAW
C
      CALL CLEAR
      CALL POINT(0,0,'*')
      CALL POINT(15,-10,'M')
      CALL POINT(-45,-20,'2')
      CALL POINT(-1,-25,'K')
      DO 10 I = 1,20
      CALL POINT(I,I,'A')
      CALL POINT(I - 40, 10 - I, '0')
   10 CONTINUE
C
C         TEST ONE INVALID POINT
C
      CALL POINT(1000,10,'E')
      CALL DRAW
      STOP
      END
```

This main program clears the board, enters four individual points, enters 40 points by way of a loop, attempts to enter an invalid point, and finally requests that the board be printed. The debugging output (Figure 11.7) helps clarify the flow of control. Figure 11.8 shows the printed board.

While the results of this program are simple, they provide a foundation for the creation of a more powerful system. The best way to construct a complex program is to write and test a small portion of the program and gradually increase the program's complexity. This evolutionary approach permits thorough testing of the program.

```
✗DEBUG✗CLEAR✗
✗DEBUG✗POINT✗              0              0              ✗
✗DEBUG✗POINT✗             15            -10              M
✗DEBUG✗POINT✗            -45            -20              2
✗DEBUG✗POINT✗             -1            -25              K
✗DEBUG✗POINT✗              1              1              A
✗DEBUG✗POINT✗            -39              9              0
✗DEBUG✗POINT✗              2              2              A
✗DEBUG✗POINT✗            -38              8              0
✗DEBUG✗POINT✗              3              3              A
✗DEBUG✗POINT✗            -37              7              0
✗DEBUG✗POINT✗              4              4              A
✗DEBUG✗POINT✗            -36              6              0
✗DEBUG✗POINT✗              5              5              A
✗DEBUG✗POINT✗            -35              5              0
✗DEBUG✗POINT✗              6              6              A
✗DEBUG✗POINT✗            -34              4              0
✗DEBUG✗POINT✗              7              7              A
✗DEBUG✗POINT✗            -33              3              0
✗DEBUG✗POINT✗              8              8              A
✗DEBUG✗POINT✗            -32              2              0
✗DEBUG✗POINT✗              9              9              A
✗DEBUG✗POINT✗            -31              1              0
✗DEBUG✗POINT✗             10             10              A
✗DEBUG✗POINT✗            -30              0              0
✗DEBUG✗POINT✗             11             11              A
✗DEBUG✗POINT✗            -29             -1              0
✗DEBUG✗POINT✗             12             12              A
✗DEBUG✗POINT✗            -28             -2              0
✗DEBUG✗POINT✗             13             13              A
✗DEBUG✗POINT✗            -27             -3              0
✗DEBUG✗POINT✗             14             14              A
✗DEBUG✗POINT✗            -26             -4              0
✗DEBUG✗POINT✗             15             15              A
✗DEBUG✗POINT✗            -25             -5              0
✗DEBUG✗POINT✗             16             16              A
✗DEBUG✗POINT✗            -24             -6              0
✗DEBUG✗POINT✗             17             17              A
✗DEBUG✗POINT✗            -23             -7              0
✗DEBUG✗POINT✗             18             18              A
✗DEBUG✗POINT✗            -22             -8              0
✗DEBUG✗POINT✗             19             19              A
✗DEBUG✗POINT✗            -21             -9              0
✗DEBUG✗POINT✗             20             20              A
✗DEBUG✗POINT✗            -20            -10              0
✗DEBUG✗POINT✗           1000             10              E

✗✗✗INVALID POINT✗✗✗          1000                    10
✗DEBUG✗DRAW✗
```

Figure 11.7

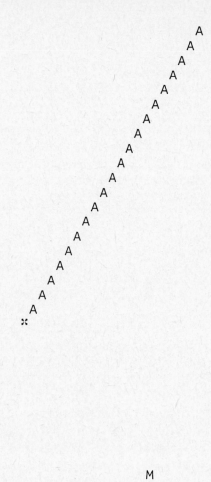

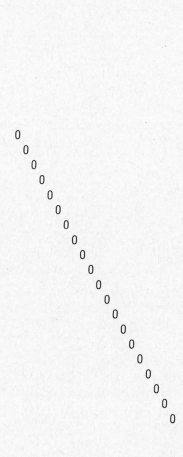

Figure 11.8

Problem 11.3

Write a main program to clear the board and draw a single horizontal line of *x*'s across the middle, then print the board.

Computer Art

At this stage we have a working main program and three subroutines:

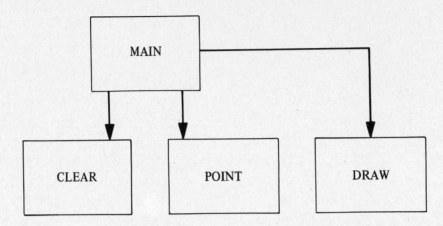

The basic system will now be extended to produce computer art based on arrangements of squares. Squares (in outline form) will be drawn by the subroutine SQUARE, and filled-in squares will be drawn by the subroutine SQFILL. SQUARE will operate by calling subroutines XLINE and YLINE. XLINE draws a horizontal line while YLINE produces a vertical line. SQFILL repeatedly calls XLINE to produce a filled-in square. Both XLINE and YLINE call POINT actually to enter a character at a point. Finally, there is a BORDER routine which enters a border around the board to frame the image. The structure of the programming system for squares is shown in Figure 11.9. Note again how a complex system is reduced to its fundamental operations by appropriate modularization. The main program to test our subprograms might be:

```
    DIMENSION NC(6)
    DATA NC/'.','+','*','X','0','W'/
    CALL CLEAR
    CALL BORDER('/')
    CALL SQUARE(-40,-20,3.0,'0')
    CALL SQUARE(0,0,3.5,'H')
    CALL SQFILL(-12,-10,2.0,'W')
    CALL SQFILL(-40,0,3.0,'S')
    CALL DRAW
    CALL CLEAR
    CALL BORDER('/')
    DO 10 I = 1,6
    IX = -50 + I*10
    IY = -24 + I*4
    SIDE = FLOAT(I)/2.0
    CALL SQUARE(IX,IY,SIDE,NC(I))
 10 CONTINUE
    CALL DRAW
```

```
       CALL CLEAR
       DO 20 I = 1,6
       CALL SQFILL(-50 +I*10, -24 + I*4, FLOAT(I)/2.0,NC(I))
   20 CONTINUE
       CALL DRAW
       CALL BORDER('/')
       CALL DRAW
       STOP
       END
```

The main program used in this version invokes the DRAW subroutine four times to produce four pieces of computer art. These works are extremely primitive, but they do convey some of the possibilities open to an "artist" using only simple forms on a printer. In the first picture (Figure 11.10) there are two outlined squares and two filled-in squares within a border. The second (Figure 11.11) contains a border to frame six increasingly large squares. The third image (Figure 11.12) contains six filled-in squares of increasing dimension and the fourth image (Figure 11.13) has the simple addition of a border.

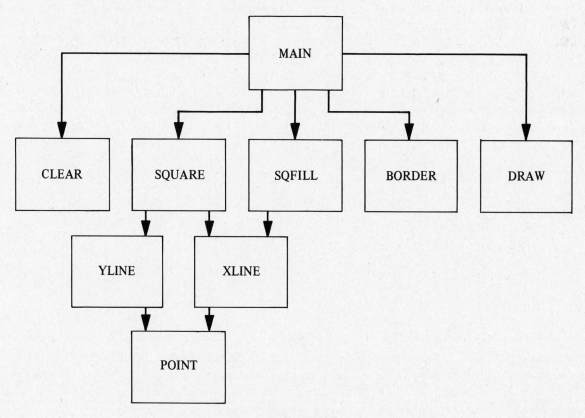

Figure 11.9

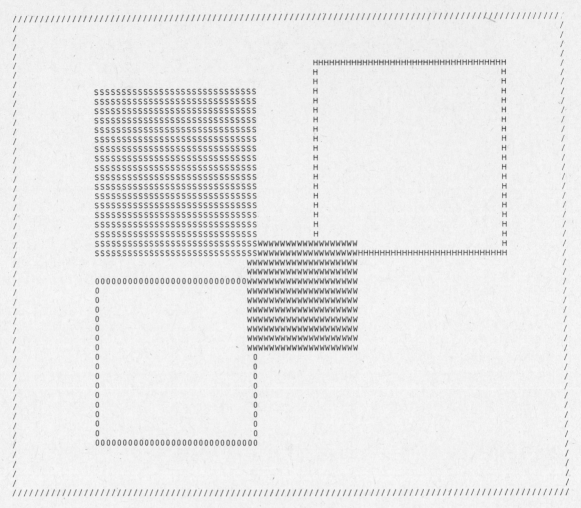

Figure 11.10

Summary

The solution of large and complicated problems is best accomplished by a divide-and-conquer strategy. First, envision the overall macrostructure of the problem and design a simplified main program to execute the solution. The main program should invoke a series of subprograms to handle the details. Subprograms may also invoke other subprograms to handle still lower levels of detail. This top-down design strategy is the easiest to understand, implement, and debug.

The computer graphics programming system is an example of this top-down technique. The main program described the placement of the squares, the inclusion of a border, and the actual drawing operation. The square drawing routines invoked line drawing routines which, in turn, invoked a routine to enter a single point.

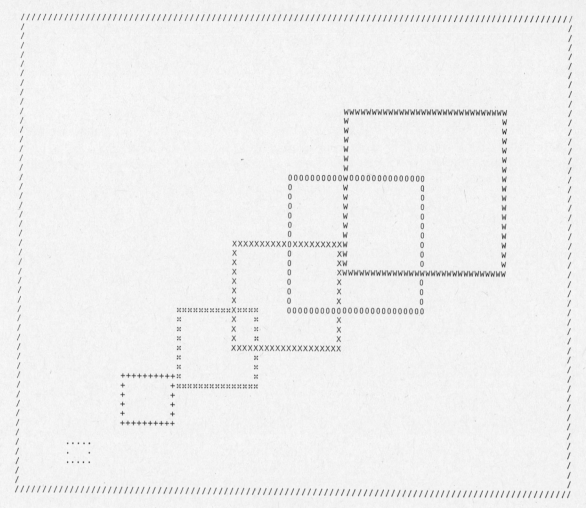

Figure 11.11

When a program is divided into units, each unit should have clearly defined, meaningful functions. Some programmers use as a rule of thumb the guideline that no subprogram should be more than one page in length.

DEBUGGING CLINIC

When you create large programs with many subprograms, the size of the program itself may be the greatest barrier. By working on a small part of the program at one time, it is possible to gain the thorough understanding necessary for effective coding and debugging. Subprograms should be debugged individually or in small groups.

"Dummy" main programs can be constructed to exercise the subprograms thoroughly. When you are convinced that the subprograms are functioning properly, they should be combined to form ever larger collections of correctly

Figure 11.12

operating programs. Eliminate bugs when you find them. Don't ignore them in the hope that they will disappear when you put the entire program together.

It is often useful to include debugging printout to trace the executive flow of the program. Such traces can be obtained by printing at least the name of each subprogram on entry. A more thorough check would print out the value of all the arguments passed to the subprogram. Be certain that the type of the dummy arguments in the subprogram definition matches the type of the arguments being passed in. Special care is warranted when passing arrays. Be sure that COMMON declarations match.

If all of your subprograms compile correctly, but you have called a subprogram that is not defined, you will get an error message. This simple mistake is the cause of many lost runs. Inserting a subprogram that is never called will usually produce a warning message, but the program will be executed.

Figure 11.13

REVIEW QUESTIONS

1. Why is modularity an element of good program design? What criteria would you use for deciding what modules a program should contain?

2. Do you think that a top-down or bottom-up approach to program design is preferable. Why? What are the advantages and disadvantages of each? If you used a mixed strategy, what types of routines would you define first?

3. What is a macro-flowchart? How would you go about designing one?

4. How can debugging problems be attacked at the design level? What debugging aids would you build into a program you were designing?

1. The computer graphics programming system discussed in this chapter can be extended in many different directions. Write subroutines to allow for these printouts. Try to make your subroutines as general as possible. Use your imagination and enjoy yourself.
   a. Isosceles triangles whose bases are parallel to the x axis.
   b. Right triangles whose bases are parallel to the x axis.
   c. A line connecting two arbitrary points.
   d. A triangle connecting three arbitrary points.
   e. A circle. (It is difficult to generate curves on a printer. Do your best.)
   f. A parabola.
   g. A sine curve.
   h. A diamond-shaped figure.
   i. A parallelogram.
   j. An ellipse.

2. Use any or all of the above figures to create these images.
   a. A city skyline.
   b. A group of sailboats on the ocean.
   c. A mountain range.
   d. A tree or group of trees.
   e. A human face.

3. Create a subroutine REDARY to read in an array of real data. The subroutine should read data cards, filling an array, until a zero data value is encountered; it should then return the array name and the number of items in the array. Allow for a maximum of 100 data items.
   a. Create a main program to call the REDARY subroutine and to print the contents of the array.
   b. Create a main program which calls the REDARY subroutine twice to put values into two different arrays.
   c. Create a MERGE subroutine which merges two arrays of data which have been sorted in ascending order. The original arrays and the merged array should be printed by the main program. Use the REDARY subroutine to read in two arrays which should be in sorted order.
   d. Use REDARY to read in two arrays of real data. Use a sorting subroutine to sort the arrays. Use a merging subroutine to merge the data. Use a printing subroutine to print the data.
   The main program is

```
DIMENSION A(100), B(100), C(200)
CALL REDARY (A,N)
CALL REDARY (B,M)
CALL SORT (A,N)
CALL SORT (B,M)
CALL MERGE (A,N,B,M,C,NM)
CALL PRTARY (C,NM)
STOP
END
```

4. Create a series of function subprograms for work in plane and solid geometry. Test them with a suitable main program.

   a. CIRCA computes the area of a circle given the radius.

   b. CIRCUM computes the circumference of a circle given the radius.

   c. SPHVOL computes the volume of a sphere given the radius.

   d. SPHARE computes the surface area of a sphere given the radius.

   e. CYLVOL computes the volume of a cylinder given the height and the radius of the base.

   f. CYLARE computes the surface area of a cylinder given the height and the radius of the base.

   g. SQAREA computes the area of a square given the length of a side.

   h. SQPERI computes the perimeter of a square given the length of a side.

   i. CUBVOL computes the volume of a cube given the length of a side.

   j. CUBARE computes the surface area of a cube given the surface area and the length of a side.

   k. Use these subroutines to determine the volume of a cube with a side of length 5 inches.

   l. A one-inch diameter hole has been bored through the cube perpendicular to the faces. Compute the volume and surface area of the remaining solid.

SPIRAL PROBLEMS

These problems have purposely been shallowly defined. Use your imagination and skill to design useful subroutines.

A. Add a RECTNG subroutine to the computer graphics programming system, whose function is to draw rectangles. Carefully specify what each of the arguments should be. Write a main program to demonstrate this feature.

B. Create a subroutine to convert the computer graphics programming system into a plotting tool. Design the subroutine to plot a series of points and to connect the points with a line of dots. Carefully specify what each of the arguments should be. Write a main program to demonstrate this feature.

CHARACTER, STRING, AND TEXT MANIPULATION

Words, words, words!
Hamlet

CHAPTER 12

Computers were originally designed for numerical calculation, but they are increasingly being used to manipulate symbols and process text. Although FORTRAN is not an ideal language for character manipulation, it is possible to perform a number of operations on text strings.

Characters are stored in REAL or INTEGER variables by means of A-format and DATA statements. By building upon simple operations of assignment and comparison, routines may be developed for counting the number of characters in a string, searching for specified substrings within a string, and copying all or parts of a string. This chapter presents these basic techniques of string manipulation.

Such manipulation forms an integral part of programs for the processing of textual information. Applications include literary style analysis, computer typesetting of books, information retrieval, business letter printing, and message processing.

WATFIV provides a CHARACTER declaration which simplifies the programming of character manipulation operations.

Introduction

Computers were originally designed to perform mathematical calculations with great speed and accuracy. Numerical calculation is important in scientific computation, but there is increasing use of computers in non-numerical situations where the "calculator" becomes a symbol manipulator. In computer science, non-numerical applications include compiler, interpreter, and assembler design. In the humanities, computers aid in the construction of word frequency lists, concordances, bibliographies, and cross-reference dictionaries. Experiments in language translation (for example, Russian to English) and man/computer dialog in English also require character manipulation procedures.

A number of special purpose languages have been designed to simplify the programming of character manipulation. The most popular of these is SNOBOL, which was developed by Bell Telephone Laboratories. The data structures and operations provided by the SNOBOL language are designed for character manipulation and text processing. While SNOBOL is a useful language for character manipulation, it is not widely available. Many general purpose algorithmic languages have some facilities for string manipulation: PL/I has character string operations, library functions, and a CHARACTER type declaration. ALGOL, COBOL, and BASIC may have varying facilities for character processing depending on the language level and implementation. Unfortunately, standard versions of FORTRAN provide few facilities for character manipulation, and this type of programming often becomes cumbersome. Nonetheless, it is sometimes desirable to code character manipulation operations in FORTRAN. The algorithms described here can be implemented easily in standard FORTRAN on a variety of computers. WATFOR/WATFIV include special facilities for character manipulation which will be discussed below.

In this chapter we shall consider the input of character strings of fixed or varying lengths and the modification of strings by *deletion, addition, replacement,* and *concatenation* (the joining of two strings). Other basic techniques discussed are the copying of all or part of a string, the comparison of two strings to test if they are identical, searching a string for occurrences of a particular substring or a certain character, and the alphabetical sorting of a group of strings. Finally, we discuss means of writing strings with output devices such as the printer.

Individually these operations are simple, but they can be combined to perform complex tasks such as the stylistic analysis of literature. Character manipulation programs have been written to count the number of words per sentence, the number of sentences per paragraph, and the frequency of occurrence of various words in a text passage. Since each author's style is unique (for example, the short staccato phrase structures of Hemingway differ greatly from the extended sentences of Proust), excerpts which have been found statistically dissimilar from the body of a work may be suspected to be additions by another author. Some such computer leads have proved correct.

Political scientists have used similar methods in analyzing historical documents. Automated literature searching systems which locate relevant scientific journal articles involve character manipulation. There are fascinating applications of non-numerical manipulation in artificial intelligence. Experiments in computerized game playing, pattern recognition, and theorem proving also rely on the ability of the computer to perform symbol manipulations. Character manipulation is also important in business applications. Management information systems, letter writing systems, and inventory control systems all use character manipulation techniques. Because of the wide applications of character manipulation techniques, it is likely that you will have occasion to use the concepts presented in this chapter.

Character Storage

The memory of the IBM 360/370 computers and other similar machines is divided into *words* and *locations* which contain four characters.

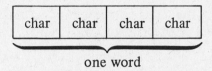

one word

To read the first four characters from an input card and store them in a word, we could use the FORTRAN statements

```
    READ(5,101) NAME
101 FORMAT(A4)
```

If the card had the name

JOHN

punched on it in the first four columns, the variable NAME would contain

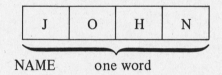

NAME   one word

It does not matter whether character information is read into INTEGER or REAL locations, but the usage must be consistent. Using INTEGER locations in some cases and REAL in others could lead to disaster. In the examples in this book, all character information is stored in INTEGER locations.

Although this input technique is efficient in that the entire word is used, operations on *single characters* are difficult since the characters are embedded in the word. Extracting characters requires complicated manipulations which are difficult to write and slow to execute. Therefore, in spite of the inefficient storage utilization, we will put only one character in each word and sacrifice storage space for ease and speed of manipulation.

To read the name "JOHN" from card columns 1 to 4 and store a single character per word, the following program fragment could be used:

```
    DIMENSION NAME(4)
    READ(5,102) (NAME(I), I = 1,4)
102 FORMAT(4A1)
```

Although the implied DO loop is not necessary it is included for the sake of clarity. Internally, the characters are stored one per word:

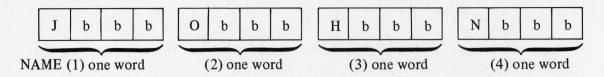

NAME (1) one word   (2) one word   (3) one word   (4) one word

There are single characters in the leftmost portion of each word and the rest of the word is padded with blanks. We will abbreviate the contents of the words by writing only the characters and ignoring the blanks:

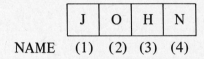

NAME   (1)   (2)   (3)   (4)

It is valid to ignore the trailing blanks that fill out each word because these blanks will never be printed if we use A1 format for output. When comparing two words which have been padded with trailing blanks, only the first character will be important since the trailing blanks will always compare equally. If N contains $x$bbb and M contains $y$bbb, where x, y are characters and b is a blank, then N = M only if x is the same as y and N > M only if x is higher than y.[1]

When a string of characters is read in A1 format, one word must be provided for each letter. To read in the seven-character string "MESSAGE" we must allocate seven words:

```
      DIMENSION NWORD(7)
      READ(5,101)NWORD
101   FORMAT(7A1)
```

Following the READ statement, the array NWORD would contain

M	E	S	S	A	G	E

NWORD   (1) (2) (3) (4) (5) (6) (7)

The array could be written on the printer by using the statements

```
      WRITE(6,102)NWORD
102   FORMAT(' ',7A1)
```

Problem 12.1

Write a program to read a string of 30 characters from columns 1–30 of a data card, and print the middle ten characters.

---

[1]The order of characters for purposes of comparison is: blank (lowest), A, B, C, . . . , X, Y, Z, 0, 1, 2, 3, . . . , 7, 8, 9 (highest).

The Assignment Statement

Characters may be manipulated by means of the assignment statement. Consider the array NWORD above with the value

M	E	S	S	A	G	E

NWORD   (1) (2) (3) (4) (5) (6) (7)

The statement

$$NWORD(2)=NWORD(5)$$

will alter the values in the array to

M	A	S	S	A	G	E

NWORD   (1) (2) (3) (4) (5) (6) (7)

Caution: Never attempt to mix modes in an assignment statement when the variables contain character values.

```
A = A    OK
I = I    OK
A = I    Wrong
I = A    Wrong
```

The compiler will attempt to convert the mode of the value from integer to real or real to integer and will scramble the bit configurations in the process.

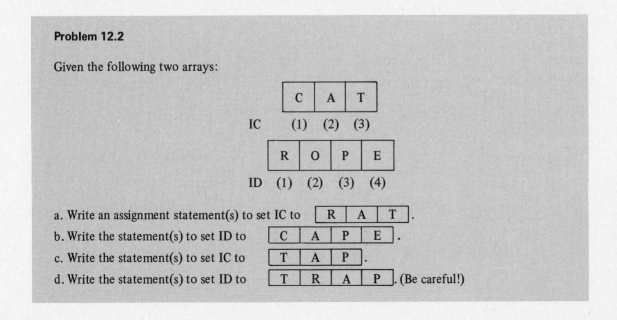

Problem 12.2

Given the following two arrays:

C	A	T

IC   (1) (2) (3)

R	O	P	E

ID   (1) (2) (3) (4)

a. Write an assignment statement(s) to set IC to | R | A | T | .

b. Write the statement(s) to set ID to | C | A | P | E | .

c. Write the statement(s) to set IC to | T | A | P | .

d. Write the statement(s) to set ID to | T | R | A | P | . (Be careful!)

String Input

Reading, writing, and modifying single characters is useful but limited. To perform more sophisticated operations, it is necessary to process strings of text. For example, it might be important to read an entire phrase from a card, such as

```
WE THE PEOPLE OF THE UNITED STATES
```

In order to do this for an arbitrary string, the program must have some way of obtaining the string's length. One technique might be to preface the character string with a two-digit integer number indicating the length. Then the above string, keypunched as

```
34WE THE PEOPLE OF THE UNITED STATES
```

could be read by the following program fragment:

```
      DIMENSION NSTRNG (78)
      READ(1,101) LEN,(NSTRNG(I),I = 1, LEN)
  101 FORMAT(I2, 78A1)
```

Since a card contains 80 columns, a string of up to 78 characters could be read if two digits were used to indicate the length, LEN.

This technique, while workable, is inconvenient since the length of the input string must be determined by counting the characters. This job is tedious and error-prone. An alternative method which eliminates the need for counting characters is to terminate each string with a special character which serves to mark the end of the string. Such a character is termed a *delimiter*. The delimiting character should be one which will not occur in the body of the string. Using an asterisk as a delimiter, the original input phrase would be coded

```
WE THE PEOPLE OF THE UNITED STATES*
```

Using delimiters, we can write a program to count the number of characters in the string. Since it is often necessary to process strings of length greater than 80, the following subroutine has been designed to read strings up to 400 characters in length which are punched on one to five cards. The subroutine reads a card and scans for an asterisk. If no asterisk is found in the first five cards, reading continues until an asterisk is reached, but only the first 400 input characters are retained. The string is returned in array LST and the length is entered in LNLST.

```
      SUBROUTINE READST(LST,LNLST)
C
C        THIS SUBROUTINE READS UP TO 400 CHARACTERS
C        FROM SUCCESSIVE DATA CARDS AND PLACES THEM
C        INTO AN ARRAY, ONE CHARACTER PER LOCATION.
C        THE CHARACTER STRING IS ENDED BY AN '*'
```

```
C            LST    IS THE NAME OF THE ONE DIMENSIONAL ARRAY
C                      IN WHICH THE CHARACTER STRING IS STORED
C            LNLST IS THE NUMBER OF CHARACTERS IN THE STRING.
C
C
          DIMENSION LST(1),N(80)
          DATA NAST/1H*/
C
C            READ UP TO FIVE CARDS
C
          DO 20 I = 1,5
          READ(5,101) N
    101   FORMAT(80A1)
          NPOS = (I - 1) * 80
C
C            LOOK FOR AN ASTERISK
C
          DO 10 J = 1,80
          IF(N(J) .EQ. NAST) GO TO 40
          K = NPOS + J
          LST(K) = N(J)
     10   CONTINUE
     20   CONTINUE
C
C            OVERFLOW  -  SCAN FOR NEXT ASTERISK
C
          LNLST = 400
     25   READ(5,101)N
          DO 30 I = 1,80
          IF(N(I) .EQ. NAST) GO TO 50
     30   CONTINUE
          GO TO 25
C
C            SET LENGTH AND RETURN
C
     40   LNLST = NPOS + J - 1
     50   RETURN
          END
```

Problem 12.3

a. What does READST do if the first data card contains an asterisk in column 1?

b. What does READST do for strings that are longer than five data cards?

Note the use of the DATA statement to preset the value of NAST. The statement results in NAST being set to

*	blank	blank	blank

Thus '*', '*b', '*bb', and '*bbb' are equivalent. (Unfortunately, the use of character data in assignment statements, such as NAST = '*', *is not permitted* in standard FORTRAN.)

Substring Search

Having developed a technique for character string input, we turn to the problem of string manipulation. One basic operation is searching the string to determine whether it contains a particular substring. A *substring* may be a single character, a group of characters, a word, a phrase, or a whole sentence. It might also be useful to compare an entire string to another string of the same length to determine whether they are the same.

Checking for a single character is easily accomplished by testing each position of the string for a given character. For example, to search for the letter H in a string NST, the following program might be used:

```
      DATA IH/'H'/
      DO 20 I = 1,LEN
      IF(NST(I).EQ.IH)GO TO 30
   20 CONTINUE
      WRITE(6,100) IH
  100 FORMAT('THE LETTER ', A1, ' WAS NOT FOUND')
      GO TO 40
   30 WRITE(6,104) IH, I
  104 FORMAT(' THE LETTER ', A1, ' FOUND IN POSITION', I3)
   40 CONTINUE
```

The program "falls through" statement 20 only if the letter H is not found anywhere. This program locates the first occurrence of the letter H but gives no indication as to whether the letter appears more than once.

A more general program, which can scan a string for the presence of a certain substring, is the function INDEX. The arguments are the array containing the main string (the string to be searched), its length, the search string array, and the length of the search string array. INDEX returns zero if the substring is not in the main string. If the substring is found, INDEX returns an integer number indicating the position at which the substring begins.

```
      FUNCTION INDEX(MST,LMST,NSR,LNSR)
C
C         THIS FUNCTION SEARCHES A MASTER STRING MST
C         FOR A SUBSTRING NSR.  IF A MATCH IS MADE,
C       . THE NUMBER OF THE POSITION IN MST IN WHICH
C         THE MATCH OCCURRED IS RETURNED.  IF NO MATCH
C         IS MADE, ZERO IS RETURNED
```

```
C
C        MST      IS THE ONE DIMENSIONAL MASTER STRING ARRAY
C        LMST     IS THE LENGTH OF THE MASTER STRING
C        NSR      IS THE ONE DIMENSIONAL SEARCH STRING ARRAY
C        LNSR     IS THE LENGTH OF THE SEARCH STRING
C
C
         DIMENSION MST(1),NSR(1)
         IF(LMST .EQ. 0 .OR. LNSR .EQ. 0) GO TO 80
         LAST = LMST - LNSR + 1
         DO 70 I = 1,LAST
         DO 40 J = 1,LNSR
         NPOS = I + J - 1
         IF(MST(NPOS) .NE. NSR(J)) GO TO 70
   40 CONTINUE
C
C             HAVE A MATCH
C
         INDEX = I
         GO TO 90
C
C             NO MATCH
C
   70 CONTINUE
   80 INDEX = 0
   90 RETURN
      END
```

If the main string is "WE THE PEOPLE OF THE UNITED STATES" and the search string is "THE," then INDEX would perform the matching process as follows:

First   `WE THE PEOPLE OF THE UNITED STATES` (No match)
Comparison   `THE`

Second   `WE THE PEOPLE OF THE UNITED STATES` (No match)
Comparison   ` THE`

Third   `WE THE PEOPLE OF THE UNITED STATES` (No match)
Comparison   `  THE`

Fourth   `WE THE PEOPLE OF THE UNITED STATES` (Successful match;
Comparison   `   THE`   return 4)

Used together, the READST and INDEX subprograms are quite powerful. Given a file of scientific journal articles, all citations that contain the word "multiprogramming" or the phrase "survival of the fittest" could be selected and displayed, or the names of all articles authored by a particular researcher could be printed out. By using similar techniques, the molecular structure of chemical compounds could be encoded and then checked for particular substructures. The résumés of employees could be scanned for background in areas such as "physical chemistry," "project management," or "systems design." College course descriptions could be checked for references to certain fields of study.

Substring Replacement and Copying

The READST and INDEX routines provide means for input and scanning of the text strings. The ability to move and alter character strings are the next techniques to be considered.

The basic operations of moving and copying strings or substrings are implemented by the SUBSTR subroutine. SUBSTR allows copying a complete string or selectively copying parts of a string into another string. The arguments to SUBSTR are the name of the sending string, the position from which the copy is to begin, the name of the receiving string, the position into which copying is to begin, and the number of characters to be sent.

```
      SUBROUTINE SUBSTR(NRECV,IPTA,NSEND,IPTB,NUM)
C         THIS SUBROUTINE MOVES NUM WORDS BEGINNING IN
C         NSEND(IPTB) TO NRECV(IPTA)
C
C         NRECV   IS A ONE DIMENSIONAL ARRAY CONTAINING ONE
C                 CHARACTER PER WORD
C         IPTA    IS THE NUMBER OF THE FIRST RECEIVING
C                 LOCATION IN NRECV
C         NSEND   IS THE NAME OF A ONE DIMENSIONAL ARRAY
C                 FROM WHICH CHARACTERS ARE SENT
C         IPTB    IS THE LOCATION IN NSEND FROM WHICH DATA
C                 ARE MOVED
C         NUM     IS THE NUMBER OF CHARACTERS MOVED
C
      DIMENSION NRECV(1),NSEND(1)
      DO 7 I = 1,NUM
      IA = IPTA + I - 1
      IB = IPTB + I - 1
    7 NRECV(IA) = NSEND(IB)
      RETURN
      END
```

Let us return to an earlier example:

```
DIMENSION NFIRST(400), NTWO(400)
CALL READST(NFIRST,LEN)
```

Suppose the string, stored in NFIRST, appears as

```
WE THE PEOPLE OF THE UNITED STATES
```

The word "PEOPLE" can be copied to the first six positions of NTWO by the subroutine call

```
CALL SUBSTR(NTWO,1,NFIRST,8,6)
```

NFIRST is unchanged, and only the first six positions of NTWO are changed; the others remain the same as they were before the subroutine call. The subroutine call

```
CALL SUBSTR(NTWO,1,NFIRST,1,LEN).
```

would copy the entire string.

The SUBSTR subprogram is simple and straightforward; it simply provides the proper array subscripts for an assignment statement. The SUBSTR routine also can be used to perform a *concatenation* (joining) operation combining two independent strings to create a new string. If NSTR1 contains

```
WE THE PEOPLE OF THE UNITED STATES
```

with LEN1 = 34 and NSTR2 contains

```
IN ORDER TO FORM A MORE PERFECT UNION
```

with LEN2 = 38, SUBSTR can be used to join the two strings:

```
CALL SUBSTR(NSTR1,35,NSTR2,1,LEN2).
```

The length of NSTR1 would be set to

```
LEN1 = LEN1 + LEN2
```

In this example, NSTR2 remains unchanged, and NSTR1 becomes

```
WE THE PEOPLE OF THE UNITED STATES IN ORDER TO FORM A
MORE PERFECT UNION
```

with LEN1 = 72.

Problem 12.4

What is the effect of

```
CALL SUBSTR(NST,2,NST,3,5)
```

followed by

```
CALL SUBSTR(NST,19,NST,18,15)
```

if NST is

WHEN IN THE COURSE OF HUMAN EVENTS

Textual Output

The subroutine WRITST is used to print a string on the printer. WRITST permits the specification of the line width to be in the range of 1 to 132 characters and the text string is fragmented to fit these limitations without splitting words in the middle.

```
      SUBROUTINE WRITST(LST,LEN,NWIDE,MM)
C         THIS SUBROUTINE OUTPUTS A STRING ON THE PRINTER,
C          USES SUBROUTINE SUBSTR.
C
C         LST        IS A ONE DIMENSIONAL ARRAY CONTAINING THE
C                    STRING
C         LEN        IS THE LENGTH OF LST
C         NWIDE      IS THE WIDTH OF THE LINE DESIRED FOR OUTPUT
C         MM  =  0   FOR SINGLE SPACING AND
C             =  1   FOR DOUBLE SPACING
C
C
      DIMENSION LST(1),LINE(132)
      DATA NBLK,NZERO / 1H ,1H0/
      M = NZERO
      IF(MM .EQ. 0) M = NBLK
      IF(NWIDE .GT. 132 .OR. NWIDE .LE. 0) GO TO 99
      I = 1
  10  DO 20 K = 1,NWIDE
      LINE(K) = NBLK
  20  CONTINUE
      IF(I + NWIDE .GT. LEN) GO TO 70
      DO 30 J = 1,NWIDE
      NPT = NWIDE + 1 - J + I
      IF(LST(NPT) .EQ. NBLK) GO TO 40
  30  CONTINUE
      CALL SUBSTR(LINE,1,LST,I,NWIDE)
      I = I + NWIDE
      GO TO 50
  40  NUM = NWIDE - J + 1
      CALL SUBSTR(LINE,1,LST,I,NUM)
      I = I + NUM + 1
  50  WRITE(6,101)M,(LINE(K),K = 1,NWIDE)
 101  FORMAT(133A1)
      GO TO 10
  70  LI = LEN - I + 1
      CALL SUBSTR(LINE,1,LST,I,LI)
      WRITE(6,101)M,(LINE(K),K = 1,LI)
  99  RETURN
      END
```

Problem 12.5

Write a subroutine call to WRITST to print a string NST of length LEN. The column width should be 50 and double spacing is desired.

A Replacement Program

To demonstrate the use of the subroutines that have been presented in this chapter, we will construct a program to replace every occurrence of a given substring with a new substring in a block of text. Suppose that a computerized announcement had been prepared for the Bean Blossom Folk Festival in March:

```
BEAN BLOSSOM FOLK FESTIVAL
MARCH 11-15 IN WOODS PARK
FEATURING PEARL RUGGS, MARCH 11; JEANNIE LEE, MARCH 12;
RANDY FELLA, MARCH 13; TOM SLOW, MARCH 14;
PHILALAEA DENDRON, MARCH 15
```

Unfortunately, a delay in the preparations has caused the festival to be moved back exactly one month to April. The following program will replace every occurrence of "MARCH" by "APRIL" in the text:

```
      DIMENSION MST(400),NOLD(400),NEW(400)
      CALL READST(MST,LMST)
      CALL WRITST(MST,LMST,80,1)
      CALL READST(NOLD,LNOLD)
      CALL READST(NEW,LNEW)
10    NPOS = INDEX(MST,LMST,NOLD,LNOLD)
      IF(NPOS .EQ. 0) GO TO 20
      CALL SUBSTR(MST,NPOS,NEW,1,LNEW)
      GO TO 10
20    CALL WRITST(MST,LMST,80, 0).
      STOP
      END
```

Terminating each input string with an asterisk, we use the READST subroutine to read in the text. Then "MARCH" and "APRIL" are obtained from successive cards using READST. Occurrences of "MARCH" are located by the INDEX function and SUBSTR is used to perform the replacement. This process continues until no further occurrences of "MARCH" are found. The new string is then printed by the WRITST subroutine. The final output is

```
BEAN BLOSSOM FOLK FESTIVAL
APRIL 11-15 IN WOODS PARK
FEATURING PEARL RUGGS, APRIL 11; JEANNIE LEE, APRIL 12;
RANDY FELLA, APRIL 13; TOM SLOW, APRIL 14;
PHILALAEA DENDRON, APRIL 15
```

This simple program does have a serious limitation—the length of the new and old substrings must be equal. A more sophisticated replacement program would account for unequal lengths by shifting the text string as required.

CHARACTER Variables (WATFIV)

WATFIV and some other FORTRAN processors permit the declaration of special *character variables*, which can contain strings of up to 256 characters. The maximum length of the string is given in the declaration statement. The following statement will declare two strings, each having a length of 80:

```
CHARACTER*80 INCARD,LINE
```

To read a full card of text into INCARD we can write

```
      READ(5,101) INCARD
101 FORMAT(A80)
```

Copying the input string to another variable may be performed by an assignment statement:

```
LINE = INCARD
```

Printing a string is accomplished by the statements

```
      WRITE(6,102) LINE
102 FORMAT(' ',A80)
```

Unlike standard FORTRAN, WATFIV permits CHARACTER constants (strings surrounded by apostrophes) in assignment statements:

```
LINE = 'THIS IS A STRING CONSTANT'
```

Another useful feature of CHARACTER variables is that they can be used in relational expressions:

```
IF(LINE .EQ. INCARD) GO TO 50
```

Since arrays of CHARACTER variables may be declared, processing lists of words is easily accomplished with their use.

Although these features are helpful in processing character information, it is still difficult to operate on portions of a string. Replacing parts of a string, searching for substrings, and combining two strings are tasks which can usually be more easily accomplished with the subprograms presented earlier in the chapter or with your own special purpose subprograms.

Summary

In order to simplify the tasks of string manipulation, we have presented a number of useful subprograms. READST reads in a string of characters, delimited by an asterisk, which may extend over five cards. The input string and its length are returned by this subroutine. The INDEX function searches a string for the first occurrence of a given substring. The value returned is 0 if there is no match. If there is a match, the value returned is the position in which the substring begins. The SUBSTR subroutine is used to copy strings. SUBSTR may also be used to perform concatenation operations or deletions. Finally, the WRITST subroutine prints a string; the width of the output and line spacing are specified as input arguments.

For those processors which permit it, the CHARACTER declaration provides a useful alternative technique for dealing with strings of characters. Although this feature is useful, its capabilities are limited.

DEBUGGING CLINIC

When using the string manipulation subprograms presented in this chapter, make sure that the arguments in the calling program match the arguments in the subprogram. Strings must be stored in INTEGER arrays, but only READST is predicated on the size of being precisely 400 locations. The other subprograms will operate on strings of any length, but care must be taken to ensure that length and position specifications are used properly. During debugging, the WRITST routine may be used frequently to display the current value of a string. The length of a string should be printed as well.

When constructing your own subprograms for character manipulation, care should be taken to ensure that the routines operate correctly for strings of length zero and strings of maximum length, and that a suitable error handling is provided for oversized strings. Make sure that substring processing routines operate properly on the beginning, middle, and end of the strings. Be especially attentive to the possibility of mixed mode operations; assigning an INTEGER value to a REAL location or any other type of location will produce incorrect results. Do not assign CHARACTER values to any other type locations.

REVIEW QUESTIONS

1. What are the advantages and disadvantages to storing one character per location?

2. How would READST have to be changed in order to process strings of up to 800 characters (ten cards)?

3. How might string processing techniques be applied to process musical notation? What kind of coding scheme could you design for encoding music scores?

4. How might string processing techniques be applied to process chemical formulas? What kind of coding scheme could you design for encoding chemical formulas?

5. In psychology, text analysis has been applied to written responses in Rohrschach (inkblot) and Thematic Apperception Tests (TAT). What kind of counts do you think would be significant?

EXERCISES

1. Improve the subroutine WRITST so that the left and the right margins are justified. Use whatever strategy you wish in deciding where to insert the extra blanks.

2. Create and test a replacement subroutine which replaces a new substring for every occurrence of an old substring within a master string. Be sure to account for variations in length between the old and the new substrings. Remember that the new substring may be of length 0.

3. Create and test a subroutine called SQZBLK which takes as arguments a string and its length, and replaces all multiple occurrences of blanks by a single blank. The length should be adjusted appropriately.

4. Create and test a function, NCOUNT, which returns the number of words in a given string. The input arguments are a string and its length.

5. Write a function similar to INDEX but having a fifth argument which indicates with which position in the string comparison is to begin. This function allows you to scan a string for multiple occurrences of a substring.

6. Write a program that reads in another FORTRAN program as data and changes the name of a particular variable every time that it occurs. The program would read in a data card with the name of the variable to be changed and its new name. Then the program to be altered would be read in and a new deck with the alteration would be printed and/or punched out.

7. Use the given and any other subprograms to create a frequency distribution for the characters in a string of text. Your output should indicate how many times each character appears in the string.

8. Use the given and any other subprograms to create a frequency distribution for the words in a string of text. Your output should indicate how many times each word appears in the text.

9. Write and test a subroutine to sort an array of words alphabetically. The selection of a suitable way to store the input array of words will significantly affect the complexity and the generality of your program. Be sure to include comment cards to describe the limitations of your subprogram.

10. Write and test a subprogram to reverse a string. If the string is

    `FULL SPEED AHEAD`

    the reversed string is

    `DAEHA DEEPS LLUF`

    The length of the string remains unchanged.

11. Write a subprogram to test for the equality of two strings. Be sure to account for the possibility of the two strings being of different lengths.

12. Write a program to read in FORTRAN and count the number of comment cards, assignment statements, IF statements, GO TO statements, READ and WRITE statements, DO statements, FORMAT statements, and so on. The output should be a listing of the program being scanned and a table of the frequency of occurrence of each kind of statement.

13. Write a program to assist in simple substitution coding and decoding for secret messages. The input should be the 26 letters of the alphabet followed by the substitution pattern

```
ABCDEFGHIJKLMNOPQRSTUVWXYZ
BCDEFGHIJKLMNOPQRSTUVWXYZA
```

This example demonstrates a simple substitution pattern which shifts the alphabet by one position. A is replaced by B, B is replaced by C, and so on. After reading this input, the program should read message cards such as

```
THE QUICK BROWN FOX JUMPED OVER THE LAZY DOG
MEET ME AT THE CORNER OF FOURTH AND TENTH STREETS
```

and produce the coded results

```
UIF RVJDL CSPXO GPY KVNQFE PWFS UIF MBAZ EPH
NFFU NF BU UIF DPSOFS PG GPVSUI BOE UFOUI TUSFFUT
```

Your program should also be able to do decoding, by merely interchanging the order of the first two cards.[1]

14. Write a program to produce computer "poetry" like the following:

```
SOFT HEAVENS MOVE PONDEROUSLY
ICY RIVERS DART HASTILY
PLEASANT FLASHES SWAY BOLDLY
DELIGHTFUL STREAMS SHOOT DEEPLY
```

Each line is composed of an adjective, a noun, a verb, and an adverb randomly selected from lists of words. The input data should include the words in Table 12.1.

Table 12.1

Adjectives	Nouns	Verbs	Adverbs
GREEN	TREES	SHOOT	SOFTLY
SWEET	STARS	SWAY	HASTILY
SOFT	LEAVES	MOVE	DEEPLY
TENDER	FORESTS	GLIDE	SILENTLY
ICY	HEAVENS	SLIP	BOLDLY
PLEASANT	RIVERS	TOUCH	RAPIDLY
FAST	STREAMS	SIGH	SCORNFULLY
SMOOTH	FLASHES	DART	PONDEROUSLY
DELIGHTFUL		EXPLODE	
SILENT			

[1] For more sophisticated discussion of coding techniques, see Helen Fouche Gaines, *Cryptanalysis* (New York: Dover, 1956).

Your program should select a word from each of the lists and compose a line of the verse. You will have to design a random number selection process to choose the words from the lists.

More elaborate schemes involving more words and more varied grammatical forms will enhance the result.

SPIRAL PROBLEMS

A. Student Records

Student records have been prepared on data cards in the form

last name, first name / major / / grades *

A sample of the input is

```
CHURCHILL, WINSTON / POLITICAL SCIENCE // A B- A- A *
MANTLE, MICKEY / PHYSICAL EDUCATION // B A B B *
BRANDO, MARLON / DRAMA // B C A A *
KISSINGER, HENRY / POLITICAL SCIENCE // A A B A- *
```

Prepare at least ten such cards, terminated by a card with an asterisk in column 1.

Write a program to scan these cards and to print out the names and grades of all students majoring in 'POLITICAL SCIENCE.'

B. Corporate Search

Information concerning the products marketed by companies have been prepared on data cards in the following form:

```
GENERAL BEAN INTERNATIONAL*
COFFEE BEANS, LIMA BEANS, SOY BEANS, SUNFLOWER SEEDS,
LICHEE NUTS, PINTO BEANS*
UNIVERSAL INTERNATIONAL*
TURRET LATHES, OIL DRILLING DERRICKS,
TURBINE GENERATORS, JET ENGINES*
GENERAL FUELS, INCORPORATED*
DIESEL OIL, GASOLINE, HEATING OIL, JET FUEL*
                    .
                    .
                    .
```

Using the subprograms defined in the chapter, write a program to print out the names of the companies which sell any oil products. Scan the product list and print out the names of the companies for which there is a match on the term 'OIL' in the product list. The end of the data is indicated by a card with an asterisk in column 1.

C. Palindrome Tester

A *palindrome* is a sentence or word which reads the same backward and forward. A few well-known historical palindromes are

```
MADAM, I'M ADAM
ABLE WAS I ERE I SAW ELBA          (—Napoleon, concerning imprisonment on
                                        the island of Elba.)
A MAN, A PLAN, A CANAL, PANAMA
```

Only the second one is immediately recognizable as a palindrome; the others require some re-working, such as the elimination of punctuation and blanks.

Write a computer program to read sentences from data cards, eliminate blanks, commas and apostrophes, and check whether the remaining string is a palindrome. Print out the sentence and a message indicating whether or not it is a palindrome. The end of the data is indicated with a period in column 1 and an asterisk in column 2.

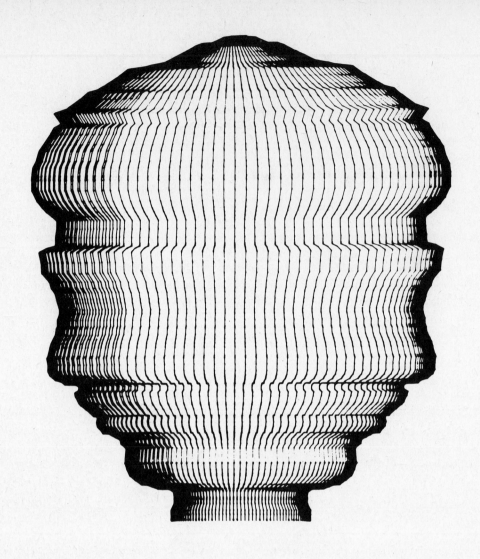

SEQUENTIAL AND DIRECT FILES

Reading serves for delight, for ornament, for ability. The crafty contemn it; the simple admire it; the wise use it.

Francis Bacon

CHAPTER 13

In this chapter we consider techniques for manipulating large data files. Sequential files are data files in which the data are read or written in a predetermined order. Data read from punch cards are sequential because the order in which the data is read depends upon the order of the cards. Cards are not ideal for very large data files, so many programs store sequential files on magnetic tape. A minor extension of the READ and WRITE statements allows the programmer to process magnetic tape files.

A direct file is one in which the records are not read and written in any predetermined order but randomly. Direct files are stored on magnetic disks. The DEFINE FILE statement allows the programmer to indicate that a file is direct rather than sequential. Reading and writing a direct file is similar to reading and writing a sequential file. When a READ or WRITE statement is programmed for a direct file, the programmer must indicate which record is to be read or written. Thus, instead of reading the records in a file in the order 1, 2, 3, 4, 5, 6, 7, . . . , a programmer may choose to read them in a completely different order such as 2, 1, 7, 4, 3, 5, 6, ...

When data files are written by a program for input to a second program and will not be read by people, the FORMAT statement need not be used. Data written by unformatted WRITE statements will be read by unformatted READ statements; this provides a simple means for passing data between programs.

Introduction

In previous chapters we have discussed most of the statements in the FORTRAN language. However, the programs that we have considered up to now have used relatively small amounts of data. While this is typical of programming exercises, it is not typical of most programs. One capability which makes the computer so powerful is that it can process large volumes of data rapidly. Unfortunately, the punch card is not an adequate medium on which to code large quantities of data. Its bulk, its small recording space (80 characters per card), and its relatively slow data transfer rate[1] makes it unsuitable for large data files. A typical card reader is capable of processing 600 to 1000 cards per minute. This means that a computer using punch cards as the means of data input could obtain no more than about 1333 characters of data per second, a rate which is far slower than the processing speed of even a modest computer. As a result, the development of faster input and output devices has been of primary concern to data processing engineers.

When large data files are to be processed, magnetic tape and magnetic disks are the usual storage media. Magnetic tapes can be read or written by the computer at speeds of one million characters per second. Magnetic disks have similarly rapid data transfer times, and, in addition, have the advantage that any particular piece of data can be located rapidly.

In this chapter we will consider ways of performing input and output for files in FORTRAN. We will discuss the use of the punch card as an output medium, the use of magnetic tape, and the use of the magnetic disk. Knowledge of these input-output devices is likely to be important should you become involved in a problem which requires large-scale data processing for its solution.

How Data Are Recorded

The basic problem in the design of a medium for recording data is to devise a means of translating characters and symbols into codes that can be recorded and read mechanically. The input medium with which you are most familiar is the 80-column punch card. Characters encoded on a punch card by the presence or absence of holes in specified positions are read by photoelectric sensors. Although the punch card is often manually prepared on a keypunch, most computers have a device which will permit programs to produce card output. Thus a program may prepare machine-readable results for input to other programs.

Although the 80-column card is by far the most popular, punch cards are available in other sizes. Some computers use small cards on which 96 characters can be recorded. It is also possible to obtain cards which are 60 columns in length. The bills which many credit card and utility companies prepare are produced on 80-column cards with a stub to be torn off and retained by the customer. The remaining 60 columns are returned with payment and are read by a special card reader. The discount coupons which many food manufacturers distribute as incentives for people to purchase their products are also nonstandard punch cards, as are some price tags which many stores use for inventory control.

---

[1] Data transfer rate is the speed with which data can be read from (or written on) a data recording medium such as punch cards or magnetic tape.

Magnetic Tape

The major restriction on the use of punch cards for input and output is that they are relatively slow. A program which must process hundreds of thousands of records would require an inordinate length of time if punch cards were the medium selected for input and output. In addition, the use of large numbers of punch cards presents handling problems. Punch cards are bulky, easily damaged, and if dropped, can cause considerable problems. For these reasons, magnetic tape is a frequently used alternative.

Magnetic tape is similar to the tape used on audio recorders although it is manufactured to higher standards. It typically comes in reels of 2400 feet although smaller reels and even cassettes are available. Characters are recorded on magnetic tape by means of magnetized spots which are sensed by a "read head" in the tape drive. Unlike the punch card, which usually requires separate units for input and output, a tape drive can both read and write magnetic tape. However, a reel of tape can be used either for input or for output in a given program—not both.

Each character is encoded as eight magnetized spots across the width of the tape. The eight positions, or *tracks*, may each be encoded with a one or a zero. Therefore, 2^8 or 256 different characters might be encoded on tape.

The number of characters recorded per inch of tape varies from 200 to 1600, with 1600 being more than usual. This number is known as the *tape density*. Although each character is encoded as eight positions, a ninth position is used for error checking. This ninth position is called a *parity check*. It works as follows: If the number of ones in the character code is even, then the ninth position is recorded as a one. On the other hand, if the number of ones in the character code is odd, then the parity position will be recorded as a zero. The number of ones in a valid character must always be odd. If the number of ones is even, then an error in recording or reading has occurred which the system will be able to detect. Parity checking is thus an automatic scheme for protecting the integrity of data. Instead of the *odd parity* scheme outlined above, some systems utilize *even parity* schemes which ensure that the number of ones in a character is always even. Figure 13.1 illustrates how the characters A through H are recorded on nine-track magnetic tape.

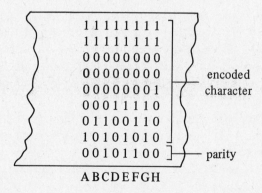

Figure 13.1

It is not possible to record the data on a magnetic tape as a continuous stream of characters. There is inertia to be overcome when starting or stopping the tape drive; it takes time for the tape to accelerate before the data reaches the read head, and to decelerate after the last character of the record has been read. The inter-record gaps (Figure 13.2) provide this extra time.

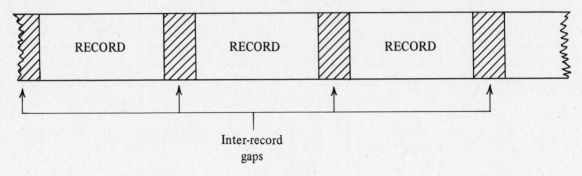

Inter-record
gaps

Figure 13.2

The data to be processed may not fill an entire reel of tape. For this reason there needs to be some means of indicating the end of data. On a card reader, of course, this occurs when there are no more cards to be read, but a reel of tape may contain many feet of unused tape. A special indicator, known as an *end-of-file marker*, is encoded on the tape when the last record has been written. When the tape is read, the end-of-file marker causes an indication that there are no further data to be read.

Blocking

When using a standard punch card for input or output, the programmer is restricted to a maximum record length of 80 characters. If shorter records are used, the remainder of the card is filled with blanks. Longer records require the use of more than one card. No such constraints are placed upon the programmer using tapes for input and output. Records may be as short or as long as desired (although the hardware may impose maximum or minimum lengths).

Since every record is preceded and followed by an inter-record gap, the length of a record is an important factor in how much data can be stored on a single reel of tape. For example, a record which is 100 characters in length would occupy one-sixteenth of an inch of tape recorded at 1600 characters per inch. A 100-character record with its associated inter-record gap would fill nine-sixteenths of an inch of tape. Thus, ten such records would use about five and a half inches of tape to encode 1000 characters. On the other hand, a single record which is 1000 characters long would require slightly more than an inch of tape, including the associated inter-record gap. If the record's length is shorter than 800 characters, more tape will be used for inter-record gaps than for recording data. Also, since tape movement is relatively slow, programs which pass over many inter-record gaps run more slowly than programs which use less tape—even when the number of characters read is equal.

In order to minimize the amount of tape which is wasted in inter-record gaps, it is frequently desirable to combine many small records into one large record or *block*. For example, ten 100-character records could be treated as one record 1000 characters long. Not only does such a procedure permit more information to be contained on a reel of tape, but it is only necessary to move the tape once for every ten records of input or output. The process of combining small records to form larger records is known as *blocking*. Blocking records is automatically performed for the programmer in most computer systems. It is necessary for the programmer to indicate (on control cards) the length of a record and how many records are contained in a block, but the programmer writes the program as though the records were not blocked.

Writing Tape in FORTRAN

In order to write tape in FORTRAN, it is merely necessary to specify an appropriate logical unit number in the READ or WRITE statement. The particular unit numbers which refer to tape depend on the installation conventions. For purposes of illustration we will use unit numbers in the range 10–20. For example, to read a tape record which is 100 characters long as 20 five-digit integers, the following program could be used:

```
      DIMENSION IVAL (20)
      READ (10,100) IVAL
100   FORMAT (20I5)
```

Although many students find it difficult to visualize a tape record, it is not conceptually difficult. If it helps you, visualize a tape record as containing 100 (or the appropriate number) columns of data. You should then have little difficulty in making up the appropriate FORMAT statements to read or write the record. The following statements could be used to write a tape record with 30 characters of data:

```
      WRITE (11,105) A,B,C,D
105   FORMAT (2F8.3,F5.1,F9.2)
```

When designing tape records, many programmers tend to use 80-character records. This allows them to test their programs by punching cards and afterwards to use tape input for actual runs. This is not a bad idea providing that the data can be accommodated in an 80-character record. However, when writing 80-character records on tape, it is usually best to block them so as to obtain maximal efficiency.

Unformatted Input and Output

Format statements permit precise control over the way that records are read and written. This control is desirable because it allows the programmer to write records in one format while reading them in another. If tapes are prepared in one program, only relevant portions of the records need be read by other programs. For example, an employee record containing employee number, department, annual salary, number of dependents, and job title could be written by using the following statements:

```
    WRITE (10,150) EMPNO,DEPT,ANNSAL,DEPEND,TITLE
150 FORMAT(I5,I4,I5,I2,5A4)
```

However, a program to list all employees, their departments, and their titles, could use the following format and read only the relevant data:

```
160 FORMAT(I5,I4,7X,5A4)
```

while a program to print employee number and annual salary could read the tape record using the following format:

```
170 FORMAT(I5,4X,I5)
```

However, such precise control of the record format is not always needed. It is frequently necessary to write data solely for the purpose of providing input to another program.

For example, a program might accumulate a large table of data which is to be passed to another program for processing. In such a case, the control provided by the FORMAT statement is not needed. FORTRAN provides an unformatted READ and WRITE statement for use in such cases. The unformatted READ and WRITE statements should not be confused with the format free input-output of WATFOR/WATFIV. The format free statements are intended primarily for card input and printed output where the user does not desire precisely controlled formats. The unformatted input-output, on the other hand, is used primarily to write large quantities of data on to secondary storage (such as tape) for input to other programs. Although it is possible to direct unformatted input-output to punch cards, it is not generally a good idea, as the results are difficult to check. It is not illegal to direct unformatted input-output to the printer, but it would be hard to make sense of the output.

Unformatted input-output statements are written like formatted input-output statements except that they do not refer to a FORMAT statement. The general form of these statements is

READ (i) *list*
WRITE (i) *list*

where i is the unit number reference and *list* is the list of variables to be read or written.

Suppose a programmer wished to preserve a matrix

```
DIMENSION A(10,5,3)
```

for use by another program. In order to write this matrix on tape, the statement

```
WRITE(10)A
```

could be used. The output tape could be read by a program fragment such as

```
DIMENSION B(10,5,3)
READ(11) B
```

Note that the same variable name need not be used, but the dimensions must be the same. The particular unit number which is used for reading or writing is determined by control cards which reflect the given installation.

The list may include scalar variables as well as arrays, and it is possible to write portions of an array by use of an implied DO loop.

Tape Manipulation Statements

There are three statements that are useful in manipulating tape data sets.

The END FILE statement is used to write an end-of-file marker on an output tape. When a program attempts to read the tape, the end-of-file marker will indicate that the end of data has been reached. The general format of the END FILE statement is

END FILE i

where i is the unit number. The unit may be specified as either an integer constant or an integer variable. Some examples of the END FILE statement are

```
END FILE 10
END FILE KTAPE
```

The BACKSPACE statement is used to go back one record on a file. This permits a record to be read a second time, possibly using a different format. The general form of the statement is

BACKSPACE i

where i may be an integer constant or a variable. On most systems it is not legal to backspace a file which is assigned to a card reader, card punch, or printer. Some examples of the BACKSPACE statement are

```
BACKSPACE 11
BACKSPACE JUNIT
```

The REWIND statement is similar to the BACKSPACE statement but repositions the unit to the first record. This move permits an entire file to be reread. The general form of the statement is

REWIND i

where i again may be either an integer variable or a constant. Some examples are

```
REWIND 15
REWIND L
```

Updating Sequential Files

Data stored on magnetic tape must be obtained sequentially. In order to get the information contained in a given record, it is necessary to read all the records which precede it on the tape. For example, if a company had 10,000 customers' records stored on magnetic tape, and it desired to read the 10,000th record, a program would have to read and ignore the first 9999 records on the tape.

A common task in commercial systems is to update the record of an individual customer. For example, a credit card company needs to know the current status of each customer's account. As each customer submits a payment or charges an item, it is necessary to alter the appropriate record to reflect the new balance due. For example, suppose

Customer account 1001 owes $ 100.00.
Customer account 1002 owes $ 150.49.
Customer account 1005 owes $ 956.89.

.

.

.

Customer account 5007 owes $ 800.01.

.

.

.

and there is one tape record for each customer showing the customer's name, address, account number, and amount owed. A file of data such as the one described above is usually known as a *master file*. As records of charges and credits are processed, they must be matched up with the appropriate master file record. A file of changes to be applied to the master file is known as a *transaction file*. The general processing scheme is to read the master record, apply any transactions to the record, and write the master record as a new file (Figure 13.3).

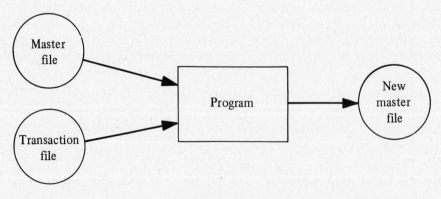

Figure 13.3

The new master file thus becomes an updated version of the old master file. Every record on the old master file must either be written unchanged or written after being updated. If only the transaction records were written, the customer records which had no activity would be lost.

In order to match the transaction records with the master records, the two files must be in the same sequence. If both files are in the same sequence, then all master records up to the one which matches a transaction record may be copied unchanged. When a master record and transaction record both refer to the same customer, then the master record is rewritten with the transactions applied to it. For example, if customer 1002 made a $200 purchase and customer 5007 made a $300 payment, then the tapes would change as in Figure 13.4.

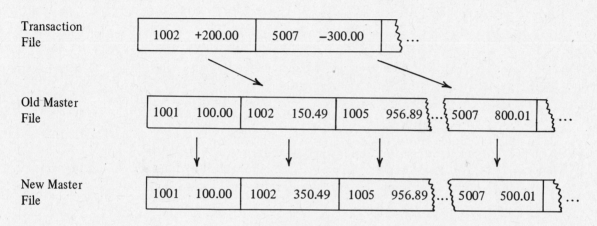

Figure 13.4

It is necessary to select some part of the record which can serve as a *key* for comparing the master record with the transaction record. It might be possible to use the customer name or address, but these may not be unique. More common is the assignment of a unique account number to each customer. Both the master file and the transaction file are sequenced on this account number. Note that the account numbers used in the example above do not necessarily correspond to the record position they occupy (for instance, there is no customer 1004). This is a frequent situation since customers open new accounts or close old accounts. Transaction records tend to arrive in random sequence because customers pay bills and make purchases at unspecified times. In order to arrange the transaction file in the appropriate sequence, it is necessary to sort the transactions prior to processing. Since sorting is such a fundamental operation, most computer manufacturers provide a flexible and efficient sorting program for their customers' use.

The general processing sequence for updating a master file is

1. Compare the number of the master record with that of the transaction record.

2. If they are equal:
   Apply the transactions indicated.
   Write the new master record.
   Read the next master record.
   Read the next transaction record.
   Go to step 1.

3. If the master record has a lower number than the transaction record:
   Write the unchanged master record.
   Read the next master record.
   Go to step 1.

4. If the master record has a higher number than the transaction record:
   Print the transaction record.
   Read the next transaction record.
   Go to step 1.

Problem 13.1

Draw a flowchart for the above algorithm and sketch out a design of a FORTRAN program to implement it.

In step four a transaction exists for a record which is not on a master file. This may indicate an error. For this reason, the algorithm states that the record in question should be printed. However, this condition can also be programmed to cause the addition of a new account to the master file.

Direct versus Sequential Files

The master file for a corporation with many customers may contain hundreds of thousands or even millions of records. For example, the master files of utility and major charge card companies are extremely large. It is inefficient and expensive to update a master file of this size when there are relatively few transactions to be processed. For this reason, corporations tend to save their transactions until they have a sufficient number to justify the expense of processing them. A group of transactions which is applied together is known as a *batch*.

Accumulating transactions until a sufficiently large batch is available saves money but creates problems. Customers' payments or charges may not be recorded for days or even weeks. The most recent copy of a customer's record may be out of date because it does not reflect transactions waiting to be processed. It would be preferable if a customer's record could be reached directly. For example, if there were a way of obtaining the 10,000th record on a file without reading the previous 9999, processing would be much more efficient. While this is not possible with magnetic tapes, magnetic disks provide an alternative.

A magnetic disk looks something like a large phonograph record. Its surface may be magnetized in a manner similar to magnetic tape. The disks revolve at high speed, and the records pass under heads which are capable of reading and writing. (Disks may be stacked one above the other to increase the storage space.) Unlike magnetic tapes, a disk record may be rewritten. It is thus possible to update a record by writing over the original. Since any record can be obtained within a few thousandths of a second, it is possible to apply transactions to a file on disks efficiently. The general algorithm for updating a master file contained on disks is

1. Read the transaction record.
2. Locate the corresponding master record.
3. Read the corresponding master record.
4. Rewrite the updated master record over the old master record.

Note that it is not necessary to process master records which have no transactions, nor is it necessary to sort the transactions prior to applying them.

Further consideration of the advantages and disadvantages of direct versus sequential organization is beyond the scope of this text. Information on this topic is frequently published in trade magazines and in manufacturers' educational manuals.

Processing Direct Files

To define and process a direct access file, the statements used are very similar to those used for processing sequential files, except that the programmer must indicate which record he desires to read or write. Both formatted and unformatted input-output is available for direct files.

In order to indicate that a particular file is direct rather than sequential, the DEFINE FILE statement is used. The general form of a DEFINE FILE statement is

DEFINE FILE $u(r, s, f, i)$

where

u is the data set reference number. This must be an integer constant and serves the same function as the reference number in a sequential READ or WRITE statement.

r is the number of records in the file. r must be an integer constant.

s is an integer constant which indicates the size of the record. s is either the number of characters in the record or the number of words in the record (words = number of characters/4, rounded up). If the records are to be read or written using unformatted input-output, then the record size is specified in words. Otherwise, the record size is specified in characters.

f indicates whether the record is to be written with or without format. If the letter "L" is coded, both formatted and unformatted input-output can be used. If the letter "E" is coded, then only formatted input-output will be used. If the letter "U" is coded, then only unformatted input-output will be used. Note that if "U" is coded the record size (s) must be specified in words rather than characters.

i is an integer variable which will be set to the record number read or written. i is called an *associated variable.*

To define a direct file which will be referred to as unit 10 containing 500 records of 90 characters to be read under format control, the programmer would code

```
DEFINE FILE 10(500,90,E,K10)
```

K10 is the associated variable. To define a file with 1000 records of 20 words (80 characters) which will be read or written without format control, the programmer would code

```
DEFINE FILE 11(1000,20,U,IVAR)
```

Problem 13.2

Write DEFINE FILE statements for the following files:

a. A file of 2000 records, 80 characters each, to be read under format control.

b. A file of 100 records, 95 characters each, to be read or written without format control.

When a file has been defined as a direct file, it may be read by a READ statement with the general form

READ (*u'recno, fmt*) *list*

where

u is the unit reference number.

recno is the record number.

fmt is the FORMAT statement number.

list is the list of variables.

This form is almost exactly the same as the READ statement for sequential files, except for the inclusion of *recno* which indicates the record to be read. *recno* may be any integer expression. To read the 100th record from unit 10, code

```
    READ (10'100,150) A,B,C

150 FORMAT (...
```

More usual is the use of an integer variable to specify the record number:

```
     DO 10 I = 1,N
     READ (8'I,3000) DATUM
3000 FORMAT ( ...
        .
        .
        .
```

To read a record without format control, the format statement reference is omitted (as in the sequential READ statement):

```
READ (22'K) CUST,DATE,AMOUNT
```

Writing records into a direct file is also straightforward. The general form of the WRITE statement parallels the sequential WRITE:

WRITE (*u'recno, fmt*) *list*

for format controlled output and

WRITE (*u'recno*) *list*

for writing without format control.

As in the READ statement, *recno* may be an expression. Since the associated variable is set to the value of the next record in the file following execution of a READ or WRITE statement, using the associated variable as the *recno* field will cause the file to be read or written sequentially. This technique is frequently used to "build" a direct file. The key (that is, relative record position) associated with each record can be recorded for use as an account or identification number when the record is updated.

When records are read in arbitrary sequence, time must elapse between the time when the READ statement is executed and the time when reading the record actually begins. This lag occurs while the disk revolves until the record desired is positioned under the read head and transmission of the data can begin. On many disks, the head must move to the appropriate *track* of the disk, much as a phonograph arm must be moved to select a particular song on a record album. Although the time required to position the read head and the disk may be measured in thousandths of a second, it is still far slower than the processing speed of the computer. It is therefore desirable to position the disk head before the record is needed. Then other processing can proceed while the disk is being positioned and the execution time of the program will be speeded up. In order to find the next record to be read in FORTRAN, a FIND statement may be used. The FIND statement is only useful before a READ statement, there is no advantage to using it before a WRITE. The general form of the FIND statement is

FIND (*u'recno*)

where *u* is the unit reference number and *recno* is an integer expression indicating the desired record.

For example, if the 50th record of a data set is to be read, then the sequence

```
FIND (23'50)
      .
      .
      .
   (other statements)
      .
      .
      .
   READ (23'50,190) X,Y,Z
150 FORMAT (...
```

will cause the 50th record to be found while the statements prior to the READ statement are being executed. The READ statement will therefore be executed without a wait for the disk head to be moved.

Summary

Although FORTRAN programs that require low volumes of data are often designed around the punch card (for input) and the line printer (for output), programs that process large volumes of data may take advantage of faster data recording media. Two commonly used media are magnetic tape and magnetic disk. Magnetic tape is used for large data files which will be read and written sequentially. When every data record is to be processed, magnetic tape is an efficient storage medium. However, when data records must be accessed in random sequence, magnetic disks are often used. Magnetic disks rotate at high speed and can, therefore, provide access to any given record within a few thousandths of a second.

Writing or reading magnetic tape files in FORTRAN is straightforward. The standard READ and WRITE statements are used; the unit number directs the data transfer to the appropriate device. When reading or writing a random (direct) access file stored on disk, the READ and WRITE statements specify the particular records to be processed in addition to the standard information used with sequential files.

If records are to be used by other programs and need not be produced in a format convenient for human interpretation, the FORMAT specification may be omitted from the READ or WRITE statement. Producing tape or disk records without FORMAT control tends to be efficient although it may create problems if the program requires extensive debugging. The problems may arise because it is difficult to check data which have been written without FORMAT control.

DEBUGGING CLINIC

Programs which use tape and disks are more difficult to debug than those which use card input, because it is more difficult to determine what data are on a tape. Most installations have "tape dump" programs which can be used to display the records on a reel of tape. If you are using unformatted output or creating an elaborate file it is usually a good idea to write a small program to display the file in a readable format. Such programs should allow records to be printed selectively (the first ten, every fifth record, and so on.).

If it is difficult to create test data for a program using tape or disks, it is often a good idea to provide card input as a means of testing the program. When the tape records are a multiple of 80 characters this is simple to do. It may also be useful to isolate the input processing as a subroutine which can either accept tape (or disk) input or generate test data from cards. Record counts are another check on the accuracy of programs; for example, in a master file updating program, the number of records written should equal the number read plus any added. Record counts should be an integral part of any program handling large data files.

REVIEW QUESTIONS

1. How are data recorded on magnetic tape? What is meant by *blocking* records?

2. What are the advantages of unformatted input-output as opposed to formatted input-output? What are the disadvantages? Under what circumstances would you choose one above the other?

3. What is a sequential file? What is a direct file? What are the differences in the strategies used to update each?

EXERCISES

1. Write DEFINE FILE statements for the following data files:
   a. A file of 500 records, of 50 characters each, to be read with FORMAT control.
   b. A file of 1000 records, of 91 characters each, to be read without FORMAT control.
   c. A file of 999 records, of 457 characters each, to be read either with or without FORMAT control.

2. Write a program to copy a deck of cards onto tape. Print the message "THERE ARE *nn* CARDS IN THE DECK." Write an end-of-file marker on the tape, rewind the tape, then print the cards by reading them from the tape.

3. Write a program to read character strings of length 400 from cards (use SUBROUTINE READST introduced in Chapter 12) and write these strings on tape.

4. Write a program to read a deck of ten cards with sentences on them and create a direct file. Print the cards in reverse order, then in the order 2,4,6,8,10,1,3,5,7,9 by using a direct READ statement.

5. Write a program to place a deck of cards on a direct file. Each data card should contain a customer name. Print a report listing the customer name and his account number (that is, record position). Then write a program to update selected records. Each transaction should contain the customer account number and an amount due. Update the records by adding the amount due to a total counter in the record. This will require rewriting the record. Be sure to handle invalid account numbers. When the last transaction has been read, print a report for all customers showing the total amount due.

6. Write a program to place a deck of cards on magnetic tape. The cards have the following format:

Columns 1–4	Customer number	(0000–9999)
Columns 5–25	Customer name	(alphabetic)
Columns 26–30	Number of items ordered	

   Set the third field to zeroes initially. Then read transaction records updating the number of items ordered and update the file. The transaction records should have the same format as the initial records, except that columns 26–30 are nonzero. If an invalid transaction is found, print it. If a transaction is found which does not exist on the master file but has zeroes in the third field, add the customer to the file. You should be able to use the same program both to create the file initially and to update it.

7. Create your own subprogram library on a reel of magnetic tape. First prepare your subprograms on cards in the following form

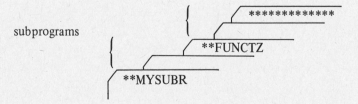

subprograms

****

**FUNCTZ

**MYSUBR

a. Write a program to copy this deck of cards onto the tape file, then rewind the file and read and print the contents of the file.

b. Create a retrieval program which accepts request cards containing the name of the desired program, locates the subprogram, and prints it.

8. Create a subprogram library using the input from the previous problem, but store the subprograms on a direct access disk file. In a separate place on the disk, you must store an index that indicates where each subprogram begins. Write a separate retrieval program which accepts request cards containing the name of the desired subprogram, look up the name in the index, retrieve and print the subprogram.

SPIRAL PROBLEMS

A. Student Grading

Create a set of cards with student identification numbers (in ascending order) and names on them. Store these cards on a sequential tape file. Create a transaction file of student grade cards containing the identification number and a grade from an exam. Read from the master tape file and the transaction card file to produce an updated master file. Allow for the case of students who did not take an exam and for erroneous student numbers. Finally, write a program to read the master file and produce a listing of identification numbers, names, and grades.

B. Banking

Create a set of cards with bank account numbers (in ascending order), customer names, and initial balances on them. Store these cards on a sequential tape file. Create a transaction file of withdrawals and deposits containing the account number, a code to indicate withdrawal or deposit, and the amount. Read from the master tape file and the transaction card file to produce an updated master file. Allow for the case of the transaction file account number which does not exist in the master file and for accounts which were inactive by printing error messages. Finally, write a program to read the master file and produce a listing of the account number, name, and balance.

C. Banking (direct access)

Create a set of 30 cards with bank account numbers (in the range 1 to 100), customer names and initial balances on them. Store these cards on a direct access file, using the account numbers as the record positions. Create a transaction card file of withdrawals and deposits containing the account number, a code to indicate withdrawals or deposits, and the amount. Read the transaction and update the direct access file. Allow for the case of the transaction file account number which has not been activated by printing an error message. Finally, write a program to read the master file in ascending order and produce a listing of the account number, names, and balances.

APPENDIX:

A REFERENCE GUIDE TO FORTRAN[1]

When writing FORTRAN programs you may want to look up some feature of the language. This appendix outlines the FORTRAN language for easy reference. The ranges specified for the values of variables are those accepted by the IBM 360/370 series of computers (WATFOR, WATFIV, FORTRAN G, FORTRAN H). For examples of the use of these statement types, consult the earlier chapters.

FORTRAN Statement Construction

Valid Source Program Characters

Any of the following characters may appear in a FORTRAN statement:

- *Alphabetic Characters*[2]

  A B C D E F G H I
  J K L M N O P Q R
  S T U V W X Y Z

- *Numeric Characters*

  0 1 2 3 4 5 6 7 8 9

- *Special Characters*

  (blank)   +   −   /   =   .   *   )   (,   &   '

Note that while these characters are the only ones used to make up source program statements, any character at all may appear in a literal.

---

[1] Adapted from *IBM System/360 and System/370 FORTRAN IV Language* #GC28-6515-10.
[2] The IBM FORTRAN compilers (G and H), as well as WATFOR/WATFIV, treat the dollar sign "$" as an alphabetic character.

Coding FORTRAN Statements

The statements of a FORTRAN source program can be written on a special FORTRAN coding form (see Figure 3.5). Each line on the coding form represents one 80-column card. FORTRAN statements are written one to a card within columns 7 through 72. If a statement is too long for one card, it may be continued on successive cards by placing any character, other than a blank or zero, in column 6 of each continuation card. For the first card of a statement, column 6 must be blank or zero.

Columns 1 through 5 of the first card of a statement may contain a statement number consisting of from one to five decimal digits. Blanks and leading zeroes in a statement number are ignored. Statement numbers may appear anywhere in columns 1 through 5 and may be assigned in any order; *the value of statement numbers does not affect the order in which the statements are executed in a FORTRAN program.*

Columns 73 through 80 are not significant to the FORTRAN compiler and may, therefore, be used for program identification, sequencing, or any other purpose.

Comments to explain the program may be written in columns 2 through 80 of a card if the letter C is placed in column 1. Comments may appear between FORTRAN statements, but a comment card may not immediately precede a continuation card. Comments are not processed by the FORTRAN compiler although they are printed on the source program listing.

As many blanks as desired may be written in a statement or comment to improve its readability. They are ignored by the compiler. However, blanks that are inserted in literal data are retained and treated as blanks within the data.

CONSTANTS

Integer Constants

An integer constant is a whole number written without a decimal point.

Maximum magnitude: 2147483647 (that is, $2^{31} - 1$)

An integer constant may be positive, zero, or negative. If unsigned and nonzero, it is assumed to be positive. (A zero may be written with a preceding sign, which has no effect on the value). Its magnitude must not be greater than the maximum and it may not contain embedded commas.

Real Constants

A *real constant* has one of three forms: a basic real constant, a basic real constant followed by a decimal exponent, or an integer constant followed by a decimal exponent.

A basic real constant is a string of decimal digits with a decimal point.

The storage requirement (length) of a real constant can be explicitly specified by appending an exponent to a basic real constant or an integer constant. An exponent consists of the letter E or the letter D followed by a signed or unsigned one- or two-digit integer constant. The letter E specifies a single precision constant; the letter D specifies a double precision constant.

Magnitude: 0 or 16^{-65} through 16^{63} (approximately 10^{-78} through 10^{75})

Precision: Single precision, approximately 7.2 decimal digits
Double precision, approximately 16.8 decimal digits

A real constant may be positive, zero, or negative (if unsigned and nonzero, it is assumed to be positive) and must be within the allowable range. It may not contain embedded commas. A zero may be written with a preceding sign, which has no effect on the value. The decimal exponent permits the expression of a real constant as the product of a basic real constant or integer constant times ten raised to a desired power.

Note that a single precision constant occupies one word while a double precision constant requires two words (eight bytes). However, even though a double precision constant can represent about twice as many digits as a single precision constant the range of values of both are the same. On the IBM 360/370 series computer, single precision real constants are also known as REAL*4 and double precision as REAL*8.

Complex Constants

A *complex constant* is an ordered pair of signed or unsigned real constants separated by a comma and enclosed in parentheses. The first real constant in a complex constant represents the real part of the complex number; the second represents the imaginary part of the complex number. Both parts must occupy the same number of storage locations (either four or eight).

The real constants in a complex constant may be positive, zero, or negative (if unsigned and nonzero, they are assumed to be positive), and must be within the allowable range. A zero may be written with a preceding sign, which has no effect on the value.

Logical Constants

A *logical constant* is a constant that specifies a logical value "true" or "false." There are two logical constants:

.TRUE.
.FALSE.

Each occupies four storage locations. The words TRUE and FALSE must be preceded and followed by periods.

Literal Constants

A *literal constant* is a string of characters, delimited as follows:

- The string can be enclosed in apostrophes.
- The string can be preceded by wH where w is the number of characters in the string.

Each character requires one byte of storage. The number of characters in the string, including blanks, may not be less than one or greater than 255. If apostrophes delimit the literal, a single apostrophe within the literal is represented by two apostrophes. If wH precedes the literal, a single apostrophe within the literal is represented by a single apostrophe.

Literals can be used only in CALL statement or function reference argument lists, as data initialization values, or in FORMAT statements.

Variables

A variable consists of from one to six alphabetic and numeric characters of which the first *must* be alphabetic. Unless otherwise declared, a variable is of INTEGER mode if its first letter is I, J, K, L, M, or N and REAL (single precision) otherwise.

Arithmetic Expressions

An arithmetic expression consists of constants and variables separated by arithmetic operators.

No two arithmetic operators may appear consecutively in the same expression. For example, the following expressions are invalid:

A*/B and A*−B

The expression A*−B could be written correctly as

A*(−B)

In effect, −B will be evaluated first and then A will be multiplied with it.

The *order of computation* is from left to right according to the hierarchy of operations shown in Table A.1.

Table A.1

Operation	Hierarchy
Evaluation of functions	1st
Exponentiation (**)	2nd
Multiplication and division (* and /)	3rd
Addition and subtraction (+ and −)	4th

This hierarchy is used to determine which of two sequential operations is performed first. If the first operator is higher than or equal to the second, the first operation is performed. If not, the second operator is compared to the third, and so on. When the end of the expression is encountered, all of the remaining operations are performed in reverse order.

However, A**B**C is treated as A**(B**C). Also, note that A = −B*C is treated as A = − (B*C).

If operands in an arithmetic expression are of different modes the result is computed in the more "powerful" of the two modes (Table A.2).

Table A.2

Results of Mixed Mode Operations

OP1 / OP2	Integer	Real	Complex
Integer	Integer	Real	Complex
Real	Real	Real	Complex
Complex	Complex	Complex	Complex

Logical Expressions

Relational Expressions

Relational expressions are formed by combining two arithmetic expressions with a relational operator. The six relational operators, each of which must be preceded and followed by a period, are shown in Table A.3.

Table A.3

Relational Operator	Definition
.GT.	Greater than ($>$).
.GE.	Greater than or equal to ($\geqslant$).
.LT.	Less than ($<$).
.LE.	Less than or equal to ($\leqslant$).
.EQ.	Equal to ($=$).
.NE.	Not equal to ($\neq$).

The relational operators express an arithmetic condition which can be either true or false. The relational operators may be used to compare two integer expressions, two real expressions, or a real and an integer expression.

Logical Operators

The three logical operators, each of which must be preceded and followed by a period, are given in Table A.4. A and B represent logical constants or variables, or expressions containing relational operators.

Table A.4

Logical Operator	Use	Meaning
.NOT.	.NOT.A	If A is true, then .NOT.A has the value false; if A is false, then .NOT.A has the value true.
.AND.	A.AND.B	If A and B are both true, then A.AND.B has the value true; if either A or B or both are false, then A.AND.B has the value false.
.OR.	A.OR.B	If either A or B or both are true, then A.OR.B has the value true; if both A and B are false, then A.OR.B has the value false.

The only valid sequences of two logical operators are .AND..NOT. and .OR..NOT.; the sequence .NOT..NOT. is invalid.

Only those expressions which, when evaluated, have the value true or false may be combined with the logical operators to form logical expressions.

The *order of computations* in logical expressions is given in Table A.5.

Table A.5

Operation	Hierarchy
Evaluation of functions	1st
Exponentiation (**)	2nd
Multiplication and division (* and /)	3rd
Addition and subtraction (+ and −)	4th
Relationals (.GT.,.GE.,.LT.,.LE.,.EQ.,.NE.)	5th
.NOT.	6th
.AND.	7th
.OR.	8th

Assignment Statements

General form: $a = b$

where a is a variable or array element.

b is an arithmetic or logical expression.

This FORTRAN statement closely resembles a conventional algebraic equation; however, the equals sign specifies replacement rather than equality. That is, the expression to the right of the equals sign is evaluated, and the resulting value replaces the current value of the variable or array element to the left of the equals sign.

If b is a logical expression, a must be a logical variable or array element. If b is an arithmetic expression, a must be an integer, real, or complex variable or array element.

Control Statements

GO TO Statement

General form: GO TO $xxxxx$

where $xxxxx$ is the number of an executable statement in the same program unit.

The GO TO statement causes control to be transferred to the statement specified by the statement number. Every subsequent execution of the GO TO statement results in a transfer to that same statement. Any executable statement immediately following this statement should have a statement number; otherwise it can never be referred to or executed.

Computed GO TO Statement

General form: GO TO $(x_1, x_2, x_3, \ldots, x_n), i$

where each x is the number of an executable statement in the program unit containing the GO TO statement.

i is an integer variable (not an array element) which must be given a value before the GO TO statement is executed.

This statement causes control to be transferred to the statement numbered $x_1, x_2, x_3,$ $\ldots,$ or x_n, depending on whether the current value of i is 1, 2, 3, $\ldots,$ or n, respectively. If the value of i is outside the range $1 \leqslant i \leqslant n$, the next statement is executed.

ASSIGN and Assigned GO TO Statements

General form: ASSIGN i TO m

$$\cdot$$
$$\cdot$$
$$\cdot$$

$$\text{GO TO } m, (x_1, x_2, x_3, \ldots, x_n)$$

where i is the number of an executable statement. It must be one of the numbers $x_1, x_2, x_3, \ldots, x_n$.

Each x is the number of an executable statement in the program unit containing the GO TO statement.

m is an integer variable (not an array element) of length 4 which is assigned one of the statement numbers $x_1, x_2, x_3, \ldots, x_n$.

The assigned GO TO statement causes control to be transferred to the statement numbered $x_1, x_2, x_3, \ldots,$ or x_n, depending on whether the current assignment of m is $x_1, x_2, x_3, \ldots,$ or x_n, respectively. For example, in the statement

```
GO TO N, (10, 25, 8)
```

if the current assignment of the integer variable N is statement number 8, then the statement numbered 8 is executed next. If the current assignment of N is statement number 10, the statement numbered 10 is executed next. If N is assigned statement number 25, statement 25 is executed next.

At the time of execution of an assigned GO TO statement, the current value of m must have been defined to be one of the values $x_1, x_2, \ldots, x_n$ by the previous execution of an ASSIGN statement. The value of the integer variable m is not the integer statement number; ASSIGN 10 TO I is not the same as I = 10.

Any executable statement immediately following this statement should have a statement number; otherwise it can never be referred to or executed.

Arithmetic IF Statement

General form: IF $(a)\ x_1, x_2, x_3$

where a is an arithmetic expression of any type except complex.

Each x is the number of an executable statement in the program unit containing the IF statement.

The arithmetic IF statement causes control to be transferred to the statement numbered $x_1, x_2,$ or x_3 when the value of the arithmetic expression (a) is less than, equal to, or greater than zero, respectively.

Any executable statement immediately following this statement should have a statement number; otherwise it can never be referred to or executed.

Logical IF Statement

General form: IF $(a)\ s$

where a is any logical expression.

s is any executable statement except a DO statement or another logical IF statement.

The logical IF statement is used to evaluate the logical expression (a) and to execute or skip statement s depending on whether the value of the expression is true or false, respectively.

DO Statement

General form:

End of range	DO variable		Initial value	Test value	Increment
DO x	i	$=$	$m_1,$	$m_2,$	m_3

where x is the number of an executable statement appearing after the DO statement in the program unit containing the DO.

i is an integer variable (not an array element) called the DO variable.

m_1, m_2, m_3, are either unsigned integer constants greater than zero or unsigned integer variables (not array elements) whose value is greater than zero. The value of m_1 should not exceed that of m_2; m_2 may not exceed $2^{31}-2$ in value; m_3 is optional (if it is omitted, its value is assumed to be 1, in which case, the preceding comma must also be omitted).

The DO statement is a command to execute, at least once, the statements that follow, up to and including the statement numbered x. These statements are called the range of the DO. The first time the statements in the range of the DO are executed, i is initialized to the value m_1; each succeeding time i is increased by the value m_3 (or 1 if m_3 is omitted). When, at the end of the iteration, i is equal to the highest value that does not exceed m_2, control passes to the statement following the statement numbered x. Upon completion of the DO, the DO variable is undefined and may not be used until assigned a value (for example, in an arithmetic assignment statement).

CONTINUE Statement

General form: CONTINUE

CONTINUE is a statement that may be placed anywhere in the source program (where an executable statement may appear) without affecting the sequence of execution. It may be used as the last statement in the range of a DO in order to avoid ending the DO loop with a GO TO, PAUSE, STOP, RETURN, arithmetic IF, another DO statement, or a logical IF statement containing any of these forms.

STOP Statement

General form: STOP
              STOP n

where n is a string of one to five decimal digits.

The STOP statement terminates the execution of the object program and displays STOP n if n is specified.

END Statement

General form: END

The END statement is a nonexecutable statement that defines the end of a main program or subprogram. Physically, it must be the last statement of each program unit. It may not have a statement number, and it may not be continued. The END statement does not terminate program execution. To terminate execution, a STOP statement or a RETURN statement in the main program is required.

Input/Output Statements

Standard READ Statement

General form: READ $(a, b,$ ERR$=c,$END$=d)$ *list*

where a is an unsigned integer constant or an integer variable that is of length 4 and represents a data set reference number.

b is optional and is either the statement number of the FORMAT statement describing the record(s) being read or the name of an array containing a format specification.

ERR$=c$ is optional and c is the number of a statement in the same program unit as the READ statement to which transfer is made if a transmission error occurs during data transfer.

END$=d$ is optional and d is the number of a statement in the same program unit as the READ statement to which transfer is made upon encountering the end of the data set.

list is an optional I/O list.

The READ statement may take many forms. The value of a must always be specified, but under appropriate conditions $b, c, d,$ and *list* can be omitted. The order of the parameters ERR$=c$ and END$=d$ can be reversed within the parentheses.

Transfer is made to the statement specified by the ERR parameter if an input error occurs. No indication is given of which record or records could not be read, only that an error occurred.

Simplified READ Statement (WATFOR/WATFIV only)

General form: READ, *list*
              READ $(a, *,$ ERR$=c,$ END$=d)$ *list* (WATFIV only)

where $a, c,$ and d are the same as in the standard READ statement.

The input card(s) contain a list of values separated by blanks and commas.

Standard WRITE Statement

General form: WRITE (a, b) *list*

where a is an unsigned integer constant or an integer variable that is of length 4 and represents a data set reference number.

b is optional and is either the statement number of the FORMAT statement describing the record(s) being written or the name of an array containing a format specification.

list is optional and is an I/O list.

Simplified WRITE Statement (WATFOR/WATFIV only)

General form: PRINT, *list*
        WRITE(a, *) *list* (WATFIV only)

The simplified PRINT allows format-free output of variables.[3]

FORMAT Statement

General form: $xxxxx$ FORMAT $(c_1, c_2, \ldots, c_n)$

where $xxxxx$ is a statement number (one to five digits).

$c_1, c_2, \ldots, c_n$ are format codes.

The format codes are

aIw	Describes integer data fields.
paD$w \cdot d$	Describes double precision data fields.
paE$w \cdot d$	Describes real data fields.
paF$w \cdot d$	Describes real data fields.
aZw	Describes hexadecimal data fields.
paG$w \cdot s$	Describes integer, real, or logical data fields.
aLw	Describes logical data fields.
aAw	Describes character data fields.
'literal'	Indicates literal data.
wH	Indicates literal data.
wX	Indicates that a field is to be skipped on input or filled with blanks on output.
Tr	Indicates the position in a FORTRAN record where transfer of data is to start.
a(...)	Indicates a group format specification.

---

[3]The form PUNCH, *list* may be used. It is equivalent to the statement WRITE(7, *) *list*.

where a is optional and is a repeat count, an unsigned integer constant used to denote the number of times the format code or group is to be used. If a is omitted, the code or group is used only once.

w is an unsigned nonzero integer constant that specifies the number of characters in the field.

d is an unsigned integer constant specifying the number of decimal places to the right of the decimal point; that is, the fractional portion.

s is an unsigned integer constant specifying the number of significant digits.

r is an unsigned integer constant designating a character position in a record.

p is optional and represents a scale factor designator of the form nP where n is an unsigned or negatively signed integer constant.

(. . .) is a group format specification. Within the parentheses are format codes or an additional level of groups, separated by commas or slashes.

Declaration Statements

Data Initialization

General form: DATA $k_1/d_1/, k_2/d_2/, \ldots, k_n/d_n/$

where each k is a list containing variables, array elements (in which case the subscript quantities must be unsigned integer constants), or array names. Dummy arguments may not appear in the list.

Each d is a list of constants (integer, real, complex, hexadecimal, logical, or literal), any of which may be preceded by i^*. Each i is an unsigned integer constant. When the form i^* appears before a constant, it indicates that the constant is to be specified i times.

A DATA initialization statement is used to define initial values of variables, array elements, and arrays. There must be a one-to-one correspondence between the total number of elements specified or *implied* by the list k and the total number of constants specified by the corresponding list d after application of any replication factors, i.

For real, integer, complex, and logical types, each constant must agree in type with the variable or array element it is initializing. Any type of variable or array element may be initialized with a literal or hexadecimal constant.

This statement cannot precede any specification statement that refers to the same variables, array elements, or arrays, but it can precede specification statements for other variables, array elements, or arrays. It also cannot precede an IMPLICIT statement. Otherwise, a DATA statement can appear anywhere in the program.

DIMENSION Statement

General form: DIMENSION $a_1(k_1), a_2(k_2), a_3(k_3), \ldots, a_n(k_n)$

where each a is an array name.

Each k is composed of one to seven unsigned integer constants, separated by commas, representing the maximum value of each subscript in the array. Each k may contain integer variables of length 4 only when the DIMENSION statement in which they appear is in a subprogram and the corresponding a is a dummy argument of that subprogram.

IMPLICIT Statement

General form: IMPLICIT $type_1 *s_1(a_{11}, a_{12}, \ldots), \ldots, type_n *s_n(a_{n1}, a_{n2}, \ldots)$

where $type$ is INTEGER, REAL, COMPLEX, or LOGICAL.

Each $*s$ is optional and represents one of the permissible length specifications for its associated type.

Each a is a single alphabetic character or a range of characters drawn from the set A, B, . . . , Z, and \$, in that order. The range is denoted by the first and last characters of the range separated by a minus sign—for example, A–D.

The IMPLICIT specification statement must be the first statement in a main program and the second statement in a subprogram. There can be only one IMPLICIT statement per program or subprogram. The IMPLICIT specification statement enables the user to declare the type of the variables appearing in the program (integer, real, complex, or logical) by specifying that variables beginning with certain designated letters are of a certain type. Furthermore, the IMPLICIT statement allows the programmer to declare the number of locations (bytes) to be allocated for each in the group of specified variables. Table A.6 shows the types that a variable may assume, along with the permissible length specifications.

Table A.6

Type	Length Specifications
INTEGER	2 or 4 (standard length is 4)
REAL	4 or 8 (standard length is 4)
COMPLEX	8 or 16 (standard length is 8)
LOGICAL	1 or 4 (standard length is 4)

Type Statements

General form: $type*s\ a_1*s_1(k_1)/x_1/, a_2*s_2(k_2)/x_2/, \ldots, a_n*s_n(k_n)/x_n/$

where *type* is INTEGER, REAL, LOGICAL, or COMPLEX.

Each s is optional and represents one of the permissible length specifications for its associated type.

Each a is a variable, array, or function name (see the section, "Subprograms").

Each k is optional and gives dimension information for arrays. Each k is composed of one to seven unsigned integer constants, separated by commas, representing the maximum value of each subscript in the array. When the type statement in which it appears is in a subprogram, each k may contain integer variables of length 4, provided that the array is a dummy argument.

Each $/x/$ is optional and represents initial data values. Dummy arguments may not be assigned initial values.

DOUBLE PRECISION Statement

General form: DOUBLE PRECISION $a_1(k_1), a_2(k_2), a_3(k_3), \ldots, a_n(k_n)$

where each a represents a variable, array, or function name (see the section, "Subprograms").

Each k is optional and is composed of one to seven unsigned integer constants or integer variables of length 4, separated by commas, that represent the maximum value of each subscript in the array.

The DOUBLE PRECISION statement explicitly specifies that each of the variables a is of type double precision. This statement overrides any specification of a variable made by either the predefined convention or the IMPLICIT statement. The specification is identical to that of type REAL*8, but it cannot be used to define initial data values.

COMMON Statement

General form: COMMON $/r_1/a_{11}(k_{11}), a_{12}(k_{12}), \ldots /r_n/a_{n1}(k_{n1}), a_{n2}(k_{n2}), \ldots$

where each a is a variable name or array name that is not a dummy argument.

Each k is optional and is composed of one to seven unsigned integer constants, separated by commas, representing the maximum value of each subscript in the array.

Each r represents an optional common block name consisting of one to six alphanumeric characters, the first of which is alphabetic. These names must always be enclosed in slashes.

The form / / (with no characters except possibly blanks between the slashes) may be used to denote blank common. If r_1 denotes blank common, the first two slashes are optional.

The COMMON statement is used to cause the sharing of storage by two or more program units, and to specify the names of variables and arrays that are to occupy this area. Storage sharing can be used for two purposes: to conserve storage, by avoiding more than one allocation of storage for variables and arrays used by several program units; and to transfer arguments implicitly between a calling program and a subprogram. Arguments passed in a common area are subject to the same rules with regard to type, length, and so on as arguments passed in an argument list (see the section, "Subprograms").

A given common block name may appear more than once in a COMMON statement, or in more than one COMMON statement in a program unit. All entries within such blocks are strung together in order of their appearance.

EQUIVALENCE Statement

General form: EQUIVALENCE $(a_{11}, a_{12}, a_{13}, \ldots), (a_{21}, a_{22}, a_{23}, \ldots), \ldots$

where each a is a variable or array element and may not be a dummy argument. The subscripts of array elements may have either of two forms. In either case, the subscripts themselves must be integer constants.

If the array element has a single subscript quantity, it refers to the linear position of the element in the array (its position relative to the first element in the array: third element, 17th element, 259th element).

If the array element is multisubscripted (with the number of subscript quantities equal to the number of dimensions of the array), it refers to the position in the same manner as in an arithmetic statement (position relative to the first element of each dimension of the array).

All the elements within a single set of parentheses share the same storage locations. The EQUIVALENCE statement provides the option of controlling the allocation of data storage within a single program unit. In particular, when the logic of the program permits it, the number of storage locations used can be reduced by causing locations to be shared by two or more variables of the same or different types. Equivalence between variables implies storage sharing. Mathematical equivalence of variables or array elements is implied only when they are of the same type, when they share exactly the same storage, and when the value assigned to the storage is of that type.

Subprograms

Arithmetic Statement Functions

General form: *name* $(a_1, a_2, a_3, \ldots, a_n)$ = *expression*

where *name* is the statement function name.

Each a is a dummy argument. It must be a distinct variable (that is, it may appear only once within the list of arguments). There must be at least one dummy argument.

expression is any arithmetic or logical expression that does not contain array elements. Any statement function appearing in this expression must have been defined previously.

Functions

General form: *type* FUNCTION *name**s $(a_1, a_2, a_3, \ldots, a_n)$

where *type* is INTEGER, REAL, DOUBLE PRECISION, COMPLEX, or LOGICAL. Its inclusion is optional.

name is the name of the FUNCTION.

s represents one of the permissible length specifications for its associated type. It may be included optionally only when *type* is specified. It must not be used when DOUBLE PRECISION is specified.

Each *a* is a dummy argument. It must be a distinct variable or array name (that is, it may appear only once within the statement) or dummy name of a SUBROUTINE or other FUNCTION subprogram. There must be at least one argument in the argument list.

Subroutines

General form: SUBROUTINE *name* $(a_1, a_2, a_3, \ldots, a_n)$

where *name* is the SUBROUTINE name.

Each *a* is a distinct dummy argument (that is, it may appear only once within the statement). There need not be any arguments, in which case the parentheses must be omitted. Each argument used must be a variable or array name, the dummy name of another SUBROUTINE or FUNCTION subprogram, or an asterisk, where the character "*" denotes a return point specified by a statement number in the calling program.

The SUBROUTINE subprogram is similar to the FUNCTION subprogram in many respects. The rules for naming FUNCTION and SUBROUTINE subprograms are similar. They both require an END statement, and they both contain the same sort of dummy arguments. Like the FUNCTION subprogram, the SUBROUTINE subprogram is a set of commonly used computations, but it need not return any results to the calling program, as does the FUNCTION subprogram. The SUBROUTINE subprogram is referred to by the CALL statement.

CALL Statement

General form: CALL *name* $(a_1, a_2, a_3, \ldots, a_n)$

where *name* is the name of a SUBROUTINE subprogram.

Each *a* is an actual argument that is being supplied to the SUBROUTINE subprogram. The argument may be a variable, array element, array name, literal, or arithmetic or logical expression. Each may also be of the form &*n* where *n* is a statement number.

RETURN Statement

General form: RETURN
　　　　　　　RETURN i

where i is an integer constant or variable of length 4 whose value, say n, denotes the nth statement number in the argument list of a SUBROUTINE statement; i may be specified only in a SUBROUTINE subprogram.

EXTERNAL Statement

General form: EXTERNAL $a_1, a_2, a_3, \ldots, a_n$

where each a is the name of a subprogram that is passed as an argument to other subprograms.

The EXTERNAL statement is a specification statement, and must precede statement function definitions and all executable statements.

BLOCK DATA Subprograms

To initialize variables in a labeled (named) common block, a separate subprogram must be written. This separate subprogram contains only the BLOCK DATA, DATA, COMMON, DIMENSION, EQUIVALENCE, and type statements associated with the data being defined. Data may not be initialized in unlabeled common.

General form: BLOCK DATA

The BLOCK DATA subprogram may not contain any executable statements, statement function definitions, or FORMAT, DEFINE FILE, FUNCTION, SUBROUTINE, or ENTRY statements.

The BLOCK DATA statement must be the first statement in the subprogram. If an IMPLICIT statement is used in a BLOCK DATA subprogram, it must immediately follow the BLOCK DATA statement. Statements which provide initial values for data items cannot precede the COMMON statements which define those data items.

Any main program or subprogram using a common block must contain a COMMON statement defining that block. If initial values are to be assigned, a BLOCK DATA subprogram is necessary.

All elements of a common block must be listed in the COMMON statement, even though they are not all initialized.

Note: Input/output statements for *direct files* are discussed in Chapter 13 as are special tape-oriented *sequential file* manipulation statements.

ANSWERS
TO PROBLEMS

CHAPTER 1

Problem 1.1 (page 11)

    a. #1 READ
           #2 READ
           #3 MULTIPLY
           #4 PRINT
    b. Add the instruction #5–"GO TO INSTRUCTION #1"
    c. No, it does not. However, we will see programs in which the *order* of the data is important.

CHAPTER 2

Problem 2.1 (page 40)

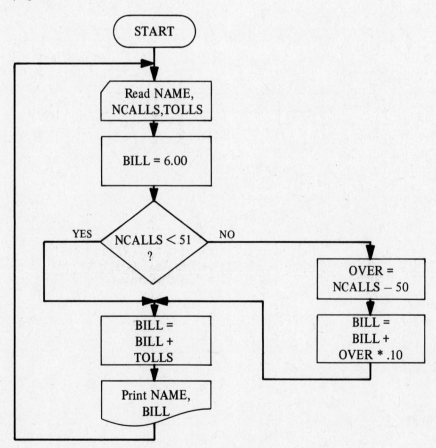

Problem 2.2 (page 43)

One possible solution is:

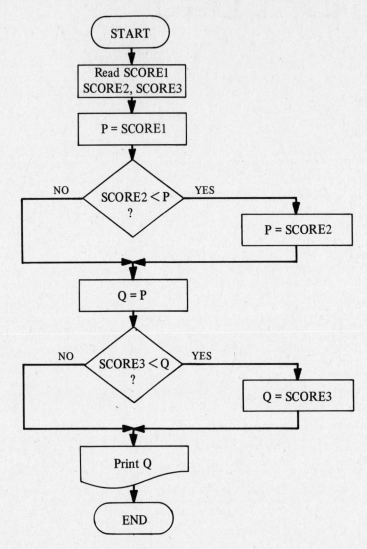

CHAPTER 3

Problem 3.2 (page 59)

a. valid
b. valid
c. invalid
d. invalid
e. invalid
f. invalid
g. valid
h. invalid

i. invalid
j. valid
k. valid
l. valid
m. valid
n. valid
o. invalid

Note that items *d, e, h,* and *o* are valid INTEGER variables.

Problem 3.3 (page 60)

a. invalid (no decimal point)
b. valid
c. valid
d. invalid (comma not permitted)
e. valid
f. valid

Problem 3.4 (page 63)

a. valid
b. invalid (valid REAL variable)
c. valid
d. invalid (too long)
e. valid

f. invalid (valid REAL variable)
g. invalid
h. invalid
i. invalid (valid REAL variable)

Problem 3.5 (page 63)

1) A: 5.4
   B: 6.3
   C: 2.4
   D: 6.3
   E: 5.4

2) N: 9
   K: 9
   K5: 5
   NOW: 9

3) RESULT: 8.675
   TEST: 9.6
   VALUE: 9.6
   X: 9.6

Problem 3.6 (page 66)

```
BUILDG = 945.5
TV = 135.2
HEIGHT = BUILDG + TV
```

Problem 3.7 (page 66)

```
MARK = 78
NEW = MARK + 5
```

CHAPTER 4

Problem 4.1 (page 91)

```
T = A/B
X = T*C
```

Problem 4.2 (page 95)

```
a. V = 4.0/3.0 * 3.1416 * R ** 3
b. S = 4.0 * 3.1416 * R ** 2
c. V = VO + A ** T
d. Y = X ** 3 + 2.0 * X ** 2 - 4.0 * X - 3.0
e. I = (J + K)/(J - K) * M
f. M = (N - 1) * (N - 2) * (N - 3)
g. X = Y ** (3.0 * A)
h. D = XM/V
i. Y = (X - 2.0) * (X + 3.0)
j. K = (N ** 2 + 1)/2 + 6
```

Problem 4.3a (page 95)

1. $a = b(c - \dfrac{d}{e})$

2. $x = y + \dfrac{w}{z}$

3. $d = d_1 + \dfrac{1}{2}at^2$

4. $p = a^2 r$

5. $x = \dfrac{1 - x}{y - x}$

6. $y = x^3 + 5x^2 - \dfrac{5x}{2} + 6$

7. $p = p + prt$

8. $j = kl - k + \dfrac{l(m+n)}{m-n}$

9. $m = \dfrac{3m}{\dfrac{i}{j} - k} - n + 6$

10. $i = \dfrac{j^{((k-3)^l)}}{7}$

Problem 4.3b (page 95)

```
1. A = B*(C - (D/E))
2. X = Y + (W/Z)
3. D = D1 + ((A*(T**2.0))/2.0
4. P = (A**2.0)*R
5. X = (1.0 - X)/(Y - X)
6. Y = (((X**3) + (5.0*(X**2))) + (2.5*X)) + 6.0
7. P = P + ((P*R)*T)
8. J = ((K*L) - K) + ((L/(M - N))*(M + N))
9. M = (((3/((I/J) - K))*M) - N) + 6
10. I = (J**((K - 3)**L))/7
```

CHAPTER 5

Problem 5.1 (page 133)

If the GO TO instruction were not present, the instructions in set "A" would be executed regardless of the condition. That is, if the condition were *true*, the sequence "A" would be executed; if the condition were *false*, the sequence "B A" would be executed. Without the GO TO the structure might be interpreted as "skip B if the condition is true."

Problem 5.2 (page 134)

a. false

b. true

c. false

d. true

e. true

f. false

Note: Because arithmetic in the computer may not always be quite precise due to *roundoff error*, a construction like that used in (b) is often avoided. See page 141.

Problem 5.3 (page 137)

```
      READ 101, X, Y
101  FORMAT(F3.0, F3.0)
      IF (X .GT. Y) GO TO 40
      IF (X .LT. Y) GO TO 50
      PRINT 102
102  FORMAT('0X IS EQUAL TO Y')
      GO TO 99
 40  PRINT 103
103  FORMAT('0X IS GREATER THAN Y')
      GO TO 99
 50  PRINT 104
104  FORMAT('0X IS LESS THAN Y')
 99  STOP
      END
```

Note the use of the carriage control character in the three FORMAT statements used for output.

Problem 5.4 (page 147)

One solution is

```
      N = 0
      SUM = 0
 92  READ 101, X
101  FORMAT(F5.0)
      IF (X .LT. 0.0) GO TO 50
      N = N + 1
      SUM = SUM + X
      GO TO 92
 50  AVE = SUM/FLOAT(N)
      PRINT 102, N, AVE
102  FORMAT('0THERE ARE ', I2,
     1' NUMBERS AND THE AVERAGE IS', F10.3)
      STOP
      END
```

CHAPTER 6

Problem 6.1 (page 168)

a.

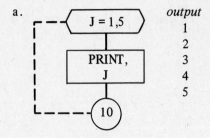

output
1
2
3
4
5

b.

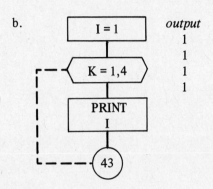

output
1
1
1
1

c.

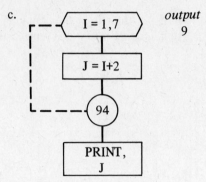

output
9

Problem 6.2 (page 177)

a. 1,2,3,4,5,6,7
b. 1,3,5,7
c. 5,6,7,8,9,10,11,12,13,14,15,16,17,18
d. 14,17,20,23,26
e. 2,4,6,8,10,12,14,16,18,20
f. 1,5,9,13,17,21,25,29

Problem 6.3 (page 180)

column 1
↓

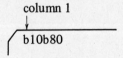

b10b80

71 lines of output would be produced.

CHAPTER 7

Problem 7.1 (page 201)

```
a.    DO 10 I = 1,14          c.    DO 44 J = 1,250
      X(I) = 0.0                    NUMBER(J) = J
   10 CONTINUE                   44 CONTINUE

b.    DO 90 KK = 1,5
      N7(KK) = 11
   90 CONTINUE
```

Problem 7.2 (page 202)

```
a. DIMENSION YY(49)
b. DIMENSION A4(7), I(15), F(1000)
```

Problem 7.3 (page 209)

```
      DIMENSION NUMS(1000)
            .
            .
            .
      READ (5,100) IFVAL
  100 FORMAT(I2)
      DO 4 I = 1,1000
      IF (NUMS(I) .NE. IFVAL) GO TO 4
      WRITE (6,101) IFVAL, I
  101 FORMAT('0THE VALUE ', I3, ' IS IN POSITION ', I4)
      GO TO 999
    4 CONTINUE
      WRITE (6,102) IFVAL
  102 FORMAT('0THE VALUE ', I3, ' IS NOT FOUND')
  999 STOP
      END
```

Problem 7.4 (page 215)

Assume X is dimensioned for 10 elements.

```
      IPOS = 1
      SMALL = X(1)
      DO 10 I = 2,10
      IF (X(I) .GE. SMALL) GO TO 10
      SMALL = X(I)
      IPOS = I
   10 CONTINUE
      WRITE (6,101) SMALL, IPOS
  101 FORMAT('0THE SMALLEST VALUE IS', F7.1,
     1   ' IN LOCATION', I3)
      STOP
      END
```

Problem 7.5 (page 219)

```
      NM = N - 1
      DO 30 I = 1, NM
      JM = N - I
      DO 20 J = 1, JM
      IF (A(J) .LE. A(J+1)) GO TO 20
      TEMP = A(J)
      A(J) = A(J+1)
      A(J+1) = TEMP
   20 CONTINUE
   30 CONTINUE
```

Problem 7.6 (page 225)

```
      DIMENSION A(4,7)
              .
              .
              .
      ABIG = A(1,1)
      ASMALL = A(1,1)
      DO 20 I = 1,4
      DO 10 J = 1,7
      IF (A(I,J) .GT. ABIG) ABIG = A(I,J)
      IF (A(I,J) .LT. ASMALL) ASMALL = A(I,J)
   10 CONTINUE
   20 CONTINUE
```

CHAPTER 8

Problem 8.1 (page 246)

```
      DO 10 I = 1,25
      ISQ = I*I
      WRITE(6,101)I,ISQ
  101 FORMAT(' ',T19,I2,T50,I5)
   10 CONTINUE
      STOP
      END
```

Problem 8.2 (page 248)

```
      READ(5,101)NA,NB,NC
  101 FORMAT(A4,A4,A4)
      WRITE(6,102)NA,NB,NC
  102 FORMAT('1',T60,A4,A4,A4)
```

Problem 8.3 (page 249)

```
(3I3)
(F4.3,F5.4,F4.3)
(F10.2,2A4,A3,I2,2F6.2)
(2I1,F2.1,2E12.6)
```

Problem 8.4 (page 254)

```
      DIMENSION ARRAY(8,20)
      WRITE(6,101)((ARRAY(I,J),J = 1,20),I = 1,8)
  101 FORMAT(8(' ',20F10.2/))
```

CHAPTER 9

Problem 9.1 (page 278)

a. function
b. function
c. subroutine
d. function

e. subroutine
f. function
g. function

Problem 9.2 (page 281)

```
a. FUNCTION A1(X)
   A1 = X + 1.0
   RETURN
   END
```

```
b. FUNCTION I1(X)
   I1 = IFIX(X + 1.0)   or   I1 = X + 1.0
   RETURN
   END
```

Problem 9.3 (page 289)

```
      SUBROUTINE PAGE(NUM)
C
C      THIS SUBROUTINE PRINTS A TITLE AND PAGE NUMBER
C      NUM SHOULD BE EQUAL TO ZERO ON THE FIRST CALL
C
      NUM = NUM + 1
      WRITE(6,101) NUM
  101 FORMAT('1THIS IS A TITLE', T80, 'PAGE', I3)
      RETURN
      END
```

CHAPTER 10

Problem 10.1 (page 310)

```
a. A.GT.B                    d. A.GT.C .OR. B.GT.C
b. A.GT.B .AND. A.LT.C       e. A.LT.B .OR. A.LT.C
c. A.GT.C .AND. B.GT.C
```

Problem 10.2 (page 310)

```
a. LOGICAL L                 b. LOGICAL L7
   L = X .GT. Y                 L7 = A.LT.1.0 .OR. A.GT.B
   IF (L) GO TO 70              IF (L7) X = 17.2
```

Problem 10.3 (page 318)

Main Program

```
DIMENSION A(1000)
COMMON A
```

Sub 1

```
INTEGER B(1000)
DIMENSION A(1000)
COMMON A
COMMON/SUBCOM/B
```

Sub 2

```
INTEGER B(1000)
DIMENSION A(1000)
COMMON A
COMMON/SUBCOM/B
```

Problem 10.4 (page 319)

```
REAL X(1500)
INTEGER IA(500), IB(500), IC(500)
EQUIVALENCE (X(1), IA(1)), (X(501), IB(1)), (X(1001), IC(1))
```
or
```
DIMENSION X(1500), IA(500), IB(500), IC(500)
EQUIVALENCE (X(1), IA(1)), (X(501), IB(1)), (X(1001), IC(1))
```

CHAPTER 11

Problem 11.1 (page 334)

    a. valid
    b. invalid. There is more than one main program.
    c. invalid. The function calls the program which invokes it.
    d. invalid. The function calls itself.

Problem 11.2 (page 337)

    a. (51,1)   c. (41,68)
    b. (1,101)   d. (4,33)

Problem 11.3 (page 343)

```
C
C         CLEAR BOARD
C
          CALL CLEAR
C
C         DRAW LINE
C
          DO 10 I = 1,100
          J = I - 51
    10 CALL POINT (J, 0, 'X')
C
C         DRAW GRAPH
C
          CALL DRAW
          STOP
          END
```

CHAPTER 12

Problem 12.1 (page 356)

```
          DIMENSION ICHARS(30)
          READ(5,101) ICHARS
    101 FORMAT(30A1)
          WRITE(6,102) (ICHARS(J), J = 11,20)
    102 FORMAT('0', 10A1)
          STOP
          END
```

Problem 12.2 (page 357)

a. IC(1) = ID(1)

b. ID(1) = IC(1)
   ID(2) = IC(2)

c. IC(1) = IC(3)
   IC(3) = ID(3)

d. ID(2) = ID(1)
   ID(4) = ID(3)
   ID(1) = IC(3)
   ID(3) = IC(2)

Problem 12.3 (page 359)

a. LNLST will be returned as zero, to indicate that the routine has read a string with no characters (a *null string*).

b. LNLST will be set to 400, the maximum length string that is allowed. Cards will be read but ignored until an asterisk is found. This serves to position the card reader to the next string to be read, if any.

Problem 12.4 (page 363)

WEN IN THE COURSEEEEEEEEEEEEEEES

Problem 12.5 (page 365)

CALL WRITST (NST, LEN, 50, 1)

CHAPTER 13

Problem 13.1 (page 382)

See flowchart on opposite page.

Possible subroutines:　READM — Read master record
WMAST — Write master record
READT — Read transaction record
ERRPRT — Print error message

```
            .
            .
            .
    100 IF (MAST - ITRNS) 200, 150, 300
            .
            .
C               MASTER AND TRANSACTION MATCH
    150 [apply transaction]
        CALL WMAST
        CALL READM
```

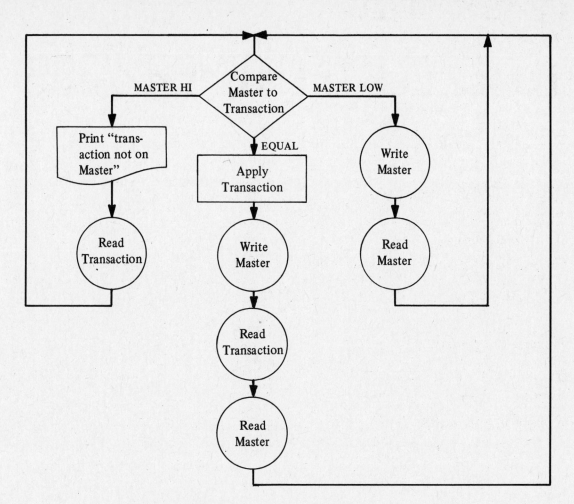

```
           CALL READT
           GO TO 100
C                 MASTER < TRANSACTION
     200 CALL WMAST
           CALL READM
           GO TO 100
C                 TRANSACTION < MASTER
     300 CALL ERRPRT
           CALL READT
           GO TO 100
                 .
                 .
                 .
```

Problem 13.3 (page 384)

```
    a. DEFINE FILE 15 (2000,80,E,IR)
    b. DEFINE FILE 19 (100,95,L,JREC)
```

ANSWERS
TO SELECTED EXERCISES

CHAPTER 1

Exercise 1 (page 25)

a. input
c. conditional, transfer
e. transfer

g. output
i. conditional, output

Exercise 2 (page 26)

b. compiler
d. ALGOL, COBOL, SNOBOL, BASIC

f. END
h. 25.0

Exercise 3 (page 26)

There are two errors in this program. The first is that statement 40 must appear before statement 30. We cannot add the value of CHANGE to STOCK before we know what it is.

The second error is one of omission. There is no END statement. *Every* FORTRAN program must have an END statement as its last instruction.

The correct program should look like this:

```
10  READ, STOCK
20  PRINT, STOCK
40  READ, CHANGE
30  NEW = STOCK + CHANGE
50  PRINT, CHANGE, NEW
    END
```

NOTE: It is all right to have an input statement (#10) followed by an output statement (#20) without having another statement in between. In fact, we recommend you do this when testing a program so you can see if you are reading in what you expect.

CHAPTER 2

Exercise 1 (page 46)

a.

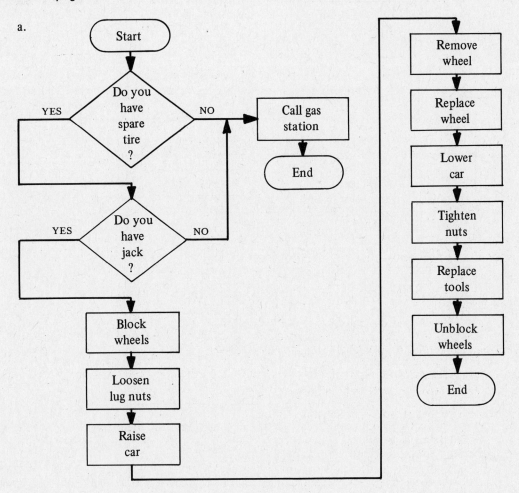

c.

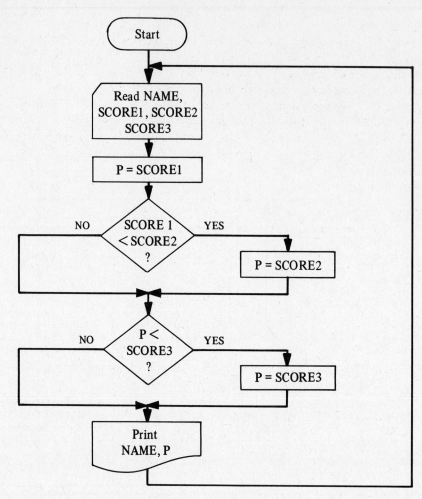

e. Read a temperature in centigrade. Convert it to Fahrenheit. Print the temperature in Fahrenheit and centigrade. If the resulting temperature is the boiling point of water then stop; otherwise read another temperature and repeat the process.

The program will terminate when a temperature of 100° centigrade is read, or when there are no more cards to be read.

Exercise 2 (page 47)

a. flowchart
c. terminate (with a message)

e. GO TO
g. 1, 2, 5, and 6

Exercise 3 (page 48)

a. (3) and (5) are correct answers. Because a program with a loop does execute some instructions more than once, it needs fewer instructions. Refer back to page 37 for examples of the advantage of using a loop.

Incorrect answers: (1) and (2) are incorrect because, while a loop may affect how many cards (if any) are read, it is the READ statement that stops a program when an end-of-file condition arises. (4) is incorrect because *all* FORTRAN programs must have an END as the last statement.

b. (1) is correct.

(2) is incorrect. No matter what the outcome of the decision statement the program branches to the process box just preceding it; this results in a program which loops forever (or until someone pulls the plug). This type of "loop" is frequently referred to as an "infinite loop."

(3) is incorrect. No statement of any kind may appear after the END statement.

(4) is correct. This program, which has no executable steps, is a perfectly valid one. Since it does nothing, though, it is wise not to write any programs like it. (There are some more advanced programming techniques in which such a "dummy program" can be useful; these are discussed later in the book.)

(5) is correct.

(6) is correct.

c. One answer is:

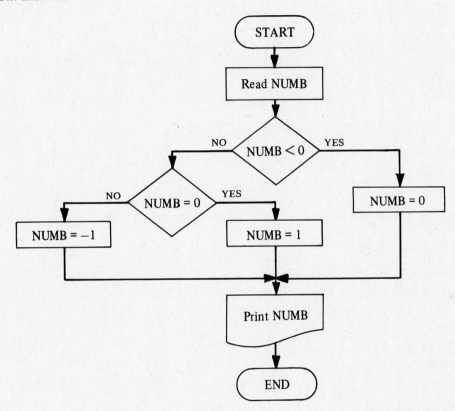

As a shorter alternative:

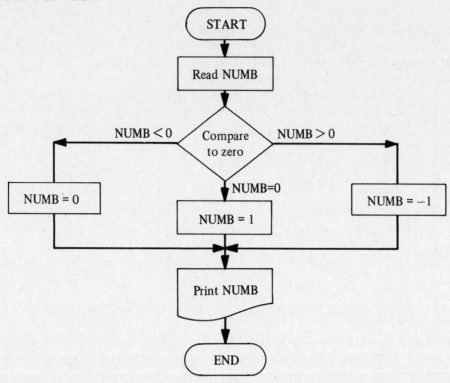

Remember that a decision block can have more than two outputs. The less than, equal to, or greater than combination is one that can be written as a single FORTRAN statement and so could be a single decision block.

CHAPTER 3

Exercise 1 (page 83)

a. valid
c. invalid (name too long)
e. invalid
g. invalid

i. invalid
k. invalid
m. valid
o. invalid

Exercise 2 (page 83)

```
b. XINT = .05 * PRINC
d. AREA = SIDE * SIDE
f. SUM = TEST1 + TEST2
   AVG = SUM/2.0
h. AREA = XLEN * WIDTH
   VOLUME = AREA * HEIGHT
```

```
j. R3 = R ** 3
   PIR3 = 3.1416 * R3
   VOL = 1.33 * PIR3
```

Exercise 3 (page 84)

a. valid　　　g. invalid
c. valid　　　i. valid
e. invalid

Exercise 4 (page 84)

a. NSTDS = 35　　　c. (1) 4.6
　 NSTDS = NSTDS + 4　　(2) 8.2
　 NSTDS = NSTDS - 2　　(3) 4.1

e. 0.350000E 01　　 0.500000E 01　　 0.200000E 01
　　(3.5)　　　　　　(5.0)　　　　　　(2.0)

Exercise 5 (page 84)

NOTE: The READ and PRINT statements in these answers are WATFOR/WATFIV language extensions. See pages 71–80.

a. READ, FEET
   XINCH = 12.0 * FEET
   PRINT, XINCH
   STOP
   END

c. READ, P, RATE
   XINT = RATE * P
   PRINT, XINT
   STOP
   END

e. READ, I, J
   K = I/J
   PRINT, K
   STOP
   END

CHAPTER 4

Exercise 1 (page 122)

a. Y = (A * B)/C
c. Y = A * B + C
e. Z = 2.0 * SIN(X) + COS(X)

g. XI = SQRT(XJ * XJ + Z) *or*
   Z = XI * XI - XJ * XJ
i. X = (A/B) / (C/D)

Exercise 2 (page 122)

b. $b = \dfrac{y + x^2}{2}$

d. $q = da + bc$

f. $m = \dfrac{1}{\dfrac{i}{j}} + k^2$

Exercises 3-6 (page 122)

The key statements are:

```
3. DIAG = SQRT(XLEN ** 2 + WIDTH ** 2)
5. XBAR = (X(1) + X(2) + X(3) + X(4))/4.0
   DEV = (ABS(X(1) - XBAR) + ABS(X(2) - XBAR)
          + ABS(X(3) - XBAR) + ABS(X(4) = XBAR))/4.0
6. VEL = R * W * COS(W * T)
   ACC = R * (W ** 2) * SIN(W * T)
```

Exercise 7 (page 122)

```
a.      READ 100, ID, TEST1, TEST2
   100 FORMAT(I6, F5.2, F5.1)
c.      READ 100, IANUM, NPRO, NEUT, WT
   100 FORMAT(I3, 2X, I3, 4X, I3, 3X, F5.1)
e.      READ 100, POP, SQM, CRATE
   100 FORMAT(F7.0, 2X, F6.2, 6X, F6.2)
```

Exercise 8 (page 123)

```
a.      PRINT 500, ID, TEST1, TEST2
   500 FORMAT('1ID', I6, 'TEST1', F5.2, 'TEST2', F5.1)
c.      PRINT 500, IANUM, NPRO, NEVT, WT
   500 FORMAT('1ATOMIC NUMBER', I3, ' PROTONS', I3,
   1 ' NEUTRONS', I3, ' ATOMIC WEIGHT', F5.1)
e.      PRINT 500, POP, SQM, CRATE
   500 FORMAT('1POPULATION', F7.0, ' SIZE', F6.2, ' CRIME
   1 RATE', F6.2)
```

Exercise 9 (page 123)

```
    10 READ 200, XMILES, GAS
   200 FORMAT(F6.1, F5.1)
       XMPG = XMILES/GAS
       PRINT 300, XMPG
   300 FORMAT('0MPG =', F5.1)
       XKILO = 0.621 * XMILES
       XKPG = XKILO/GAS
       PRINT 400, XKPG
   400 FORMAT('0KPG = ', F5.1)
       XLIT = 3.785 * GAS
       XKPL = XKILO/XLIT
       PRINT 500, XKPL
   500 FORMAT('0KPL =', F5.1)
       GO TO 10
       END
```

Exercise 10 (page 123)

```
 b.      READ 100, POUNDS
   100 FORMAT(F5.0)
         XKILO = POUNDS/2.2
         PRINT 200, POUNDS,XKILO
   200 FORMAT('0', F5.0, ' POUNDS =', F6.0, ' KILOGRAMS')
         STOP
         END
 d.      READ 100, R
   100 FORMAT(F5.0)
         PRINT 200, R
   200 FORMAT('0RADIUS =', F6.0)
         AREA = 3.1416 * R ** 2
         PRINT 300, AREA
   300 FORMAT('0AREA =', F8.2)
         CIR = 2.* 3.1416 * R
         PRINT 400, CIR
   400 FORMAT('0CIRCUMFERENCE =', F8.2)
         STOP
         END
```

CHAPTER 5

Exercise 1 (page 155)

```
a. IF (X .GT. 25.0) X = 25.0
c. IF (I .LE. N) READ (5,300) X, Y, Z
e. IF ((2 * (J/2)) .EQ. J) GO TO 99
```

Exercise 2 (page 155)

```
a. READ (5,1000) X, Y, Z
c. WRITE (6,14) FICA, TAX
e. READ (5,*) V8    (WATFIV only)
```

Exercise 3 (page 155)

```
XMAX = X1
IF (XMAX .LT. X2) XMAX = X2
IF (XMAX .LT. X3) XMAX = X3
```

Exercise 5 (page 155)

```
        IF (AVERAG .LT. 70.) GO TO 20
        IF (AVERAG .LT. 80.) GO TO 30
        IF (AVERAG .LT. 90.) GO TO 40
        WRITE (6,102)
    102 FORMAT('0YOUR GRADE IS A')
        GO TO 50
     20 WRITE (6,103)
    103 FORMAT('0YOUR GRADE IS F')
        GO TO 50
     30 WRITE (6,104)
    104 FORMAT('0YOUR GRADE IS C')
        GO TO 50
     40 WRITE (6,105)
    105 FORMAT('0YOUR GRADE IS B')
     50    .
            .
            .
```

Exercise 7 (page 155)

```
     10 READ (5,100) VAL
    100 FORMAT(F5.0)
        RATE = 0.03
        IF (VAL .LT. 10000.0) GO TO 20
        RATE = 0.04
        IF (VAL .LT. 30000.0) GO TO 20
        RATE = 0.05
        IF (VAL .GE. 60000.0) RATE = 0.06
        CHG = RATE * VAL
     20 WRITE (6,110) CHG
    110 FORMAT('0TAX CHARGE IS', F7.2)
        GO TO 10
        END
```

Exercise 9 (page 156)

```
        IF (NREQ .LE. NAVAIL) GO TO 10
        WRITE (6,100)
    100 FORMAT('0REQUEST CANNOT BE FILLED')
        GO TO 20
     10 NAVAIL = NAVAIL - NREQ
     20    .
            .
            .
```

Exercise 10 (page 156)

```
     10 READ (5,101) AVERAG
    101 FORMAT (F3.0)
        IF (AVERAG .GT. 95.) GO TO 20
        IF (AVERAG .GE. 90.) GO TO 30
        IF (AVERAG .GE. 85.) GO TO 40
        IF (AVERAG .GE. 80.) GO TO 50
        IF (AVERAG .GE. 75.) GO TO 60
        IF (AVERAG .GE. 70.) GO TO 70
        IF (AVERAG .GE. 65.) GO TO 80
        WRITE (6,102)
    102 FORMAT('0FINAL GRADE IS F')
        GO TO 10
     20 WRITE (6,103)
    103 FORMAT('0FINAL GRADE IS A+')
        GO TO 10
     30 WRITE (6,104)
    104 FORMAT('0FINAL GRADE IS A')
        GO TO 10
     40 WRITE (6,105)
    105 FORMAT('0FINAL GRADE IS B+')
        GO TO 10
     50 WRITE (6,106)
    106 FORMAT('0FINAL GRADE IS B')
        GO TO 10
     60 WRITE (6,107)
    107 FORMAT('0FINAL GRADE IS C+')
        GO TO 10
     70 WRITE (6,108)
    108 FORMAT('0FINAL GRADE IS C')
        GO TO 10
     80 WRITE (6,109)
    109 FORMAT('0FINAL GRADE IS D')
        GO TO 10
        END
```

Exercise 11 (page 156)

```
        DIFF = ABS (TEMP - 98.6)
        IF (DIFF .GE. 0.5) GO TO 10
        WRITE (6,100)
    100 FORMAT('0NORMAL')
        GO TO 90
     10 IF (DIFF .GE. 1.5) GO TO 20
        WRITE (6,200)
    200 FORMAT('0REST IN BED')
        GO TO 90
     20 WRITE (6,300)
    300 FORMAT('0CONTACT DOCTOR')
     90 .
        .
        .
```

Exercise 13 (page 156)

```
 10  READ (5,200) XN
200  FORMAT(F10.5)
     IF (XN .LT. 0.0) STOP
     WRITE (6,300) XN
300  FORMAT('1INPUT VALUE IS', F11.5)
     APPROX = XN/2.0
 20  WRITE (6,400) APPROX
400  FORMAT(5X, 'APPROXIMATION', F11.5)
     ALAST = APPROX
     APPROX = (APPROX + XN/APPROX)/2.0
     IF (ABS(APPROX - ALAST) .GE. 1.0E-5) GO TO 20
     WRITE (6,500) APPROX
500  FORMAT('0SOLUTION IS', F11.5)
     GO TO 10
     END
```

CHAPTER 6

Exercise 1 (page 192)

a. invalid   i. invalid
c. invalid   k. invalid
e. invalid   m. invalid
g. invalid   o. invalid

Exercise 2 (page 192)

a.	1			g.	0.0	−4.0
	2				10.0	126.0
	3				20.0	456.0
	4				30.0	986.0
					40.0	1716.0
c.	3	3	5		50.0	2646.0
	4	3	5			
	5	3	5	i.	1	
					2	
e.	3				3	
	5				5	
	7				6	
	9				7	
					8	

CHAPTER 7

Exercise 1 (page 231)

b. valid   h. invalid
d. invalid   j. invalid
f. invalid

Exercise 2 (page 232)

```
      DIMENSION AREA(200)
      DO 10 I = 1,50
      AREA (I) = 0.0
   10 CONTINUE
```

To zero out the last 40 locations as well, add

```
      DO 20 I = 161,200
      AREA(I) = 0.0
   20 CONTINUE
```

An alternative (though much less efficient) solution would have been to replace the first DO loop with

```
      DO 10 I = 1,200
      IF (I .LE. 50 .OR. I .GT. 160) AREA(I) = 0.0
   10 CONTINUE
```

Why is this less efficient?

Exercise 4 (page 232)

The most efficient solution is

```
      DIMENSION IAREA(50)
      DO 10 I = 1,50,2 (NOTE: I = 1,49,2 would also work)
      IAREA(I) = -1
   10 CONTINUE
      DO 20 I = 2,50,2
      IAREA(I) = 1
   20 CONTINUE
```

Exercise 6 (page 232)

```
      READ (5,100) NAREA, MAREA
  100 FORMAT(I5)
      I = 1
      J = 1
      NPM = N + M
      DO 30 K = 1,NPM
      IF (I .GT. N) GO TO 20
```

```
        IF (J .GT. M) GO TO 10
        IF (NAREA(I) .GT. MAREA(J)) GO TO 20
10 NMAREA(K) = NAREA(I)
        I = I + 1
        GO TO 30
20 NMAREA(K) = MAREA(J)
        J = J + 1
30 CONTINUE
```

Note the tests for I and J exceeding their ranges immediately following the DO statement. This is to make certain that when one of the arrays is exhausted the third IF statement does not become meaningless.

Exercise 8 (page 232)

a. One of the most efficient procedures is as follows (assume N is the dimension of the array IAREA):

```
        MAX = IAREA(1)
        MAX2 = IAREA(2)
        IF (MAX .GE. MAX2) GO TO 10
        MAX = IAREA(2)
        MAX2 = IAREA(1)
10 DO 30 I = 3,N
        IF (IAREA(I) .LE. MAX) GO TO 20
        MAX2 = MAX
        MAX = IAREA(I)
        GO TO 30
20 IF (IAREA(I) .GE. MAX2) MAX2 = IAREA(I)
30 CONTINUE
```

The result will be in MAX2. Note that MAX2 may be equal to MAX if the largest value occurs two or more times in the array. How could you avoid this?

CHAPTER 8

Exercise 1 (page 261)

```
a.      READ (5,100) K, X
   100 FORMAT(I6, F8.2)
c.      READ(5,100) SOUP, VEGE, TABLE, MEAT
   100 FORMAT(F6.2, 2X, F8.1, 4X, F6.4, 2X, I4)
e.      READ (5,100) ((TABLE(I,J), J = 1,4), I = 1,4)
   100 FORMAT(4F5.1)
```

Exercise 2 (page 261)

```
b.      WRITE (6,100) (I, N(I), I = 1,4)
   100 FORMAT('0', 4 ('N(', I1, ') =', I2, 3X))
d.      WRITE (6,100) (NEGGS(I), I = 1,12)
   100 FORMAT(12I1)
```

Exercise 3 (page 261)

   a. bbbbb78.35bb88643.14bbbbbb1.00

   c. TESTb483421bbbb483421bbb483421

   e. AIRbb707.747bbbbbbbb0.70775Eb03bbb**********

CHAPTER 9

Exercise 1 (page 296)

```
b. CALL NUMBER (IANS, IR, NUM1, IND)
   CALL NUMBER (3, 896, 16295, 4)
   SUBROUTINE NUMBER (I1, I2, I3, I4)
d. CALL XMIN (X1, X2, X3, X4)
   CALL XMIN (3.5, -7.0, 0.147E-05, ZZ)
   SUBROUTINE XMIN (X1, X2, X3, X4)
f. DIMENSION IAREA(100), IBVEC(100)
   CALL MERGE (IAREA, IBVEC, NA, NB)
   CALL MERGE (IAREA, IBVEC, 100, 100)
   SUBROUTINE MERGE (IVEC1, IVEC2, NSIZ1, NSIZ2)
h. DIMENSION X(50,100), Y(50,91)
   CALL CONST (X, 50, 100, IC)
   CALL CONST (Y, 50, 91, 7)
   SUBROUTINE CONST (AREA, N1, N2, ICON)
j. CALL PAGE
   CALL PAGE
   SUBROUTINE PAGE
```

Exercise 2 (page 296)

The word "SUBROUTINE" should be replaced by the word "FUNCTION" throughout. Examples of valid function invocations are as follows:

```
a. Z = FUNCT (X, Y, 6)
b. N = NUMBER (8, IR, N1, 3)
c. MIN = MINVAL (4, IN, IOUT, II, J)
d. ZZ = XMIN (2.5, XX, Y, BAR)
e. Y = XMINAR (AREA, 500, RES)
f. I = MERGE (IBVEC, IAREA, N, N)
g. N = COMPAR (Y, X, I, I)
h. C = CONST (X, N, 100, I)
i. MCK = MATMUL (X, Y, 10, 20, N)
```
j. This cannot be done because **PAGE** has no argument.

CHAPTER 10

Exercise 1 (page 322)

```
a. RESULT-   F   F        d. T NOT EQUALF
b. LOGIC=T               e.  NOT ALL TRUE
c. MAPLE
```

INDEX

L 2
M 3
N 4
O 5
P 6
Q 7
R 8
S 9
T 0
1